WOMEN AND CHANGE IN LATIN AMERICA

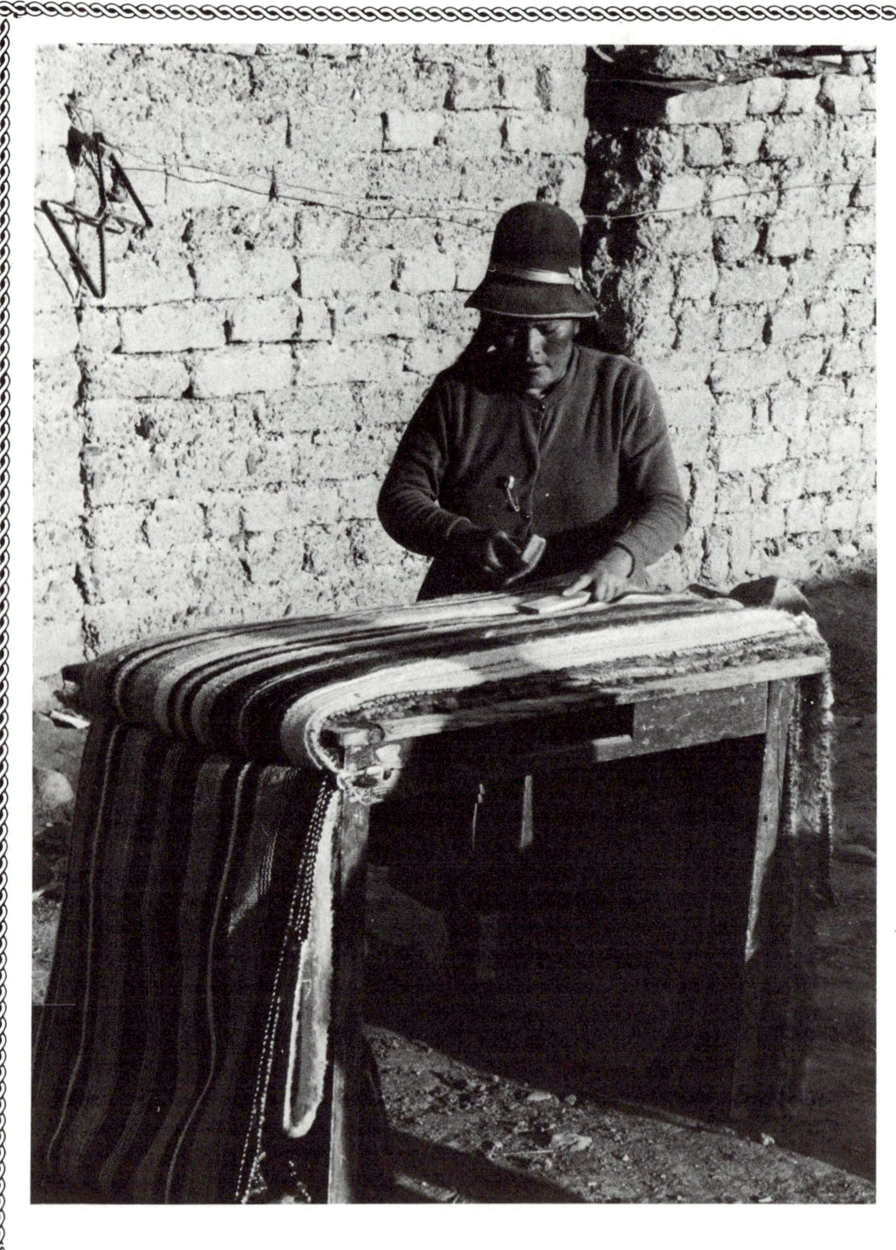

Aymara woman preparing alpaca woven cloth, El Aldo. La Paz, Bolivia.
PHOTO BY JUDITH-MARIA BUECHLER

WOMEN AND CHANGE IN LATIN AMERICA

June Nash
Helen Safa
and contributors

Bergin & Garvey Publishers, Inc.
MASSACHUSETTS

First published in 1986 by
Bergin & Garvey Publishers, Inc.
670 Amherst Road
South Hadley, Massachusetts 01075

56789 987654321

Printed in the United States of America

Library of Congress Cataloging in Publication Data
Main entry under title:

Women and change in Latin America.

Includes bibliographies and index.
1. Women—Latin America—Economic conditions—Addresses, essays, lectures. 2. Women—Latin America—Social conditions—Addresses, essays, lectures. 3. Women—Employment—Latin America—Addresses, essays, lectures. 4. Sexual division of labor—Latin America—Addresses, essays, lectures. 5. Feminism—Latin America—Addresses, essays, lectures. I. Nash, June C., 1927– . II. Safa, Helen Icken.
HQ1460.5.W6 1985 305.4'098 85-18563
ISBN 0-89789-069-8
ISBN 0-89789-070-1 (pbk.)

Contents

Preface

As the title suggests, this collection follows upon an earlier volume edited by us entitled *Sex and Class in Latin America.* That book grew out of a conference organized by the editors in Buenos Aires in 1973, which brought together Latin American and U.S. scholars who were interested in research on women in Latin America. The conference and subsequent volume served to stimulate that interest, and to help open up a new field of research and action, which today has attracted many scholars and practitioners in both North America and Latin America.

In *Women and Change in Latin America* we have tried to give the reader a glimpse of this new scholarship and some of the major issues confronting feminist research. Scholars have passed beyond the descriptive phase of earlier studies, which carried out the important task of documenting the contribution women made to family and society, both in their productive and reproductive roles. The concern now is to use women's contributions as leverage for change in Latin America, which is undergoing one of the worst economic crises in its history. As always, women are falling victim to this crisis, and are looking for new survival strategies, such as migration, industrial employment often in the newer export-processing plants, and mobilization through various forms of collective action in both capitalist and socialist countries. The contributors to this volume document the struggles of peasant and market women in the Andes; of female factory workers in Brazil, Mexico, Puerto Rico, and Jamaica; and of Colombian and Dominican migrants in New York City. Women living under military dictatorships in Latin America have suffered severe repression and no longer enjoy a protected or privileged status—evidence that women are part of a national struggle for change. Now that the official U.N. Decade on Women is drawing to a close, political mobilization may well hold the key to the success of the women's movement in Latin America, as the comparative gains in gender equality achieved in socialist Cuba demonstrate.

Many of the contributors to this volume are drawn from a younger generation of scholars who were initiated into feminist research during the last decade. This is our best assurance that the field does not represent a passing fancy or fad, but is a source of new knowledge, paradigms, and models for society. As June Nash indicates in her introductory essay, many of the contributions made by research on women in Latin America have yet to be incorporated into the mainstream literature. It is still all too prevalent to read about the peasantry, migration, or the informal economy in Latin America without recognition of the importance of gender differences. But this ideological cultural lag can only be overcome by the kind of sound scholarship we have tried to offer here.

One of the most important outcomes of this research has been the bond formed between Latin American and U.S. researchers working on the topic. From the beginning, this has been a true collaboration that has attempted not to objectify women, but to view all women as partners in the struggle. We are deeply indebted to our Latin American colleagues and to those Latin American women who have opened their lives and hearts to us. We hope that this volume may represent a small contribution toward greater understanding among the sisters of the Americas.

JUNE NASH
HELEN I. SAFA

I Theoretical and Methodological Progress

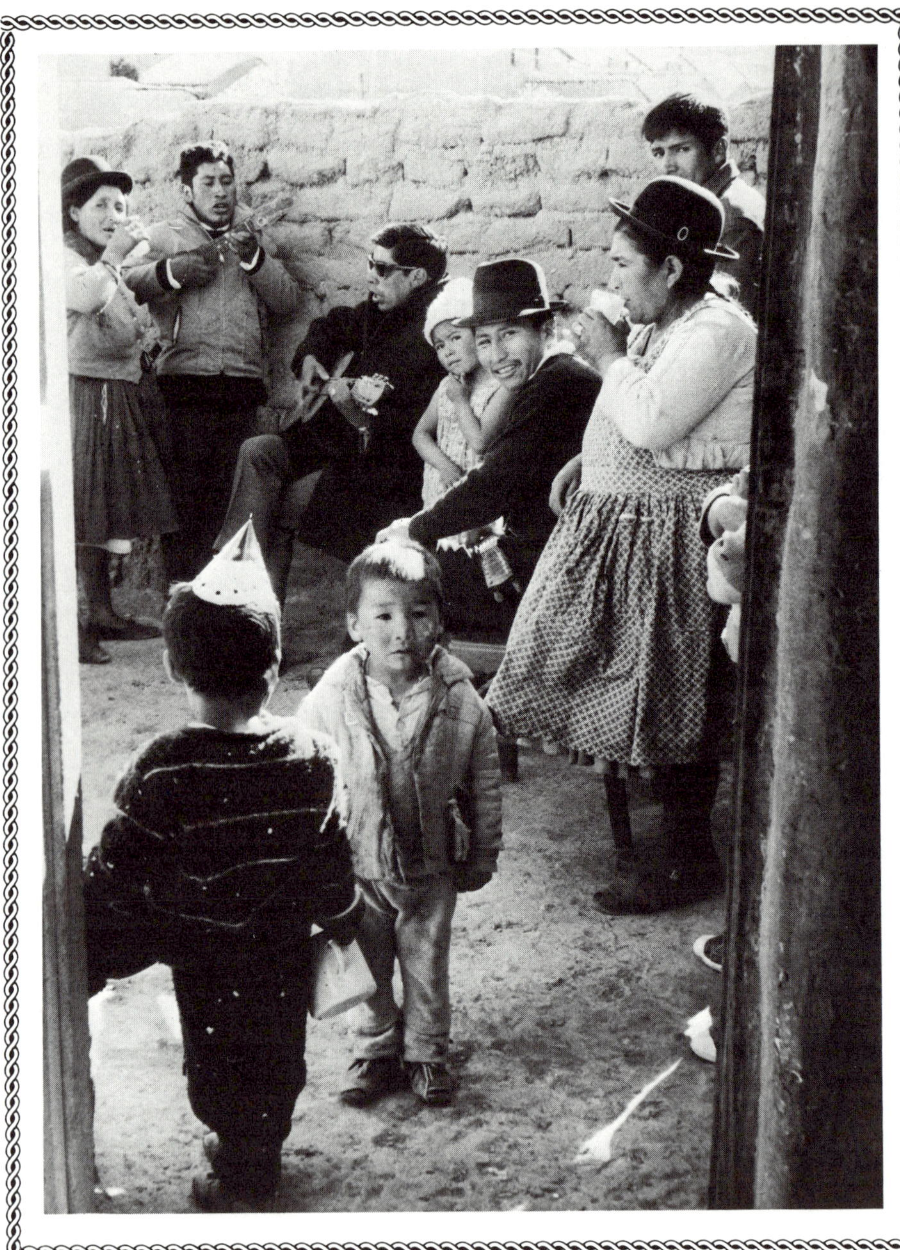

Women are central to the household and neighborhood scene, providing the 'chicha', food, and occasions for festivities that revitalize Bolivian tin mining communities.

PHOTO BY JUNE NASH

1 A Decade of Research on Women in Latin America

June Nash

We have witnessed over a decade of research and writing focusing on women in Latin America since the first conference organized around the theme of feminine perspectives held at the Torcuato de Tello Institute in Buenos Aires in 1974. One of the problems in organizing that meeting was to identify the people who had done empirical research on women, since the researchers, like their subjects, were with few exceptions invisible. What made the organization of the conference problematic was, in fact, the reason motivating it. The lack of data reflected a consistent lack of interest or attention to women's contribution to economic, political, and social life. Whether investigators were influenced by neoclassical, Marxist, dependency or developmentalist paradigms, they tended to stop short of an analysis of women's condition in any but the most stereotyped roles in the family and biological reproduction.

In the intervening decade, many of the original contributors to that conference have made major contributions to the study of Latin American society, and they have been joined by many other researchers, whose work will be discussed in their book. Some of this work has been presented at conferences held in Bogota in 1976, in Mexico City and in San Juan in 1977, in Rio de Janeiro in 1978, and in Montevideo and in Caracas in 1979. In 1981 there were four conferences concerned with women: in Bogota, San Jose, Havana and Rio de Janeiro. International conferences that included important papers on Latin America were held in the United States--at Wellesley College in Massachusetts--in 1976, in Copenhagen in 1980, Mexico City 1983 and during the meetings of the Latin American Studies Association. The publications resulting from these conferences[1] show a progressive focus on methods and problem formulation to advance the economic and social status of women in Latin American society. Research and publication centers emphasizing data collection, welfare, and the legal aspects of work and family have developed in Mexico City, Bogota, Lima and other major Latin American cities.

Concern with the ideological, economic, and political context in which female subordination is generated and sustained has been present from the very beginning. I shall summarize some of the contributions made by scholars up to the present and go on to discuss future directions. Developments promoted in the intervening decade of studies concerning gender roles have stimulated research and debate in the following areas: (1) the differential gains made by sectors of the work force segmented by gender and ethnicity; (2) the interplay between social reproduction, production for the market, and biological reproduction; (3) the comparative advantages of women in different modes of production, and (4) the newly emergent international division of labor, with its sharp reversal of gender employment in multinational corporations. Methodological approaches have been advanced along with the sharpened conceptualization of philosophical issues related to the social construction of gender, the dialectics of change in which women were excluded from the central hierarchy of institutional domains, and the relative importance of cultural versus economic determinants in conditioning their status and role in society. These four areas will be discussed in relation to the advance in theory and method.

SEGMENTATION OF THE WORK FORCE

In advanced industrial centers, segmentation of the work force by gender refers to the allocation of low-paid, nonunion and routine dead-end jobs to women. In Latin America, it applies most frequently to nonmarket, subsistence sectors of production versus capitalist enterprises. While returns are lower in the subsistence sector, the products are directly channeled into social reproduction.

The devaluation of this sector of production by most economic analysis is due to lack of data about nonmarket activities. A conference held in Rio de Janeiro in 1978 addressed the problem of data gathering at its source: the census enumerations of activity rates. Neuma Aguiar's article in this volume points out two biases in research: (1) the inadequacy of categories used in most census surveys, and (2) the failure to capture nonmarket inputs. Both failures reflect the patriarchal biases in the census bureaucracies that define the categories in use. As a result, existing stereotypes related to designation of "household head" become reified in data collection. Added to this is the classist and racist perspective that obscures the reference points for ethnically differentiated groups.

The limited perspective in data-gathering agencies can be

overcome with the following recommendations made at the Rio conference. First, in terms of a chronology for comparative research and its importance, is the need for ethnographic studies to complement survey research. Unless on-the-ground studies are carried out to determine what in fact is being done by women and men in different economic settings, the questions asked by census takers will not capture the range and diversity of female and male activities. The primary tenet of ethnographic studies is the framing of questions in relation to observed regularities. Census takers and those who rely on their findings construct questionnaires that tend to reify their assumptions about society. One of these has been that women do not work in basic farming of a subsistence type but on "help" in periods of harvesting.

This takes us to the second recommendation, stressing the need for women as census takers and interviewees. The fact that most census takers are male and seek out the male "household head" reaffirms their assumptions that the work is in the domain of male activity. Even if women are asked what they do, they might reaffirm the men's statements. In those cultures where women are categorically enjoined from doing men's work, particularly that which involves using "men's" tools such as the hoe and plow, one must develop the research tactics of a detective to catch them in the act. Such is the case with Maya women of traditional communities in Chiapas, Mexico, who, if they are left without menfolk to do the work of their fields and do not have money to hire help, sneak out to work in the fields at night so that they will not be seen (Nash 1970). However, when Guatemalan Maya women migrate to the coast to work in agroindustrial fields, these inhibitions are relaxed as women work alongside men in the coffee and cotton harvests (Bossen 1984).

Third World countries are experiencing an unprecedented expansion of capitalist institutions in rural and urban areas. Subsistence agriculture, where it survives, has not fully been evaluated as to its contributions to reproduction of the labor force. However, studies that provide a data base for a fundamental reevaluation are now available and must be incorporated in aggregate analyses at national and international levels. Outstanding among these is the work of Carmen Diana Deere and Magdalena Leon de Leal. Three volumes published by the Asociacion Columbiana para el Estudio de la Poblacion span the local, regional, national, and international levels of economic integration, bringing to bear data on the economic, social, and cultural conditions in which women act to reproduce the society (Leon de Leal and Deere 1980; Leon and Deere 1982a and 1982b).

Segmentation of the labor force in Third World countries is clearly related to different modes of production. Sectors of the labor force that enter into the different modes of production are often integrated within the family (Nash 1982). It is in this context that we can appreciate the crucial importance of women's roles in articulating distinct modes of production. Women's economic objectives often differ from those of men who may welcome wage work in commercial agriculture since it is they who try to preserve the subsistence cultivation that permits survival of their children (Rubbo 1975). Women engaged in piece work and putting out systems in their homes weave together the production schedules of highly capitalized and mechanized firms with their familial chores in the home, as Judith-Marie Buechler demonstrates in her chapter on Bolivian artisans in this volume. In their trading activities, women are the mediators in bringing commodities produced on the world market to women who produce handcraft items for that market. As managers of household expenditures, they convert men's wages earned in capitalized enterprises into use values for household consumption. This task has become increasingly more difficult as forced labor migrations and the increase in female-headed households break traditional redistribution channels in the family.

Disaggregation of employment data by sex and class sets into relief the differential effects of the penetration of capitalist enterprises in Latin America. In a comparison of the countries in the southern cone of South America, Ruth Sautu (1981) shows that there is an increase in countries with an expanding tertiary sector, creating a demand for women in clerical and service occupations at the same time that there is a decrease in the activity rates of lower-class women. Urban educated women in Argentina are responding to the increasing demand for women in finance, commerce, and government at the same time that women are losing jobs in industry. However, in Bolivia, where women had always maintained high activity rates in agriculture prior to the 1952 land reform, they are no longer forced to work in fields of the large landholders. The lower rates of participation recorded in recent censuses may reflect the failure of the census enumerators to account for nonmarket activities. In Bolivia, as elsewhere, it is well recognized that "the whole peasant family participates in the cultivation of the land . . . . [and] women also assume the task of selling the farm produce in the local market" (Sautu 1981:157).

SOCIAL RELATIONS IN PRODUCTION AND THE REPRODUCTION OF SOCIETY

Reasoning from census data is only a beginning toward defining the problems for microstatistical analyses relating directly to what is going on in the field. Macrostatistical analysis enables us to see the contradictions of a process that displaces rural populations from a given subsistence mode of production that fails to reintegrate people in new forms of employment. What we must look at more intensively is the specific adaptation of women to the changes in the social relations of production.

It is precisely because women's roles in production are

conditioned by their reproductive roles that we learn more about the contradictions inherent in capitalism. Lourdes Beneria and Gita Sen (1981) clarify this relationship between the processes of accumulation and changes in women's work: "The tendency of capitalist accumulation is to separate direct producers from the means of production and to make their conditions of survival more insecure and contingent" (288).

The contradiction in capitalism between production for use in a household economy and production for exchange was obscured in the resurgence of feminist intellectual movements in the post World War II period by the proposition that the subordination of women is universal. Simone de Beauvoir (1953) was prominent among those theorists who asserted the universality of women's subordination as a corollary of their reproductive role. Margaret Mead reversed her earlier analysis of New Guinea sex roles as culturally patterned in *Sex and Temperament in Three Primitive Societies* (1935) to promote a more universal biologically based gender construction in *Male and Female; A Study of the Sexes in a Changing World* (1953). The postulate of women's condition as a "natural" extension of biological reproduction was amenable to the ideological pressures exerted upon women to revert from wage work in war production to domestic roles.

Heleieth Safiotti was one of the first Latin American scholars to critique universalistic pronouncements about the construction of gender, stating that Mead, "in failing to look at the sociohistoric determinants of a social reality . . . . invested that reality with a permanence it does not have." Archetti and Stolen (1978) criticized a later version of the thesis (Rosaldo and Lamphere 1974) in their review of the great differences in the situation of women in Argentina over time and in different modes of production. Yet Franchetti et al. (1981) persist in defending the premise of universal sexual subordination despite evidence to the contrary.

There is a growing literature questioning the biological premises of gender role construction. Florence Babb's chapter in this volume shows how the cultural elaboration of reproduction defines women's functions in the labor market. The informal sector permits women to bring children with them even as it exploits their labor, a theme developed by Ximena Bunster (1982). The flexibility of place and time in informal work opens up space for women to fulfill their responsibilities in both productive and reproductive spheres.

The critique of the thesis of universal subordination has also been related to historical developments. *Women and Colonization* (1980), edited by Mona Etienne and Eleanor Leacock, refutes the thesis and calls for a historical perspective relating gender roles and status to specific historical formations. The chapters dealing with different colonial encounters show that the undermining of the egalitarian status women enjoyed in many indigenous societies occurred at different rates and different chronologies. Whereas the erosion of women's position among the Aztecs preceded the Spanish conquest as the egalitarian relations in production ensured in the calpulli, the territorially based kinship group, yielded to militarism and agnatic power structures (Nash 1980), among the Inca the Spanish conquest was responsible for the systematic undercutting of parallel male and female descent structures that provided both sexes with access to land and other resources (Silverblatt 1980). Tribes remote from Spanish colonization, such as the Carib Bari, retained egalitarianism until the 1960s, when the government succeeded in making a truce with them, with the result that male chiefs were named and the communal hearths came under male dominance (Buenaventura-Posso and Brown 1980).

Ethnohistorical studies showing the specific processes relegating women to subordinate status in pre- and postcolonial times disprove the universalistic thesis of women's subordination. At the same time, they show that patriarchal institutions are not exclusively related to capitalist penetration but may contribute to the accumulation of capital (Dalla Costa 1971, Jelin 1980). The evidence from contemporary studies of capitalist penetration reinforces the conclusion that it is the loss of control over the means of subsistence production and the failure to integrate them in wage work that make women the most oppressed victims (Vasquez de Miranda 1977: 273; Leon and Deere 1980).

Older forms of patriarchy that persisted in peasant households on haciendas were broken down with the spread of capitalist agriculture but were often replaced with new forms. In Peru, as Deere (1977) has shown, the impoverishment of female-headed households reduces their autonomy and many women must resort to extended household residence with their parents. Deere shows that, like Russian peasants analyzed by Chayanov (1966), prior to the land reform of 1969, these peasants maximized domestic accumulation of capital by increasing the number of children available as workers on the lands of the lord. With the succession of commodity production and wage work, the value of both child and female labor is reduced without the compensating access to new opportunities that men enjoy. Bolivian women have experienced a similar decline in activity rates in rural agriculture as the services required of them on the old landed estates were nullified by passage of the land reform act in the 1950s (Sautu 1981).

The changes in familial social relations are even more dramatic when there is a shift from subsistence farming to modern industrial employment. The spread of import-substitution industrialization after World War II resulted in the preferred employment of men in capital-intensive industries (Sautu 1981; Orrego de Figueroa 1976; Vasquez de Miranda 1977). The loss of value for child labor that could be integrated into farm production and the concomitant increase in the "cost" of raising children create a trend in the direction of smaller families that, according to Frances Rothstein (this volume), can be seen in Mexico today. This parallels earlier trends in industrialized countries, but in Mexico the overall impact is far less than in advanced industrial countries. Safa's (1983) comparison of New Jersey and Sao Paulo garment workers illustrates this contrast in perceived benefits.

WOMEN IN THE ARTICULATION OF MODES OF PRODUCTION

In discussing women's productive and reproductive roles, we have anticipated the problem of how they are integrated in different modes of production. Analytical modes for the insertion of women in production vary from the Marxist "reserve labor pool" to that of the segmented labor market. Saffioti's (1969) study of women in capitalist production analyzes women's labor as a reserve maintaining itself in "outmoded" modes of production. This labor is commanded by the dominant mode of production when demand for labor increases. In their marginally utilized roles, women bear the brunt of social malintegration as the first to be fired and the lowest paid. The studies in the decade sharpen the historically specific contexts that condition women's entry into the labor force. Whereas women's labor appeared to be a reserve when the ideology of patriarchy characterized their commitment to domestic labor as primary, their labor has always been an essential part of specific labor markets. With the integration of production at a global level, women are the preferred labor force. The growing unemployment of men and the superemployment of women changes the dynamic of expolitation of women in the labor market and in the households (Fernandez-Kelly 1983; Nash and Fernandez-Kelly 1983). This will be discussed below in relation to the new international division of labor.

Brazil remains a crucial arena in which to explore the contradictions in women's position resulting from the uneven expansion of capitalism. Saffioti (this volume) shows this in her comparison of women in two garment factories representing different levels of technological application. She concludes that women are consistently losers with technological introduction since their control over jobs that demand craft skills, and even the job itself, is lost as automation proceeds. Another level of uneven development is analyzed by Aguiar (1983) in her comparative study of women in a plantation system, a government irrigation project, and an industrial capitalist enterprise. Differential access to the housing and food resources supplied as payment in kind in the first two of these enterpises exacerbated the marginality of the women engaged in production. Men were given house lots and a wage for the labor of the entire family. Widowed and divorced women were cut out of the community as well as out of work in the plantation. Social workers in the government-controlled project tried to discourage women from working in agriculture, in contrast to plantation settings where women were superexploited. The transnational textile firm that

Aguiar studied used only wage incentives to attract workers, but as the most subject to layoffs, women workers suffered even more than male workers. They could not cultivate community ties in this setting because of the constant moves conditioned by short employment periods, and they lost this important strategy compensating for their vulnerability in the labor market.

The importance of the multiplicity of economic activities carried out by women in meeting domestic needs is rarely conceptualized as an opportunity cost for female wage employment. Marianne Schmink in her study of Brazilian urban women (this volume) succeeds in posing this problem of the conflicting demands put on women in the wage earning market and the domestic economy. As Schmink shows, household mediation of the resources and income generated in the domestic context merits serious study because of the light it sheds on the articulation of productive and reproductive spheres.

Development is also uneven in those Latin American countries that have not experienced the remarkable growth of Brazil. Women have shown a great deal of flexibility in adapting to economic changes that expelled them from the agricultural domestic economy. Laurel Bossen (1984) and Florence Babb (this volume) describe how women in a wide variety of economic contexts in Guatemala and Peru supplement household incomes with petty commodity production. Class position modifies the impact of capitalist transformations. In Guatemala, upper class women in the capital have more autonomy and control over resources than proletarianized women in the sugar plantation even though the penetration of capitalist institutions is greater in the former setting. Bossen (1984:320) concludes that "Both structurally and culturally, capitalism has brought about a redivision of labor which has relatively penalized women." Young (1978) found a similar transformation in Oaxaca as women lost their handicraft production with the introduction of factory-made goods.

As we note such changes in particular contexts, we must recognize that the destruction of craft production is not inevitably a consequence of the penetration of capitalist production. Buechler (this volume) shows the entry points women have devised to gain an entry into the market with their craft production even while fulfilling domestic roles. Her chapter underlines the importance of recognizing the specific historical context of capitalist penetration and local resistance to the destruction of the economy. Distinct modes of production within a social formation provide the stage but do not determine the actions of men and women. The dynamic interplay between women's economic contribution and the way it is perceived and negotiated in social interaction is also illuminated by Susan Bourque and Kay Warren (1981). In their analysis of two highland Peruvian communities at different altitudinal levels representing different degrees of penetration of capitalism, we are able to assess the complexity of factors that influence the division of work and the relations between the sexes. In Mayobamba, a potato-growing, cattle- and sheep-herding community, the tradition of communal works with a core of adult male family heads who serve as representatives of nuclear or extended families involves a gender division of labor that overlaps but at crucial points excludes women from taking advantage of communal resources such as irrigation. With an increase in the number of cash transactions in this agricultural village, women's control over the management of domestic resources is weakened. However, when we turn to Chiuchin some two thousand feet lower and more involved in trade, the cash economy opens new opportunities for women to enter capitalist exchange systems. Although their husbands still have the greater contact and opportunities to advance economically through truck transportation, women have more opportunity to maintain their position in the household and community than those at a higher altitude. In this comparison, we can see that while capitalist exchanges disturb the complementarity that is noted in highland society, they may also provide compensating opportunities as women gain entry in the new system.

Although many tend to draw a linear causal relationship between the economic system and strategies for survival, ethnographic case studies show the importance of cultural factors--the patterning of class positions, marital relationships, and the varying strength of kinship networks--that reciprocally contribute to and are reinforced by economic differences. Schminck and Bolles, among others in this volume, show how the dialectic of gender relations informs and shapes the larger dialectic of class formation in the process of capitalist penetration. In Jamaica, households formed by permanent unions are able to reinforce income generation. Similarly, relative degrees of poverty in Bello Horizonte, Brazil, are attributed in part to the inability to utilize available workers in the household. The economic status of the family influences, and in turn is influenced by, the composition of its membership.

WOMEN IN THE GLOBAL INTEGRATION OF PRODUCTION

The importance of an approach focusing on women is even more apparent in the analysis of the global integration of capital. In the recent expansion of industry across national boundaries, the "comparative advantages of women's disadvantages," in Lourdes Arizpe and Josefina Aranda's (1981) felicitous phrasing, become more explicit. Their disadvantaged position in the labor markets of the less developed countries and their greater availability give them a preferential status in the multinational corporations' search for cheap labor.

Increases in the number of women employed in the wage labor force continue to reflect the greater concentration of women in the service section, where 67.2 percent of Latin American women were employed a few years ago (ILO 1980). Brazil, like other more industrialized Latin American countries, showed a rise in women employed in manufacturing, where there was a 181 percent growth in manufacturing in the period from 1970 to 1980. Their increased participation rates rose from 13.6 to 29.6 in 1976, reversing earlier trends showing declining or stablizied rates of employment in industry (Schminck this volume). In Mexico, women's participation in the wage labor force rose from 240,000 in 1930, when they were 4.5 percent of the work force, to 2,892,000 in 1974, when they constituted 19.1 percent of the work force (de Leonardo 1976) reflect the rise in their employment in border electronic and garment industries. In 1982, border industries employed a predominantly female work force of 156,000 (Fernandez-Kelly 1983). With high male unemployment, women are increasingly the main support of families. Fernandez-Kelly found that three out of four women provided the only means of support for their families in the border garment industries she studied (1983:4). In the newer electronic shops, young unmarried women are preferred in part because it is assumed that they do not have family reponsibilities. However, these young women are often the prinicpal support of their parents and siblings under working age, and one in three families is headed by a woman. Despite the large share of household expenses borne by women working in the *maquiladoras* (assembly industries), they still do most of the housework. Fernandez-Kelly found that the average working day of these women was fifteen hours (1983:137).

The runaway shops raise the level of competition among workers to an international level, as Safa contends (1981:433). These industries in flight from high wage areas are ever ready to depart if labor starts to make demands in their new sites. Their preference for women workers is, in fact, built into their mobility since it is assumed that young women are only temporary members of the work force.

With the new international division of labor brought to Latin American countries by multinational corporations operating in free trade zones, women are the preferred labor force for low skilled assembly jobs. These trends may now be reversed as men seek government backing to demand jobs in the *maquiladoras*. Arnulfo Castro Munire, President of the Association of Maquiladoras, was quoted by Richard J. Meislin, a reporter for the *New York Times* (March 19, 1984 D8.), as saying, "We had become a matriarchy. It had ruptured the social equilibrium." A deliberate effort is now being made in Ciudad Juarez to hire men, and Castro reported that one-third of the workers are male. Up to the present time, only 10 percent of the shops are organized, and even organized shops tend to be conciliatory in an area of high unemployment (*ibid*). It will be interesting to note whether the increasing proportions of male workers assumed to have a greater commitment to permanent employment will result in pressures for greater job stability.

An important facet of the international movement of investments is the fluctation in the exchange rate for currency. The steady devaluation of the Mexican peso has made labor costs increasingly attractive to American business. An assembly line worker now earns $28 for a forty-five-hour week. Differential currency exchanges also stimulate migration in Latin America. Margalit Berlin (1983) has shown that because of the favorable exchange rates in Colombia for Venezuelan currency, Colombian women are willing to work in Venezuelan factories paying too low a wage to attract natives. Migration from labor-exporting countries such as Bolivia, Colombia, Ecuador, and Peru can be expected to continue, both in direct migration to the U.S. and to the more industrialized countries of South America. The uneven development of Latin American countries and regions in the period of import substitution from the end of World War II to the end of the 1960s can be expected to intensify these movements in the eighties.

Those who feel most poignantly the effects of the integration of production on a global level are the migrants. Women differ from men in their assessment of the new social and cultural setting. As Patricia Pessar shows in her chapter of this book, women from the Dominican Repbulic often prefer to remain in the U.S. because of the enhanced appreciation of their role in the household. Their work outside the home enables them to make a greater economic contribution to the household expenses than they could expect in their home country. Contrary to expectations, women's work heightens their self-esteem as wives and mothers, affording them an opportunity to participate as equals and thus actualize these roles more fully. Like Dominican migrant women, Colombian women maintain close ties with their families in Colombia even when they intend to stay. Their familial lives influence their decisions to work and to remain in the U.S. or return to Colombia just as in the case of Dominican women (Berlin, this volume).

These personal accounts of migrants remind us that the structural parameters derived from aggregate data must eventually be interpreted in terms of the decisions made by human beings who have the illusion, if not the reality, of autonomous control over their lives. Structuralist premises are good for postmortems. They can rarely predict what people will do in response to changes in their environment or even what any individual will opt to do. Our case study approach will make it possible to indicate the links between action and motivations that are too often absent from the literature.

Our final section deals with the political behavior of women in Chile, Cuba, Bolivia, and Peru. Bunster Burotto vividly describes the strategies of military regimes in the southern cone to discourage political participation by women. Culturally sustained ideologies concerning women are the basis for transforming women who have resisted the military regimes from the ideal of womanhood to its opposite by systematic raping and torture debasing female prisoners.

Women's entry into political life frequently begins with culturally accepted notions of what they should do as wives and mothers, but when crisis periods are passed, they may be summarily dismissed. Gloria Ardaya, who surpassed these strictures in her own life, describes the careers of Bolivian women in the Movimiento Nacional Revolucionario in Bolivia, who brought the revolution to fruition in 1952, only to be dismissed when they were no longer needed. Carmen Deere's comparison of Chile, Peru, and Cuba gives us some understanding of how structural changes permit the deepening of the revolution, admitting women to a wider arena for the economic and political participation. The more effective integration of women in the Cuban land reform is a fundamental reason given by Isabel Larguia and John Dumoulin for the success in advancing the position of women.

FUTURE DIRECTIONS IN RESEARCH FOCUSING ON WOMEN

Nadia Youssef called for a "new theoretical orientation [that] seeks to find the golden mean between economic determinism, and absolute cultural relations" (1977:276). We feel that the solution does not lie between these two models but in a dialectical analysis of relations in production and reproduction. The key to this approach is the contradictions in class relations in production, modified and intensified by gender and race in the work place, as well as at home and in the community.

The advances marking the past decade of research have not overcome the need to focus on women in the coming decade. The need persists because of two factors: (1) we have not yet moved far enough beyond a structural definition of gender role to encompass the cultural transformations that are symbols of and continue to affect women's subordination in many societies; and (2) the many contributions made in research on women to the understanding of Latin American society have not been incorporated in mainstream literature. A research agenda focusing on the interplay of cultural and structural factors can advance theory and method in all disciplines whether the field of enquiry is gender or any other principle.

A dialectical perspective is of particular importance in studies focusing on women because their lives as workers are imbedded in the total domestic and community context. Survey analyses of census figures show that female activity rates are conditioned more by marital relationships than by the presence of dependent children alone, although the two factors combined serve to limit entry into and length of stay in the labor market (Sautu 1981). When we go into in-depth studies of women's working lives and their options, we begin to appreciate the complexity of ideological and sociocultural constraints that affect women's economic behavior.

I shall illustrate these propositions with the studies that show the potential for a dialectical analysis of cultural and structural interrelations in the future. Such a perspective embraces values, beliefs, and expectations conditioning behavior and attitudes about society at the same time that it relates to the structural constraints of a given mode of production and level of capital accumulation. We are not limiting the culture concept to that which is transmitted from one generation to another, but rather we shall assert that culture is the generative base for adapting to and redefining basic relations in production and reproduction. Self-perceptions enter into and form collective ideologies, but individual consciousness is rarely homologous with all other individuals in the group. Furthermore, sharp contradictions may be contained within the individual or group world view without a sense of cognitive dissonance. The latter emerges from group discussions coalescing around issues and movements in crisis situations.

Given these propositions about consciousness, culture, and material conditions, we can return to our case studies and raise questions posed by Bourque and Warren (1981). What are the links between the social ideologies, sexual division of labor and differential access to central institutions? Do women's perceptions contribute to their oppression? Do they act on consciousness of sexual hierarchy? Do they contribute to strategies for change?

The study of households and the life histories of women who manage them reveal the dialectical interrelationship of class, gender, ethnicity, constructed around these social categories. Class position sets the framework for the degree of activity in agricultural tasks, but then it is necessary to go on to show how the patterning of class positions, marital relationship, and the varying strength of kinship networks all contribute to economic differences. As all the contributors to this volume show, women activate the kinship, fictive kinship, and friendship ties to reinforce and even transform their economic position and that of their children more frequently than do men. This is particularly marked in the migration studies of Mary Castro, Margalit Berlin, and Patricia Pessar, but it is also present in the different class levels described by Judith-Maria Buechler in Bolivia and Florence Babb in Peru.

The very fact that, in most societies, "men's power is institutionally based" while "women's influence involves culturally formalized strategies recognized as legitimate" (Bourque and Warren 1981:53) means that a focus that takes women into account must analyze the cultural sources of power and privilege as well as the relations in production that give expression to them and reproduce the power. Cultural norms that reinforce hierarchy break down in economic crises. They are weaker in their impact on poor people, as Deere (1977) demonstrates in the relationship between economic-class position and gender behavior. She has also shown the importance of persistent ideological patterns of patriarchy that counteract revolutionary ideals of the Nicaraguan revolution. In these dramatic transformations of societies we can see more clearly the reciprocal influence of class and culturally prescribed gender role activity in all of the matrices in which they occur. A theory of the economic determinism of consciousness is patently less adequate in explaining female identity and behavior than in the study of male conduct.

The second point on our agenda for this decade--getting women's research into the mainstream of social science--we see a slow but not consistent percolation of the data amassed. For the most part, it has affected the description of but not the models concerning society. Despite the need for disaggregated data, more than one-half of Latin American countries reporting to the United Nations do not give gender breakdowns. The World Bank and other international lending agencies admit concern with women's productive roles but continue to lend money principally to capital intensive projects (Nash 1982). The tendency for scholarship to emphasize economic models derives from the polarization of wealth that makes such factors salient. However, it is important to go beyond such paradigms for a deeper understanding of society. While production for exchange in a capitalist market dominates the present reality of most Latin American economies, we still have contemporary reminders of cultures that produce for direct use, and women are most often those who are engaged in such efforts.

As Elsa Chaney suggests, when women's issues are made paramount, then we must question development goals that emphasize production for profit rather than concern for quality of life (1979:60). In the decade of the seventies, women experienced the loss of control over resources even more poignantly than did men since they bear the principle burden of subsistence production. If we are to envision a society in which social production meets the needs of all the population, it will be based on models that take into account the productive potential of the entire society and ways of engaging the human resources in which Latin America has such great potential.

NOTES

Helen Safa made many suggestions that elaborated upon and improved this chapter.

1 Among these are Maria del Carmen Elu de Lenero (1975); Nash and Safa (1976); *America Indigena* 1978; *Nueva Antropologia* 1977; Leon de Leal and Deere 1980, 1982a, and 1982b.

REFERENCES

Aguiar, Neuma. 1983. "Household, Community, National and Multinational Industrial Development." In Women, Men and the International Division of Labor. J. Nash and M. P. Fernandez-Kelly, eds. pp. 117-137. Albany: State University of New York Press.

Archetti, Eduardo and Kristo Anne Stolen. 1978. "Economia domestica, estrategias de herencia y acumulacion de capital: la situacion de la mujer en al norte de Sante Fe, Argentina." America Indigena 38:383-403.

Arizpe, Lourdes and Josefina Aranda. 1981. "The 'Comparative Advantage' of Women's Disadvantages: Women Workers in the Strawberry Export Business in Mexico." Signs 7:453-473.

de Beauvoir, Simone. 1953. The Second Sex. New York: Alfred Knopf.

Beneria, Lourdes and Gita Sen. 1981. "Accumulation, Reproduction, and Women's Role in Economic Development: Boserup Revisited." Signs 7:279-298.

Berlin, Margalit. 1983. "The Formation of an Ethnic Group: Columbian Female Workers in Venezuela." In Women, Men, and the International Division of Labor. J. Nash and M. P. Fernandez-Kelly, eds. pp. 257-270. Albany: State University of New York Press.

Bolles, Lynn. 1983. "Kitchens Hit by Priorities: Employed Working-Class Jamaican Women Confront the IMF." In Women, Men, and the International Division of Labor. J. Nash and M. P. Fernandez-Kelly, eds. pp. 257-270. Albany: State University of New York Press.

Bossen, Laurel Herbena. 1984. The Redivision of Labor: Women and Economic Choice in Four Guatemalan Communities. Albany: State University of New York Press.

Bourque, Susan C. and Kay Barbara Warren. 1981. Women of the Andes: Patriarchy and Social Change in Two Peruvian Villages. Ann Arbor: University of Michigan Press.

Buenaventura-Posso, Elsa and Susan E. Brown. 1980. "Forced Transition from Egalitarianism to Male Dominance." In Women and

Colonization: Anthropological Perspectives. Mona Etienne and Eleanor Leacock, eds. pp. 109-133. South Hadley: J. F. Bergin Publishers, Inc.

Bunster, B. Ximena. 1982. "Market Sellers in Lima, Peru: Talking about Work." In Women and Poverty in the Third World. Mayra Buvinic and Margaret A. Lycette, eds. Baltimore: Johns Hopkins Press.

Chaney, Elsa. 1979. Supermadre: Women in Politics in Latin America. Austin: University of Texas Press.

Chayanov, A. V. 1966. The Theory of Peasant Economy. D. Thorner, B. Kerblay, and R. E. F. Smith, eds. Homewood, Ill.: Irwin.

Dalla Costa, Mariarosa. 1972. "Women and the Subversion of the Community." In The Power of Women and the Subversion of the Community. M. Dalla Costa and Selma James, eds. Bristol: Falling Wall Press.

Deere, Carmen Diana. 1977. "Changing Social Relations of Production and Peruvian Peasant Women's Work." Latin American Perspectives 4 (Spring):48-69.

______. 1984. "La mujer en las cooperativas agropecuarias en Nicaragua." Centro de Investigaciones y Estudios de la Reforma Agraria. Managua: Division de Comunicaciones.

Elizaga, Juan C. 1976. "The Participation of Women in the Labour Force of Latin America: Fertility and Other Factors." Women Workers and Society. Geneva: International Labor Organization.

Elu, Maria del Carmen. 1975. La Mujer en America Latina. Mexico: Sep-Setentas.

Etienne, Mona and Eleanor Leacock, eds. 1980. Women and Colonization: Anthropological Perspectives. South Hadley: J. F. Bergin Publishers, Inc.

Fernandez-Kelly, M. Patricia. 1983. For We Are Sold, I and My People: Women and Industry in Mexico's Frontier. Albany: State University of New York Press.

Franchetti, Bruna, Maria Laura V. C. Cavalcanti, and Maria Luiza Heilbom. 1981. "Antropologia e Feminismo." In Perspectivas Antropologicas da Mulher. Rio de Janeiro: Zahar Editores.

Graciarena, Jorge. 1975. "Mujeres en America Latina: Aportes para una Discusion." Mexico: Fondo de Cultura Mexico (CEPAL).

International Labor Office. 1980. Women in World Development. Geneva.

Jelin, Elizabeth. 1980. "The Bahiana in the Labor Force in Salvador, Brazil." In Sex and Class in Latin America. J. Nash and Helen Safa, eds., pp. 129-146. South Hadley: J. F. Bergin Publishers, Inc.

Leon de Leal, Magdalena and Carmen Diana Deere. 1980. Mujer y Capitalismo Agrario. Bogota: Asociacion Columbiana para el Estudio de la Poblacion (ACEP).

______. 1982a. Las Trabajadoras del Agro: Debate sobre la Mujer en America Latina y el Caribe, Vol. 2. Bogota: Asociacion Columbiana para el Estudio de la Poblacion (ACEP).

______. 1982b. Sociedad, Subordinacion y Feminismo: Debate sobre la Mujer en America Latina y el Caribe, Vol. 3. Bogota: Asociacion Columbiana para el Estudio de la Poblacion (ACEP).

de Leonardo, Margarita. 1976. "La mujer y las clases sociales en Mexico." In La Mujer: Explotacion, Lucha, Liberacion. Clara Eugenia Aranda, et al., eds. pp. 1-58. Mexcio: Editorial Nuestro Tiempo.

Mead, Margaret. 1935. Sex and Temperament in Three Primitive Societies. New York: William Morrow.

______. 1950. Male and Female: A Study of Sexes in a Changing World. New York: William Morrow.

Meislin, Richard. 1984. Mexico's Border Industries. New York Times. March 19.

Nash, June. 1970. In the Eyes of the Ancestors. Belief and Behavior in a Maya Community. New Haven: Yale University Press.

______. 1980. "Aztec Women: The Transition from Status to Class in Empire and Colony." In Women and Colonization. M. Etienne and E. Leacock, eds. pp. 134-148. South Hadley: J. F. Bergin Publishers, Inc.

______. 1982. "Implications of Technological Change for Household Level and Rural Development." In Technological Change and Rural Development in Developing Countries. Peter M. Weil and J. Elterich, eds. pp. 429-476. Newark, Delaware: University of Delaware Press.

Nash, June and M. Patricia Fernandez-Kelly, eds. 1983. Women, Men and the International Division of Labor. Albany: State University of New York Press.

Nash, June and Helen Safa, eds. 1976. Sex and Class in Latin America. South Hadley: J. F. Bergin Publishers, Inc.

Orrego de Figueroa, Teresa. 1976. "A Critical Analysis of Latin American Programs to Integrate Women in Development." In Women and World Development. Irene Tinker and Michele Bo Bramsen, eds. Washington, D.C.: Overseas Development Council.

Rosaldo, Michele ad Louise Lamphere. 1974. Women, Culture, and Society. Stanford: Stanford University Press.

Rubbo, Anna. 1975. "The Spread of Capitalism in Rural Columbia: Effects on Poor Women." In Toward an Anthropolgy of Women. Rayna R. Reiter, ed. pp. 333-358. New York: Monthly Review Press.

Safa, Helen. 1981. "Runaway Shops and Female Employment: The Search for Cheap Labor." Signs 7:418-434.

______. 1983. "Women, Production and Reproduction in Industrial Capitalism: A Comparison of Brazilian and U.S. Factory Workers." In Women, Men, and the International Division of Labor. J. Nash an M. P. Fernandez-Kelly, eds. pp. 95-116. Albany: State University of New York Press.

Saffioti, Heleieth. 1969. Women in Class Society. New York: Monthly Review Press.

Sautu, Ruth. 1981. "The Female Labor Force in Argentina, Bolivia, and Paraguay." Latin American Research Review 16:152-159.

Silverblatt, Irene. 1982. "Andean Women under Spanish Rule." In Women and Colonization. M. Etienne and E. Leacock, eds. pp. 149-185. South Hadley: J. F. Bergin Publishers, Inc.

Vasquez de Miranda, Glaura. 1977. "Women's Labor Force Participation in a Developing Society: The Case of Brazil." In Women and National Development: The Complexities of Change. Wellesley Editorial Committee. Special Issue of Signs 3:261-274. Chicago: The University of Chicago Press.

Young, Kate. 1978. "Modes of Appropriation and the Sexual Division of Labour: A Case Study from Oaxaca, Mexico." In Feminism and Materialism. Annette Kuhn and Ann Marie Wolpe, eds. pp. 125-154. London: Routledge and Kegan Paul.

Youssef, Nadia H. 1977. "Introduction." In Women and National Development: The Complexities of Change. Wellesley Editorial Committee. Special Issue of Signs 3:275-277. Chicago: The University of Chicago Press.

2 Research Guidelines: *How to Study Women's Work in Latin America*

Neuma Aguiar

Latin American research has contributed many new perspectives on how to collect data on women in the work force. Although enthnographies themselves may serve to improve knowledge on women's work, they may also be used to complement survey research by asking deep questions that cannot be raised through survey research (Jain 1978).

This paper is based on the experience of Latin American researchers investigating the position of women through a combination of survey research and ethnographic methods to estimate the reach of census data and national household surveys in the representation of women in population and labor statistics.

Women's economic activities are underestimated because of two basic sets of premises. The first is cultural factors derived from kinship organization and patriarchal rule. The second has to do with the difficulty of conceptualizing women's productive activities in a positive manner. Since they are noncapitalist activities, not measured by market indices, they are either ignored or dumped in a residual category such as "the informal labor market." These two problems will be discussed below in the effort to outline a strategy of analysis when space and time provide positive references for studying women's work in Latin America.

ANALYZING WOMEN'S WORK CATEGORIES: THEORETICAL PERSPECTIVES

The categories selected for studying women's work have been criticized from different theoretical perspectives. One criticism, derived from phenomenology, suggests that classificatory systems used to aggregate data on society reflect the organizational context that produces them. The classifications are developed by analysts who may reproduce current stereotypes drawn from everyday life in their attempts to grasp reality (Garfinkel 1967; Cicourel 1976).

Marxist analysts, on the other hand, have tended to attribute the choice of categories for the study of aggregate data to theoretical concepts and methods used by the producers of statistics (Hindess 1973). Others link organizational reference points to the theoretical preferences of state bureaucrats. This is the approach of Miles and Irvine (1979), who analyze statistical agencies as part of the administrative apparatus of capitalist societies to deal with matters such as developmental planning, the provision of a trained labor force, intervention in a socioeconomic crisis, and the maintenance of basic services related to transportation and energy. These are all possible areas for state planning, management, and control. A comparative study of the choices of categories, particularly dimensions such as gender and work in censuses in capitalist and socialist countries would further elucidate such assumptions and reveal in each case the existing organizational preferences and stereotyping procedures.

Stereotyping in data-gathering procedure affects the perception of social problems and the attention directed toward them by government agencies. Conditions related to gender, ethnicity, or age can be masked by failure to disaggregate data in accord with these variables. Gonzales (1978) demonstrated the significance of census enumeration policies in the long-term neglect of ethnic variables by Brazilian census agencies, which ignored the varied racial composition of a given population in a national group.

Demographers themselves are inserted in social positions that they universalize as the premises of societal action. The institutions in which they operate reflect patriarchal preferences, since men are the principal incumbents in statistical agencies in charge of most decision making on data-gathering procedures. Their decisions are often derived from their everyday life experience, the major premise of which is that men are the major bread earners and women the major child-rearing adults in a household, performing unremunerated domestic work.

Stereotypes derived from patriarchal assumptions also intrude when census agencies enumerate the members of the household according to their kinship position in relation to one component of it: the head of a household, generally conceived to be a male adult. Sampling by household is a much less costly strategy than addressing questions to every adult member of a population. When a person listed as the male head is also the informant, this may result in incorrect information about women's activities.

Researchers concerned with the adequate measurement of women's participation in the work force are raising questions that can improve the collection of data on women's work. There is nothing inherently more accurate in having female researchers formulate the questions in census taking, yet to overcome cultural biases it may require such a corrective in perspective. Historically, it is feminist scholarship that has challenged traditional assumptions about the sexual division of labor in such a way as to throw light on women's activities that are commonly made invisible.

Some Latin American census agencies, including those in Brazil, have recognized the importance of addressing specific questions related to women when they want to improve the level of information about infant mortality. Unfortunately, this concern has only been developed in relation to reproductive matters, although other examples show how the selective interview strategy may also operate in other domains.

Household-survey strategies developed by Vera and Laird (1978) have shown how selecting a woman in each household as the informant may improve the level of information about women's activities. Problems may appear when there are several women adults in a household. A random-choice strategy may help to decide, in this case, which person should be selected.

INTERNATIONAL AGENCIES GUIDELINES

International agencies have imposed the categories of work developed in industrial capitalist countries on the data-collecting procedures of developing nations. The guidelines developed for market economies often disregard different coexisting modes of production in developing regions. They have also tended to ignore the many different ways in which households enter into production.

Focusing attention almost exclusively on market transactions, census enumerators fail to account for work performed in the household, whether it is paid or unpaid. However, as microanalytic studies have demonstrated, this is a work environment where women have been predominant.

The problem has two dimensions. The first has to do with patriarchal assumptions about the sexual division of labor by which women are shunted out of the public sphere, resulting in the underrepresentation of women. The other has to do with the almost exclusive focus on activities characteristic of a highly developed capitalist society. This does not take into account work situations pertinent to agricultural societies or to societies where there are a large number of domestic industries in the productive apparatus. National governments trying to stimulate capitalist growth or heavy industrialization as a developmental model often pay little attention to household labor, domestic industries, and domestic employment, where women's activities are highly concentrated. As a result, women's activities tend to be underrepresented and underreported.

We can summarize the factors that determine the choice of work categories influencing the measurement of women's work as follows:

(1) the position of agents, including their gender, in the organization that produces the statistics; (2) the position of the agency in the sociopolitical structure--the concepts, theories, and techniques that orient the practices of data collection performed by agencies; and (3) the degree to which dimensions that characterize the household in industrial and agrarian economies are taken into account.

THE HEAD OF HOUSEHOLD ISSUE

The question of who is selected as the head of household binds together two realms of concern: the gender organization of households and the position of households in the structure of production. These problems are crucial in the improvement of data-collection strategies, particularly in relation to women. One dimension has to do with the structure of production and the other with the gender arrangements for the control of reproduction. The first relates to the domain of labor statistics and the second to population.

The concept of the head of household is particularly important in the analysis of the small mercantile production developed in the domestic sphere under the command of the owner of the house. In the plantation economy, household head refers to the male workers who receive housing for their families as representatives of the family labor force, which each residential unit comprises for the plantation. In the capitalist economy, the concept implies that there are highly differentiated roles in the residential unit, when men work outside the house and women perform the domestic tasks of looking after the children and giving emotional support to the members of the family.

In either of these cases, the concept of the head of household hides the authority that women exert in the house and results in inadequate information on women's work. When male and female members work outside the house or are jointly responsible for domestic decisions, the situation is ignored by the Latin American censuses. The situation is further aggravated when married women are the major bread earners of a family or when women are the single heads of a household. In this last case, the data are collected in a way that makes it almost impossible to apprehend their major source of earnings (Barroso 1978).

HOUSEHOLD COMPOSITION

Changes occur among family components according to the level of economic development. The Latin American census has adopted a system of classification that distinguishes nuclear, extended, and composite families. This last category is a residue, including cases that simply could not fit into the other categories.

As families may have nonresident members, for census purposes the nuclear family is composed of female and male members of a conjugal society with the single daughters and sons who live under the same roof, that is, coresidents. It is recommended that these be coded in the following manner: (1) a person of reference and the spouse or companion; (2) the single daughters and sons of (1); (3) the married daughters and sons of (1); (4) the spouses or companions of (3); (5) the sons and daughters of (3) and (4); (6) grandchildren of (1); (7) the parents of (1); (8) the relatives of (1); (9) other residents unrelated to (1).

The type of family encountered may be classified according to the following system, detailed sufficiently to give an adequate composition: (1) single individuals; (2) no family; (3) simple family; (4) extended family; three generation--matrilateral, patrilateral, bilateral; two generation--matrilateral, patrilateral; other extended multiple family--matrilateral, patrilateral, bilateral; non-kin-related families.

The challenge here lies in enumerating the variation in household composition in such a way as to account for extended families, nuclear families, composite families that result from several matings of the person of reference, and the increasingly varied sexual preferences reflected in household composition that are found today. The situation should also allow for the depiction of varied single statuses as well as childless unions.

RESIDENTIAL UNIT AND PRODUCTION UNIT

In industrial capitalism, the residential unit becomes differentiated from industrial production in the factory, and the latter becomes the key arena in which production takes place. The social organization of the ancillary production that goes on in the interior of the residential unit, as well as the gender division of labor in other household services, makes it easier for some and harder for others to leave the housing environment to work in the enterprise or other unit of production external to the residence.

In the case of large agricultural enterprises where commercial crops are grown, we find a complex relationship between housing and production. When the enterprise allocates residential units to the workers as part of the work contract, the residential unit is coexistent with the productive unit (Aguiar 1983). When the residents of these big properties are expelled, the families may establish sharecropping or rental contracts with the landowners. The residential unit becomes separated from the production unit, and the plots of land are generally small. Although there is a dissociation between the house and the productive unit, these spaces are either contiguous or the unit of production may be temporarily rented by members of a household. This should not be confused with the dissociation between the residential unit and the unit of production that characterizes industrial capitalism, since household members participate as unpaid family workers to allocate goods to the market.

In small mercantile production, the residential unit and its surrounding areas are means of production. To classify this form of social organization as capitalist may lead to the assumption that the unpaid family workers are domestic workers instead of workers at home for cash.

All analysis of work should take into account the following situations: the residential unit is the unit of production; the residential unit is differentiated and dissociated from the unit of production; the residential unit is differentiated from the unit of production but is contiguous with it; the residential unit is contained within the productive unit. Residential "collectives", or units where people who live together may not necessarily have kinship ties, may be studied in the same manner, according to the position of the household in society's productive system.

The designation of the position of the household in the productive system provides knowledge of the social organization of work at the same time that it indicates how the category "head of the household" has been constructed. It clarifies the distinction among domestic work, domestic employment, work in the domicile or at home, and domestic industry. The classification of the work site in terms of space also allows the distinction of work that is performed in the streets.

WORK AND EMPLOYMENT

The analysis of the relationship between work and employment should clarify the meaning of the concepts of work and employment. The categories used by the Latin American census are more adequate to measure employment, or salaried work (Levitan 1979), in detriment to the apprehension of work tied to small mercantile production.

Leon and Deere (1975) differentiate between salaried work and unremunerated family work in accordance with the social reltions of production prevailing. They point to the impact of capitalist production on small-scale "subsistence" production, indicating that the two forms may coexist in different degrees. From this perspective, they compare two different regions in Colombia, stratifying small production according to the penetration of capitalist production in the productive apparatus. Observations on the differentiation of small-scale production have also been pointed out in the analysis of women's work developed by Schmuckler (1978) and Hermitte and Segre (1978).

All these studies point to the need for differentiation between work and employment. Research on women's work should specify differentiation among small production units since the size of the production unit and technology employed in it vary and the female participation in the work force may also vary according to these dimensions.

The Latin American literature on women's work has brought to light the work performed at home in the production of food or garments destined for the market. Such activities were formerly classified indiscriminately with the domestic activities related to them and as a result were not enumerated in the census. Furthermore, when questions on women's work are addressed to men, the work is underreported. This may also be true even if the questions are addressed to the women themselves. For instance, in many peasant areas, "work" refers only to remunerated activities. A solution to this problem may be to give women a precodified set of activities, asking them to provide information on whether they performed any of them in a determined period of time taken as reference. Vera and Laird (1978) suggest that if an exploratory study is made prior to the definitive study, a precoded list of the most frequent activities may be elaborated. Sautu (1978) indicates that these activities may be identified with the kinds of agricultural production performed in a certain area. She also notes that it is possible to identify activities developed in large, as well as in small, productive units and that they may be studied as an articulated work system. All analyses of female work should allow for an accounting of the activities that may be done at home but are oriented toward the market.

A comparative analysis of the occupational categories used in Latin America carried out by the United Nations (1978:108-27) showed that Latin American countries group together the activities performed by workers and artisans. The continuity that is given emphasis by this combination is contrasted with the handling of domestic work that lumps together many differentiated tasks. Ethnographic techniques and open-ended questions in exploratory surveys or pilot census may be necessary to sort out these activities, since the existing categories do not cover the whole gamut of activities performed by women. These exploratory studies aimed at attaining a high level of occupational specification might well be taken as a standard for incorporation in large-scale surveys.

PERIOD OF REFERENCE IN THE ANALYSIS OF WOMEN'S WORK

The period of time used as a reference to verify whether the interviewee belongs to the economically active labor force may affect the labor force composition encountered in census data (D'Souza 1978; United Nations-CEPAL 1978; Lattes and Wainerman 1979). When a larger period of time is taken as a reference, for instance, when a question about the main activity refers to the twelve months prior to the census, more women will be shown in the composition of the labor force since there is a high female component in rural seasonal activities. These are not captured if the question refers only to the week prior to the census (D'Souza 1978; United Nations 1978; Souza and Silva 1978; Lattes and Wainerman 1979).

Investigations in the rural Latin American context demonstrate the importance of using questions that refer to several time periods presented simultaneously during the interview: one relative to the moment of the interview, another relative to the week prior to the census, one seasonal, one annual, and finally one that refers to the life cycle. These allow for improved international comparisons and for the improvement in measurement based on more adequate accounting within each nation.

The Number of Hours of Paid Work

Censuses typically have shown little concern with part-time work. Since women more often than men are engaged in part-time work, this lapse also contributes to the diminished perception of their contribution. The number of hours of work is crucial in the accounting of women as participants in the economically active population. Socioeconomic class variations exist here as in other variables. In the case of Nicaragua, Rojas (1978) points out that women in high occupational positions tend to work part time, while low status women tend to work many more hours than that considered to be average for full time work.

Research should elaborate clearly specified questions on women's work for each of the house components. The interviews must be addressed not only to the main activities of women, but also to their secondary activities. The amount of work should be measured in terms of the numbers of hours of work.

Age and Life Cycle

When age is taken as a limitation in investigating the condition of women related to their activities, the composition of the economically active population is affected, as a comparative analysis developed by Lattes and Wainerman (1977) demonstrate. For example, in rural areas and urban contexts of poor regions, many children work (Neto 1978).

The life cycle stage is also a factor of decisive importance in the determination of female work. In this should be included the time of marital union (when there is one); the average age of the companions or spouses; the number of children and their ages, particularly of the oldest and of the youngest; the ages of the female and of the male at the time of birth of the last child; and the sexual and generational division of labor in the domestic context and outside it. The life-cycle stage is also important for the understanding of the intensity of work done by the several members of the domestic group in the rural or in the urban context (Rodrigues 1978).

It is recommended that these dimensions be comparatively analyzed in relation to the female and male responsible for the house when there are members of the two sexes holding such responsibility.

In this case the relationship between the domestic context and the work performed by the same persons outside that context should be accounted for as well. Data on the educational level and income should also be collected for all the members of the domestic group. If there is only one person of reference instead of two, those data should still be included.

THE IDENTIFICATION OF DOMESTIC ACTIVITIES

One of the main tasks in studying women's work consists in the identification and codification of the activities performed in the domestic context. Official statistical agencies in several nations (none of them in Latin America) have conducted household surveys to find out the amount of time allocated by the members of the domestic units in relation to the activities performed in the domestic context, as well as outside it. Time-budget studies have been conducted in three Latin American peasant societies. They furnish useful guidelines and may be applied on a larger scale by statistical agencies.

Despite the limitation of many time budget studies to peasant women's work, there are specific accounts from widely differentiated contexts (Lingsom 1975; United Nations CEPAL 1978; Figueiredo 1980). Based on them, we may classify women's activities in the following categories: domestic activities; activities which contribute to family subsistence; economic activities which are addressed to the market but which may be alternated with housework; commercial activities, that is, activities related to the buying and selling of goods.

Domestic activities comprise feeding the family, cleaning the kitchen and the house, and sewing and cleaning clothing, and caring for the young children. Activities that contribute to family subsistence include gardening, animal husbandry, and obtaining water and fuel for the house. Several studies have also developed more complex classificatory systems that take into account the time dedicated to leisure and to physiological activities. Other studies may expand the set of categories to include urban activities, and among these, time spent traveling to work. Whenever possible samples of time allocation should be obtained since they provide a thorough description of activities differentiated by gender.

The identification of female activities should be obtained through questions addressed to women, making it possible for them to consult with other members of the domestic unit so that they give more precise information on their activities. One strategy consists in choosing women in charge of decision making in the domestic unit as the respondents when doing household surveys. This procedure is radically distinct from that discussed above, where the person chosen to be interviewed is generally a male, based on the premise that males are the heads of households.

Another strategy for depicting female activities consists in choosing female interviewers who are well acquainted with the cultural universe of the interviewees (Vera and Laird 1978). One alternative to this form, for comparative purposes, may be the use of interviewers of both sexes to check on the effect of the sex of the interviewers on the response rate and content.

The identification of new ways of asking questions raises the problem of the comparability of data throughout time. However, the immutability of concepts makes it difficult to capure societal changes. The new questionnaires may be pretested through in-depth interviewing, done with the purpose of checking the adequacy of census or household surveys.

In the Paraguayan census of 1972, only 13 percent of the women in the rural areas were shown as economically active (Vera and Laird 1978). One household survey, developed by the census agency in 1976, with additional questions on work, was addressed to women who would have been classified as economically inactive in the previous census (Vera and Laird 1978), raising their level of participation to 24 percent. A new sample, intended to provide information for a socioeconomic profile of rural women, indicated that 86 percent of the women interviewed engaged in cash producing activities during the week taken as reference through the strategy mentioned above (Republica del Paraguay 1979).

It is recommended that the suggestions advanced here, based on the experience of data users, constitute research guidelines to improve the measurement of female work, making it possible for the rates of labor-force participation obtained through household surveys and other reserach to reflect accurately the activities performed by women.

REFERENCES

Aguiar, Neuma. 1983. "Household, Community, National and International Development," In Women, Men and the International Division of Labor. J. Nash and M. Patricia Fernandez-Kelly, eds., pp. 117-137. Albany: State University of New York Press.

Barroso, Carmen. 1978. "Sozinhas ou Mal Acompanhadas: A Situacao des Mulheres Chefes de Familia." Paper presented to the Seminar: Women in the Labor Force in Latin America. Rio de Janeiro: IUPERJ.

Carvalho, Maria Luiza, and Rosa Maria Ribeiro Silva. 1978. "O Trabalho Feminino em Areas Rurais da America Latina: Uma Revisao da Literatura." Paper presented to the Seminar: Women in the Labor Force in Latin America. Rio de Janeiro: IUPERJ.

Cicourel, A. V. 1976. The Social Organziation of Juvenile Delinquency. London: Heinemann.

D'Souza, Stanislas. 1978. "Head of Household: Sex Based Stereotypes, Sex Biases and National Data Systems." Paper presented to the Seminar: Women in the Labor Force in Latin America. Rio de Janeiro: IUPERJ.

Figueiredo, Mariza. 1980. "O Papel Socio-Economico das Mulheres Chefes de Familia, numa Comunidade Pesqueira do Litoral Norte da Bahia." Cuadernos de Debates 6:35-78.

Garfinkel, Harold. 1967. Studies in Ethnomethodology. Englewood Cliffs, New Jersey: Pentice Hall.

Gonzales, Lelia de Almeida. 1978. "Qual o Lugar da Mulher Negra Enquanto Force de Trabalho?" Paper presented to the Seminar: Women in the Labor Force in Latin America. Rio de Janeiro: IUPERJ.

Hermitte, Esther, and Malvina Segre. 1978. "Unidad Productiva y Formas de Articulacion con el Mercado Nacional: El Caso de las Artesanas Textiles en la Region del Noroeste Argentino." Paper presented to the Seminar: Women in the Labor Force in Latin America. Rio de Janeiro: IUPERJ.

Hindess, Barry. 1973. The Use of Official Statistics in Sociology. London: Macmillan.

Jain, Devaki. 1978. "Recommendations to the 1981 Census of India." Institute of Social Studies: Data Users Conference.

Lattes, Zulma Recchini de, and Catalina H. Wainerman. 1977. "Empleo Femenino y Desarrollo Economico: Algunas Evidencias." Desarrollo Economico 66, 17:301-317.

______. 1979. "Informacion de Censos y Encuestas de Hogares para al Analisis de la Mano de Obra Femenina en America Latina y el Caribe: Evaluacion de Deficiencias y Recomendaciones para Superarlas." United Nations-CEPAL: E/CEPAL/L.206.

Leal, Leon de, Magdalena and Carmen Diana Deere. 1978. "La Proletarizacion y el Trabajo Agricola en la Economia Parcelaria: Estudio de la Division del Trabajo por Sexo en Dos Regiones Colombianas." Paper presented to the Seminar: Women in the Labor Force in Latin America. Rio de Janeiro: IUPERJ.

Levitan, Sar A. 1979. "Labour Force Statistics to Measure Full

Employment." Society 16, 6 (September/October): 68-71.

Lingsom, Susan. 1975. Household Work and Family Care: An Analysis of Time Budget Data. Oslo: Arbeidsnotater- Statistics Sentral Byra.

Miles, Ian, and J. Irvine. 1979. "The Critique of Official Statistics." In Demystifying Social Statistics. John Irvine; Ian Miles and Jeff Evans, (eds.) 113-129. London: Pluto Press.

Neto, Zahide Machado. 1978. "As Meninas: Sobre o Trabalho da Crianca e da Adolescente em Familia Proletaria." Paper presented to the Seminar: Women in the Labor Force in Latin America. Rio de Janeiro: IUPERJ.

Republica del Paraguay-Direccion General de Estadistica y Censos. 1979. La Mujer Rural en el Paraguay: Dimension Socio-Economica. Asuncion: Ministerio de Hacienda.

Rodrigues, Arakcy Martins. 1978. "O Padrao de Distribuicao de Papeis em Familias Operarias." Paper presented to the Seminar: Women in the Labor Force in Latin America. Rio de Janeiro: IUPERJ.

Rojas, Antionio Ybarra. 1978. "La Estructura Ocupacional de la Fuerza de Travajo Femenina en Nicaragua: 1950-1977." Paper presented to the Seminar: Women in the Labor Force in Latin America. Rio de Janeiro: IUPERJ.

Sautu, Ruth. 1978. "Formas de Organizacion Agraria, Migraciones Estacionales y Trabajo Femenino." Paper presented to the Seminar: Women in the Labor Force in Latin America. Rio de Janeiro: IUPERJ.

Schmuckler, Beatriz Elba. 1978. "Mujer y Familia Comerciante." Paper presented to the Seminar: Women in the Labor Force in Latin America. Rio de Janeiro: IUPERJ.

United Nations Comision Economica para America Latina (CEPAL) Statistical Commission. 1978. Progress Report on the Development of Statistics of Time Use. Report of the Secretary-General. E/CN. 3/519.

Vera, F. David, and Judith Laird. 1978. "Metodologia Empleada en la Encuesta del Perfil Socio-Economico de la Mujer Rural en el Paraguay." Paper presented to the Seminar: Women in the Labor Force in Latin America. Rio de Janeiro: IUPERJ.

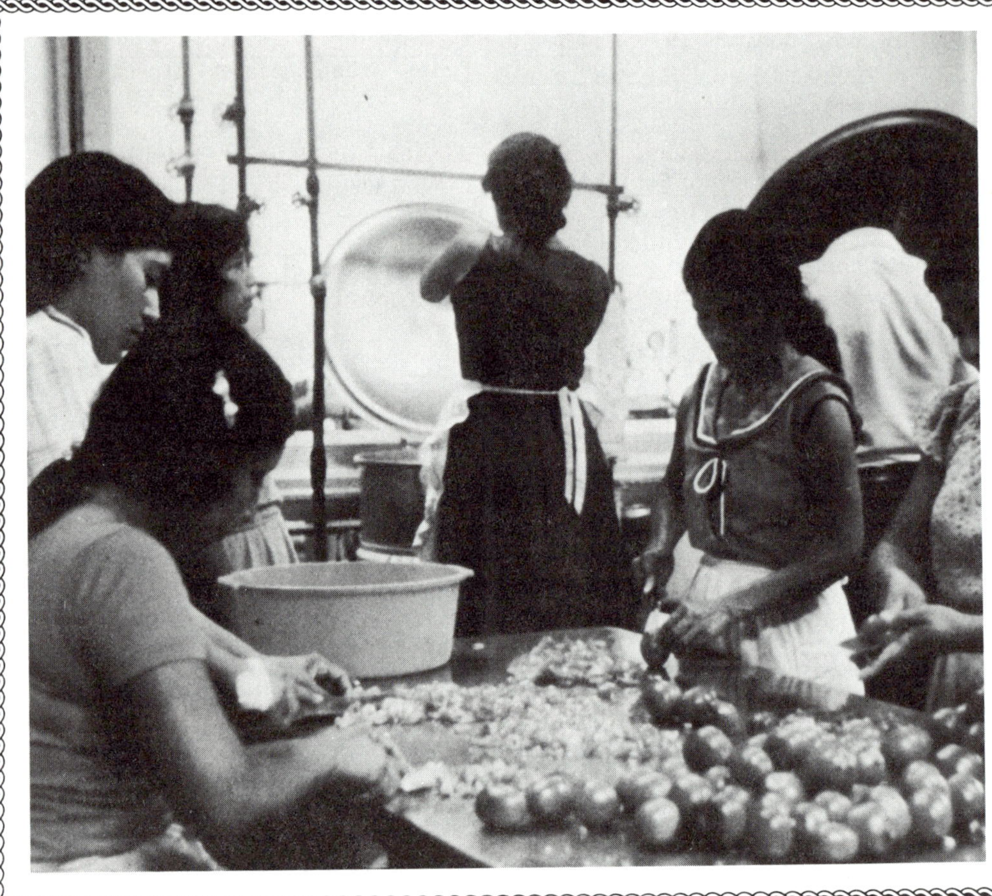

These women are part of a food-processing cooperative financed by OEF in rural El Salvador.

II Production for the Market, Social Reproduction, and Biological Reproduction

The interrelatedness of productive and reproductive systems, particularly when analyzed from the perspective of women, makes it impossible to separate the analyses in different sections of an anthology. Frances Rothstein poses the related issues of market, social, biological reproduction in the most blunt terms: how does the cost of bearing and rearing children affect childbearing in an industrializing sector of Mexico. Florence Babb shows the underside of development where the extremely marginalized economic roles of women in a provincial city of Peru make children's contribution to income an important asset in the penetration of capitalism. The counterpoint in the two articles shows the importance of a multifaceted, cross-cultural comparative approach to the study of the relationship between modes of production and modes of reproduction. These contrasts are of crucial importance in assessing societies undergoing extreme pressures on domestic budgets as a result of national indebtedness, as Lynn Bolles shows in her study of Jamaican households. The burden women bear in the reproduction of working class families is still underestimated. Helen Safa assesses what that underestimation means in economic terms when women enter the paid labor force.

Sometimes marketing is a family affair. Two sisters and their husbands bring their children with them to this small restaurant.

PHOTO BY FLORENCE BABB

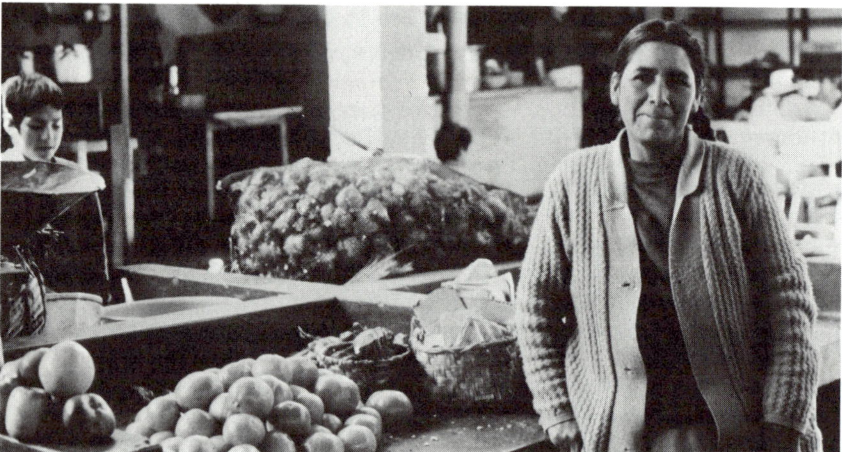

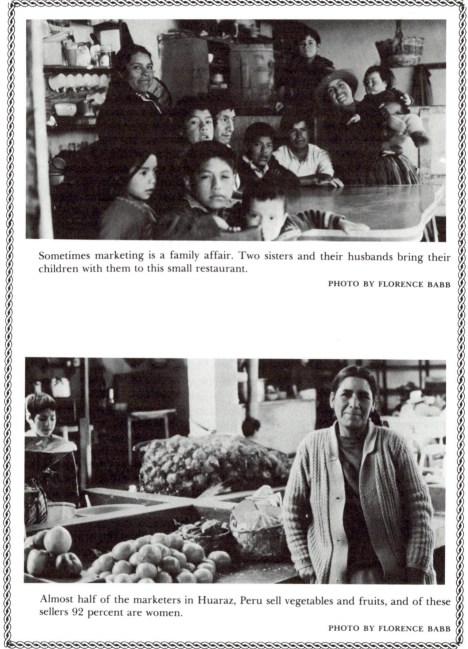

Almost half of the marketers in Huaraz, Peru sell vegetables and fruits, and of these sellers 92 percent are women.

PHOTO BY FLORENCE BABB

3 Capitalist Industrialization and the Increasing Cost of Children

Frances Rothstein

Historical studies of the family since the seminal work by Aries (1962) have shown that European industrialization was associated with the emergence of the idea of childhood, the centering of the family on children, and an increasing concern with education. A number of studies have further suggested that these changes in childhood and child rearing are related to the development of wage labor and proletarianization (Tilly, Scott, and Cohen 1976; Tilly n.d.; and Tilly and Scott 1978; Minge-Kalman 1978).

More specifically, recent studies suggest two patterns of response to wage earning. First, in early industrialized cities, a high fertility strategy was the response to the imperative for multiple wage earners (Tilly n.d.:12). Second, in a later phase of industrialization, the demand for educated labor put a new demand on the family as producers of that labor. Children "subtly but rapidly developed into a labor-intensive product of the family" (Minge-Kalman 1977:88). Minge-Kalman shows how, in this second stage, the direct financial cost of children and the indirect costs of their foregone labor continued to rise with industrialization (1977).

Although there have been a number of historical studies of the impact of industrialization on the family that shed some light on the relationship among industrialization, market conditions, and childhood, many of these studies have necessarily been based on the method of family reconstitution that reconstructs family patterns from parish registers. Although family reconstitution has proven to be a valuable approach, as Levine notes, it has "some very real shortcomings . . . revolving around the limited, narrowly statistical nature of the information that can be derived from this form of analysis" (1977:2).[1] Other historical studies, such as those by Aries

(1962) and Shorter (1975), although more qualitative and holistic, have had to rely primarily on limited portraits, memoirs, family reference books, and brief descriptions by casual observers.

Anthropological discussions of the impact of industrialization on the family have shown changes, but these studies tend to concentrate on the relations among different families or domestic units and often ignore the relations within the family (e.g. Carlos and Sellers 1972). Many anthropological studies have examined child rearing, but they have been concerned mainly with the consequences of various child rearing practices on personality and they focus on mother-child interaction rather than adult-child interaction (e.g. Minturn and Lambert 1964; Whiting and Whiting 1975). Because of these various limits on studies of the family and industrialization, the transition from what Shorter calls indifference (1975:169) to child-centeredness requires further clarification.

The anthropological literature hints that children in the Third World are also becoming "a labor-intensive, capital-intensive product of the family" (Minge-Kalman 1977:88). This fits with the recent expansion of industrial capitalism. As capitalists search for cheap labor, industrial or productive capital is increasingly replacing merchant capital in the Third World, and the relations of production in underdeveloped countries such as Mexico are increasingly mirroring the capitalist relations of production in the center. Few studies, however, have focused on the emergence of child-centeredness in the underdeveloped world.

This chapter, based on eighteen months of field work, describes and analyzes changes in childhood, the centering of family resources and efforts on children, and an increasing concern with education among proletarians in San Cosme Mazatecochco, an industrializing community in the central Mexican Highlands[2]. The purpose of the chapter is twofold. As indicated earlier, our understanding of the development of child-centeredness in the nineteenth century is limited. Because the process is occurring today in San Cosme, it can provide suggestions as to what that process was like in the last century. The first half of this chapter describes child-centeredness and suggests some of the important characteristics of that process. The second half examines the possibilities for mobility, or the gains from child-centeredness. Many studies explicitly or implicitly suggest that education is the means to mobility in both the advanced and dependent capitalist countries. It is beyond the scope of this chapter to examine the validity of this assertion in the advanced capitalist world, but the analysis of Mexico suggests that under conditions of dependent industrialization the possibilitiies for mobility are very limited.

Until the early 1940s, San Cosme was a relatively homogeneous peasant community. Even by 1950, according to the national census, 90 percent of the population walked barefoot, 85 percent spoke Nahuatl, and 56 percent were illiterate. Except for a few families that supplemented small-scale agriculture with a mill or a general store and a handful of factory workers who worked in Mexico City, about sixty miles away, or Puebla, ten miles away, San Cosmeros relied on subsistence agriculture.

As a result of the national textile boom during the Second World War, men from San Cosme began making inroads into factory work. From less than ten industrial workers in 1940, participation in the industrial sector grew to almost three hundred, or 27 percent of the economically active population in 1970 (Direccion General de Estadisticas). By 1980, 60 percent of the economically active males aged twelve and over were factory workers. By 1980 also a small proportion of young women were working in such transnationals as Majestic and Exquisiteform.

Initially, men from San Cosme were able to obtain first unskilled and then semiskilled factory jobs in the textile industry by knowing someone in the factory. Increasingly, however, job applicants, even for unskilled labor in these same factories, are expected not only to know someone but also to have completed at least a primary school education. At the same time, participation in the industrial sector has also made workers aware of the educational requirements for such other jobs as nurses, engineers, teachers, and lawyers. In an attempt to prepare their children for the skilled labor force and the growing requirements for unskilled labor, the families of San Cosme have increasingly become child-centered. Child-centeredness is especially apparent among the proletarians but peasants, who have no direct experience with factory work, are also devoting more and more of thier resources to their children.

CHILD-CENTEREDNESS IN SAN COSME

Childhood in San Cosme has changed in three respects. First, children are less integrated into the adult world than they used to be. Second, they are integrated into the adult world at a later age. And third, parents are devoting more time, energy, and resources to their children.

A Separate World for Children

Studies of the family in Europe prior to industrialization have suggested that in the preindustrial family children were integrated into the adult world of work and play by the age of seven. Several contemporary studies also suggest that children's labor is an important part of the peasant family economy (e.g. Nag, Peet and White 1978; Minge-Klevana 1980; Rothstein 1983). With industrialization, however, the demand increased for skilled or educated labor[3]. Not only is wage work under industrial conditions performed in a separate world of the factory but children are, as Aries (1962) argues, separated from the adult world as they are placed in a world of school and other children.

All the families of San Cosme, proletarian and peasant, cultivate small plots of land mostly for subsistence, but the children of San Cosme are spending more and more time in school and away from the family and the family farm. This is apparent in the level of education now achieved. As Table 1 indicates, among those fifty years of age and older, 97 percent did not complete primary school. Among the fifteen to nineteen year olds, however, 94 percent did complete primary school. The change is even more pronounced among proletarian families. Among the children of obreros, between the ages of twelve and nineteen, and therefore including some students who are still in primary school and will finish in a year or two, 94 percent have already completed primary school (See Table 2).

School attendance means that children are away from home and farm, and thus unavailable, not only for the five hours a day that they are in school. There is no postsecondary school in San Cosme, so after the ninth year students must spend time traveling to other communities. Since the local secondary school is a "tele-secondaria" school and some families prefer to send their children to a secondary school where teaching is direct, a number of children go elsewhere even before postsecondary school. Frequently, students live where they study and return to San Cosme only on weekends. Homework and studying for entrance examinations also keep children from the work and play of adults.

Presumably, since students are not in school all day and every day, children could help in the fields or in household chores during their free hours. Many of the children of San Cosme do. The children of factory workers, however, are less likely to do so. Among campesinos only 38 percent of the children seven years of age and older had not yet begun to help their families in the harvest. Among obreros 64 percent of those seven and over had not yet begun to help in the harvest. Even during the summer vacation, when most of a series of "spot observations"[4] were done, proletarian children were less likely to help with agricultural tasks. Among campesinos there was only one family out of eight in which children did not do any agricultural work during the study period. Among the fifteen proletarian families, children did not do any agricultural work in five families.

In part the withdrawal of proletarian children from field work is due to a general lowering of agricultural participation for all the family members of proletarian families. Although most of the proletarian families have continued to cultivate some corn for family consumption and sale, because of the unproductivity and unprofitability of small-scale agriculture,[5] they are less likely to also plant such other products as squash and beans, they weed and check their fields less, and are more likely to hire workers to replace men, women, and children of the family for most agricultural tasks. That the lesser work of proletarian children is not entirely due to more hired labor and fewer agricultural tasks in general, however, is sugguested by the fact that proletarian children are also less likely to do household chores. In eight of the fifteen proletarian households, children did no housework during the observations. There was only one peasant household in which children did no housework.

A More Prolonged Childhood

Childhood is not only increasingly separate from the adult world but children are also entering the adult world later and in a less graduated fashion.

In the family economy of peasants, children begin such productive and domestic tasks as caring for animals, sweeping, and running errands by the age of six or seven. Gradually, they assume more responsible jobs. For example, at about the age of eight, they may cut weeds and make tortillas. By ten or twelve, they can plant, harvest, and make meals. By the age of thirteen, the children have already begun doing the tasks that will be their life's work.

Increasingly, however, many children are still in school at the age of thirteen. Almost a third of the fifteen- to nineteen-year-olds in San Cosme have gone beyond the sixth grade. They may occasionally participate in adult activities but often they cannot. Some families try to do their harvesting on the weekends so that schoolchildren can help. Many, however, just do without the labor of their children.

The prolongation of childhood is most apparent among proletarian sons, for whom some postprimary school has become the norm. More of the sons of factory workers between the ages of fifteen and nineteen have gone beyond primary school than not (See Table 3).

Thus, the children of San Cosme are now less integrated into the adult world, the boys especially, and are integrated into the adult world at a later age. The costs in foregone labor are high. Nor are these the only costs. San Cosmeros, especially proletarians, are paying more for childhood in other ways as well. Increasingly, a variety of their efforts and resources are devoted to children.

Other Costs of Childhood

To say that proletarians are increasingly devoted to children is not to say, as Shorter (1975) suggests, that peasants are indifferent to or neglect their children. It is only by ignoring the high costs involved that one can characterize peasants as indifferent or negligent. As Bartra (1974) has pointed out, most Mexican peasants are pauperized. They not only lack excess resources to devote to children but are often living below a subsistence level. One peasant family, for example, cut out meat entirely so that they could send their daughter to school. Factory workers, who earn a minimum of 1,200 pesos a week compared to a peasant's maximum of 720 pesos can forego the labor of children and hire workers or buy some of the products, such as alfalfa instead of weeds to feed animals[6] that the labor of children might otherwise provide. Proletarians can also use their relatively higher earnings to buy a television for a child who cried for a TV, to buy school uniforms or costumes so that their child can dance or be queen in a school performance, and to pay four or five hundred pesos a month for tuition for a private school, plus books, bus fare, registration fees, and clothes.

Obreros also have the political contacts, usually through their unions, to fight for improved educational facilities. Educational facilities are scarce in Mexico, especially in rural areas. Over the last ten years, San Cosmeros, usually factory workers, have increased the local educational facilities from one primary school to two primary schools, a kindergarden, and a "tele-secondaria" school. Their efforts are reflected in the fact that in 1974, when almost a fifth (18 percent) of the municipios in Tlaxcala still had no general secondary school and 73 percent of the secondary schools were private (Secretaria de Educacion Publica 1975), San Cosme had a federal secondary school. San Cosmeros have made numerous trips to Tlaxcala and Mexico City to plead their case for more schools. They have helped construct and finance the schools. They also serve on school committees, sweep classrooms, and cook and sew for school fiestas.

In sum, San Cosmeros are now devoting a great deal of their time, effort, and resources to childhood. Rather than being a period of gradual and increasing integration into the adult world, childhood has become a long and costly period of preparation away from the adult world of wage labor. This costly preparation has involved the efforts of individuals, families, and the community. It is important to stress that all members of the family are involved. There has been a tendency in much of the literature on child-centeredness to focus on mothers (e.g. Shorter 1975; Minge-Kalman 1978). The data from San Cosme indicate that the nature of their efforts differ, but that child-centeredness is a costly process for all--women, men, and children. The efforts of women for their children take place largely in the private, less prestigious, domestic sphere, where they cook and clean for children and take over the domestic chores that children would do if they were not in school. Fathers go to work in factories and go to see state and national politicians. Meanwhile, children try to get through an educational system that must, because educational facilities are scarce, eliminate many. Despite the different nature of their efforts, however, they share common expectations about the rewards for their efforts.

THE GAINS

What are the gains? Studies of child-centeredness, as well as studies of the educational system, have suggested that the industrial workplace gains because widespread education serves as a means of uniform socialization, which teaches discipline (Minge-Kalman 1978) as well as new skills. Explicitly or implicitly, many studies also suggest that workers get better jobs. This view is also expressed by San Cosmeros. Many people said that through education their children would have better lives. Few San Cosmeros expect their children to be peasants, and many do not want their children to be factory workers. One proletarian father, for example, when asked whether it was better to be a peasant or a factory worker replied: "Neither. It is better to have a career." San Cosmeros see education as a means by which their children will achieve some social mobility.

The Myth of Mobility

San Cosmeros, like many proletarians elsewhere, (See Cardoso and Reyna 1968; Sennett and Cobb 1972; Scrimshaw 1975; Vellinga 1979) are aware that there are better jobs than the ones they have, and they want their sons, and to a lesser extent, their daughters, to have those jobs. They are also aware that the better jobs require more education. Toward that end they have devoted a great deal of their time, effort, and resources. Numerous sacrifices are made. For example, one storeowner closed down his store because the constant interruptions of customers disturbed his grandchildren while they were studying in the room adjacent to the store. Many families sacrifice meat so that they can send their children to school. One man in his early fifties said that his brother often asked him why he continues to work so hard as a factory worker. He said it is because he wants his children to be well educated so that they will not have to be factory workers. Among the young adults, those in their twenties and early thirties, many intend to have only two children so that they can afford to educate them. Most of the parents, however, already have four, five, or six children. They had their children when infant mortality was still very high and children were not a labor and capital-intensive product of the family. A high fertility rate was necessary to compensate for the high infant mortality rate, and children, rather than being the object of much of the family's resources, could with their labor, increase the family's resources. Although some of the older children help their parents and siblings by contributing part of their wages to the cost of educating their siblings, the major burden falls on the parents. As Sennett and Cobb suggest for workers in Boston, parents bear this burden because "The strains of one's own life become justified by the privilege work will create for their children" (1972:124).

The hopes of the San Cosmeros mirror the models of mainstram theorists and reformers who maintain that education is an equalizer in modern society. Such theorists see education as equalizing the gap between nations as well as within nations and often attribute underdevelopment to the lack of education. Hughes, for example, suggests that the poverty of nations is attributable to the lack of education and this lack of education keeps poor nations poor (1970).

This view of education is part of the mainstream picture of modern society and the modern world as open, mobile societies in which equality and opportunity abound. According to this view, public education reduces traditional inequalities (Moore 1963:107) and blurs the distinction between masses and elites (Kahl 1968:5). Differences that persist despite this presumed equality are seen as the inveitable inequality of individual differences in individual ability.

This view, which hides, justifies, and legitimates inequality, does not explain the increasing gap between rich and poor in Mexico. Nor does it explain why most of the men of San Cosme, despite their greater education, are still doing the same work, and earning the same salaries, in the same textile factories, on the same temporary contracts as the generation before them. The women, too, are still homemakers dependent on their husbands' insecure and low-paying jobs.

The original factory workers in San Cosme, that is, the first generation, experienced mobility with the shift from peasant to obrero. Sons of peasants may still move upward as they, too, become factory workers. Most likely, however, the rate of absorption will slow down. The number of textile workers has decreased despite an increase in the value of production. (Juarez 1979:138). As capital becomes increasingly concentrated and foreign capital continues to grow, unemployment has risen. In the late 1970s, manufacturing in general had its capacity to generate employment reduced by a 1.6 percent cut in the personnel employed (Economic Commission for Latin America 1978:338). There is also a growing tendency to hire the most educated workers. Since peasant sons tend to be less educated, they may not be able to enter the industrial sector as easily as the first-generation obreros.

Women, too, despite their greater education, will suffer from the growth of credentialism. Girls have not been unaffected by the development of child-centeredness. As indicated in Table 4, proletarian daughters are less likely to do domestic chores than are peasant daughters. They are also more educated than are peasant daughters. In comparison to proletarian sons, however, they are less educated. Whereas most proletarian sons have finished secondary school (ninth grade), most proletarian daughters have not (see Table 5). Not only will their lesser education put them at a disadvantage in the labor market and thereby encourage marriage as their major goal, but it will further increase the gap between proletarian husbands and wives.

Some sons and daughters of peasants and semiskilled factory workers have become middle-class teachers, nurses, lawyers, and engineers. The son of one factory worker, who is still in high school but has some mechanical training, works in the same facotry as this father and earns almost as much at sixteen as his fifty-year-old father, who has been an obrero for thirty-five years. Most, however, will not be so fortunate. As indicated in Table 6, the sons of most factory workers still become semiskilled factory workers. They work in the same textile industry, which is one of the lowest-paying industries in Mexico. Inflation has meant that their real wages are less than the wages of workers in the past. The introduction of new, more advanced, machinery, usually imported, has meant also that they operate more machines but cannot fix them as they used to. Not only have their jobs become simplified, but they are not paid while they are waiting for a mechanic to repair the machinery. Their jobs have become redefined, but rather than taking advantage of their improved education, their jobs are simplified, and they, the workers, are more easily replaced. In addition, as many young obreros in San Cosme pointed out, since the price of land in the community has risen, they cannot afford to buy land as their fathers did, and they cannot supplement their wages and carry themselves and their families through periods of unemployment with subsistence production. As factories are built in San Cosme, a process that began in the early 1980s, the possibility of supplementing wages with subsistence production will be even further reduced. Education has not improved the standard of living.

The daughters of San Cosme are also unlikely to have experienced any significant changes in life-style through improved education. A daughter of a campesino may experience a rise in her standard of living by becoming the housewife of an obrero. The majority of proletarian daughters become homemakers like their mothers (see Table 6). Some will work in "women's factories" before they are married, but since these factories, usually transnationals, hire only young women and offer only the least skilled and lowest-paying job possibilities, they are not channels for mobility.

Most likely, also, subsistence production, which gave their mothers a small amount of economic independence, will as indicated above, continue to decline. Unlike their mothers, for whom proletarian domesticity usually meant a higher standard of living then that of their peasant parents, most proletarian daughters do not experience mobility through marriage.

CONCLUSION

According to Wells, peasants are characterized by a sense of powerlessness and see the world as uncontrollable. Those with modern values, on the other hand "believe not only that the world is knowable and controllable, but that it is to an individual's advantage to plan his or her life and to attend to the future. To merely avoid trouble is no longer enough (as it was in traditional society) for the modern individual; such a person wants to advance" (1978:521).

Child-centeredness is an attempt by San Cosmeros to plan for the future and to deal with the strains of the present. They have hopes for advancement, largely through education. The ideas that through education one's children can experience mobility is a common theme in the literature on modernization as well as in the appeals of social workers, nurses, and other reformers. And there are numerous examples of such mobility. What is often neglected, however, is the fact that although education has become necessary, it is not sufficient. By its very nature, a capitalist class structure limits the number of successes. In a dependent capitalist system, such as that of Mexico, mobility is further limited.

The success stories of San Cosme are qualitiatively impressive. Unfortunately, however, despite their improved education and the costly efforts of all, the majority of the youth will do the same semiskilled, or less skilled, factory work that men from San Cosme have been doing since the 1940s. Their wives, too, will do the same domestic tasks as their mothers, except that their domestic work will be less diverse and confined even more to consumption. Without more education than their parents, the children of San Cosme will sink. But the obverse is not true. More education does not mean they will rise.

NOTES

This chapter is a revised and shortened version of some of the material in Three Different Worlds: Women, Men, and Children in an Industrializing Community, Westport, Conn.: Greenwood Press.

[1] Several critics have suggested that the limits on these studies have more to do with the questions asked and the assumptions made than with the methodology. See Berkner (1973) and Rothstein (1982:ch.2)

[2] Field work was conducted in San Cosme from June 1971 to June 1972, from May 1974 to August 1974, and from July 1980 to September 1980. I am grateful for the assistance of the Wenner-Gren Foundation for Anthropological Research, which made it possible for me to return in 1980.

[3] See Braverman (1974) for an excellent discussion of the functions of education under industrial capitalism.

[4] A modified version of the "spot observations" suggested by Johnson (1978) was used in 1980. Selected families were each visited eight times on randomly selected days in August and September. The activities of all family members were recorded for a specified hour of the day.

[5] See Bartra (1974) and Rothstein (1982:ch.3) for discussions of the low productivity of subsistence production.

6 In 1980 there were 22.5 Mexican pesos to the U.S. dollar.

REFERENCES

Aries, Phillippe. 1962. Centuries of Childhood. New York: Vintage.

Bartra, Roger. 1974. Estructura Agraria y Clases Sociales en Mexico. Mexico: Serie Popular Era.

Berkner, Lutz. 1975. "The Use and Misuse of Census Data for the Historical Analysis of Family Structures." Journal of Interdisciplinary History 4:721-728.

Braverman, Harry. 1974. Labor and Monopoly Capital. New York: Monthly Review Press.

Cardoso, Fernando and Jose Reyna. 1968. "Industrialization, Occupational Structure and Social Stratification in Latin America." In Constructive Changes in Latin America. C. Blasier, ed. pp. 21-55. Pittsburgh: University of Pittsburgh.

Carlos, M. and L. Sellers. 1972. "Family, Kinship Structure, and Modernization in Latin America." Latin American Research Review 7:95-125.

Direccion General de Estadisticas. 1940. VI Censo General de Poblacion. Mexico: Secretaria de Industria y Comercio.

______. 1950. VII Censo General de Poblacion. Mexico: Secretaria de Industria y Comercio.

______. 1960. VII Censo General de Poblacion. Mexico: Secretaria de Industria y Comercio.

______. 1970. IX Censo General de Poblacion. Mexico: Secretaria de Industria y Comercio.

Economic Commission for Latin America. 1978. Economic Survey of Latin America: 1977. Santiago, Chile: United Nations.

Hughes, John. 1970. Industrialization and Economic History. New York: McGraw-Hill.

Johnson, Allen. 1978. Quantification in Cultural Anthropology. Stanford: Standford University Press.

Juarez, Antonio. 1979. Las Corporaciones Transnacionales y los Trabajadores Mexicanos. Mexico City: Siglo Veintiuno.

Kahl, Joseph. 1968. The Measurement of Modernism: A Study of Values in Brazil and Mexico. Austin: University of Texas.

Levine, David. 1977. Family Formation in an Age of Nascent Capitalism. New York: Academic Press.

Minge-Kalman, Wanda. 1977. The Evolution of Family Productive Changes During the Peasant to Worker Transition in Europe. Ph.D. Dissertation, Department of Anthropology, Columbia University.

______. 1978. "The Industrial Revolution and the European Family." Comparative Studies in Society and History 20:454-468.

Minge-Klevana (Minge-Kalman), Wanda. 1980. "Does Labor Time Increase with Industrializaton?" Current Anthropology 21:279-298.

Minturn, L. and W. Lambert. 1964. Mothers of Six Cultures. New York: John Wiley and Sons.

Moore, Wilbert. 1963. Social Change. Englewood Cliffs, New Jersey: Prentice-Hall.

Nag, Moni, R. C. Peet, and Benjamin White. 1978. "An Anthropological Approach to the Study of the Economic Value of Children in Java and Nepal." Current Anthropology 19:293-306.

Rothstein, Frances Abrahamer. 1982. Three Different Worlds: Women, Men and Children in an Industrializing Community. Westport, Conn.: Greenwood

______. 1983. "Women and Men in the Family Economy: An Analysis of the Relations between the Sexes in Three Peasant Communities." Anthropological Quarterly 56:10-23.

Scrimshaw, Susan. 1975. "A Study of Changing Values, Fertility, and Socio-Economic Status." In Population and Social Organization. M. Nag, ed. pp. 135-151. The Hague: Mouton.

Secretaria de Educacion Publica. 1975. Tlaxcala: Systema Educativa. Mexico City: Direccion General de Planeacion Educativa.

Sennett, Richard and Jonathan Cobb. 1972. The Hidden Injuries of Class. New York: Vintage.

Shorter, Edward. 1975. The Making of the Modern Family. New York: Basic Books.

Tilly, Louise. n.d. Production and Reproduction. Unpublished manuscript.

Tilly, Louise and Joan Scott. 1978. Women, Work and the Family. New York: Holt, Rinehart and Winston.

Tilly, Louise, Joan Scott and M. Cohen. 1976. "Women's Work and European Fertility Patterns." Journal of Interdisciplinary History 6:447-476.

Vellinga, Menno. 1979. Industrializacion, Burgesia y Clase Obrera en Mexico. Mexico City: Siglo Veintiuno.

Wells, Robert. 1978. "Family History and Demographic Transition." In The American Family in Social-Historical Perspective. M. Gordon, ed. pp. 516-532. New York: St. Martin's.

Whiting, Beatrice and John. 1975. Children of Six Cultures. Cambridge: Harvard University Press.

TABLE 1
Years of Schooling of San Cosmeros

Age	Less Than Six		Six		More Than Six		Total	
	#	%	#	%	#	%	#	%
50 And Over	104	97	3	3	-	-	107	100
40-49	84	87	12	13	-	-	96	100
30-39	68	80	15	18	2	2	85	100
20-29	19	41	26	57	1	2	46	100
15-19	8	6	85	63	41	31	134	100

Source: Rothstein 1982, Table 17.

TABLE 2
Education of Children of Peasant and Factory Workers
(12-19 years old)

Years of School	Peasants		Factory Workers	
	#	%	#	%
Less Than Six	15	21	7	6
Six or More	55	79	101	94

Source: Rothstein 1982, Table 19.

TABLE 3
Postprimary Education of 15- to 19-Year Olds in San Cosme

	Six Years Or Less		Seven Years Or More		Total	
	#	%	#	%	#	%
Peasant daughters	17	81.0	4	19.0	21	100.0
Peasant sons	16	80.0	4	20.0	20	100.0
Proletarian daughters	28	75.6	9	24.3	37	99.9
Proletarian sons	11	36.7	19	63.3	30	100.0

Source: Rothstein 1982, Table 20

TABLE 4

Work Done by Children

	Proletarian Families				Peasant Families			
Agricultural Work	Sons		Daughters		Sons		Daughters	
	#	%	#	%	#	%	#	%
Yes	8	66.7	4	30.8	6	85.7	2	28.6
No	4	33.3	9	69.2	1	14.3	5	71.5
Total	12	100.0	13	100.0	7	100.0	7	100.0
Domestic Work								
Yes	2	16.7	7	53.8	1	14.3	6	85.7
No	10	83.3	6	46.2	6	85.7	1	14.3
Total	12	100.0	13	100.0	7	100.0	7	100.0

Source: Rothstein 1982, Table 18.

TABLE 5

Education of 15-19-Year-Olds

	Peasant				Factory Workers			
	Sons		Daughters		Sons		Daugthers	
	#	%	#	%	#	%	#	%
Less Than Nine Years	16	80.0	19	90.5	14	46.7	33	89.2
Nine Years or More	4	20.0	2	9.5	16	53.3	4	10.8
Total	20	100.0	21	100.0	30	100.0	37	100.0

Source: Rothstein 1982, Table 16.

TABLE 6

Social Mobility

	Father's Occupation			
	Obrero		Campesino	
	#	%	#	%
Occupation of Son (16 and over)				
Obrero	32	62.7	59	80.8
Campesino	0	--	4	5.5
Student	18	35.3	4	5.5
White collar	0	--	3	4.1
Miscellaneous	1	2.0	3	4.1
Total	51	100.0	73	100.0
Occupation of Daughter (16 and over)				
Homemaker	22	62.9	37	72.5
Obrera	1	2.8	4	7.8
Campesina	0	--	1	2.0
Student	7	20.0	5	9.8
White collar	3	8.6	4	7.8
Maid	1	2.8	0	--
Miscellaneous	1	2.8	0	--
Total	35	99.9	51	99.9

Source: Rothstein 1982, Table 26.

4 Producers and Reproducers: *Andean Marketwomen in the Economy*

Florence E. Babb

For the last decade, since the florescence of research on women in society, the sexual division of labor has been viewed as a key to understanding women's socioeconomic position. By the mid-1970s, the view held sway that women's cross-cultural subordination could be explained by their universal or near-universal attachment to the domestic sphere of activity while men enjoyed the higher prestige of the public sphere. A flurry of studies appeared, documenting the unequal and undervalued role of women in the family and household. By calling attention to the previously "invisible" activities carried out daily by women, analysts undertook to transform the androcentric social sciences (e.g. contributions to Rosaldo and Lamphere 1974; Reiter 1975; Rohrlich-Leavitt 1975).

But just when the domestic/public framework was gaining support by many researchers, it was called into question by others. Evidence was brought forth from fieldwork in a variety of settings that showed women to move in a far broader sphere than the term "domestic" would suggest. Reports of women's participation in agriculture, in marketing, and in the wage labor force surfaced, and we began to hear more accounts of women's *dual* work roles, within *and* outside the home (e.g. Sudarkasa 1973; Chinas 1973). By the late 1970s, the domestic/public framework was regarded by many as inadequate to account for women's socioeconomic position (Young et al. 1981). There were simply too many cases of societies where women had active roles both inside and outside the home.

Even so, it was agreed that there are significant cross-cultural patterns in the work performed by women, and researchers dissatisfied with the available theoretical frameworks undertook to formulate a new one. In the last few years, the production/reproduction conceptual framework has emerged as the most powerful analytical tool that we have to account for women's socioeconomic condition. The identification of production and reproduction as focuses of analysis may be traced to earlier writers, notably Engels ([1884] 1972), but in contrast to scholarly interest in (male) production, serious attention has only recently been directed to the reproductive activities carried out by women (Beneria 1979; Safa and Leacock 1981).

The widespread acceptance of this framework seems due in large part to the power of the expanded concept of reproduction. In this context, reproduction refers to several levels of women's participation in society: as biological reproducers of children, as social reproducers of labor power on a daily and generational basis, and most broadly as reproducers of society itself (Edholm et al. 1977). There is then a recognition of certain cross-cultural patterns in the sexual division of labor; for reasons generally regarded as socially determined, women perform more of the maintenance work in society, freeing men to engage in other, productive, activity.

Beyond this, however, there is less clarity in the distinction between reproductive and productive work. For some (e.g., Deere 1982), the difference lies in whether the work creates use values or exchange values. Women's involvement in subsistence production for family consumption is regarded as reproductive, while men's exchange-value production for the market is more strictly productive. Others (e.g., Schmink 1977; Vasques de Miranda 1977), however, expand the definition of reproductive work to encompass women's income-generating activities, both in and out of the home. It is argued that women's work as domestic servants, laundresses, seamstresses, or sellers of food represents an extension of work carried out in the home and fulfills the same fundamental needs on the societal level. This is contrasted to men's leading roles in such areas as commercial agriculture, manufacturing, and trades such as carpentry and masonry.

In this chapter I want to suggest that while the production/reproduction framework has moved us forward to important new lines of inquiry, taking these conceptual categories as unproblematic may result in some confusion. I will turn now to consider the case of marketwomen in Andean Peru, to illustrate what I view as the strengths of the concepts discussed here, as well as some shortcomings, for an examination of these Latin American women workers.

THE CASE OF ANDEAN MARKETWOMEN

In many ways, Andean marketwomen appear to be a classic example of women whose reproductive domestic work roles have extended to the public sector. Their involvement in the procurement, preparation, and distribution of basic needs such as food, clothing, and other household items may be viewed as commercialized housework (Jelin 1980; Arizpe 1977). What is more, the marketers often have infants and young children in tow, creating an even stronger impression that these are homemakers who have simply moved their activities to the marketplace. On the other hand, the efforts of marketwomen to provide their families with income brings them into a relationship with society and economy very different from that of unpaid workers in the home. It is this contradictory role of marketwomen that will be explored here.

The research that forms the basis for my observations was carried out in the Andean city of Huaraz, about 200 miles north of Lima. For half a year in 1977 and two months in 1982, I lived with a marketer and her family in Huaraz, and through a combination of participant observation and open-ended interviewing in the city's markets, learned about the work and social lives of marketwomen. My primary interest was in market sellers and street vendors, but interviews with shopkeepers, producers, consumers, and market officials were included as well.

Huaraz is a city of some 45,000 Quechua-Spanish-speaking people, and the capital of Peru's department of Ancash. It serves as the commercial and administrative center for the Andean valley known as the Callejon de Huaylas. The kinds of economic activity generally available to the working class and poor majority in Huaraz include subsistence agriculture, wage labor, and petty commodity production, commerce, and services. Domestic work should be included as well and analyzed with subsistence agriculture as unpaid household labor for direct consumption. Consequently, most marketwomen and their families that I came to know in Huaraz depend on several different sources of livelihood. Before I turn to examine marketing more closely, I will consider familial strategies for economic diversification.

Landholdings surrounding Huaraz are generally very small, rarely as large as one hectare. The *chacras* (fields) are important sources of foodstuffs for many families, but far from sufficient to meet household needs. Though men are identified as most actively involved in agricultural work, women perform many tasks on the land, and tend household animals.[1]

Housework, of course, must be performed in every household. Unlike middle class Peruvians who employ domestic help, the poor of Huaraz supply their own household labor, and this falls chiefly to women. In addition to child care and meal preparation, other time-consuming activities include fetching wood and water (many lack the urban conveniences), washing clothes, knitting, and sewing.

Unskilled and skilled wage work around Huaraz includes agricultural day labor, work in construction, small-scale manufacture of such goods as chairs and adobe bricks, and employment in a soda bottling plant and fishery. These jobs are primarily available to men, who may earn about US$1.00 daily as laborers. Occasionally, women are hired to work as seamstresses in household manufacturing, and some young women work as domestic servants, earning only marginal incomes.

With unmet family needs and few alternatives for earning an income, many women in Huaraz turn to petty commerce. On the busiest days of the week, the city attracted upward of 1,200 sellers to its markets and streets in 1977, and almost 1,600 by 1982. Close to 80 percent of sellers are women, and they include rural producer-sellers who come periodically to the city, as well as a much larger number of full-time marketers, who live in Huaraz and purchase all or most of their stock from wholesalers. Women, in contrast to men, are highly concentrated in the retail sale of vegetables, fruits, and prepared foods, which together constitute the bulk of goods sold in the market. Both women and men sell staple foods like rice, pasta, flour, sugar, and salt, as well as meat, fish, live animals, clothing, and household items such as pots and other kitchen utensils, although men generally do so on a larger scale. When men engage in marketing, they may often draw on resources generated from other forms of employment, and they may have greater mobility to travel directly to production sites to buy their goods. Consequently, men often sell larger quantities of goods at lower prices than women, and they are far more likely than women to sell manufactured goods from the coast.

Women's earnings in the marketplace are quite low, often around half the earnings of a male day laborer. Still, the need to diversify means that it is common to find families that engage in all three forms of production mentioned here, subsistence farming and household labor, petty production and commerce, and capitalist wage labor.[2]

Many times the skills that a woman takes to the market are ones she acquired at home. She may in fact offer on the market the same product that she prepares at home for family use. Such diverse items as knitted baby caps, shirts, processed grains, cornstarch pudding, tamales, or prepared drinks are found in the markets. It is not uncommon for a marketer to take some food prepared in her household to the market while she leaves the remainder for her family. In the marketplace itself, a seller's work resembles housework. For example, the sellers of fruits and vegetables, who predominate in the markets, generally spend time cleaning and arranging their goods, and some go a step further, to chop portions of vegetables, sold in small quantities for use in soups. Other women cook simple dishes over kerosene stoves in their market stalls, offering on-the-spot meals to the public.

The content of marketing work and its serving character have much in common with domestic work. It is not surprising that marketing work is frequently described as a "natural" extension of women's work at home. Moreover, there are other features of marketing that lend themselves to comparison with housework. Marketwomen usually have some flexibility in determining when and where they work and what products they offer. They can organize marketing activities around other responsibilities, most importantly child care. Indeed, for many women the principal advantage of marketing is the possibility of taking children along with them. Just as they manage to watch their children while they work at home, women manage to look after their children in the marketplace. Infants may be breastfed, toddlers can play with other young children, and older children can be given breakfast and sent off to school.

In the most obvious sense, then, we see that marketing may be regarded as a reproductive activity similar to domestic work. Besides being similar in content, both kinds of work function to reproduce the labor force and, more broadly, society. Housework provides essential, yet unpaid, services, and marketing brings needed goods and services to consumers at relatively low prices. Together, these activities keep down the cost of reproducing the labor force in Peru and in this way contribute to the accumulation of capital at the societal level.

Nevertheless, I think there may be problems when the limits of the concept of reproduction go unexamined or when reproductive work is taken to be coterminous with women's work. When all of women's work beyond the home is viewed as defined by and reflective of the work women do in the household, we fail to see that many skills necessary to sellers are not learned at home and are not extensions of housework. Locating goods to purchase from wholesalers when retailers are crowding the markets and successfully attracting regular customers must be learned from other marketers or from experience in the marketplace, as must transporting, bulking, pricing, and other types of market work. Securing earnings adequate to pay the multitude of daily and annual fees necessary to stay in business, and, sometimes, evading the officials who seem so eager to increase city revenues by fining sellers for minor infractions also require special skills. Finally, these sellers participating in organized activity in the market unions require experience and knowledge obtained on the job through the work of marketing.

Using the concept of reproduction, we run the risk of failing to differentiate subsistence activities, or the production of use values, from the production of exchange values. It is important to remember, of course, that these are not always clear-cut categories of analysis. While the household may be the center of production for use, we have already seen that marketers often produce or prepare goods at home for market exchange. Similarly, the marketplace is the center for exchange par excellance, but we may discover subsistence activities in that sphere as well. During their hours of work in the markets, women find time to do the family shopping, care for their children, and spin or knit for their families, as well as for sale. Furthermore, it is common practice for food sellers to take some food home to their families, especially when it is spoiling or not selling well, turning one of the risks of selling perishable goods into an advantage. One woman, who operates a small restaurant in the marketplace, told me that she chose that particular area of commerce because it meant that her husband and young daughter could come and have a good meal at her stand. In this way production for market exchange generates use values as well.[3]

The point I wish to emphasize here is that calling women's work at home and in the market "reproductive" in an undifferentiated way obscures the degree to which women participate in production for exchange. Where women are principally engaged in income-generating activity, as in marketing, the reproductive label may divert attention away from the significant role of marketwomen in the national economy.[4] Huaraz marketwomen themselves do not speak of marketing as an extension of their role in the home but rather describe it in quite a different way, as a separate job that is essential for the earnings it provides. This has implications for women's views of themselves as workers and for researchers' understanding of women's work in society.

Furthermore, with so broad a concept of reproduction--one which encompasses work that reproduces labor force and society--it is difficult to see where to draw the line. Almost all productive work, it would seem, could be subsumed under reproductive work. Certainly, it would be hard to claim a significant analytical difference between the work of female and male marketers, even if the latter sell larger quantities, travel greater distances, and deal in different products.[5] Like women, men who sell provide essential services and help to maintain society. Men and women in other lines of work, in the trades, as agriculturalists, or as wage workers, may also be regarded, in the fullest sense, as reproductive.

It may be most useful to consider the reproductive *and* productive aspects of both women's and men's work, in as well as outside the home.[6] In the discussion that follows, I will suggest that we view production and reproduction in dynamic relationship, as integrated social processes.

PRODUCTION AND REPRODUCTION AS SOCIAL PROCESSES

Just as the controversy over the relation of domestic work to the production process--or the "housework debate"--was laid to rest, the concept of reproduction came to the fore, challenging us to see how far we could progress in theorizing about women's work. Unlike the debate over whether women's unpaid work was productive, which revolved around Marxist categories that could be supported, refuted, or revised, the current discussion over women's reproductive work calls for clarification of a concept that only recently came into use.

The power of the concept of reproduction lies in the way it explains the sexual division of labor as the cultural elaboration of women's role in biological reproduction; women's diverse economic activities are seen as extending from and linked to their role in bearing and nursing children. Whether the cross-cultural tendency for women to engage in reproductive work is adequate to explain their *subordination* is another question, and it may be only in class-based societies that such activities are devalued (Leacock 1978). Some writers have suggested that women's subordination may be explained by their reproductive roles (e.g. Beneria 1979:222), though they note the weak separation of productive and reproductive roles in noncapitalist societies (Beneria and Sen 1981:292; Deere and Leon de Leal 1981:360). Leaving aside the problem of the universal applicability of this framework, let us consider how it may be most useful in examining dependent capitalist societies, where most marketwomen are found.

As mentioned before, it appears more fruitful to view productive and reproductive activities as integrated in society than as sharply divided along sex lines. Like other forms of dualist thinking,[7] the production/reproduction dichotomy may veil the interconnectedness of these social processes. On the other hand, understood dialectically, these categories of analysis permit us to examine the way that the division of labor in society and household allocation of labor are fundamentally linked. For example, several writers (e.g. Deere 1982) have noted that if women more often than men carry out subsistence activities, this may be explained by more than cultural tradition or male dominance; often familial strategies for economic diversification are based on rational assessments of the greater income-generating power of men in capitalist society. Even so, when women are drawn into the labor force, their work load may double as they continue to meet major responsibilities in the home. Consequently, it is essential that our analysis encompass the total context within which women and men work and make work-related decisions in society.

Bujra has called for attention to "interlocking productive and reproductive processes" (1982:20). Arguing against the descriptive, and polar categories of domestic and public, she presents a case for analysis of the articulation of domestic work with different modes of production. Bujra's emphasis on the need to investigate the *relationship* of these spheres of social action pertains closely to the issues raised in this chapter.

The task ahead, it seems to me, is first to clarify our use of the terms production and reproduction and then to accept the likelihood that social activity cannot be neatly divided into these two distinct spheres. Mackintosh makes this point, noting that the concepts in question are not of the same order, with reproduction subsuming many productive activities (1981:10). From this point, as Mackintosh shows, we may turn to the issue that most concerns us: the concentration of women in so many of the undervalued activities in dependent capitalist societies--in the household and in the labor force.

CONCLUSIONS

As the suppliers of society's basic needs, Andean marketwomen--often pictured with babies carried on their backs--would appear to present a classic case of women's reproductive role extended to the wider socioeconomic sector. It is certainly true that a distinct advantage of marketing is that it may be organized around domestic responsibilities, notably child care. Looked at another way, however, marketwomen present a clear example of the way that reproductive and productive work roles may be integrated when women enter the work force. In this chapter I have suggested that a recognition of the reproductive aspect of women's work in petty commerce should not force us to compartmentalize work in society in such a fashion that women's share in production for exchange is rendered "invisible".

The theoretical progress signaled by the reproduction/production model should not be diminished. As used by feminists, and often Marxists, it has added to our understanding of the sexual division of labor, familial economic strategies, and the subordination of women. Like the domestic/public spheres model before it, the reproduction/production model makes sense of much cross-cultural material that previously seemed confusing. The earlier model was found limiting, however, in its ahistorical form and inadequate for analysis of such categories as marketwomen, which seem to defy classification. For the conceptualization of women and work throughout societies, the "new" model offers the advantage of describing the character of women's work rather than narrowly delimiting the place where it occurs, and its analysts have generally considered the historical context of reproduction and production in society. However, there may be a tendency once again to rigidify our concepts in a way that obscures our view of the interrelatedness of social processes.

All of this concerns most closely how we view women as workers in society. In Huaraz, marketwomen themselves reveal an identification as workers, important to both family and the national economy. When they told me "Without marketers, Huaraz couldn't survive," they were expressing themselves, perhaps, as sustainers or social reproducers, but they were also recognizing their productive contribution to the economy and society.

ACKNOWLEDGMENTS

Earlier versions of this chapter were presented in Lima in 1982 at the Peru Mujer Congress on Research on Women in Andean Latin America and in Mexico City in 1983 at the Congress of the Latin American Studies Association. I gratefully acknowledge the useful comments of participants at these conferences. Gabriela Nunez and Stan Ziewacz offered constructive criticisms of the present version.

Field research in 1977 was supported by a grant-in-aid awarded to William W. Stein by the State University of New York Research Foundation. In 1982, travel funds were provided by Peru Mujer. I am especially indebted to the marketers of Huaraz, Peru, for without their friendship and cooperation this research would not have been possible.

NOTES

1 For discussion of male bias in assessing women's work in agriculture in the Andes, see Bourque and Warren (1981) and Deere and Leon de Leal (1981).

2 Household diversification may be viewed at the family level as a strategy for coping with poverty and for spreading the risk of failure in any one endeavor, but it should be viewed at the broader level as a response to economic underdevelopment in Peru (Babb 1981).

3 This occurs in a way parallel to that described by Deere (1982). She noted that the household in the Peruvian Andes yields use values and exchange values; here I note the similar phenomenon in the Huaraz markets, where both exchange values and use values are created.

4 Esculies et al. (1977) point out that 99 percent of retail activities in Peru are in the hands of small sellers.

5 Despite the shared labor process of male and female marketers, there *are* critical differences between the situation of women marginalized in the least remunerated sales and that of men in capital-intensive commerce. This is discussed further in Babb (1984).

6 See Mercado (1978) and Bunster (1982) for discussion of Lima marketwomen and street vendors. Their Lima research calls attention to the integrated work activities of women who carry the double load of household responsibility and petty commerce. Figueroa and Anderson (1981) also include women in commerce in their useful overview of Peruvian women.

7 For example, the dual society, or traditional/modern sector, view (Frank 1969), or the informal/formal economy model (Bromley 1978).

REFERENCES

Arizpe, Lourdes. 1977. "Women in the Informal Labor Sector: The Case of Mexico City," Signs 3 (1):25-37.

Babb, Florence E. 1981. Women and Marketing in Huaraz, Peru: The Political Economy of Petty Commerce. Ph.D. dissertation, SUNY Buffalo.

______. 1984. "Women in the Marketplace: Petty Commerce in Peru." Forthcoming in Review of Radical Political Economics 16(1).

Beneria, Lourdes. 1979. "Reproduction, Production and the Sexual Division of Labour," Cambridge Journal of Economics 3:203-225.

Beneria, Lourdes and Gita Sen. 1981. "Accumulation, Reproduction, and Women's Role in Economic Development: Boserup Revisited." Signs 7 (2):338-360.

Bourque, Susan C., and Kay B. Warren. 1981. Women of the Andes: Patriarchy and Social Change in Two Peruvian Towns. Ann Arbor: University of Michigan Press.

Bromley, Ray (ed.). 1978. The Urban Informal Sector: Critical Perspectives. Special issue of World Development 6(9-10).

Bujra, Janet M. 1982. "Introductory: Female Soldiarity and the Sexual Dvision of Labour." In Women United, Women Divided, edited by Patricia Caplan and Janet M. Bujra. Bloomington, Indiana: Indiana University Press.

Bunster, B., Ximena. 1982. "Market Sellers in Lima, Peru: Talking about Work." In Women and Poverty in the Third World, edited by Mayra Buvinic and Margaret A. Lycette. Baltimore: Johns Hopkins University Press.

Chinas, Beverly L. 1973. The Isthmus Zapotecs: Women's Roles in Cultural Context. New York: Holt, Rinehart and Winston, Inc.

Deere, Carmen Diana. 1982. "The Allocation of Familial Labor and the Formation of Peasant Household Income in the Peruvian Sierra." In Women and Poverty in the Third World, edited by Mayra Buvinic and Margaret A. Lycette. Baltimore: Johns Hopkins University Press.

Deere, Carmen Diana, and Magdalena Leon de Leal. 1982. "Peasant Production, Proletarianization, and the Sexual Division of Labor in the Andes," Signs 7(2):338-360.

Edholm, Felicity, Olivia Harris, and Kate Young. 1977. "Conceptualizing Women," Critique of Anthropology 3(9-10):101-130.

Engels, Frederick. 1972. [orig. 1884] The Origin of the Family, Private Property, and the State. New York: International Publishers.

Esculies Larrabure, Oscar, Marcila Rubio Correa, and Veronica Gonzalez del Castillo. 1977. Comercializacion de Alimentos: Quienes Ganan, Quienes Pagan, Quienes Pierden. Lima: Centro de Estudios y Promocion del Desarrollo (DESCO).

Figueroa, Blanca, and Jeanine Anderson. 1981. "Women in Peru," International Reports: Women and Society. London: Change International Reports.

Frank, Andre Gunder. 1969. "Dialectic, Not Dual Society." In Latin America: Underdevelopment or Revolution, By Andre Gunder Frank. New York: Monthly Review Press.

Jelin, Elizabeth. 1980. "The Bahiana in the Labor Force in Salvador, Brazil," in Sex and Class in Latin America. Edited by June Nash and Helen Icken Safa. New York: J. F. Bergin

Leacock, Eleanor. 1978. "Women's Status in Egalitarian Society." Current Anthropology 19(2):247-276.

Mackintosh, Maureen. 1981. "Gender and Economics: The Sexual Division of Labour and the Subordination of Women." In Of Marriage and the Market, edited by Kate Young, Carol Wolkowitz, and Roslyn McCullagh. London: CSE Books.

Mercado, Hilda. 1978. La Madre Trabajadora: El Caso de las Comerciantes Ambulantes. Serie C, No. 2. Lima: Centro de Estudios de Poblacion y Desarrollo.

Reiter, Rayna Rapp (ed.). 1975. Toward an Anthropolgy of Women. New York: Monthly Review Press.

Rohrlich-Leavitt, Ruby (ed.). 1975. Women Cross-Culturally: Change and Challenge. Chicago: Mouton Publishers.

Rosaldo, Michelle, and Louise Lamphere (eds.). 1974. Women, Culture, and Society. Stanford, California: Stanford University Press.

Safa, Helen I., and Eleanor Leacock, eds. 1981. Development and the Sexual Division of Labor. Signs, Special Issue 7(2).

Schmink, Marianne. 1977. "Dependent Development and the Division of Labor by Sex: Venezuela," Latin American Perspectives 12-13:153-179.

Sudarkasa, Niara. 1973. Where Women Work: A Study of Yoruba Women in the Marketplace and in the Home. Ann Arbor: The University of Michigan Press.

Vasques de Miranda, Glaura. 1977. "Women's Labor Force Participation in a Developing Society: The Case of Brazil," Signs 3(1):261-274.

Young, Kate, Carol Wolkowitz, and Roslyn McCullagh (eds.). 1981. Of Marriage and the Market, Women's Subordination in International Perspective. London: CSE Books.

5 Economic Crisis and Female-Headed Households in Urban Jamaica

A. Lynn Bolles

Feminist scholars have estimated that between 25 and 33 percent of all households in the world are de facto female-headed units (Buvinic and Youssef 1978). Although this phenomenon is appearing on an international scale, its most dramatic increase has occurred in Third World societies (Tinker and Bramsen 1977:37). Therefore, further feminist research on female-headed households, in both advanced capitalist and Third World countries becomes a compelling and significant issue. We must refer to specific case studies of the productive and reproductive activities of female-headed households within specific historically based social and economic contexts. Then, by way of comparison, we must use these examples to direct our attention to the nature of particular social forces that influence women's lives and those of their dependents.

In this chapter, I want to show how Jamaican female-headed households cope with dependence in an insecure and inadequate wage economy based on international monopoly capital. A variety of income-generating activities and non-wage subsistence bases have been relied upon since the end of the economy based on slave labor but the agrarian base of these activities has consistently deteriorated. By focusing on a group of working-class women and their households in Kingston, Jamaica, I will illustrate the varied relations between women and work and between households and a national economy. I will demonstrate that urban working-class households, with a male partner/spouse in residence, have greater access to resources and are less dependent on alternative income strategies found in the informal sector of the economy than urban working-class households headed by women and dependent on their labor.

Regardless of composition, all urban working-class women and the members of their households tend to use a variety of economic activities to compensate for the lack of full employment and to guarantee their survival. The economic constraints placed on them stem from the political economy of Jamaica, which, in turn, is determined directly and indirectly by the movements of international capital. The coexistence of the formal and informal economic sectors in Jamaica serves as an example of the level and location of international capital in the economy. In addition, this perspective allows us to pinpoint what component of the labor force utilizes, in various degrees, these two economic entities.

The first section provides background to the economic crisis experienced in Jamaica during the 1970s.[1] The second describes the household composition of these working-class women. The third analyzes their economic activities and those of members of their households. Here I show that these Kingston households must be resolute and utilize multiple resources to overcome the economic disadvantages of their situation. In the final section, I discuss the overall effect that rising unemployment and underemployment have had on the Jamaican women who head the households represented in this research.

DEPENDENT DEVELOPMENT AND WORKING CLASS HOUSEHOLDS

Here we seek to examine how the movements of international capital affected the structure of Jamaica's economy. Jamaica's post World War II expansion, like that of several Third World countries, has been deemed a "miracle." The Jamaican "miracle" occurred between 1950 and 1970, when the economy's annual rate of growth was 8 percent (Jefferson 1972). In the late 1940s, Jamaica legislated a development plan called "industrialization by invitation." Following Puerto Rico's Operation Bootstrap as a model for growth, the plan was designed to attract international investment by offering income tax concession, duty relief and other incentives. This plan resulted in the rapid expansion of the mining, construction, tourism, and manufacturing sectors, financed by direct capital inflows from North America. Jamaica, therefore, tied her economy to the predicaments of international capital through these investments and through the structure of its developmental model.

Investors in the manufacturing sector were attracted to Jamaica by numerous incentives available and also by the fact that they could remove their profits, with little, if any, government restrictions. In addition, the manufacturing sector enjoyed a reliable, comparatively cheap labor force, particularly in the women whom they hired for most labor-intensive operations. Generally, the "miracle" years were characterized by international investment, which heightened the expectations of the government and the people, but, in fact, encouraged increasing economic dependence.

Jamaica was the testing ground for the characteristically footloose export processing plants. These plants were likely to withdraw their monetary investment and dismantle their physical plants at any moment with no regard to the impact on the economy. They relied heavily on imported raw materials and specialized in assembly, repackaging imported components, and production of semifinished goods. Emphasis on this type of production earned them the appelation "screw-driver" manufacturers.

Because of its insufficient tax base, even the Jamaican government had to depend on foreign investors to finance public expenditure. By the 1970s, Jamaica's dependence on foreign investment, together with a growing debt-servicing burden and an inability to generate its own internal finances, brought the country's "miracle" growth to a halt.

The economic stiuation was further exacerbated by the world financial and "oil" crisis of 1973. In the international markets, Jamaica's products--bauxite and sugar--declined in price. And the tourist trade suffered a drastic reduction in visitors. The changes in the demands of the world market, the burden of deficiencies in the Jamaican economy overall, and the high price of government programs resulted in a balance-of-payments problem for the country.

A number of events affected Jamaica's course of action and its prime minister, Michael Manley (1972-80). When Manley was elected in 1972, his goverment called for a policy that would realign Jamaica's currently inequitable position in the international market, in addition to easing the social and economic disparities in the society. His commitment to the New International Economic Order (NIEO), his becoming a spokesperson for the Third World, and Jamaica's renewed friendship with Cuba raised questions about the country's receptivity to foreign investment, especially in those who required a stable anticommunist government and cheap labor, as well as generous incentive packages. In 1976, Michael Manley was reelected to office by a landslide. Later that same year, Henry Kissinger, then secretary of state of the United States, visited Jamaica in an attempt to persuade Manley to change his course of action. Coincidentally, shortly after the failed Kissinger mission, Jamaica's credit rating by the Export-Import Bank was lowered from a top to a bottom category. That date also marks the beginnings of the destablization of the Manley administration (1977-80) (Beckford and Witter 1982:91). It also marks the beginning of Jamaica's dealing with the International Monetary Fund (IMF).

The terms negotiated in 1978 for the three-year IMF agreement with Jamaica included a one-year "crawling peg" 15 percent devaluation (a gradual reduction of 1.5 percent per month from U.S. $1.00=J$1.05 to U.S. $1.00=J$1.55). Also included as a part of the IMF stabilization or anti-inflation program were strict controls on lines of credit given by commercial banks, a requirement that the Bank of Jamaica (the central bank) maintain a certain level of foreign exchange, liberalization of import regulations, restraints on wage increases, a weakening of consumer price controls, and increased hospitality to foreign investment. Generally, the IMF program controlled foreign exchange expenditures by both government and private enterprise, and maintained a domestic policy that in essence increased the national rate of inflation. On the basis of a monthly credit rating conducted by the IMF, Jamaica could procure other loans and lines of credit, a practice that Payer has called the "debt trap" (Payer 1975).

With the destabilization of the Manley administration, strained political relations between Jamaica and the U.S. (its major economic supporter) and general economic instability on both domestic and national levels, in 1980 the conservative Edward Seaga was elected prime minister of Jamaica. The Seaga administration has made tremendous efforts to put Jamaica back on its "miracle" path, utilizing strategies very similar to those that were effective in the 1950s and 1960s. These efforts have the support of the Reagan White House via the Caribbean Basin Initiative (CBI).[2] The CBI program encourages foreign investment in providing a twelve-year, one-way, duty-free access to the U.S. from Jamaica and other Caribbean and Central American countries, excluding Cuba, Nicaragua, and Grenada.[3]

HOUSEHOLD COMPOSITION

As a preliminary step, to clarify the relations of production and reproduction within the study's household units, the composition of these residences must be analyzed. We can then demonstrate how household based activities are connected to the larger economic structure already discussed.

The established literature on Jamaican household organization extensively documents the high incidence of female-headed households in the society. Recently, scholars have noted that the trend of women heading households has been more prevalent in the metropolitan area of Kingston and in the eastern sections of the island than in rural areas (Powell 1976:3:234-58). Scholars have also recognized the connections between women household heads, urban employment, and impoverishment.[4] But there has been less of an attempt to place those interconnected factors into the wider social and economic framework in which they are enmeshed.

When I analyzed the composition of 127 working-class households according to the marital status of the woman respondents, I found three types: (1) stable coresidential unions (legal marriage and common-law union of respondents, both denoting a degree of permanence); (2) visiting unions (women who head households and have steady visiting boyfriends); and (3) single women (women who are heads and sole supporters of households, including widows, women separated after marriage or consensual unions, and other women without current mates).

There was an equal number of stable coresidential households (N=52), and visiting-unions households (N=52). In the former category, nineteen women were legally married while thirty-three were in common-law relationships. The remaining respondents were in the single-woman category (N=23).

Stable-union households, with an average of 8.5 persons, were the largest units. Next came the single-woman households, averaging 5.6 persons. The smallest were the visiting-union households, averaging 5.1 persons per unit. The households headed by women (visiting-union and single-woman households) in general incorporated a greater number of adult kin in their domestic units than did the stable-union households (those with male heads of household)--forty-four out of fifty-two visiting unions and twenty out of twenty-three single-woman households included other adult kin versus only twenty-eight out of fifty-two stable union households (see Table 1). The reason that stable-union households nevertheless had the greatest number of members per unit was that they had more dependent kin, i.e., children and grandchildren, in residence.

Another important element contributing to the difference between woman-headed households (visiting-union or single-woman) and stable-union households was the factor of age. Stable relationships were more common among older women while their younger counterparts were found more often in less permanent unions. Of those currently married, 58 percent had been in visiting unions prior to their marriage while 14 percent had been in consensual unions--all with the same man they eventually married. More than half of these legally married women were forty years of age or older. Clearly, as they aged, these women settled down with their partners, established long-term relationships based on emotional and economic support, and eventually married thir mates (Rubenstein 1977:2: 202-16).

Another indication of the correlation between age and marital status can be seen in the fact that 70 percent of the total stable union group (both legally married and consensual) were over the age of thirty-six. In comparison, more than 50 percent of the women in visiting unions were under thirty years of age. It is evident then that the women found in more permanent conjugal unions were at the end of their child-bearing days--a later life-cycle phase. Hence, the factor of age and marital type had pronounced effects on household composition, which then created other differential characteristics between the household in this research.

Among the characteristics related to the age of the woman respondent were the age of the children in the household, and the number of siblings of the respondents who were household members. For example, women who headed their households (the younger group) had more siblings in residence than households with resident partners/spouses. All of these factors display a certain degree of interplay as we examine how the members of these households try to maintain themselves as individuals and try to maintain their residences as viable productive and reproductive units.

MAKING A LIVING

These working-class households combined two strategies to support themselves: using multiple incomes and engaging in informal economic sector activities. In a country where unemployment and underemployment are chronically high, resources few, and the wages in question usually low, it takes more than one wage to provide anything approaching a "livable income" for the domestic unit as a whole. All 127 respondents were women currently employed in low-level factory jobs, in sixteen various firms (subsidiaries of multinational corporations, joint ventures run by local and foreign investors, local enterprises, and one government-owned concern). However, while woman-headed households relied more often on one wage and adult informal activities for economic viability, their stable-union counterparts showed multiple wage earners per unit as their source of livelihood.

Of the 127 residences, there were fifty with only *one* wage earner--the woman respondent. It was especially common to find only one wage earner per unit in the female-headed households, much more so than in the stable-union units. Twenty-six of the fifty-two visiting unions and also half of the single-woman households depended on one wage. In contrast, a much smaller number, twelve of fifty-two stable unions were supported solely by the worker-respondent.

An example of a one-wage-earner, woman-headed household was the residence of "Barbara Williams" (a pseudonym). Barbara and her two sisters share a rented flat not far from the factory where she works. Barbara's daughter, a toddler, has been sent to the country to be raised by Barbara's mother until the child gains a "reasoning" age. That is, until the daughter is old enough to be more responsible for herself (about school age), she will live with her grandmother in a rural area. Barbara sends money to her mother for the child's upkeep. In Kingston, the youngest sister in the household attends high school on the early shift. Barbara pays for her sister's books and uniforms. In the afternoon when the youngest sister returns from school, she starts the dinner. Barbara's other sister had been employed as a casual worker at a factory and worked only during peak periods. At one time this sort of work was reliable, but in the past year there has been little work for extra help. At present, Barbara provides the sole income (approximately U.S. $38.00 per week)[5] to support the three-person household as well as to send money to her mother for the care of her child.

In contrast to the single-wage subsistence pattern, which is predominant among female-headed households, nearly half (twenty-four out of fifty-two) of the stable-union households had three wage earners per unit, and 7 percent had four wage earners per unit. In comparison, two wage earners were in evidence in only 40 percent of all female- households.

Although four of the fifty-two visiting union households had four sources of income derived from the formal economy, this situation was in sharp contrast to the majority of households headed by women. For the majority, a most striking fact was that there was a smaller percentage of households with three or more wage earners among the woman-headed groups then among their stable-union counterparts. Seven (7) out of fifty-two of the single woman category and only three out of fifty-two of the visiting union households had three wage earners. Obviously for the majority, the number of wage earners per household accounted for distinct income differences and divergent consumption levels found among the three types of urban working-class households.

When the salaries of the women workers are compared, the critical position of the wage earner in these working-class units becomes explicit. Taking the income levels of the women under study and dividing them into high and low subsectors, we see that half of the respondents in the single-woman and stable-union households earned less than J$70 per week (U.S.$39.55). In contrast, over 61 percent of the women in visiting unions fell into that low-income category. Moreover, of the eleven women who earned the highest salary (over J$100 per week, U.S.$56.60), six were in the stable-union category, compared with three in visiting-union households and two in single-woman households. Without a doubt, women who were heads of households had fewer financial resources than women in stable unions.

Multiple wages are the clue to the differences in the levels of consumption and household composition among these working class households. Recalling the Barbara Williams case, let us compare that situation to the following description of the "Thompson" household. "Dorothy Thompson" (a pseudonym) has been employed in the biscuit factory since it opened its doors in 1959. Her salary is U.S.$38.00 per week. Her partner, Nigel, has an equally lengthy employment record at the oil refinery. Their combined weekly salary is approximately J$200.00 (U.S.$113.00). In addition, an adult son resides with them and contributes J$20 to the household kitty. Two teenage sons attend technical school. Both teenagers and their mother have visited their married sister/daughter in the United States. The older of the teenagers hopes to emigrate when he leaves school. The Thompsons live in their own home in a housing development near the airport. They possess all the modern household appliances available, having purchased them on the installment plan, a common buying habit for the working class. Everything is now paid in full.

It is important not only to note the numbers of wage earners per unit, but also to ascertain which household members were wage earners (see Table 1). For example, in the stable-union households, forty-two of the fifty-two spouse/partners were employed. Another benefical factor for the stable-union residences was the fact that sixty-three children had jobs. These children represented the eldest of all the children in the study. Children found in the female-headed households, especially in visiting unions, were, for the most part, in primary school and definitely dependents in their households.

In the female-headed households, however, another situation occurs in regard to the wage-earning capacity of those units. In the case of visiting unions, siblings of the respondents were often second wage earners. Among the visiting unions, fourteen of the twenty-six resident sisters were wage earners while eleven of the twenty-five brothers were also sources of household income. The distribution of wage earners in single-woman households was much the same as for visiting-unions. Five of seven sisters of respondents and two of the five brothers were active wage earners for single-woman residences. Like stable-union households, single-woman households contained some older children, and fifteen of these were wage earners.[6] The presence of these older children was the result of previous marital unions among a number of these single women, for example, those who had been widowed or separated. A study of Mrs. Gordon's household provides an example of older children's activities.

A widow for the past ten years, since her husband died of pneumonia, "Mrs. Gordon" (a pseudonym) lives in her own home with her three children and a niece. They reside in an upper-working-class/ middle-class area of town. The niece (deceased husband's brother's daughter) is completing her teacher's training course. Mrs. Gordon's youngest child is a son who is in the fifth form in secondary school, and Mrs. Gordon hopes to send him to a university in the United States.[7] Her older daughter (the eldest child) is a secretary and is engaged to be married. The second daughter is also a secretary. Both daughters contribute money to the household kitty and do housework and other domestic chores. The niece and son also help out around the house but do not contribute economically to the unit. Mrs. Gordon enjoys one of the higher salaries among the sample of respondents.

The presence of multiple wage earners provides a means by which working-class households may derive essential income. One must keep in mind, however, the levels of unemployment and comparative earning capacities of men and women in Jamaica. In the October 1979 labor force statistics, 19.9 percent of the males, in comparison with 43.5 of the females, were unemployed. These indices become even more striking when we note that the male labor force was almost twice as large as that of its female counterpart: 507,700 men compared with 256,900 women (Jamaica, Dept. of Statistics 1982:3). Therefore, when we see how dependent the female-headed households are on women's employment opportunities, their predicament becomes even more problematic, particularly since there are more women resident in those units. Excluding the respondents and children, among the female-headed households, twenty-two of the thirty-nine documented members whose gender could be identified were female and listed as being employed. In comparison, one sister alone could be identified as an employed female household member in the stable-union residences. Clearly, those conjugal-pair households do not rely on remunerative activities of additional kin as much as their female-headed counterparts.

Another measurement of the hardships faced by female-headed households can be seen by comparing wage rates by gender. Wage differentials between men and women are quite evident in Jamaica. Again, using 1979 data, the median wage of women was 13 percent less than that for men (J$33.33 compared to J$40.05) although the wage rate is low for both (Jamaica, Dept. of Statistics 1982:4). Such comparative information also indicates a lower economic base for women who head households or whose wages help support such residences in comparison with households with a female wage earner and a better-paid male worker.

THE INFORMAL ECONOMY

Up to this point we have focused on formal sector employment, exemplified by the jobs of women factory workers and the remunerative labor carried out in sectors of the formal economy by other household members, whether on a full-time or occasional basis. Now we will assess another set of income-generating activities, which falls within what is known as the informal economic sector. The differences between the formal and informal sectors in Kingston, Jamaica, lie in the size of each sector, state sanctioning, and ownership of production (Bolles 1981:83-96). The formal sector means of production is usually large-scale and capital-intensive, uses imported technology, and most often is financed by foreign capital. In contrast, the informal sector encompasses small-scale activities, conducted outside state and state-regulated private sectors. The orthodox economic view of informal activities has emphasized that these are backward Third World holdovers from the premodern era. That perspective maintains that until the entire population catches up and benefits from the trickle-down of new techniques promoted by the "modern" formal economy, the food-peddling, "chiclet"-selling and shoe-shining level of activities will continue.

However, more recent evidence has eroded the stereotype of the informal market that stressed such activities as merely traditional means of production brought to the city from the rural areas. In contrast, the new trend on the subject focuses on the articulation between the two economic sectors. The informal sector continuously changes to meet the needs and opportunities available in the "modern" formal economy. The locations and structure of informal activities are such that they operate in close conjunction with, or as appendages to, formal economic activities. They are not parallel to or unrelated to formal sector activities as expressed in the orthodox perspective, but are subordinated to them.[8]

In a recent state-of-the-art summary of the current research on the informal sector, Portes states, "Informal sector activities are neither traditional nor transitional, but very modern features of the system of capitalist accumulation, and, as such, continuously reproduced by the operations of the system" (Portes and Walton 1981:86). When we focus in on the supplies of labor in the theory of capitalist accumulation, it becomes clear that the informal sector provides subsistence for that surplus labor force. Labor is made surplus when it is not utilized by the formal sector.

Moreover, the supply of labor must always exceed the demand for labor in order to keep labor costs at a minimum--a prerequisite for capitalist accumulation. One of the reasons that multinationals, export processing plants, and local industry can be competitive on the international market is the depressed wages of workers and the complementary army of surplus labor at that location. The cheapness of labor then increases the levels of unequal exchange between advanced capitalist countries and Third World economies. And on a subsistence level, the informal sector supports the reproductive costs of surplus labor (usually the majority of potential workers) at no cost to the formal economy. It becomes most beneficial for international capital to maintain such a system.

The following examples will demonstrate the various operations of the informal economy in Jamaica. These cases will also describe the activities of some of the members of the working-class households in the research as members of the urban surplus labor pool.

Miss Mary's (a pseudonym) daughter is still employed in the garment factory where Mary had been laid off for two years because the demand for production was slow. While her daughter continues on her job (she was kept on because her piecework rate was *lower* than her mother's), Miss Mary sews school uniforms at home for clients with whom she attends church. She buys bulk fabric through her connections in the apparel business. Her church-member clients know how well she sews and that her uniforms will be cheaper than the ready-to-wear uniforms in the stores, or those made by other seamstresses. When fabric was readily available on the market, Miss Mary stocked up on basic colors such as khaki and navy, financing her purchases with her daughter's income. She was in a good position, therefore, when uniform material became scarce but demand was still high. Although her relatively expensive labor was made redundant in the formal sector, the informal sector provides for Miss Mary's subsistence. She also capitalizes on the correspndence between her former position (entailing skill, access to goods, etc.) and her daughter's wages (financial backing and cash) and then successfully competes for her share in the local apparel market, satisfying a community need because of the inadequacies of Jamaican industry.

A different example illustrates that the economic benefits provided by informal sector activities are not necessarily in monetary form but may consist of the direct procurement of goods and services.

Neville (a pseudonym) is the brother of Marlene, (a pseudonym) a worker in a food-processing plant. Neville lives with his girlfriend and their son and a child of hers by a previous relationship. He works as a stockman in a bread-baking firm. As an employee, Neville can buy bread at cost when there is an overrun in production. Whenever this occurs, Neville takes as many loaves home as he can. He keeps a loaf or two for himself, gives a few loaves to his sister, and then sells the rest to neighbors, who know that he has this connection. Although Neville does not financially support his sister--a woman who heads a household with two young children--he does provide her with a dietary staple that she would otherwise have to purchase.

A third example of informal economic activities demonstrates another way that working-class people use this sector. "Robots" are unlicensed minibuses that travel regular bus routes in Kingston, picking up passengers. Although the fares are a bit more expensive than those for state-licensed mass transport, these buses are quicker, often more convenient and flexible in destination, and most reliable for commuting workers. The following is a case in point.

About ten women workers live in a newly developed area of St. Catherine Parish, neighboring on metropolitan Kingston. Although the tract where they live was developed by urban planners, no bus routes were included in the scheme. Since all ten women are employed at the same multinational, they have made an informal contract with a robot to pick them up, take them to work, and bring them back at the end of the day. Since their work day begins at 7:00 a.m. and ends at 4:00 p.m., the robot driver can make a steady income from these commuters, and still do a full day's work driving regular bus routes and taking on other engagements.

Another important factor in the functioning of these households is the sharing of wage and other income-gathering activities. Not surprisingly the figures show that residents of the female-headed households (visiting-union and single-woman categories) are most heavily engaged in the informal sector. Moreover, when we look at which household members are involved, we find that for visiting-union households, they are most often resident adult kin; for stable union units, spouse/partners, and for single-woman residences, they are evenly distributed between children and other adult kin. Since resident kinspersons wered included as wage earners, we gain a better understanding of the reliance of female-headed households on the informal sector. We find households headed by women had two-thirds more participants in the informal sector than those in stable-union residences. Interestingly, the eight husband/spouses who participated in the informal economy did so in a fashion similar to the case of Miss Mary: they performed work that was similar to or identical with the work they did while employed in the formal sector. This was especially true for unemployed construction workers, who still had access to supplies and could be self-employed contractors.

The manner in which the individuals in the preceding cases

participated in both formal and informal activities demonstrates two perspectives on the subject. The first has already been discussed--how the informal sector provides the reproductive costs of surplus labor. The second, however, shows how the two sectors are utilized as working-class survival strategies (Tilly 1977:3). These strategies vary in scope and purpose: from family strategies, such as Neville's assistance to his sister; to those of the group commuters, who have organized their own transportation because of the absence of mass transport in their residential area. Decisions and choices are made with regard to the individual's circumstances within their families or by their position as members of the working class, whose maintenance, including transport to and from work, is left up to them.

Because of uneven development and dependency--both based on Jamaica's peripheral position in the world market--informal economic activities are necessary and they thrive. This phenomenon is not surprising, given the chronic unemployment problem in Jamaica, where the formal labor sector has never been able to even approach fulfilling the demands of a labor-surplus economy (see Beckford and Witter 1982).

MACRO-LEVEL LINKAGES

The working-class women represented in this research are connected to the larger economic picture outlined above by the type of work in which they are employed, the structure of the Jamaican economy, and the level of dependency they face as economic supporters for their households.

First, all the women in the research were industrial workers employed in the manufacturing sector established during the "miracle" years. Hence the IMF program had particular implications for the manufacturing sector, as a segment of the structure of the Jamaican economy.

These women were employed mainly in subsidiaries of multinational corporations, joint investment ventures by foreign and local capitalists, and to a smaller extent, locally owned firms. Because of the sector's dependence on imported components, raw materials, and foreign investment (the structure of production), it became vulnerable to constraints placed on any aspect of the operation by IMF restrictions. Domestic sales were depressed because of higher consumer prices. The devaluation raised the costs (in local currency) of imported components--the essence of the "screw-driver" type of operation. Paying for and buying imported materials became more difficult, and high interest rates placed bank loans beyond the reach of most manufacturers.

The female industrial employees under study felt the IMF impact on industry quite directly. Its constraints were passed on to employees as production cuts or slowdowns, layoffs, forced terminations, and pay freezes. These, in turn, often led to labor union disputes and factory foreclosures. No industrial employee could afford to have his or her job made redundant--least of all women who headed households.

The impact of the economic crisis on these groups of women is also underscored by a comparison of the circumstances of those currently heading their households to the earlier life-cycle situation of the women in stable unions, who were then heads of their households. As may be recalled, women in stable unions, because of their age, have had the longest industrial employment histories. When they entered the factories, Jamaica was at the height of the "miracle" years. The opportunity to be steadily employed in a comparatively well-paying job for ten to twenty years afforded these women financial security, the ability to save and purchase a variety of consumer goods, including houses and to pay for the education of their children (Safa 1983:110). In the late 1950s and early 1960s, the expansion of the economy also provided regular employment for those women's then boyfriends and partners. Fifteen to twenty years of essentially steady working-class wage labor offered those men the kind of financial security and opportunities available to their female counterparts (Whitehead 1976). During that period, these women and the men made commitments to one another, strengthened by their economic circumstances. They married or established long-term companionships, i.e., stable unions.

In contrast, the women who headed households while the research was being carried out entered factory work at the moment when the economy began its downward trend. They had relatively few years in which to enjoy the financial security, buying power, and perhaps saving opportunity afforded to the set of older women. The younger group of women heads of households were five to ten years too late. Likewise, their boyfriends and partners were often unemployed or underemployed in contrast to the men in stable unions, who were for the most part steadily employed. Thus, the financial insecurity of the younger group has led to the dissolution of a number of relationships. For example, only 23 percent of women in visiting unions receive regular support from their children's fathers or their own boyfriends, while a little over half get cash on an infrequent basis. None from the single-woman group receives regular assistance from former boyfriends, partners, and children's fathers, and only five of the twenty-three receive cash once in awhile.

We have shown earlier that households headed by women had the fewest wage earners. Insecure factory employment puts extreme pressure on women workers who provide the sole steady support for their domestic units. For the most part, they have little education and no marketable skills that would enable them to pursue a wider range of opportunities. Thus, there are no formal sector economic alternatives for these women. However, recent Jamaican labor force statistics show that one particular group of occupations stands out from the rest for females--self-employment and independent occupations. In 1982, over 100,000--more than a third of the employed female labor force--were listed as self-employed. (Jamaica, Dept. of Statistics 1982:48) This category includes women performing services such as selling food, hairdressing, doing private household work (as maids), raising vegetables, baby-sitting, taking in laundry, etc. These informal-sector activities can be located outside or inside the home, in a nearby or far-removed neighborhood, depending on the nature of the work. As a matter of fact, in the households headed by women, a third of their female kin, excluding children, participated in this sector. Thus, as with other examples of informal economic activity, the family, neighborhood, and coworker-based social networks can provide for the survival of the individual, as well as the extended household unit, through their patronage of informal economic enterprises. The primary objective is to provide an adequate income for the household in an attempt to make up for the unavailability or inadequacy of a formal wage.

One example of female self-employment is the maintenance of a backyard nursery, the most popular form of day care among working class Jamaicans. Ann (a pseudonym) runs a backyard nursery in her home, which includes a small yard with a mango tree. She has two children. One attends elementary school; the other is a toddler. Her younger brother lives with her, and an older brother often stops by to visit but lives with his girlfriend. Ann worked as a sewing machine operator for seven years, until she had her last child. When she returned from her maternity leave, the factory had shut down. The trade union could not help Ann receive her redundancy pay because the firm had filed for bankruptcy. Ann started telling people that she took care of children during the day for $2.00 a day, if they brought their own lunch.

Soon she had three young children in her day care, plus her own child. Now and then a former coworker will drop her child off just for the day, which provides additional income. Although Ann no longer earns the $50.00 a week that she did as a garment worker, the $30.00 that she now receives as operator of a backyard nursery provides her household's necessities. And if we deduct Ann's own child-care costs from her former earnings, then her present income nearly equals that lost in formal-sector employment.

Again, this example supports the notion that the informal sector provides subsistence for surplus labor in dependent capitalist economies because of the way wages and services are circulated in working-class communities.

There can be little doubt that the Jamaican urban informal sector will be utilized more than in the past by working-class households, especially those headed by women. Women have higher rates of unemployment, are usually responsible for dependent children, and when they are heads of households, bear the full or a substantial portion of the household financial burden (see Valentine 1980). Also, since Jamaica has no income maintenance program for those in need, the only source of income for working-class women is whatever they generate themselves with the aid of other household members, extended family, neighbors, and friends.

CONCLUSION

The goal of this chapter has been to provide an approach to clarifying survival strategies involving working-class households, some headed by women, some with partner/spouses in residence, in Kingston, Jamaica. Households have been viewed as units comprising members whose relations of production and reproduction are affected by the political economy of Jamaica, which in turn is affected directly and indirectly by the international movement of capital.

The urban working-class households in this study utilized strategies over which they had some control--including household membership and participation in informal-sector economic activities. One of the chief factors differentiating this group of 127 working-class households was membership and participation in informal-sector economic activities.

Another difference was the number of wage earners per unit. Households with partner/spouses in residence showed the greater number of wage earners per residence. Households headed by women showed more adult kin--particularly women kin--in residence than did their stable-union counterparts. And, due in part to the high rate of female unemployment, those adult kin generated household income by their participation in the informal economy. Such activities provided necessary subsistence for female-headed working-class households and contributed to the circulation of cash, goods, and services, within their familial networks, among friends and in their neighborhoods. The way in which the reproductive costs are borne by the informal sector corresponds to the nature of monopoly capital, which depends on depressed wage rates and its control of the supply and demand of labor in the formal economy. Cheap and plentiful labor is necessary for the accumulation of capital and also reinforces the levels of unequal exchange of international capital between advanced capitalist countries and the Third World.

A final point that should be emphasized is that poverty is relative. Therefore, one must qualify where economic demarcations lie in specific societies in order to determine which group is in the most disadvantaged position of any two or more populations being compared (Green 1970:267-272). Poor and working-class female-headed households in Jamaica have been widespread in the society since the mid-nineteenth century. They are able--and forced--to deal with their circumstances without state intervention. Comparisons of female-headed households must consider the degree of cultural acceptance, in addition to the range of limited economic options available to them, to better understand the implication of the increase of women heading households on a worldwide scale.

NOTES

1 Research for this chapter was conducted in Jamaica for eighteen months in 1978-79. Fieldwork was funded by National Institute of Mental Health grant 1F31 MHO7997-01 and the Inter-American Foundation. The working-class women who participated in this study represent those factory workers and household members who agreed to be involved in the project. Interviews were conducted at their places of work and for a smaller number, also at their homes. During the research period, the social, economic and political situation was tense, and I am indebted to these working women for their time, patience and kindness. For their editorial assistance and support, I would like to thank Monica Gordon, Faith Mitchell, June Nash, Noma Petroff, Helen Safa and Carol Stack. A special note of gratitude is due to Carmen Diana Deere and Karen Sacks for their liberal use of red pen where I needed it most.

2 The theory behind the C.B.I. is to shore up the U.S.'s "third border" (the Caribbean and Central America) against communist infiltration, and advance the international division of labor by promoting private enterprise in countries whose populations have been illegally migrating to the United States in increasing numbers (causing related U.S. domestic immigration problems). In this way, three major problems can be addressed under one umbrella course of action.

3 As of the events of 25 October 1983, Grenada is definitely included in the C.B.I.

4 Guy Standing, Unemployment and Female Labour: A Study of Labour Supply in Kingston, Jamaica, and Malcolm Cross, Urbanization and Urban Growth in the Caribbean provide data on these subjects.

5 Exchange rate applied here is U.S.$1.00=J$1.77.

6 Women in the single women's category included former common-law and married persons. The number of children were similar to those found in the stable union type.

7 Following the British educational model, the 5th form is approximately the equivalent of U.S. grades 11/12.

8 See Keith Hart, "Informal Income Opportunities and Urban Employment in Ghana"; Michael Witter "Hustle Economy: Essay on Conceptualization" and Betty Lou Valentine Hustling and Other Hard Work in the Ghetto.

REFERENCES

Beckford, George, and Michael Witter. 1982. Small Garden, Bitter Weed. London: ZED Press.

Bolles, A. Lynn. 1981. "Household Economic Strategies in Kingston, Jamaica," in Women and World Change: Equity Issues in Development. Naomi Black and Ann Baker Cottrell, eds. Beverly Hills: Sage Press.

Buvinic, Mayra and Nadia H. Youssef. 1978. Women-Headed Households: The Ignored Factor in Developing Planning. Washington, D.C.: International Center for Research on Women.

Cross, Malcolm. 1979. Urbanization and Urban Growth in the Caribbean. New York: Cambridge University Press.

Green, Vera M. 1970. "The Confrontation of Diversity within the Black Community" in Human Organization 29:4:267-272.

Hart, Keith. 1973. "Informal Income Opportunities and Urban Employment in Ghana," in Journal of Modern African Studies 11:61-89.

Jamaica, The Government Department of Statistics. 1982. The Labour Force.

Jefferson, Owen. 1972. The Post-War Economic Development of Jamaica, Kingston, Jamaica: Institute of Social and Economic Research, University of the West Indies, Mona.

Payer, Cheryl. 1975. The Debt Trap: The IMF and the Third World. New York: Monthly Review Press.

Portes, Alejandro and John Walton. 1981. Labor, Class, and the International System. New York: Academic Press.

Powell, Dorian. 1976. "Female Labour Force Participation and Fertility: An Exploratory Study of Jamaican Women," in Social and Economic Studies 25:3:234-258.

Rubenstein, Hymie. 1977. "Diachronic Inference and the Pattern of Lower-Class Afro-Caribbean Marriage," in Social and Economic Studies 26:2:202-216.

Safa, Helen I. 1983. "Women, Production, and Reproduction in Industrial Capitalism: A Comparison of Brazilian and U.S.

Factory Workers," in Women, Men and the International Division of Labor, June Nash and Maria Patricia Fernandez-Kelly, eds., (Albany, NY: SUNY Press).

Standing, Guy. 1981. Unemployment and Female Labour: A Study of Labour Supply in Kingston, Jamaica. New York: St. Martin's Press.

Tilly, Louise. 1978. Women and Family Strategies in French Proletarian Families. Michigan Occasional Papers, No. 4, Ann Arbor, Michigan.

Tinker, Irene and Bo Bramsen, eds. 1977. Women and World Development, Washington, D.C.: Overseas Development Council.

Valentine, Betty Lou. 1980. Hustling and Other Hard Work in the Ghetto, New York: The Free Press.

Whitehead, L. Tony. 1976. Men, Family and Family Planning: Male Role Perception and Performance in a Jamaican Sugartown, Ph.D. dissertation in Anthropology, University of Pittsburgh.

Witter, Michael. 1980. "Hustle Economy: Essay in Conceptualization." Department of Economics, University of the West Indies, Mona, Jamaica.

TABLE 1

Wage and Other Activities by Household Position

	Single Woman (N=23)					Stable Union (N=52)					Visiting Union (N=52)				
	Numbers Engaged In					Numbers Engaged In					Numbers Engaged In				
	Totals	Formal Job	School	House-Work	Infrml Job	Totals	Formal Job	School	House-Work	Infrml Job	Totals	Formal Job	School	House-Work	Infrml Job
Respondent	23	23	--	--	--	52	52	--	--	--	52	52	--	--	--
Spouse/Partner	--	--	--	--	--	52	42	--	2	8	--	--	--	--	--
Children	86	15	42	26	3	220	63	138	15	4	138	11	95	24	8
Sister	7	5	--	2	--	1	1	--	--	--	26	14	4	7	1
Brother	2	2	--	--	--	1	1	--	--	--	19	11	--	2	6
Respondent's Mother	2	--	--	2	--	3	--	--	3	--	8	1	--	1	6
Niece	8	1	4	2	1	7	--	5	2	--	26	1	15	7	3
Nephew	1	2	4	--	1	2	1	1	--	--	9	1	5	1	2
Other	5	2	--	3	--	4	--	--	4	--	14	4	--	8	--
Respondent's Daughters Child's Father	2	1	--	--	1	1	1	--	--	1	1	1	--	--	--
Grandchild	7	--	--	--	--	10	--	--	--	--	--	--	--	--	--
TOTALS	148	50	50	35	6	353	161	144	26	13	293	96	119	50	26

Source: Bolles 1981:92

6 Female Employment in the Puerto Rican Working Class

Helen I. Safa

By now the role that women play in the social reproduction of working class families through the maintenance and reproduction of the labor force is fairly well acknowledged. However, the contribution that they make in terms of paid employment still tends to be minimized. Women of working-class families tend to be seen as supplementary wage earners, dependent on men as the primary breadwinners. This "supplementary" role has been used to justify the continued inequality in wages of men and women, as well as occupational segregation in low-paying, unskilled jobs in the manufacturing, clerical, and service sectors.

This chapter is an attempt to assess the contribution women make to the social reproduction of working-class families in Puerto Rico, a society that has undergone rapid industrialization and urbanization in the period since 1940. Certain features of the industrialization program in Puerto Rico, which will be detailed later, intensified the demand for female labor and women's role in social reproduction. However, since the Puerto Rican model of economic growth through export-based industrialization has been followed by so many developing countries, particularly the smaller economies of the Caribbean, the lessons from the Puerto Rican experience are certainly applicable elsewhere. This is particularly true now that the Caribbean Basin Initiative is advocating an extension and reinforcement of the Puerto Rican model of export-based industrialization for the rest of the region.

---

* A slightly revised version of this chapter first appeared in the *International Migration Review* special issue on women in migration.

Critics of export-based industrialization as a development model have tended to ignore the crucial role played by female labor in this process, both in Puerto Rico and elsewhere. With the initiation of Operation Bootstrap, as the Puerto Rican industrialization program is known, the rate of female employment increased from 22.1 percent in 1960 to 27.8 percent in 1980 according to official labor statistics. In part, this was due to an increased demand for female labor, not only in manufacturing, but also in the service sector and government employment, which by 1980 constituted the primary source of employment for women. More than half the new jobs created between 1960 and 1980 went to women (Departamento del Trabajo 1981:2-4), while the labor force participation rate for Puerto Rican men declined sharply, from 80 percent in 1950 to 60 percent in 1975. Many of these men are disadvantaged workers, who withdrew from the labor force rather than continuing to seek employment. It was difficult for men to find jobs, due to both the decline in agriculture and to the industrialization program which made factory employment more available to women than to men. Heavy outmigration rates starting in 1950 often affected men more than women, particularly in certain regions (Monk 1981).

The change from an agricultural to an urban, industrial economy displaced men from agricultural employment but did not offer them a suitable alternative in factory employment, much of which favored women. This was particularly true of the garment industry, which has been the leading industrial employer on the island since the 1950s, employing over one-fourth the labor force. In this chapter, we shall pay special attention to the garment industry because of its key role in female employment and because it demonstrates many of the problems that the industrialization program in Puerto Rico is now encountering. We shall also examine the results of a study of a small sample of women garment workers in the western part of the island conducted by the author in 1980. By combining macro-level data with the micro-level results of our study, we shall attempt to demonstrate the role that women are playing in the social reproduction of Puerto Rican working-class families.

MANUFACTURING AND THE APPAREL INDUSTRY IN PUERTO RICO

The demand for female labor was critically affected by the growth and subsequent stagnation of the industrialization program in Puerto Rico, known as Operation Bootstrap. Started in the 1940s, Operation Bootstrap was an ambitious program designed by the Commonwealth goverment to alleviate high unemployment brought about primarily by the stagnation of the rural plantation economy heavily dependent on sugar cane, coffee, and other export crops. It offered foreign investors, 90 percent of whom came from the United States (U.S. Department of Commerce, 1979:vol. 1, 21), tax holidays of ten years and more, infrastructure such as plants, roads, running water and electricity, and above all, an abundant supply of cheap labor.

Women provided much of this labor, though this fact has largely been ignored in the extensive research on the Puerto Rican economy. Many of the earlier industries were labor-intensive, such as apparel, textiles and food, all of which employ a high percentage of women. In the 1960s, in an attempt to avoid the high instability and low wages associated with labor intensive employment, the Commonwealth government made a concerted effort to encourage more capital-intensive plants, such as petrochemicals, pharmaceuticals, electrical machinery, and instruments, to move to the islands. While this effort was partially successful, the garment industry remains by far the largest industrial source of employment on the island. In 1957, with nearly 20,000 employees, it represented 25.6 percent of total manufacturing employment in Puerto Rico; in 1977, with 36,200 employees, its share of this employment remained high--"The employment provided in 1977 was 2.7 times that of electrical machinery, 3 times that of instruments, and almost 4 times that of pharmaceuticals notwithstanding the rapid growth in employment in those industries after 1967" (U.S. Department of Commerce 1979:vols. 2, 31).

Industrialization transformed Puerto Rico from an agrarian to an urban manufacturing economy. In 1940, manufacturing contributed 12 percent of total net income and agriculture 31 percent; in 1980, the shares were 47.1 percent and 4.4 percent. In 1940, agriculture provided employment to 44.7 percent of the labor force and manufacturing to 10.9 percent; in 1980, agriculture had declined to 5.2 percent while manufacturing had risen to 19 percent (Dietz 1982:5).

While growth in manufacturing increased nearly threefold from 1950 to 1977, it still could not offset the enormous employment declines in agriculture over this period. Even during the 1950s and 1960s, with rapid industrialization and heavy outmigration, unemployment remained at 10 to 12 percent of the labor force. Industry in Puerto Rico was severely hit by the 1973-75 recession in the United States and has not fully recovered. As a result, after the recession, unemployment in Puerto Rico reached about 20 percent, with the sharpest drops occurring in construction and manufacturing jobs (U.S. Department of Commerce 1979:vol. 1,40).

Unemployment rates for men have risen more rapidly than for women and in 1980 stood at 19.6 percent and 12.3 percent, respectively. This largely reflects the fact, noted previously, that the industrialization process and other changes in the occupational structure of Puerto Rico have tended to favor women over men. In 1980, the participation of men and women in the manufacturing sector was nearly equal (Departamento del Trabajo 1981:3), and even some of the newer capital-intensive industries such as pharmaceuticals employ large numbers of women. Jobs have opened up for women in the service and white-collar sectors, particularly in the burgeoning government bureacracy, where women represent over half of the labor force (ibid.:4). At the same time, men have suffered from the sharp decline in agriculture and later in construction, traditional sectors of male employment. Here we see how macro-level changes in the economy affect the demand for female and male labor.

Women have not been totally exempt from the effects of growing unemployment in Puerto Rico, but they have been less affected than men due to their concentration in sex-typed "female" occupations. As in the United States during the great depression (cf. Milkman 1976:76), these "female" occupations in clerical, service, and certain manufacturing jobs have suffered less contraction than male blue-collar jobs in the same period. Nevertheless, employment has declined in the garment industry, the leading industrial employer of women on the island since the 1950s. The garment industry never fully recovered from the recession of 1973, when employment fell from 40,300 workers in 1973 to 33,900 workers in 1980 (Departamento del Trabajo 1981:Table 1).

Part of this is due to competition from cheaper wage areas in Asia (e.g., Hong Kong, Korea, Singapore), as well as in Latin America and other areas of the Caribbean (Safa 1981). With an average hourly wage in the garment industry of $3.39 in 1980, Puerto Rico has lost its competitive advantage vis-a-vis these other developing countries. If President Reagan's Caribbean Basin Initiative succeeds, this movement of production abroad is likely to be accelerated, since much of the program is based on incentives to export processing industrialization. There is also some evidence of a twin-plant syndrome developing between Puerto Rico and other Caribbean islands like the Dominican Republic, with the cheaper, less skilled operations being performed in free trade zones like La Romana in the Dominican Republic, to be shipped to Puerto Rico for final processing. Such a twin-plant syndrome has proved eminently successful along the Mexican border (Fernandez Kelly 1980).

Though wages in the garment industry in Puerto Rico are much higher than in these other areas, they are still considerably lower than in the United States. In 1977, the wage differential was $1.07 an hour, or 69 percent of the United States average hourly wage (U.S. Department of Commerce 1979:vol 2, 257). The goal of the Fair Labor Standards Act was to bring all industries in Puerto Rico up to the U.S. minimum wage by January 1981, whereas previously they were set specifically for each industry. As in the United States, the garment industry is the lowest-paid industry on the island, with an average annual salary per worker in 1977 of $4,885 (ibid.:vol. 2, 46). Given the living costs in Puerto Rico, this is scarcely enough to support a single person, no less a family. Thus, we shall find that many garment workers in Puerto Rico have to depend on additional workers or other sources of income to sustain an adequate standard of living.

Growing unemployment has led to increasing reliance on federal transfer payments to sustain the Puerto Rican economy. With the collapse of Operation Bootstrap, Puerto Rico has become a prime example of an advanced welfare state, with heavy reliance on social security, veterans benefits, unemployment insurance, food stamps, etc. In 1976, the net injection into Puerto Rico reached $2,182.9 million, or about $900 per Puerto Rican resident (Dietz 1979:28). Because of low wages, even the working poor are eligible for food stamps, and it is estimated that almost 70 percent of the population now receives some benefits under this program, which in 1977 cost the federal government $802.1 million (ibid.:29). Though seen as a subsidy to the poor, food stamps and other income transfer payments may also be viewed as a subsidy to low-wage industries, like the apparel industry, which would otherwise leave the island. Federal transfer payments to the island accelerated rapidly after 1970, and had grown to 28 percent of personal income by 1977 (ibid.:69).

Clearly, the Puerto Rican economy is in deep trouble. While industrialization provided a partial alternative to the decline in agriculture during the 1950s and 1960s, it has slowed down considerably due to competition from other areas, high wages (compared to these areas), and high fuel and energy costs. The commonwealth government attempted to combat this problem by shifting into more capital-intensive industries, yielding higher profits and greater productivity. These capital-intensive industries generally employ more men. However, these industries also do not employ as many workers as labor-intensive plants, resulting in continuing declines in male labor force participation rates and rises in unemployment. The government also attempted to counter the negative effect of rising unemployment and low wages by offering workers a variety of subsidies, such as food stamps, unemployment insurance, public assistance, and programs in health, education, and human development services. While the federal government provides the major source of funding for these subsidies, the public debt of the commonwealth government has also grown enormously, and reached 80 percent of GNP in 1976 (Dietz 1979:29).

The crisis of the Puerto Rican economy has placed an even greater burden on women. The high rate of male unemployment and male outmigration left many families without a primary breadwinner, and women were often forced to assume this role. We shall look at the impact of female wage earnings on the household economy in the next section.

WOMEN GARMENT WORKERS AND THE HOUSEHOLD ECONOMY

While garment workers cannot be considered representative of the female labor force in Puerto Rico, the apparel industry gives us a unique opportunity for examining the long-term effects of female industrial employment on women and working-class families on the island. Both in the United States and Puerto Rico, the garment industry employs mostly women (90 percent according to a recent islandwide sample of workers in the International Ladies Garment Workers Union). Many of these women have been employed since the first plants opened in the early 1950s.

The data presented here were collected in 1980 on a sample of 157 women working in three different branches of the same garment firm in Puerto Rico. This firm was chosen because a study had already been conducted among women in the oldest plant and headquarters of this firm in New Jersey and therefore offered interesting possibilities of comparison. However, our analysis here will focus on the Puerto Rican sample, with a brief comparison with New Jersey in the conclusion.

Because of our initial interest in long-term employment, the sample was chosen on the basis of length of time the workers were employed. Approximately one third of the 157 women interviewed were long-term employees, who had been working for the company ten years or more, starting between 1950 and 1969. The remainder of the sample were short-term employees, who had worked for the company ten years or less, being employed since 1970 (Table 1). It was felt that ten years was a sufficient time for the effects of long-term employment to be evident.

However, upon analysis it appeared that length of employment did not appear to be a crucial determinant of any crucial variables in this sample of working women. In fact, length of employment is highly correlated with other demographic factors such as age, marital status, and rural-urban residence, which appear to be far stronger determinants of differences in this sample than length of employment. Thus, short-term employees tend to be predominantly young, single, rural women, while long-term employees tend to be predominantly older, urban, married or formerly married women (Table 2). If we break the sample into three age groups, under thirty, thirty to forty-four, and forty-five and over, we can see that we are dealing with a full developmental cycle, from single girls still living with their parent(s), to middle-aged women married and living with their husbands and children, to older women, 65 percent of whom are still married and 35 percent of whom are formerly married. These stages of the life cycle appear to be a major determinant of the role women play in the social reproduction of these working-class households.

Life cycle affects women's role in social reproduction at two levels. First, life cycle is a major factor in labor recruitment policies and thus strongly affects who is hired for particular jobs. Second, it affects the way in which women regard their earnings and the contributions they make toward the household economy. The importance of their contribution must be measured against the contributions of other household members as well as other sources of income, such as transfer payments, which also vary over the life cycle.

We shall begin with labor recuitment policies and then look at the differences between younger and older women workers.

It is clear that labor recruitment policies in the apparel industry have favored younger workers in recent years. Thus, in our analysis of the islandwide sample of ILGWU workers, almost 90 percent of the workers under thirty were recruited in the last five years (Table 3). This is also evident by examining demographic differences in the three plants in which this study was conducted (Table 4). The oldest employees are concentrated in the oldest plant (Factory 1) that opened in 1952 in Mayaguez, a major city on the west coast of Puerto Rico. As might be expected, most of the women working in this plant are urban residents, and only one in the sample is single. In the newer plants (Factory 2 and 3), however, there is a much higher percentage of young, single workers, especially in Factory 3. Though both plants opened at about the same time (in 1964 and 1965, respectively), the higher percentage of middle-aged married women in Factory 2 is due primarily to transfers from Factory 1, because of a slowdown in production in the latter plant. Since these plants are located in rural towns a few miles from the city, we might expect that their employees are primarily rural. Many of these women garment workers came from outlying rural areas rather than from the rural towns.

Why does management seem to prefer these young, single, rural workers? Facile explanations of more nimble fingers or greater visual acuity are clearly inadequate. Management says that older women complain more and are not as productive as younger women. It has often been noted that younger women constitute a more docile labor force. Why should this be so? What helps account for the difference in attitude, if any, between the younger and older women workers? Can this partly be explained by their role in social reproduction?

The contrast will be primarily between young women under thirty, who constitute 43.9 percent of the sample, and older women forty-five and over, who constitute 23.6 percent. A comparison of these two groups may help us explain why management has such a distinct preference for young, single women in labor intensive industrial employment, not only in Puerto Rico, but in many parts of the Third World.

Young, Single Women

The single women in this sample, tend to be members of large rural households, consisting of more than four and in 40 percent of the cases, more than seven persons (Table 5). As a result, there are often three to five persons working in each household, usually in factory employment. The effects of this multiple wage-earning strategy can be seen in the relatively high family incomes among these single women, where more than 40 percent of the households have annual incomes over $14,000 (Table 6). On a per capita basis, however, incomes are considerably lower. Thus, in households where the daughter lives with her parents and siblings and contributes to the family income, per capita income never runs over $6,500 annually. Still this is easier than supporting even a small household on this income, as we shall see many older, formerly married women do.

The decline in agricultural employment is clearly evident in the case of these rural houeholds. Ninety percent of our sample say it is easier for a woman to find a job than for a man. Their fathers often worked as agricultural laborers in sugar cane or coffee cultivation, before low wages (compared to other sectors), low profits, and hurricanes brought about a decline in this activity. Some continue to rent houses or land, but few families cultivate land, even for subsistence purposes. Most of these men are too old to work and live off their children's earnings and social security, food stamps, and other supplementary sources of income. In our sample, the households of young, single women receive a larger share of nonwage sources of income than those of older married or formerly married women (Table 7). This may be due to the larger size of these rural families, the older age of the head of household, and other factors. However, it should be noted that only about 20 percent of our sample receive supplementary sources of income, chiefly food stamps.

The western region has also experienced heavy outmigration, starting in the 1950s, caused largely by the decline in male agricultural employment. In our entire sample, over 60 percent of the women have siblings and husbands who have migrated to the United States. In a study conducted in this area in 1977, outmigration is directly related to lack of employment opportunities, which affected men more than women. Work opportunities for high school educated women are better than for men, particularly in factory employment, and result in a lower rate of female outmigration and a lower rate of female unemployment (Monk 1981:41).

These rural peasant households are still strongly patriarchal, despite the man's loss of earning potential. As they marry, rural women transfer patriarchal authority to their husbands, who are still considered the boss in most households. Husbands often pay the bills, and the wife may turn her paycheck over to her husband. Nevertheless, husbands tend to help out around the house and share important decisions with their wives.

Female employment is critical to the family's survival. As in most working-class families, women see work as a way of contributing to the family income rather than as a way of establishing their own indepedence. Newly married couples commonly start out in the parental home until they have money to buy or build a home of their own, often on parental land. Although they may keep part of their salary for their own expenses and savings, women's earnings in this sample never constitute less than 40 percent of the total family income, and in a fourth of the households where the daughter is working, she is the sole support of her parents and siblings (Table 8).

Older women bear an even heavier financial responsibility in the household. Among female-headed houeholds, all the women living alone and over half of the women living only with their children are the sole source of support for their families. Most married women contribute 50 to 60 percent of the total family income. No wonder most of these women say their families could not afford to have them stop working.

In these large, rural households, tasks are shared among all the members, following a strict sexual division of labor. Young working girls, however, are often relieved of major housework responsibilities by their mother, who does the cooking, cleaning, and other domestic tasks. Such help is not available to older, married women, who often also have young children to care for.

Where children are working, parents generally pay the household expenses out of their pooled income. Judging by their possessions, these families are not poor. Most families have cars (now a necessity in the rural area), washing machines, televisions, and even stereos. Many of these consumer goods are purchased on the installment plan, and over 80 percent of our respondents have debts ranging from under $100 to over $200 per month. Very few families have savings.

These rural households are part of tightly knit network of kin and neighbors, who help each other out in many ways, including child care, house building, and shopping. Nearly all the women (96 percent) under 30 have relatives living nearby, owing to a kin-based settlement pattern in the rural areas. Relatives frequently travel to work together in the same car, sharing expenses, and over 60 percent of the women working in Factory 2 and 3 have relatives working in the same factory. The first hired usually tries to secure employment for her relatives, but management has recently tried to discourage this policy, ostensibly because it contributes to greater absenteeism.

Most of these young women were hired in the past five years, and this is often their first job. Most started working between the ages of eighteen and twenty, after completing all or most of high school. They are very satisifed with their jobs and with their salaries, which average between $120 and $129 weekly. (There is no salary increase with length of employment, but some earn considerably more, depending on piecework). They have a strong work ethic and do not complain about production cutbacks and problems with the union or management.

If they lost this job, most of these young women would look for another job rather than staying home, because they need the money. Many of the younger, married women are now renting and are working to help buy or build their own home (still a tradition in rural areas, with one room added at a time). Although 71 percent of these young women consider themselves working class (Table 9), they hope their children will be middle-class and do not want their children, especially their daughters, to work in factories. They generally think it has been easier for them to advance than for their parents and think it will be easier still for their children.

Older Married and Formerly Married Women

Older married and formerly married women tend to be far less cheerful and optimistic. Many of them are employed in the old Factory 1, which experienced severe curtailments in production and employment in the 1970s and finally closed. In January 1981, there were only thirty-six operators working, compared to 128 in 1980, when we chose the sample, and over 300 when the plant was at its peak. Management blames the curtailment on the unpopularity of styles in the plant and the lack of training of the women to produce other styles. However, the fact that women workers from this plant are offered the possibility of transferring to one of the newer plants where these new styles are produced tends to belie this argument. Despite a rather extensive building rehabilitation program three years earlier, supported by the Puerto Rican government, management also complains about the poor condition of the plant, which has suffered floods, robberies, and similar misfortunes. Management gradually eliminated production from this plant entirely, retaining the building for offices and a storehouse and moving all employees to the newer plants, which still enjoy several years of tax exemption.

Women workers in Factory 1 are not happy about having to travel several miles to a nearby town to work, but many are forced to because they are not eligible for unemployment or retirement if they stop working now. Such a move is considered reorganization rather than a plant closing, which would entitle them to unemployment compensation. Most of these women feel that they are now too old to find another job, especially outside the garment industry, in which some of them have worked for nearly thirty years. They are very worried about job stability and security and dissatisfied with the promises that management and the union have made them. Most of them feel that conditions in Factory 1 have worsened in recent years and are unlikely to get better. They complain strongly about production cutbacks, the union's medical plan, and other problems.

Older women are also in a more precarious economic situaton, particularly if they are no longer married. Most formerly married women are divorced or separated from their husbands and over half live in small households of one to three persons (Table 5), either alone or with their children or other relatives. This limits the number of wage earners per family, and as we have seen, many of the formerly married women depend entirely on their own salary for a living (Table 8). Since family income is highly dependent on the number of persons working per family (Table 10), over half of these formerly married women have the lowest incomes, $5,000 to $8,000 annually (Table 6).

However, older women who are married and whose husbands also contribute to the family often enjoy incomes as high as $12,000 to over $14,000 annually (Table 6). Many of these men make over $175 a week and may be employed as managers or lower-level professionals.

Most of these older women live in the city and are clearly more isolated than their younger, rural counterparts. Not only do they live in smaller households, but they have fewer kin living nearby and tend not to socialize as frequently with neighbors or fellow workers than rural women. They often do all the household chores themselves, including paying the bills, and are very worried about inflation, which is eating up their meager incomes. In terms of savings, debts, and household possessions, these older women are no worse off than the younger women, except for some of the formerly married. In fact, a higher percentage of older women identify as middle class (Table 7), but these are generally the married women with higher incomes, noted above.

Nearly 80 percent of these older women have only a primary school education, which they admit has limited their possibilities of advancement. Although they believe strongly in education and have encouraged their children to finish high school and even go on to college, many say that inflation and unemployment are making it harder for their children to advance. Many of the older women think factory work is good for women, but, like the younger women, they would not like to see their daughters work in factories.

CONCLUSIONS

From this brief comparison, it is easy to see why management might prefer young, single women as workers over the older, married and formerly married women. Young women are better educated, they work harder, and they complain less. As single women, they are not likely to be burdened with household or child-care responsibilities, which can lead to fatigue or even absenteeism on the job. Many come from strong patriarchal rural traditions, where they readily transfer the authority of their fathers or husbands to the company manager, whose word is seldom questioned. They are aware of problems in the plant, such as production cutbacks, but they have not been as affected by this as the women in Factory 1, and they are more confident that they can find another job if they should be laid off or given very little work. In fact, many of the younger women think they could obtain better-paying factory jobs in electronics or in a pharmaceutical company, while older women feel closed off from this possibility because of their lack of education or experience. For younger women, the primary concern is not job stability but money. They need money for their parents, if they are still living at home, and for their future plans, which usually include a husband, children, and a new home.

In contrast, older women are more demanding. They have worked longer and have little opportunity of obtaining another job outside the garment industry. Therefore, they are very concerned with job stability and feel extremely threatened by production slowdowns and the closing of Factory 1. This could tend to make them more docile, but apparently among these older women, work has contributed to their sense of self-worth and independence and to a breakdown of the patriarchal tradition still prevalent in the rural area. Thus, they are more likely to question management's authority and to argue for their rights than the younger, rural women.

Older women have more at stake in their jobs. In the case of formerly married women, often their entire livelihood depends on their continued employment, since they are the sole source of income in the household. Married women at least share this responsibility with their husbands, and single women generally share it with a relatively large number of siblings. Thus, the contribution working women make to the social reproduction of Puerto Rican working-class households in most cases varies with their life cycle. Not only do older married women carry a heavier financial burden, but they also assume a larger share of household responsibilities.

There are other distinct advantages to management in hiring young, single workers. They do not have to pay maternity benefits (which are quite generous through the ILGWU) or retirement benefits to women who are forced to retire before completing ten years on the job. The union benefits from this as well, since the larger the number of older workers, the greater the drain on the retirement fund. At the same time, by shifting production to the newer plants, management can take advantage of several more years of tax exemption, which has already expired at the older plant.

In contrast to Puerto Rico, in the New Jersey sample of this same firm, almost all the women were older, married, and urban residents. In part, this was due to the movement of production abroad, to Puerto Rico and elsewhere, sharply reducing the number of women workers in the parent plant. Rather than firing workers, management followed a slow process of attrition, so that the workers remaining were usually the older, long-term workers, similar to the older workers in Factory 1 in Puerto Rico.

However, in the United States there are also more alternatives open to most working women, so that young women often shun the low-paying, unstable jobs in the garment industry. Historically, the garment industry in the United States has attracted immigrant workers, such as Jews, Italians, or now Hispanics, who have fewer job alternatives due to their limited knowledge of English, lack of job experience, and low educational levels. Many of the older women in the New Jersey plant were second-generation white ethnics, who had started working in the garment industry as young girls.

Neither in Puerto Rico nor New Jersey do we find a high level of class consciousness among these working women, even the older women who have been employed twenty years or more. Most women in both areas still define themselves primarily in terms of their family roles as wives and mothers rather than as workers. Paid work is still seen as a "male" sphere, despite the increasing contribution women are making to the household economy. In part, this stems from the nature of our sample, since the garment industry is a highly sex-segregated, female occupation, and much of the work routine in a garment plant tends to reinforce the paternalism of the patriarchal household. This patriarchal tradition is breaking down among older Puerto Rican women, but this breakdown appears to be due less to the length of employment per se than to the process of proletarianization accompanying the urbanization and industrialization process in Puerto Rico. While conributing to the breakdown of patriarchy, proletarianization also tends to isolate the family, break down the kin group, and increase the individual women's burden of maintaining the household economy.

It will be difficult for women to acknowledge their contribution to the household economy until their role is recognized by the larger society. Faced with an ideological contradiction between women's family and work roles, society has tended to emphasize the former since it still benefits from women's unpaid work in the home. This ideology also makes it easier to push women back into the home in times of economic contraction or to use them as a cheap labor reserve. However, the increasing number of women in the paid labor force, both in Puerto Rico and in the United States, is likely to accentuate this contradiction (Milkman 1976) and eventually lead to increasing demands by women for equality in the work sphere and for a recognition of the role they are playing in social reproduction.

REFERENCES

Departamento del Trabajo y Recursos Humanos, Estado Libre Asociado de Puerto Rico. 1981. La Participacion de la Mujer en la Fuerza Laboral, Informe Especial E-27.

Dietz, James L. 1979. "Imperialism and Underdevelopment: A theoretical Perspective and A Case Study of Puerto Rico." The Review of Radical Political Economics 11, 4:16-32.

_____. 1982. "Delusions of Development: International Firms in Puerto Rico." Pensamiento Critico, August/September.

Fernandez Kelly, M. Patricia. 1980. "Maquiladores" and Women in Ciudad Juarez: The Paradoxes of Industrialization under Global Capitalism. Mimeographed (Department of Sociology, University of California, Berkeley, 1980). Published in abridged version as "The 'Maquila' Women," NACLA Report on the Americas 14, No. 5, 14-19.

Milkman, Ruth. 1976. "Women's Work and Economic Crises: Some Lessons of the Great Depression." The Review of Radical Political Economics 8:73-97.

Monk, Janice J. 1981. "Social Change and Sexual Differences in Puerto Rican Rural Migration." Papers in Latin American Geography in honor of Lucia G. Harrison. Muncie, Indiana: Special publications of the conference of Latin Americanist Geographers, Vol. I, 28-43.

Safa, Helen I. 1981. "Runaway Shops and Female Employment: The Search for Cheap Labor." Signs, Vol. 7, No. 2.

U.S. Department of Commerce. 1979. Economic Study of Puerto Rico, Vols. I and II.

TABLE 1

Total Number of Employees and Interview Sample Sizes
by Length of Employment in
Three Puerto Rican Garment Plants

Factory		Number Employed more than 10 yrs.	Number Employed under 10 yrs.	Total
Factory 1				
	Total	90	38	128
	Sample	23	8	31
Factory 2				
	Total	66	218	284
	Sample	18	43	61
Factory 3				
	Total	44	271	315
	Sample	11	54	65
Total Sample		52	107	157

TABLE 2
Length of Employment
by Rural/Urban Residence, Age, and Marital Status

Selected Characteristic	Length of Employment			
	Over 10 Yrs.		Under 10 Yrs.	
	No.	%	No.	%
Age:				
Under 30	1	1.9	68	64.8
30-44	22	42.3	29	27.6
45 and over	29	55.8	8	7.6
Total	52	100.0	105	100.0
Rural/urban Residence:				
Residing in rural Setting	17	32.7	70	67.3
Residing in urban Setting	35	66.7	35	33.3
Total	52	100.0	105	100.0
Marital status:				
Married	38	73.1	67	63.8
Formerly married	13	25.0	12	12.0
Single	1	1.9	26	24.7
Total	52	100.0	105	100.0

TABLE 3
Age by Length of Employment for
International Ladies Garment Workers Union

Age	Length of Employment									
	Under 5 Yrs		5-10 Yrs		10-15 Yrs		15-20 Yrs		Over 20 Yrs	
	No.	%	No.	%	No.	%	No.	%	No.	%
Under 30	186	40.9	22	19.6	0	0.0	0	0.0	1	50
30-44	215	47.3	62	55.4	12	75.0	1	33.3	0	0
45 and over	54	11.9	28	25.0	4	25.0	2	66.7	1	50
Total	455	100	112	100	16	100	3	100	2	100

TABLE 4
Demographic Characteristics of Interview Samples in Three Puerto Rican Plants

Demographic Characteristic	Factory 1		Factory 2		Factory 3	
	No.	%	No.	%	No.	%
Age:						
Under 30	4	12.9	25	41.0	40	61.5
30-44	11	35.5	24	39.3	16	24.6
45 and over	16	51.6	12	19.7	9	13.8
Total	31	100.0	61	100.0	65	100.0
Marital Status:						
Married	20	64.5	44	72.1	41	63.1
Formerly Married	10	32.3	8	13.1	7	10.8
Single	1	3.2	9	14.8	17	26.2
Total	31	100.0	61	100.0	65	100.0
Rural/urban Residence:						
Residing in rural setting	2	6.5	35	57.4	50	76.9
Residing in urban setting	29	93.5	26	42.6	15	23.1
Total	31	100.0	61	100.0	65	100.0

Total Number: 157

TABLE 5
Marital Status by Number of Persons in Residence

No. of Persons in Residence	Marital Status: Married No.	%	Formerly Married No.	%	Single No.	%
1, 2, or 3 persons	38	36.2	13	52.0	5	18.5
4, 5, or 6 persons	63	60.0	11	44.0	11	40.7
7 or more persons	4	3.8	1	4.0	11	40.7
Total	105	100.0	25	100.0	27	100.0

Total Number: 157

TABLE 6

Marital Status by Total Annual Family Income

Annual Family Income	Marital Status: Married No.	%	Formerly Married No.	%	Single No.	%
$5,000 to 7,999	8	7.6	13	52.0	4	14.8
$8,000 to 9,999	11	10.5	4	16.0	6	22.2
$10,000 to 11,999	27	25.7	1	4.0	4	14.8
$12,000 to 13,999	33	31.4	4	16.0	2	7.4
$14,000 and over	26	24.8	3	12.0	11	40.7
Total	105	100.0	25	100.0	27	100.0

Total Number: 157

TABLE 7

Other Sources of Income by Age

Other Source of Income	Under 30		Age 30-44		Over 45	
	No.	%	No.	%	No.	%
None	32	46.4	35	68.6	27	73.0
Social Security	6	8.7	5	9.8	5	13.5
Food stamps	18	26.1	9	17.6	2	5.4
Other	13	18.8	2	3.9	3	8.1
Total	69	100	51	100	37	100

TABLE 8

Women's Earnings as Percentage of Family Income by Family Type*

	Percentage of Family Income													
	40-50		50-60		60-70		70-80		80-90		100		Total	
	No.	%	No.	%	No.	%	No.	%	No.	%	No.	%	No.	%
Nuclear:														
Woman alone	0	0.0	0	0.0	0	0.0	0	0.0	0	0.0	5	100.0	5	100
Woman and her husband	7	41.3	6	35.4	1	5.9	1	5.9	1	5.9	1	5.9	17	100
Woman, husband, and children	29	46.4	21	32.8	5	7.8	5	7.8	1	1.6	3	4.7	64	100
Woman and children alone	1	9.1	1	9.1	1	9.1	2	18.2	0	0.0	6	54.6	11	100
Extended:														
Woman, husband, children, parents, and/or other relatives	2	18.2	1	9.1	1	9.1	4	36.4	0	0.0	3	27.3	11	100
Woman head, children, and other relatives	4	80.0	0	0.0	0	0.0	0	0.0	0	0.0	1	20.0	5	100
Daughter, parents, and siblings	4	25.2	4	25.2	1	6.3	3	18.8	0	0.0	4	25.2	16	100
Daughter, parents, siblings, and other relatives	0	0.0	0	0.0	0	0.0	1	100.0	0	0.0	0	0.0	1	100

*These figures represent a comparison of women's earnings with total family income and may not represent the actual contribution made by these women.

TABLE 9

Class Identification by Age

Class	Age: Under 30 Yrs. No.	%	30-44 Yrs. No.	%	45 and Over No.	%
Middle	12	17.4	20	39.2	19	51.4
Working	49	71.0	26	51.0	15	40.5
Poor	8	11.6	5	9.8	3	8.1
Total	69	100.0	51	100.0	37	100.0

Total Number: 157

TABLE 10

Total Annual Family Income by Number of Persons Working

Number of Persons Working	Annual Family Income									
	$5,000-$7,999		$8,000-$9,999		$10,000-$11,999		$12,000-$13,999		$14,000 and over	
	No.	%	No.	%	No.	%	No.	%	No.	%
Only 1	15	60.0	6	28.6	4	12.5	1	2.6	3	7.5
2 persons	6	24.0	13	61.9	25	78.1	31	79.5	27	67.5
3 or more persons	4	16.0	2	9.5	3	9.4	7	17.9	10	25.0
Total	25	100.0	21	100.0	32	100.0	39	100.0	40	100.0

Total Number: 157

Andean women tend their babies while they watch their flocks on the altiplano.

PHOTO BY FERNANDO SORIA

III The Articulation of Modes of Production in Industrial and Agricultural Change

The integration of production on a world scale and the penetration of capitalism to the farthest reaches of urban and rural areas of Latin America have had a profound effect on male and female roles. The different levels of entry of women in industry vary over time and in space in ways that require historical and cross-cultural comparisons. Heleieth Saffioti shows that the value of women's work is more debased in industries that are the most advanced technologically in her comparison of a modern textile firm and a craft-based garment firm in Brazil. Marianne Schmink corroborates Saffioti's findings that men are more favored in the developing sectors of Brazils' economy. With the breakdown of the modernizing sector that one sees in Bolivia, there is a revitalization of women's participation in petty capitalist production that Judith-Maria Buechler elucidates in her chapter. In her comparison of Peruvian and Chilean land reform programs with that of Cuba, Carmen Diana Deere indicates the structrual contrasts in the incorporation of women in development in private capitalist and socialist nations. Cornelia Butler Flora and Blas Santos consider the specific aims of agricultural development and the techniques that favor incorporation of women in the developing projects.

Aymara woman plaiting reed adornments for Easter. La Paz, Bolivia.
PHOTO BY JUDITH-MARIA BUECHLER

7 Technological Change in Brazil: *Its Effect on Men and Women in Two Firms*

Heleieth I. B. Saffioti

Technological change and mechanization of production has had a different impact on the labor process for men and women workers. Generalizations drawn from major sectors of the economy are inadequate bases for analysis since differences exist within each. In order to understand the interrelationship between the ideologies concerning the allocation of jobs by gender and technological innovation, we must examine the concrete social relations existing in particular enterprises within each sector. This chapter is based on a comparative analysis of a textile and a garment factory in Sao Paulo, Brazil.

In Brazil the transformation of production brought about by the technological revolution since 1940 has reinforced the gender gap in employment opportunities and earnings. The major trend is the concentration of the female labor force in the service sector as it was expelled from agricultural work with the introduction of mechanized wage labor. Technological change has reduced the proportion of both male and female workers in the primary sector, but while the percentage of male workers has gone from 70.4 in 1940 to 50.4 in 1970, that of female agricultural workers has declined from 46.8 to less than half, or 20.8 percent. The majority of migrants to the cities are recruited into the service sector. The proportion of women who work in this sector in Brazil increased from 42.6 percent in 1940 to 68.6 percent in 1970.

Throughout this period, the industrial sector has shown great stability in employment. Although there were insignificant oscillations, women working in industry represented 10.6 percent of the total number of Brazilian female workers in 1940 and accounted for 10.4 percent in 1970. However, within the secondary, or industrial sector, there were significant changes in female employment in enterprises with different levels of technological investment. These changes point to interesting phenomena in relation to the differential effects of industrial modernization on the structure of female employment.

I shall review the overall trends in the textile and garment industry and then examine the process in two enterprises in Sao Paulo with different rates of technological innovation.

THE TEXTILE AND GARMENT INDUSTRIES

Each of these branches of industrial activity has developed its own specific characteristics in response to technological change. In spite of the impact of machines. the garment industry is still very much a craft activity, particularly when it serves the well-to-do classes. It calls for a labor force trained for highly skilled manual tasks, even though many of these are performed with the aid of machines. These requirements account for the high proportion of women, since they were taught dressmaking skills at home. In the past, the majority of women with these skills were self-employed; the number declined to 365,00 in the 1970 census but these independent activities are gradually being absorbed by firms with different levels of capital intensity. An unknown but large number of women assemble garments in the putting-out system. But although the labor process persists, its cadence is now determined by the demands of the garment manufacturers in fixing delivery deadlines and establishing piecework forms of payment. Other women have gone into garment factories where, although changes introduced by machines have been limited, the penetration of technology itself has created a new need for specialized maintenance. As a result, the relative number of men in the garment industry has increased, altering the gender composition of the labor force. By 1970, women accounted for only 50.2 percent of the workers in the country's garment industry, in comparison with 70 percent in 1920. The inclusion of footwear manufacturing in the census numeration of the garment industry swells the proportion of male participation, since women constitute only 14.7 percent of this subbranch, but even without these increments women have lost ground in the garment industry over time.

In contrast, the textile industry is more prone to technological innovation. At the time of the first census in 1872, 96.2 percent of the permanent employees in small textile factories were women. But by 1940 they constituted 65.1 percent, with 189,080 employed, and by 1970 their numbers had dropped to 149,810, or 47.8 percent, while male participation rose from 101,208 to 162,507, a percentage increase from 34.9 to 52.2 (Censos Economicos, 1940, 1970 IBGE). The proportion of males to females varied by occupation within the industry: the highest proportion, 67.0 percent, of threaders and bobbin winders were women; women also made up 64.7 percent of spinners, 51.8 prcent of weavers, and 44.4 percent of "other" occupations (Censo Demografico IBGE 1970). In summary, we can state that in the course of two decades, between 1950 and 1970, approximately one-fourth of the women employed in textiles were expelled, while the total number of men employed increased by over 60 percent. Indeed, women's limited access to technology and their difficulty in overcoming the demands made by enterprises characterized by a high level of technology can best be shown in the textile industry, although it is also demonstrated in other sectors (Chaney and Schmink 1975).

In the state of Sao Paulo, around 56 percent of the female labor force in manufacturing was in the textile and garment industries in 1970. The largest contingents of the female work force were in textile firms, where Almeida (1974) reported that 94,605, or 51.5 percent of the 183,577 employees were women. The Industrial Census of Sao Paulo reported 53 percent for the same year. The garment industry employed 41,189, or 61.4 percent of those directly engaged in production. There were more women among the technicians in the garment trade, where they accounted for 17.3 percent of all garment technicians, than in textiles, where they were no more than 5.4 percent.

Technological innovation in textiles outstrips that of the garment industry, although the former is today classified as a "traditional" industry. The real product in the textile industry increased by 73 percent between 1949 and 1959 even while the number of workers declined by 2.5 percent. In comparison with all industrial growth, where the product grew an average of 9.4 percent per year and the increase of jobs was 2.8 percent, the remarkable relationship between production increases and employment declines in textiles provides us with a clue to the changing rates of male and female employment. Given the stereotypes concerning gender aptitude in machine maintenance, one can begin to understand why women gave way to men. As manual looms were replaced by mechanical ones and sophisticated machinery substituted for simpler looms, the need for specialized machine maintenance personnel increased, while the higher productivity achieved with new technology led to the expulsion of those workers directly linked to production.

With the relatively high concentration of the female labor force in manufacturing of textiles and garments, these industries were less organized and paid less. This situation was due not only to the lack of political education among women, but also to their double workday, which did not allow them the free time necessary to participate in activities not strictly related to work. The dominant ideology obviously plays an extremely important role in this in curbing women's involvement in politics.

Wage discrimination is the best index to the women. Although data on wages in Brazil are usually compiled without distinction by gender, there are data on some periods for which this distinction is made. These data reveal that the gap between male and female wages among adult workers is greater in garment manufacturing than it is in the textile industry, and it is growing. In 1919, at a national level, women adult workers in the textile industry earned 70.1 percent of the male wage, although female minors earned about the same as male minors--101 percent. In the State of Sao Paulo this was less acute: women earned 81.7 percent of the wage of adult male workers, with female minors making 102 percent as much as male minors. When we turn to the garment industry, in 1920 national wages for female adult garment workers were 54.4 percent of male adult and female minors 86.7 of male minor workers and about the same for the State of Sao Paulo: 54.3 of adult and 82.8 of minor male workers (1920 Census). By 1970, women in Brazil earned around 61 percent of male workers' wages. In the intervening decade of inflation, the gap widened at the same time that it increased more for women with high levels of education than for women with low levels. According to unpublished data (Pastore and Carmo Lopes 1978) male workers with low educational levels in the secondary sector enjoyed a 154 wage ratio to that of women and those in the high educational level held a 168 ratio. This gap increased by 1976, when the ratio of wages of male workers of low educational levels in the secondary sector were 178 that of women's wages while those in high educational levels received a ratio of 222. In the tertiary sector men had less of an advantage: in 1970 the ratio of male to female wage in the low educational sector was 139, and the gap widened by only 9 points, to 148, in 1976. For high educational levels, the gap actually decreased in those same years, from 148 to 138.

These wage comparisons lead to two significant conclusions. First, women in industry suffer more discrimination than those in the service sector. Second, the differential increases with economic growth and modernization. As women break through the major obstacles to schooling, wage discrimination has become more acute. Thus, whereas in 1970 women on the average earned 61.2 percent of what men earned, by 1976 women's wages had fallen on the average of 48.6 percent of men's. The gap was thus expanded by nearly 13 points, making the average male income double that of women.

Women not only received lower wages, but they had the longest workday in industry. In 1970, while 89.0 percent of the men worked between forty-five and forty-nine hours a week, this was the case of 92.4 percent of the women. There is little evidence that the social situation of women is improving. It appears that in the present economic recession there is even greater discrimination against women. The empirical research carried out in 1977 provides a picture of the life of some of these working-class women and of the perception of the problems.

FIBROTEX AND CASULO

After a lengthy examination of house journals of Brazilian and foreign firms operating in Brazil and after numerous conversations with entrepreneurs in the textile and garment industries, two firms in Sao Paulo were singled out for investigation. One of them, to which we gave the fictitious name of Fibrotex, is a fairly large fabrics manufacturer belonging to a powerful foreign group with various textile firms and one garment enterprise in Brazil, as well as investments in various other branches of the Brazilian economy. Fibrotex is one of the ten largest textile enterpises operating in the country, and at the time of our research it had 867 employees, of whom 214, or 24.7 percent, were women.

The other enterprise chosen was a small textile and garment manufacturer that employed fifty-three people, thirty of whom were women. The firm's name, also fictitious, shall be Casulo. Although its owners are foreigners, they have lived in Brazil for many years and the invested capital is national.

Of the total of 244 women workers in the two firms, we managed to establish an excellent relationship with about 100. Although the firms offered all sorts of facilities to allow their employees to be interviewed during working hours, we preferred to look them up in their own homes. We established an excellent relationship with the eighty-one female workers from Fibrotex and nineteen from Casulo, whom we interviewed. Many employees from Fibrotex were evasive and refused to answer the questions since they seemed to fear jeopardizing their position at the firm where they worked, and for this reason, we interviewed only 37.5 percent of that work force. The receptivity of the women from Casulo was remarkably greater, and inteviews were carried out with 63.3 percent of the female workers employed there between July and September 1977. The sample was not, then, chosen on the basis of a given set of criteria, but rather, consisted of women to whom we had access and who wanted to collaborate in this study.

CHARACTERISTICS OF THE FIRMS

Casulo was established in 1969 in a residential neighborhood in Sao Paulo. One of its partners had already had experience in another firm in the same industry, set up in 1964 and closed down in 1968. Knitted fabrics are manufactured at Casulo, the fabric is cut, and the clothes are made. Its specialty is winter clothes manufacturing, although it also works with clothes for midseason and even for summer. In 1977, the unusually warm winter in Sao Paulo caused a serious crisis in such a small firm with capital assets of Cr$1,500,000. In order to meet the crisis, the factory bought light fabrics and manufactured a summer-clothes line. The company normally employs about 15 percent of its personnel through the putting-out system. But in 1977, it did not make use of this labor system, as it was already having difficulty maintaining its factory employees. Despite the crisis it managed to get through the period keeping all the employees it had already hired.

The production process at Casulo is quite craft-based. The knitted fabrics are manufactured with old-fashioned looms, each of which requires one operator. The patterns are designed exclusively by one woman, who is both a partner and the production manager of the firm. There are textile machines and typical knitwear machines such as finishers. Women operating the latter have to be skilled at the meticulous task of gathering one thread at a time from the edges of a garment in order to finish it on this special machine. Other types of clothes, which are finished on a sewing machine, are also manufactured. Because these tasks have a more craft than industrial character, they require proficiency, attention and patience. At the same time, there is a marked division of labor: each person specializes in one specific job. Some of these are very similar to the work normally performed by housewives in their homes. The ironing woman's job is a case in point. This task requires very little training, but like most tasks in the factory demands a certain amount of know-how acquired at home. But as people tend increasingly to purchase ready-made clothes, this type of socialization is disappearing, making it more difficult to recruit young women. Only older women have the know-how necessary to perform well the majority of the tasks at Casulo.

The problems of recruiting skilled labor are not the results of changes in women's socialization process alone. The fact that the factory is located in a middle-class neighborhood and is very close to the city's downtown area makes it extremely difficult for the firm to find labor power, for there are no potential female workers in the nearby area. Consequently, recruitment of new female workers takes place through existing networks of the firm's female workers' families and friends. New female workers are admitted after passing a practical test. The firm is only interested in checking whether the candidate is able to perform the tasks for which she will be responsible. No psychological or reading and writing tests are applied. It seems that in terms of personnel recuitment, the firm's only advantage is that it operates on a one-shift basis.

The owners did not plan to modernize or increase the size of their firm. They believed that they must maintain the craft character of the production process if they were to continue producing quality clothing. They were, however, thinking of expanding exports as a means of stabilizing the production cycle of the firm, thus solving the chronic crisis that this type of firm faces with a national market.

In contrast to the craft based production limited to a national market in the case of Casulo, Fibrotex belongs to a strong economic group. Most of this group's capital came from abroad, but since the firms in the group are corporations, there is a large number of small Brazilian shareholders. This group operates in three different main branches of the Brazilian economy: foodstuffs, the chemical industry and textiles. Of the group's net worth, 41.5 percent is in the textiles and more than half (23.5 percent) of net amount is in the firm under discussion. The group owns six factories in this industry. In 1976, the net sales of the group's textile firms increased 39 percent, totaling US $141,453,000.

The raw materials used at Fibrotex are cotton, wool, and synthetic fibers. The fact that cotton fabric production predominates seriously affects the workplace environment. Besides the unbearable noise made by the machines, the air is saturated with small cotton fibers, which penetrate people's mouth and nose. In 1977, Fibrotex was equipped with 34,700 ring spindles, 360 open-end turbines, and 475 automatic shuttle looms. Only one person was needed to operate an average of twenty-six looms simultaneously. Because the firm operated on a three-shift basis, this equipment was used twenty-four hours a day. The female labor force in this firm has largely been replaced by men. Women, in fact, did not even account for one-fourth of the employees in 1977, while on the average they reached more than double this proportion in the textile industry of the whole country. Fibrotex is very advanced in the process of replacing female with male labor--as the organic composition of capital continues to grow. This phenomenon was also observed by another researcher (Rodrigues 1979) in Sao Jose dos Campos, although it has not yet arrived at the figures we found in Fibrotex. Taking all the textile firms owned by the group into account, we found that as we move from the older to the more modern factories, women's presence decreases: only 28.6 percent of the workers in all of the group's textile firms are women. In the oldest firm, their numbers rises to 35.24 percent, while in the newest firm, which is equipped with more sophisticated technology, only 13.60 percent of the labor force are women.

It is important to note that together this group of textile firms employs a significant number of women under the age of eighteen. Whereas only 0.25 percent of the total number of male workers are minors, females under eighteen represented 31.19 percent of the female work force. The proportion of female minors at Fibrotex itself was even greater, reaching 44.6 percent of the firm's female labor force.

Because Fibrotex is a large company with a broad national and international market, it was less affected by the economic crisis that exploded in Brazil as a result of the end of the "miracle" in the mid-seventies when problems caused by the oil price increases precipitated a crisis in the world capitalist economy. Between 30 June 1976 and 30 June 1977, the firm's capital actually increased from 270 to 400 million cruzeiros. During that period, the firm's sales totaled 5253.8 million cruzeiros, and in the subsequent period, it invested about 164 million cruzeiros. It seems, then, that not only did the firm manage to survive this period of acute crisis, but it also greatly increased both its activities and the bulk of its profits. When it published its balance sheet in 1977, the firm wrote a letter to its shareholders informing them that its net billings had increased by 94 percent and its exports had increased 115 percent during the last period. Thus, the firm can be said to have experienced great prosperity, in spite of the serious economic crisis in the country. Female workers in the firm did not benefit from this prosperity since their wages remained the same despite the inflation that reduced buying power.

THE WORK PROCESS AND ITS CONSEQUENCES

There are marked differences in the work processes at the two firms investigated. As pointed out above, the process of fabric production and clothes manufacturing at Casulo has a strong craft character, requiring specialized human skills. Because only 20 percent of the machines are automated, female workers play fundamental roles in production. Articles are manufactured either individually or in small numbers, but are never mass produced. The need for professional skills has led the firm to develop a policy aimed at holding on to those women whom it considers to be specialized and responsible workers. The owners of the firm are aware that it is not easy to find women who know how to sew these days because this skill is the result of a certain type of female socialization that practically no longer exists. The idea that the firm should itself undertake to qualify its employees is not entertained, for this type of skill requires training on a long term basis. Thus, because young women as a rule do not have this know-how, Casulo's owners have chosen to develop and implement a policy aimed at maintaining the older employees in the factory.

Casulo grants all the benefits required by law and rigorously adheres to the legislation on special leaves of absence for pregnancy. The owners state--and their female workers confirm this--that women who get married or become pregnant are not fired. There was even one case reported of a women with eleven children, many of whom had been born during the time she worked for Casulo. The relative number of married female workers at Casulo is more than double those at Fibrotex. If we add together widows and married women, Casulo has over three times more women in these two marital categories than Fibrotex. These figures indicate a low turnover in the smaller firm and many of the older female workers have been in Casulo's labor force since it was founded in 1969.

The working environment, although cramped in physical terms, seems more hospitable and is considered almost a second home. It is common to see the female workers chatting together as they do their jobs, for all production takes place in a single room, and the rules of conduct are not as rigorous as in large automated firms. There is little evidence of technical control exerted through machines to reach higher rates of productivity since machines are operated manually and can not be used to impose any given rhythm on human labor. Given the craft character of the productive process, the female workers have greater freedom to determine their own work rhythm. The presence in the production room of the woman mentioned earlier, who is both one of the partners and the production manager, acts as a constraint to ensure the fulfillment of what the firm considers an adequate rhythm for production without technical control built into machines.

The heating-up and eating of the food taken to work in lunch boxes by the women represents a moment of fraternization and, as such, acts as an element that "humanizes" the labor process. The very fact that the owners work before the eyes of the female workers (the male partner is the firm's business manager and works in a small office next door to the production room) itself reduces the social distance between the employees and their bosses. All these factors together produce an intense identification with work and with the firm, so that the number of women at Casulo who plan to leave the work force is indeed very small. In response to questions on plans for future participation in the work force most responded that they planned to continue to be economically active until they retire. Others stated that they would only stop working if some fantastic change in their family lives occurred: for example, some said they would leave if they won a large sum of money on the lottery. Considering the burdens of domestic work following their labor in the factory, this phenomenal desire to leave work can be appreciated. However there were no statements that could lead us to infer that these women do not have job identification--despite the fact that the firm's wages are not only considered low by the employees, but are in comparison with those in other firms. We can conclude, therefore, that wages are not the most important factor in job satisfaction. Other factors enter in a much more intense way to shape the feelings female workers develop toward the job they perform. One indirect way of measuring job satisfaction, although a precarious one, could be absenteeism. Although industriousness can be linked to profound economic necessity, it can also manifest an interest in the job performed. There is practically no absenteeism at Casulo.

In terms of job satisfaction, it must also be said that the tasks performed at Casulo are not monotonous or repetitive. There is no question of responses becoming automatic, or of reproducing stereotyped responses eight hours every day. The work required competence, specialization, and skill. The way the female worker relates to her work seems to be enhanced in the work process itself. There are no complaints about the work; they are directed more toward the wages, as 60 percent of the respondents asserted. Heavy or dirty aspects of the work are not even mentioned, whereas they are referred to by female workers who operate more modern machines in Fibrotex. The work process allows for a certain amount of creativity, for fuller personal involvement, and for a rejection of the fragmentation of social roles. It is certainly owing to these characteristics, rather than as a result of the wages paid by the firm, that women at Casulo are able to feel greater identification and satisfaction with their work.

In contrast to Casulo, Fibrotex is a fairly modern factory, with automatic equipment and standardized tasks. Female workers there do not require any training to operate the machines, other than making certain muscular movements at a rhythm determined by the machine itself. As a result, there is no need for qualification in the strict sense of the term, but rather for a short period of training. All they have to do is to obey the equipment, which determines everything: the rhythm of labor, the sense of the smallness of human beings, the material discomfort resulting from the loud noise produced. As noted earlier, discomfort is also produced by the fibers released by the cotton. Human beings thus seem to be an appendix of the machine.

Besides, the fact that anyone can operate this equipment creates profound insecurity at work. There is an enormous industrial reserve army ready to replace any female worker who may make a mistake or demand that her rights guaranteed by law be respected. Once again the work process spills over the physical boundaries of the work situation itself. A sense of the transitory nature of her job, of the instability of her employment, and of her imminent replacement becomes ingrained in the female worker. Thus, she is unable to establish a deep sense of job identication, and there is a high rate of turnover. Given that prior qualification is unnecessary, the firm can recruit new workers annually and thereby keep payroll increases to a minimum. Hence some of the reasons for the massive presence of minors (much greater at Fibrotex than at Casulo) and of single women. The presence of married women is minimal, and these are older women whose children have already grown up (only two cases) or young women who have just married and therefore have no children. The only case at Fibrotex of a woman with a young child was a single mother who lived with her parents and whose pattern of life, therefore, did not differ at all from that of single female workers who were not responsible for any dependents. This case exemplifies the type of policy followed by the firm: the women was fired when she became pregnant and rehired later because her mother was willing to take care of her child. In spite of the existing legislation guaranteeing employment for those who marry or become pregnant, Fibrotex systematically fires any woman who decides to have children, as this implies greater absenteeism. Thus, the work process does affect the firm's policy on female workers' recruitment.

Although wages at Fibrotex are much higher than at Casulo, there is deep dissatisfaction with the work. Female workers often talk about its monotonous and repetitive nature and about its dirty and heavy character. No deeper link between the female workers and their own work seems to exist. It is merely considered a job that guarantees survival at the moment. Even though the job represents a relatively certain guarantee of a wage at the end of the month (the majority earn by production), it is still seen as something transitory in their lives. The majority plan to leave their job when they get married or have children. Thus, while only 15.8 percent of female employees at Casulo plan to retire from the labor force when they get married or begin to have children, 53.1 percent of those at Fibrotex have already decided to do so.

The nature of the work process, then, plays a major part in how the female workers at Fibrotex evaluate their jobs. Reasons for staying on given by the female workers who plan to keep their jobs vary at the two firms, presumably as a result of the production process. While at Fibrotex there was a higher number of women who felt that the firm's pay was good, at Casulo justifications for keeping the job were more along these lines: "the conditions of work are good," "the job is stable," "it's a job where you have freedom."

Responses to questions in the interviews indicate that the easier the work process becomes, as a result of the massive use of machines, the more uninteresting and monotonous it is. Asked to point to the element that pleased them most in their jobs, the Casulo employees overwhelmingly stressed two aspects: "the work is interesting" (37.5 percent) and "the relationship with both workmates and supervisors is good" (43.8 percent). At Fibrotex, the greatest consensus was found in the statements "the wages are good" (33.8 percent) and "the work is easy" (29.9 percent). The percentage of women at Fibrotex who consider the work there interesting and who refer to their relationship with their workmates and supervisors is very low. The firm's prime concern is its functional rationality. At Casulo, on the other hand, the number of employees who refer to their work as easy and to their wage as good, is very small.

When asked what they least like about their jobs about one-third of the workers at Fibrotex complain about their work being heavy; 22.2 percent about its being dirty; and 15.5 percent about its monotony. Of the total number of women studied, 52.0 percent had some self-perception with regard to work outside their home and saw it as a positive factor in their qualification as human beings prepared to confront life. Work is seen and felt in an ambiguous way: it represents an extra burden in the sense that other duties exist in addition to it, but it also represents the widening of horizons, a means of confronting life, a source of individualization. More than half the women interviewed were aware that they drew a significant part of their own identity from being wage-workers in a world where the process of individualization has acquired such deep-rooted characteristics. Yet there are moments in which this awareness seems obscured by the fatigue caused by the double workday and by the asymmetrical nature of relations with the opposite sex. The ambiguity, therefore, is present to a great extent and is indeed common among women who are socialized along Brazilian and even Western lines. This ambiguity cultivates a guilty conscience when women who are forced to work are unable to fulfill cultural standards of performance in the home and at work. This makes them easy prey for manipulation ideologies both as consumers and as workers, thus broadening the control exerted over them by capitalist society. Work is thus a source of security and a means of raising self-esteem, but women are nevertheless often ready to give it up in exchange for the position of housewife, spouse, and mother.

It is indeed very difficult to reconcile these two roles in a society that has no interest in freeing from domestic service labor power that exceeds the needs of capital. At the same time, this reconciliation becomes necessary, at least for a period, in the life of women who come from underprivileged socioeconomic strata. These women begin to live within a space created by the convergence of two forces: one demanding that they meet the responsibilities they acquire in the world of work as they search for the means of subsistence necessary to ensure and/or improve their livelihoods and the other requiring a more passive female, always ready to obey and prepared to dedicate herself full-time to her roles as wife and mother. It is indeed cruel to oblige women to confront this option: either follow a career or marry and have a family. That is the dilemma. In the underprivileged strata of society, however, this impasse is not even reached, for there is no alternative other than to fulfill both roles. Women experience their simultaneous roles as full of conflict and wearying, cultivating guilt feelings so characteristic of women who work outside the home and "neglect" domestic chores.

It is within these ambiguous terms that work becomes a criterion for these women's self-evaluation, as well as the source of their self-confidence. From this we can conclude that the security a single woman derives from working serves to show her the paths to follow but it fails her when she has any relationship with a man. The ambivalence benefits capitalist society by subjecting women to manipulation. While it provides a woman with the means of breaking through new frontiers and ensuring her means of survival as long as she is on her own, it simultaneously elminates or minimizes the problem of women who are dependent. Through creating obstacles to freedom and reducing her autonomy as long as she is linked to a man, it serves to keep the patriarchal family alive, with all its implications. Thus, capitalist enterprises have no interest--nor could they tolerate--elimination of the differences that separate the socialization processes of men and women. These differences guarantee the possibility of manipulating women according to what is convenient during any given socioeconomic conjuncture.

As a result, women lack one essential element in their personality to situate themselves in the world of work on equal terms with men: competitiveness. Perhaps this is why only about one-fifth of the women interviewed thought of obtaining professional qualifications when they were asked what they considered the best way of getting on in a job. They seem to project onto the world of work their habit of advancing through detours and shortcuts rather than taking the main highway to their desired aim. By placing professional qualification and, above all, professional practice on a secondary plane, they tend to see work outside the home as something compulsory and, hence, undesirable. Nevertheless, this activity at the same time constitutes a source of satisfaction insofar as it gives these human beings the means for their own self-assertion. In this way, women offer the essential requirements for the superexploitation of their labor power and thus lose their already small possibilities of advancement in the world or remunerated work.

THE FEMALE WORKERS' STANDARD OF LIVING

Although the average per capita income of the families of female workers at Fibrotex (Cr$869.00) is a little more than half that of the Casulo workers' families (Cr$1,676.00), it is the former families who make up the highest percentages of owner-occupiers of their own house. Indeed, 50.6 percent of the families of female workers at Fibrotex are owner-occupiers, while 48.2 percent rent their houses, and 1.2 percent live in rent-free houses provided by friends or relatives. Only 15.8 percent of the families of female workers at Casulo, on the other hand, are owner-occupiers, while 63.2 percent pay rent and 21.0 percent live in rent-free houses. The houses are quite modest, particularly those owned by the worker's family. Many of them are found in neighborhoods that have no normal street planning or that have only recently and/or illegally been sold off in lots for residential purposes and thus have unpaved streets and no basic sanitation facilities. In order to have an idea of the type of housing bought by the female owers' families, we have only to mention that those who were still paying off their mortgage were spending less than Cr$500.00 a month at a time when the minimum wage was Cr$768.00. Among the families who paid rent, however, 15.0 percent spent less than Cr$500.00 per month, while the largest contingent (42.0 percent) was in the Cr$500.00 to Cr$1,000.00 bracket. The rest of the families were distributed as follows: 38.0 percent paid between Cr$1,000.00 and Cr$2,000.00 and only 2.0 percent paid above Cr$2,000.00. It must be stressed that since the per capita income of the Casulo worker's family was greater, the presence of these workers in the higher rent brackets was unquestionably more marked, for there were no families of female workers at Fibrotex paying more than Cr$2,000.00 for rent.

The number of people living in each house was higher among the Fibrotex workers' families, the mode being at six residents, with high percentages of families with five or seven members: 12.5 percent, in each case. Among Casulo employees' families, however, the mode falls in two-member families--26.3 percent--while there were 21.1

percent with three members, 10.5 percent with four, and 10.5 percent with seven. The greatest concentration of women living alone was found among Casulo workers: 5.3 percent. Only 2.5 percent of the female workers sampled at Fibrotex were in this situaton. It must be noted that the proportion of large families in both firms was fairly significant. Among Casulo employees, 10.5 percent had families with nine members while the figure was 11.3 percent for female workers at Fibrotex.

Figures on the composition of the female workers' families clearly show how insiqnificant was the number of married women with children at Fibrotex. Data on the other firm are much more significant in this respect.

The data indicate clearly the response of women to company policy regarding their marital status only. Women at Fibrotex work until they get married, at best, until they have children. The family structure of those from Casulo is very different. Table 1 shows that women in both samples are at different stages in their life cycles. While Fibrotex workers, being so young, were still living with the families that had brought them up, the Casulo employees, were at a different stage in their lives and lived in much greater proportion with their procreative families. This fact to a large extent also explains the per capita income differential found among the families of both samples. Among Fibrotex workers' families, there was a large percentage of minors in the labor force, and they were contributing with low wages to the family income. There was a larger proportion of adults contributing to the family wage among the families of the Casulo workers. Thus, the average per capita income of the Casulo workers' families can be almost double that found among the families of those in the other sample.

The life-cycle stage in which the majority of the women in either sample were at the time must also influence the type of relation found between the female workers and their work. While the young girls of Fibrotex expected to "free themself" form compulsory labor outside the home through marriage, the Casulo workers had already lived through the marriage experience and the need to reconcile both workdays. Thus, they did not nurture the illusion of being able to dedicate themselves exclusively to domestic chores to the same extent as the female workers from the large firm. Life had provided them with more realistic criteria to shape their expectations.

The sampled female workers began their work lives very early. Indeed, 89.0 percent entered the labor force as minors. Table 2 shows this phenomenon.

There are significant differences in the proportion of female minors at work in the families of both samples interviewed. Almost all the female workers in families linked to Fibrotex began to work before they were eighteen years old. This percentage is much lower among those working at Casulo. The fact that more than one-fourth of the female workers in the small firm entered the labor force only after they turned twenty is significant when compared to the negligible percentage of those in this age bracket in the other sample. In any case, when the contingent of female workers interviewed is taken as a whole, it can be inferred that the female workers recruited for this kind of badly paid and traditionally female occupation come from families in which the labor of underage sons and daughters is fundamental to the relative well-being of the family group.

The nature of these female workers' first job itself points to significant differences between the two contingents studied. The figures in Table 3 indicate the different fields through which these interviewees were initiated into a life of work outside the home.

The above table shows that in the large firm the mass of female workers had already become involved, from the beginning of their working lives, in jobs found within the capitalist mode of production. Five of them even had jobs with greater prestige than factory work, although this did not necessarily imply higher wages. There was not even one worker in this sample who had begun her active life in the countryside. By contrast, rural labor is represented in the sample of female workers at Casulo, though on a small scale. A considerable number of these women began their active life as domestic servants, a job at times more rewarding then others financially but bearing the stigma of servitude. Besides, it is not common in Brazil for female factory workers to be recruited from among domestic servants (Saffioti 1978). The fact that Casulo does absorb a relatively high number of domestic servants can be explained in terms of its craft and family character, for otherwise the forms of recruitment at both firms are similar and quite traditional.

The recruitment of new female workers takes place overwhelmingly through relatives and friends who already work in the factory (84.2 percent at Casulo and 77.8 percent at Fibrotex). A notice board is put up at the factory gate as well, but no use is made of radio or newspaper advertising or of employment agencies. The forms of recruitment result in a signifcant involvement with the firm on the part of the female worker's family, allowing for a greater acceptance of its norms and producing a deeper sense of identification. Generally speaking, there is more than one member of the family working for the same employers, which in a sense serves to prevent rebelliousness, or at least to make it more difficult. The data clearly show that this type of job was what was within the reach of these women, given the connections they could make use of in getting a job and their small chances of finding a better occupation relative to their level of formal knowledge. In fact, when examining the data on these female workers' professional aspirations when they were still at school, it can be seen that 93.7 percent of them had had hopes of engaging in some kind of nonmanual activity, whether a traditionally female nonmanual job or one traditionally not open to women. The organization of the data in Table 4 allows the interviewees occupational aspirations to be better visualized.

As Table 4 shows, only 14.3 percent of the female workers in the small firm were doing the kind of work they had been counting on since their school days. Paying particular attention to the craft character of the work process in the small firm selected, we can see that the activities of these female workers are profoundly characterized as being both female and traditional. Perhaps it could be questioned whether a job in a highly sophisticated textile firm is actually traditionally female. But this is not so at Casulo, where there is a lot of detailed work or needlework. Less than 5 percent of the employees at Fibrotex planned, while they were at school, to penetrate male manual labor areas. The barriers, however, were stronger than the possibilities open to these few women who ventured to aspire to this kind of job, in terms of breaking though the sexual segregation of the labor market. This stronger aspiration to transform the sexual division of social labor becomes apparent in the data relative to the female workers at Fibrotex. Besides the small prcentage of those who identified with manual activites that were not traditionally female, there was a large contingent of female workers at Fibrotex who wanted to enter predominantly male nonmanual activities. The aspirations of the largest contingent at Casulo were more modest and were limited to activities with greater social prestige, while still remaining within the framework of the sexual division of labor sanctioned positively by society. Perhaps this fact helps to explain the greater identification of the smaller firm's female workers with an economically active life; it may thus be a factor that nurtures their staying longer in the labor force.

However, the fact that the majority's hopes of undertaking nonmanual work went unrealized meant that this group of women did not feel adjusted to or satisfied with their jobs. This was true of 81.0 percent of the inerviewees. For the sampled female workers--whether those who expected to abandon the labor force only when they reached retirement or those who saw work as temporary--the guarantee of a monthly income already represented great financial stability that other kinds of occupations did not provide. Having labor rights ensured by legislation meant not submitting to the helplessness in which the domestic servant, for example, finds herself when she is fired. Having FGTS meant the same as having unemployment benefits in other countries. The answers to questions about job satisfaction suggest that these women's greatest aspiration is to have a fixed and guaranteed income, however meager it may be. It is this guarantee of a certain amount of money that allows them to plan their existence and to confront the problems that life presents to those at the bottom of the social pyramid. Indeed, very few of the women interviewed managed to break through the three-times-the-minimum-wage barrier. Generally speaking, as Tables 5 and 6 show, the wages are low. What follows is an attempt to compare the data of the two investigated samples with those of the FIPE survey, taking from the latter those textile firms whose size corresponds to the firms surveyed for this chapter.

Overall, the women sampled for the present research were in a better position in terms of wages than were, on the average, those researched by FIPE in Greater Sao Paulo. In the case of the small firm chosen here, the percentage of women earning only one minimum wage was far lower than the proportion of those in the FIPE survey who received less than this amount. At the same time, the number of women in Casulo who managed to overcome the three-times-the-minimum-wage barrier was almost twice the number of those in the FIPE survey who made up this category. For these reasons, the contingent of Casulo employees in the 1-3 minimum wage bracket was much larger in relation to the overall average of those in this bracket.

In terms of the large firms with between 500 and 1,000 employees, the wage discrepancies between the firm chosen for this chapter and those in the FIPE investigation are even greater. In spite of the high percentage of minors employed at Fibrotex, none of the female workers sampled earned less than the minimum stipulated for adult workers by Brazilian law. This in itself is enough to place the Fibrotex female workers in above-average wage brackets. The number of women who managed to transgress the three-times-the-minimum-wage barrier was three times greater at Fibrotex than the average for firms of a similar size. This explains why there were about 10 percent fewer women at Fibrotex in the 1-3 wage bracket than the corresponding proportion in the average for firms with the above-mentioned size in Greater Sao Paulo.

A comparison of the wages of female workers in both the sampled factories shows that the larger firm pays better than the smaller firm. This does not mean, however, that the smaller one exploits its employees more. On the contrary, given the high organic composition of capital and the greater productivity of labor and machines at Fibrotex (it must be recalled that while each machine operator at Casulo was in charge of one machine, each operator at Fibrotex was in charge of an average of twenty-six machines), this firm can afford to pay better wages and even so have higher profits. It must also be remembered that by serving a domestic and international market Fibrotex operates on low unit price scales, while Casulo's smaller size gives it high production costs.

It must also be stressed that although female workers at Fibrotex were in a better position in terms of wages than those at Casulo, the average per capita income of the families of the latter represented almost twice that of the Fibrotex workers' families. This means that the latter families included other workers with differentiated wage levels. One of the factors that explains the higher income of the Casulo families is the stage of their life cycle. The average age of the members of these families was higher than for families in the other sample. The greater presence of married women at Casulo also partially explains this phenomenon. The husbands' earnings are much greater than those of the women, which contributes to the increase of the average per capita income of these families and reinforces the ideas that the female wages are only important in terms of complementing their husbands' income. In the case of the single women, the presence of brothers receiving wages that were much higher than the average for the female interviewees constitues an enormous contribution toward the appearance of the average per capita income in a higher bracket. In any case, leaving the details aside, the type of family that characterized the Casulo female workers clearly explains their being in a higher income bracket, in spite of the fact that on the average, they earned less than the other female workers interviewed. To illustrate this point, Table 7 shows the income earned by the husbands of the fifteen married women in the two samples.

The wage differentials between men and women to a great extent account for the higher male earnings, in spite of the fact that the individuals of both sexes had similar schooling levels: women employed at Casulo were linked to men (husbands in Table 7) whose incomes were greater than those of the husbands of Fibrotex workers. This same phenomenon was repeated in relation to the other members of the family and is not included here in a table only in order to avoid overloading the test with statistical data. Once again, it should be stressed that the composition of the family and the stage of the life cycle of the majority of its members clearly account for the wage differences seen above.

The standard of living of the female workers' families results from the fact that all of the members' wages are added together within the family group. However, each person would have enormous difficulties in surviving on his or her own earnings. The family thus becomes a microcosm of the reproduction of a certain way of life created by capitalism among the proletariat. Besides reproducing cheap labor, the family permits the daily production of labor power. This survival takes place on a small scale when only one or two of the family's members are working, but it still permits them to buy industrialized products--both those for immediate consumption and durable goods.

Although it involved sacrificing a part of consumption that could be reduced--food, for example--these families managed to acquire appliances that facilitate women's labor during their second (domestic) workday and even to have leisure equipment within their home. Almost all of the female workers' families researched (92 percent) had a radio. This proportion was somewhat higher in the small firm (94.7 percent) than in the larger one (91.4 percent). Only two female workers from Fibrotex had a telephone in their home. Telephones were considered an unnecessary luxury for the kind of lives these female workers led, since communication takes place person to person, through the network of relatives living nearby, workmates, and friends. Contact with relatives living at a distance is made by mail or through messages delivered by friends or their relatives traveling on visits. Television and radios were considered the most important electrical appliances, simultaneously making available information about the world outside the family and providing a means of using leisure time. This leisure activity within the domestic sphere was considered very important, since leisure activities outside the home involved expenses beyond these families' budgets. Of the homes covered by this survey, 88.0 percent had a television, its presence being greater in the Casulo worker's homes (94.7 percent) than in those of the Fibrotex workers (86.4 percent).

There was also a rather high percentage of homes with floor waxers: 73.5 percent. That more of the Casulo workers' families (82.4 percent) had one of these appliances than the Fibrotex workers' families (71.6 percent) can be attributed to the fact that the former sample had a greater density of married women. These women had less free time available for housework, whereas such work was spread out in families with a greater number of adult daughters. Cake mixers, which are not essential objects for poorer families, were present in a surprising significant number of homes (37.1 percent). Once again, the Casulo worker's families, who had a higher per capita income, were ahead in the ownership of this appliance: 50 percent of their homes had one, while only 34.6 percent of those working at Fibrotex owned one. The case of tape recorders is similar: 28.9 percent of all the families had one, but the Casulo percentage (37.5 percent) was much higher than the Fibrotex numbers (27.2 percent). Record players had an even more significant presence: 55.7 percent of all the families owned one, 75.0 percent from the small firm and 51.9 percent from the larger one. And although in small numbers, there were even automatic washing machines in these families' homes: 17.3 percent of the Fibrotex families had one. Casulo families didn't have one. As for cars, 16.7 percent of all the families had them, 13.3 percent belonging to the small firm's families, and 17.3 percent to those from the large firm.

The composition of the family income and, within it, the significance of the wage contribution of the female workers become more explicit when the financial responsibilities held by the interviewees are analyzed in terms of the basic items in the domestic budget. For example, asked who contributed the most toward food purchase in the home, 24.1 percent of Fibrotex employees, as against only 5.3 percent of those from Casulo, answered that their wage was overwhelmingly used for this purpose. Thus, a large part of these female workers were responsible for guaranteeing the families' food. Given that the average per capita income of their families was a little over half that of families in the other sample, their wages were naturally required to ensure the physical survival of the family members. In fact, as far as all the items on the domestic budget are concerned, with the exception of clothes, the female workers from Fibrotex contributed more to the expenses that were common to all the family members than the workers from Casulo. The latter, in many cases, worked to complement the income of their parents and brothers, or their husbands, or even to ensure a better standard of living for the whole family, whereas in the Fibrotex sample the very physical survival of the families depended on the female workers' wages. The problem is thus to be found at the level of the different survival mechanisms developed by these families.

The data indicate that the quality of the survival level is higher when some of the workers in the family are linked to the liberal capitalism of small firms, while others are involved in work schemes that have not yet been organized along capitalist levels. It seems that insofar as the whole family or a high percentage of its economically active members is active in the sphere of monopoly capitalism, its level of survival will be determined by the needs of capital and as such by its rhythm of accumulation. In other words, the characteristics of what is referred to as monopoly capitalism in Brazil are much closer to savage capitalism than are those in the small-scale capitalism of family businesses, which give more value to skilled female employees and develop mechanisms to keep them in the factory even after they become wives and mothers. The large firms with sophisticated technology, however, have a high rate of labor turnover, which is perhaps even used as a way of keeping down wages.

CONCLUSIONS

The development of technology has contradictory consequences for women's lives. On the one hand, work within the family sphere becomes less burdensome. Even if domestic appliances do not economize time, they undoubtedly save physical energy, making many domestic chores more bearable. On the other hand, the impact on the public economy--as opposed to the domestic one--allows women to undertake factory tasks. Nevertheless, the need for specialized equipment maintenance personnel increases. Women are not trained for this type of task, nor does the official ideology encompass women's possible entry into this field. Thus, the massive penetration of technology into industry expels large female contingents within it. These contingents move into pockets of craft industries, whose activities still have characteristics compatible with the old-fashioned type of socialization. Jobs requiring detailed manual labor with needles continue to attract generations who had access to this type of apprenticeship within their family sphere. The new generations, however, have been socialized for a different world and thus obtain employment in firms with highly sophisticated technology, which can easily train newcomers. Work becomes uninteresting and monotonous; above all, it creates a deep insecurity in female workers, since they can be replaced without great difficulty by the enormous industrial reserve army demanding employment.

Consequently the transformations in the work process resulting from the application of modern technology have dramatic repercussions not only on the execution of the activites themselves, but also on the capacity of industry to absorb female workers. While in the garment industry, which is less susceptible to technological innovations, women have already lost ground as clothes began to be mass-produced, the highly labor-saving technology being used in the textile industry has had the immediate consequences of expelling women from the production process. The conclusion that can be drawn from the historical statistics and from the empirical data collected in the present survey is that women have not had access to technology in the sphere of the public economy. Thus, while women are able to surround themselves with technology in order to facilitate their domestic chores and in this sense can be said to have benefitted from technical development, they simultaneously become extremely vulnerable as female workers in firms with high technological sophistication.

Besides their vulnerability as unskilled workers and the monotonous and wearisome character of the tasks they must carry out in the factory, women are forced to confront the more dramatic aspect of this historical process--unemployment. Indeed, the historical data show that the rhythm of the absorption of women by manufacturing industries not only slackens with technological development but becomes negative in certain periods. In the transition from a craft to an industrial basis, women lose what is perhaps their only advantage: the skills they acquired at home. Women's economic function are relatively more numerous and important when production is organized along craft lines; their importance and their relative number decrease as craft activities give way to industrialization.

It must also be considered that the feminine condition multiplies the female worker's condition, which in turn increases discrimination against women. The discrimination against women and the discrimination against poor people belonging to the lower working class add up to double the discriminatory effects on these female workers. The social and cultural conditions of working-class women produce discrimination and mutually multiply each other's effects. In this context, the double workday becomes a challenge to women's ability to produce and reproduce each day the labor power required for the extended reproduction of capital. It is in this challenge and in the endeavor to overcome it that the working woman gathers the strength to face her exhausting and menacing everyday existence with courage. It is in this way that she reproduces the working class.

REFERENCES

Almeida, Jose. 1974. Industrializacao e emprego no Brasil. Rio de Janeiro: IPEA.

_____. 1976. A formacao profissional da mulher trabalhadora no Brasil. Rio de Janeiro: MTB/SENAI/SENAC. (As it is a collective book written by employees of the 3 institutions, there are no names of authors.)

Barroso, Carmen. 1978, "Sozinhas ou mal acompanhadas - a situacao das mulheres chefes de familia." In Anais do Primeiro Encontro Nacional da Associacao Brasileira de Estudos Populacionais. Campos de Jordao.

Chaney, Else M. and Marianne C. Schmink. 1979. "Las mujeres y la modernizacion: aceso a la tecnologia." In La Mujer en America Latina. Mexico: SepSetentas.

_____. 1976. "Women and modernization: access to tools." In Sex and Class In Latin America. June Nash and Helen Icken Safa eds. pp. 160-182. New York: Praeger Publishers.

Ferrante, Vera L.S.B. 1978. FGTS: Ideologia e Repressao. Sao Paulo: Editora Atica.

Lewin, Helena, Jaqueline Pitanguy and Carlos Manuel Romani. 1977. Mae-de-Obra no Brasil. Rio de Janeiro: Vozes/PUC/OIT.

Loureiro, Ubirajara. 1980. "O governo e pressionado para nao distribuir renda." In Folha de Sao Paulo. Sao Paulo: May 18, 1980, Economic Section.

Pastore, Jose and Joao do Carmo Lopes. 1973. A Mao-de-Obra Especializada na Industria Paulista. Sao Paulo: IPE (Institute for Research in Economics)

_____. 1978. "Relacao de Empregados de Lei dos 2/3 do Ministerio do Trabalho." In Expansao e Recessao: Implicacoes de um ciclo de conjuntura na Estrutura de Emprego e Salario no Estado de Sao Paulo--1970-1976. Sao Paulo: SEP (unpublished).

Rodrigues, Jessita Martins. 1979. A mulher operaria (Um estudo sobre tecelas). Sao Paulo: Editora HUCITEC.

Saffioti, Heleieth Iara Bongiovani. 1975. "Relaciones de Sexo y de Clases Sociales." In La Mujer en America Latina. Mexico: SepSetentas.

_____. 1975. "O Fardo das Brasileiras." In Escrita/Ensaio, No. 5.

_____. 1976. "Relationships of Sex and Social Class In Brazil." In Sex and Class in Latin America. June Nash and Helen Ecken Safa eds. pp. 147-159. New York: Praeger Publishers.

_____. 1978. Women in Class Society. New York: Monthly Review Press.

_____. 1978. Emprego Domestico e Capitalismo. Petropolis: Editora Vozes.

Versiani, Flavio Rabelo. 1972. "Industrializacao e emprego: o problema da reposicao de equipamentos." In Pesquisa e Planejamento Economico e Social. Rio de Janeiro: IPEA (Institute of Social and Economic Planning).

List of Abbreviations

IBGE = Instituto Brasileiro de Geografia e Estatistica

FIBGE = Fundacao Instituto Brasileiro de Geografia e Estatistica. Brazilian Institute of Geography and Statistics

F.G.T.S. = Fundo de Garantia por Tempo de Servico. It was created by a law, in 1966, and permits employers to fire workers without just cause, in return for a sum of money, and repeals earlier tenure guarantees.

IPE = Instituto de Pesquisas Economicas

FIPE = Fundacao Instituto de Pesquisa Economicas. Institute for Research in Economics Foundation.

PNAD = Pesquisa Nacional por Amostras de Domicilios. National Research by residence sample (made by IBGE) or National Household Survey (Made by IBGE).

TABLE 1

Composition of Female Workers' Families, by Factory
(Residents In Each House In Percentages)

Type of Family	Casulo	Fibrotex
Single interviewee	5.3	2.5
Single interviewee and husband	0.0	11.1
Single interviewee, husband and children	16.0	1.2
Single interviewee and children	10.4	0.0
Single interviewee and other relatives	26.3	14.8
Single interviewee, husband, and other relatives	10.4	4.9
Single interviewee and parents	10.4	1.2
Single interviewee, parents, and other relatives	15.9	64.3
Single interviewee and other nonrelatives	5.3	0.0
Total	100.0	100.0

TABLE 2

Age of Female Workers on Entering the Labor Force

	Casulo		Fibrotex	
	No.	%	No.	%
Under 18 years old	13	68.4	76	93.8
From 18 to 20	1	5.3	2	2.5
From 21 to 23	2	10.5	2	2.5
From 24 to 29	3	15.8	1	1.2
Total	19	100.0	81	100.0

TABLE 3

Nature of the Female Workers' First Job, by Factory

Type of Job	Casulo	Fibrotex
Wage-earning rural laborer	5.3	0.0
Domestic servant	26.3	11.1
Urban factory worker	68.4	82.8
Office worker	0.0	1.2
Sales Clerk	0.0	4.9
Total	100.0	100.0

TABLE 4
Occupations Female Workers Expected to Take up On Leaving School (%)

Type of Occupation	Casulo	Fibrotex
Manual, traditionally female	14.3	0.0
Manual, not traditionally female	0.0	4.9
Nonmanual, traditionally female	71.4	41.4
Nonmanual, not traditionally female	14.3	53.7
Total	100.00	100.00

TABLE 5

Percentage Distribution of Female Textile Workers, By Income Bracket, at Companies With 50-100 Workers and at Casulo (In Minimum Wage Units)

Wage Bracket	Firms With 50-100 Employees	Casulo	Wage Bracket
Less than 1	18.0	5.3	1
1-2	53.4	42.1	1-2
2-3	19.8	36.8	2-3
3-5	5.0	10.5	3-4
5-8	3.2	5.3	+ than 4
8 and +	0.6	0.0	
Total	100.0	100.0	

TABLE 6

Percentage Distribution of Female Textile Workers, by Income Bracket, at Companies With 500-1000 Workers and at Fibrotex (In Minimum Wage Units)

Wage Bracket	Firms With 500-1000 Employees	Fibrotex	Wage Bracket
Less than 1	11.8	19.0	1-2
1-2	53.3	49.0	2-3
2-3	24.1	25.0	3-4
3-5	8.6	7.0	+ than 4
5-8	1.2		
8 and +	1.0		
Total	100.0	100.0	

TABLE 7

Monthly Income of Female Workers' Husbands, In Minimum Wage Units

Monthly Income	Casulo	Fibrotex
2-4	60.0	80.0
4 - 7	20.0	10.0
7 and +	20.0	10.0
Total	100.0	100.0

8 Women and Urban Industrial Development in Brazil

Marianne Schmink

Among developing countries, Brazil has long been viewed as a success story of economic development. During the decade of the Brazilian "miracle", from mid-1960 to mid-1970, the country achieved high rates of growth, attracting both praise and scrutiny. Statistics on aggregate output seemed to vindicate the effectiveness of the economic policies adopted. At the same time, critics denounced the increasing concentration of income, and the restriction of political rights that was central to the implementation of strategies to contain wages and curtail the strength of organized labor. More recently the economic recession, and a seemingly unmanageable foreign debt, have raised additional questions about the long-term wisdom of the so-called Brazilian model of development. With the relative "opening up" (*abertura*) of debate over Brazil's political future, these issues have become topics of central concern.

This chapter explores some aspects of the Brazilian model of development insofar as women's economic activities are concerned. A historical overview of the impact of economic changes on the structure of female employment will be presented by way of introduction. The process of urban industrial development has not, on the whole, improved the labor market position of women in Brazil. Yet low-income women continue to play a productive role in contributing to the material support of their families, especially in periods of economic stress. Individual-level patterns of labor-force participation are therefore mediated by the insertion of women (and men) into different kinds of domestic groups with diverse economic strategies. These issues are discussed in the following section. Empirical data from two industrial working class communities are then explored to show how women's outside employment is related to the characteristics of the domestic group of which they are a part. The chapter's concluding section examines more closely some of the research questions raised by the focus on domestic unit mediation of women's labor-force behavior.

EVOLUTION OF THE FEMALE LABOR FORCE IN BRAZIL

Although data are scanty on women's economic activities in Brazil before this century, what evidence there is suggests that their participation in the labor force was significant. Women represented 37.4 percent of the active labor force in the 1872 census, rising to 45.3 percent by 1900 (Saffioti 1969:253). In that year they were a full 91.4 percent of the secondary industrial sector, which was heavily dominated by household-based textile production. Kuznesof's (1980) study of nineteenth-century Sao Paulo found female-headed households to be important in cotton textile manufacture. However, most female workers were either in domestic service or in the agricultural sector, which represented roughly half and one-quarter of women workers, respectively, in 1900 (Saffioti 1969:253).

Beginning at the turn of the century, manufacturing activities carried out in sweatshops and factories displaced home-based production in Sao Paulo. During the first two decades women and minors played an important role in this transition, much as they had during the initial phases of the industrial revolution in Britain and the United States. Female workers constituted more than half of the labor force employed in textile production in Sao Paulo from 1912 to 1920 (Moura 1982:141-46). Along with minors, they were concentrated in the lower-paid, unskilled occupations of the industry (Moura 1982:35-39; Saffioti 1969:250). Between 1914 and 1918, the nation's industrial work force grew by 83.3 percent, but most of these new workers were males. By 1920 women represented only 15 percent of the total work force and had fallen to 27.9 of workers in manufacturing (Saffioti 1969:253). As the factory form of textile production expanded, females were replaced by male workers or absorbed in sweatshops and home-based putting-out systems, a factor that made their work less visible to collectors of official statistics (Spindel 1983:97; Teixeira et al. 1983:116-17). These trends continued with industrial growth during the 1930s. By 1940 the census reported only one female out of every four industrial workers (Saffioti 1969:254).

Overall female participation rates tended to stabilize after 1940, but the structure of the female labor force continued to change as the Brazilian economy evolved (Saffioti 1978:11). World War I and the great Depression reduced the imports available to Brazil from European suppliers, which no longer filled the demands of the Brazilian consumer market. The result was to stimulate domestic industrialization based on consumer goods production, shifting the demand for imports from finished manufactured goods to the capital goods that supplied Brazilian factories. During this early stage of Import Substitution Industrialization (ISI), textile and clothing industries were dominant, and both still served as important sources of female employment. In 1950, a full 92 percent of female industrial workers were in these two industries (Lewin, Pitanguy, and Romani 1977:110).

The character of Brazilian industrialization, as in many Latin American countries, changed during the post-World War II period with the "internationalization" of capital (Deere, Humphries, and Leon de Leal 1978:61-64). Compared with the European nations, the United States suffered little from the war and soon expanded its investments in the industry sector of Latin America. The growing importance of the multinational corporation during this period was one aspect of the increasing involvement of the United States in economic, financial, political, military, and technical issues in the developing world (Ianni 1977:145).

Kubitschek's election to the presidency in 1956 and his promises of "fifty years of progress in five" intensified the pace of industrialization. His policies profoundly transformed the economy, stimulating already existing government and private investment patterns (Ianni 1977:142-48). State initiatives were increasingly designed to accelerate development, particularly in industrial production, and to stimulate national and foreign investments in the private sector. Getulio Vargas's earlier development policies had emphasized the growth of national capitalism. Kubitschek's major planning document, the ***Programa de Metas***, sought to transform the nation's economic structure through the creation of basic industry and through the reformulation of interdependent relations with the world economy (Ianni 1977:149-80). Direct state infrastructural investments aimed to eliminate bottlenecks to growth, while foreign capital and technology were actively recruited. Thus, despite the import-substitution orientation, industrialization under Kubitschek created new needs for imports of machinery, implements, accessories, know-how, and raw materials. These policies consoldiated a new stage in the internationalization of the Brazilian economy through the participation of the multinational corporation, while the state essentially assumed the role of guarantor of private sector investments.

Brazil's labor force in both urban and rural areas began to change rapidly in the 1950s. In regions where industry grew, the urban work force expanded and became more male-dominated, leaving a higher proportion of women workers in agriculture (Lewin et al. 1977:89; Madeira and Singer 1973:53; Saffioti 1969:255). Most of these female agricultural workers were involved in family-based subsistence production as unpaid family workers (Oliveira 1978:5-6). Only after the passage of new land and labor statutes in 1963 and 1964 did women in Brazil's developing regions enter the rural market, primarily as day workers (*volantes*) without regular workers' benefits, often residing in urban areas and combining argicultural and urban forms of employment (Martinez-Alier 1975; Oliveira 1978:10).

The "new" industrialization of the Kubitschek era was characterized by the use of electric power and capital-intensive technologies, an orientation toward the production of capital goods, and an increasing emphasis on large-scale firms (Pereira 1962:321; Rodrigues 1970:XV-XVI; Singer 1977; Soares 1968:190). While women were initially drawn into textile factories, they were absorbed less and less as technology transformed the organization of production in the industry (Madeira and Singer 1973:34-37). According to official statistics, between 1950 and 1970 the textile industry dispensed with one-quarter of its workers but nearly doubled the number of males (Lewin et al. 1977:110-11). The proportion of women workers employed in the industry fell from 15.6 percent to 8.9 percent in this period (Bruschini 1978:13). As industrial capital penetrated the textile sector beginning in the late 1950s, the putting-out system expanded with the proliferation of intermediary sweatshops (Spindel 1983:97). The proportion of women employed in the food and drink-processing factories declined from 2.7 percent to only 0.3 percent while their proportion in manufacturing overall fell from 18.6 percent to 11 percent (Bruschini 1978:13).

During the postwar period, female workers moving out of agriculture were employed primarily in a few "female" occupations in the service and commerce sectors of the economy: primary school teachers, office workers, sales clerks, seamstresses, and domestic workers (Abreu 1977:16). The first three categories, along with others in the capitalist sector, primarily recruit young, single, more educated women. Older, married women, on the other hand cluster in female-dominated "refuge" jobs in domestic work and informal activities (Arizpe 1977; Moser 1978; Scott 1981). Domestic service alone accounted for nearly one out of three women workers (Saffioti 1978).

More recent statistics indicate a reversal of the long-term trend that shows a decline in the proportion of women in factory employment. The demographic censuses of 1970 and 1980 reveal that women's participation in industry in Brazil grew by 181 percent during that decade (Humphrey 1983:47, cited in Scott 1983). Most of this growth has been concentrated in the highly industrialized Sao Paulo area, where young, single women are penetrating such masculine sectors as steel and metalwork, in both clerical and production jobs (Leite 1982). Most women who work outside the home, however, cluster not in industry but in the tertiary sector, which accounted for 69.1 percent of the female labor force in 1976, up from 54.1 percent in 1950 (Barroso 1982:18).[1]

Overall female participation rates, as captured by the census and periodic household surveys, also increased from 13.6 percent in 1950 to 18.5 percent in 1970 and 29.6 percent in 1976 (Barroso 1982:17). If women's unpaid domestic chores are included as productive work, however, their participation rates are over 70 percent, identical to or higher than those of men (Barroso 1982:37). Only about one-fourth of working women (so defined) are paid employees, while more than half report domestic work as their occupation (Barroso 1982:38). Furthermore, many women listed as "housewives" or "students" in official statistics may be among the ranks of the disguised unemployed as there are no jobs for them (Madeira and Singer 1973:1).

Despite the limited capacity of official statistics to capture their work patterns (Wainerman and Recchini de Lattes 1981), it is evident that low-income women play an active, productive role in contributing to the material support of their families. Brazil's economic crisis of the last several years, bringing increasing unemployment and rising costs of living, has accentuated the need for their labor. As in other contexts, women help to serve as "shock absorbers" for the economic stress that threatens their family's well-being. Because of the pressing need for additional income, women in poor families must seek work wherever they can find it, which is usually outside the capitalist sector. Particularly given the limits to their direct employment, outlined above, the recognition of women's role in strategies of labor allocation at the household level is crucial to understanding their productive activities in urban industrial Brazil (Jelin 1974:68; Saffioti 1978:185).

HOUSEHOLD ECONOMIC STRATEGIES

The discussion must begin with a working definition of household economic strategies, a concept that calls attention to a host of related issues. The boundaries and functions of domestic units vary across societies and through time. In some cases coresidence is coterminous with kinship relationships. Domestic units may also be the principal locus of production and/or of biological reproduction. In many cases coresidence defines the unit of most forms of consumption, where a final pooling and redistribution of resources to individuals takes place. These elements of material consumption usually provide the basis for defining the household. As it is used here, the household (or domestic unit) refers to a coresident group of persons who share most aspects of consumption, drawing on and allocating a common pool of resources (including labor) to ensure their material maintenance and reproduction.

In contrast to societies where households are the principal units of production, domestic groups in industrial working-class communities are characterized by their dependence on wage income (Macedo 1979; Tilly and Scott 1978:105). In a capitalist system, labor power produced by the domestic unit is embodied in individuals who sell their capacity to work to the owners of the means of production. Theoretically, the cost of producing labor power is borne by the capitalist sector, through direct or indirect wages sufficient to support workers and their potential replacements (children). In reality, the salary tends to cover only a portion of the long-term consumption needs of the household, that of the maintenance of workers during their working years (Meillassoux 1981:102).

The notion that the satisfaction of material needs of working-class households is primarily a function of the capitalist wage should be viewed merely as a point of departure for analysis (Rapp 1978). The focus on the "wage" may imply a nuclear family model comprising of a male breadwinner, his nonworking wife, and dependent children. In reality, many women in working-class households are the sole support of the household or important contributors to household income. The tendency for salaries to be insufficient to cover consumption needs forces families to resort to strategies to stretch and supplement the wage (Deere et al. 1978). These strategies draw upon a multiplicity of resources aside from a primary wage. Thus the domestic unit's overall standard of living will be derived from a combination of monetary income from different sources, benefits associated with employment, collective services provided by the state and private sector, and nonmonetary inputs from home production and from wider exchanges.

In the wage-dependent context, both the meaning and relative importance of these multiple components will be a function of the level and stability of the monetary wage (Macedo 1979:34). Households with regular monetary income are also more likely to have access to the nonwage benefits associated with formal labor market employment and to the infrastructural advantages available in more affluent neighborhoods. Poorer households, compelled to stretch and supplement an inadequate wage, are deprived of access to many of these collective goods and services. Nonmonetary inputs from domestic work and from interhousehold exchanges may also serve different functions depending on a household's income level. In poor households such activities help to substitute for purchased goods and services and to diversify social resources for meeting day-to-day material needs (Anderson 1983: Fausto Neto 1982; GETEC 1978; Lomnitz 1977; Oliveira 1975; Singer 1977). Middle-class households may invest domestic labor or manipulate extra-domestic networks in pursuit of longer-term class and kin interests (Leeds 1974; Lomnitz 1971; Miller 1976; Vaneck 1974). Migration also varies for different income groups, a fact obscured by studies of individual-level patterns. Resource levels determine both the ability and the motivation to migrate, while the demographic structure of the household is an important intervening variable in the migratory behavior of individuals (Aramburu 1981; Dinerman 1978; Pessar 1982; Selby and Murphy 1982; Wood 1981 1982).

Salary levels, together with these other inputs, define the standard of living, which is the reference for the economic strategies developed by households. It can therefore be argued that qualitative differences distinguish what are often called "survival" strategies from what might be called "mobility strategies" (Schmink 1982). The two forms differ not only in the level of monetary income but also in the time frame that shapes their strategies (short vs. long-term), and in the diversity of activities that comprise them. In essence, financial pressures lead households to intensify strategies for generating income, using available labor and resources as fully as possible. Migratory strategies are often an important element in such schemes. Multiple economic activities are thus particularly important in resource-poor households, where the monetary wage is insufficient (Leite 1982:89). In this intensification effort, women play a central role. In general, whereas adult men tend to specialize in the generation of monetary income, women's roles in household strategies are typically multiple (Birdsall and McGreevey 1983:5). These include unpaid domestic labor, manipulation of extra-domestic networks and patron-client relationships, and negotiation of access to collective services, as well as generation of income--often on an irregular, intermittent basis (Anderson 1983; Schmink 1982).

Measurement of income levels is complicated by the need to take into account the characteristics of the household as a whole, not just the individual income-earner (Ben-Porath 1982; Kuznets 1976). The success of a given household in generating a sufficient monetary salary will broadly depend on the fit between household composition (available labor and consumption demand) and existing labor market opportunities. Since both household and labor market structures are continually evolving, the fit is necessarily a changing one. On the one hand, some households may have low incomes based on their internal composition and the ratio of producers to consumers within the unit. Households with small children, for example, are generally more subject to financial pressures. The younger generation is as yet unable to contribute to household income and, at the same time, adult female labor time must be invested in the care of dependent household members. Other kins of households, such as those headed by women, may be vulnerable for structural reasons unrelated to what are generally treated as phases in the typical family life cycle. Finally, internal patterns of income pooling and allocation will intervene in determing the welfare of individuals within the unit.

While the internal dynamic of household units is important in determining their standard of living at any given moment, the character of the household's insertion into the social structure is decisive. A study of household composition in Belo Horizonte, Brazil, found poverty to be largely the result of a domestic unit's inability to effectively utilize its available stock of potential adult workers (Sant'Anna, Merrick, and Mazumbar 1976). The high proportion of poor households headed by women (Barroso 1978; Buvinic and Youssef 1978) can also be interpreted as a lack of fit with existing labor market opportunities (Buvinic 1983:17). Not only are the heads of these households disadvantaged in the labor market (because they are women), but the other members are also less likely to be prime-age male workers (Merrick and Schmink 1983). The structure of the labor market, in short, is a primary determinant of the potential for income generation of households with varying demographic characteristics.

The study of household strategies must therefore be informed by the analysis of structural forms of insertion in the organization of production. This task is complicated by the use of the household, instead of the individual, as the unit of analysis. Assigning social actors to categories that approximate discrete class positions presents conceptual difficulties under any circumstances. These problems are compounded to the extent that the domestic unit is conceived as mediating social class definitions for household members (Borsotti 1977:16-17; Rey de Marulanda 1982:59; Torrado 1981:209-11). Because of the role of the domestic unit in the final redistribution of income for consumption, its members seem somehow to share a common economic relationship to society. Yet the household may combine heterogeneous relations to the productive structure, which themselves change over time. The potential contradiction between income generated from individual labor market activity and the collective needs of the household is attenuated by the strong ideological pressure of kin obligations (Jelin 1982:24).

It has been argued that in the urban industrial setting the most important component of household full income is the monetary wage from one or more workers. In the wage-dependent context, the intensity and form of other members' economic activities are partly a function of the wage level and contribution to the common pool of the primary earner. For this reason, households are often assigned to class categories on the basis of the primary earner's relation to production (Garcia et al. 1982:179). The same procedure can be used when all working members share the same class characteristics. Since nonworking members such as housewives and dependent children are dependent on the breadwinner's wage, they too are often defined in terms of that person's class position. Insofar as the housewife's unpaid labor contributes directly to consumption, it substitutes for purchased goods and services and partly compensates for the breadwinner's insufficient wage or for incomplete pooling.

Supplementary workers also indirectly subsidize the insufficient wages of the primary worker, yet their independent relationship to the productive system makes it less appropriate to assign them to class categories on the basis of the household head's occupation (Bilac 1978; Garcia, Munoz, and Oliveira 1979). The concept of "total family income" and the emphasis on the income of the household head can mask the diversity of sources from which income is derived (Jelin et al. 1982:4). Any given household may include workers of different structural characteristics and wage potential, who pool their earnings to different degrees: salaried employees in different formal sector occupations, self-employed workers in the informal market, and unpaid family workers. A low or unstable income flow or inadequate pooling tends to provoke an intensification of the household's income-generating strategy, which often leads to a greater internal heterogeneity of class and occupational positions within the domestic unit (Garcia et al. 1982; Margulis 1980:55-59; Margulis et al. 1981:295; Schmink 1979).

CASE STUDY IN BELO HORIZONTE

Several studies of Brazilian industrial workers' families have recently been published based on work in the nation's largest industrial center, Sao Paulo (Macedo 1979; Rodrigues 1978). Studies of working-class families have also been carried out in other, less industrialized urban areas of Brazil (Banck 1980; Jelin 1974; Machado Neto 1978; Madeira 1979; Perlman 1969; Scott 1979). Belo Horizonte is a particularly appropriate site for the analysis of the effects of Brazil's recent development patterns on the ecological and social processes that constitute the urban space. It is the only major Latin American city founded in the postcolonial period, and its impressive growth has been linked to increased industrial investments since 1940.

In the industrial community studied by the author, proximity to employment was clearly the neighborhood's biggest attraction. A large multinational steel-processing plant located in the neighborhood had 12,000 employees by 1978, absorbing nearly one in four of local workers. Over half were employed either in the steel plant or elsewhere in the neighborhood's relatively well-developed business and commercial center. Another 19 percent worked in the adjacent industrial centers of Contagem and Betim, while only 23 percent had jobs in Belo Horizonte's city center. This distribution demonstrates the industry orientation of the majority of the community's work force.

More accurately, it is the *male* labor force that is truly industry-oriented, while women workers are more typically clustered in the jobs described above as the female refuge. Women's occupational distribution is quite different from that of men and more clearly polarized by age. First, nearly one-half of all women workers are self-employed, compared with about one-fifth of the men; these women are primarily domestic servants, laundresses, and seamstresses. Women workers under the age of thirty, who represent more than 70 percent of all economically active women, also show higher proportions than man in professional and technical occupations, due to women's employment as teachers and nurses. Women in this age group are also, like men, employed in unskilled white-collar occupations. After the age of thirty, however, most women are not in the active labor force; those who remain are virtually restricted either to unskilled manual work or to autonomous employment.

Age and sex differences, as they define each individual's position in the household and the labor market, lead to distinct employment patterns. Male household heads were the largest economically active group (See Table 1). Management and (manual) supervisory occupations, both relatively high-income, are almost exclusively the domain of this category of worker; only two secondary workers, both female directors of primary schools, held management jobs. Nonhousehold heads taken together accounted for more than half of all workers, but showed different occupational patterns according to their relationship to the household head. Half of all secondary workers were sons, approximately one-fifth each were wives or daughters, and the remaining 10 percent were other household members. Nearly one-half of all working wives were autonomous workers, and another one-third (all under the age of thirty) were professionals. Daughters were also concentrated in the autonomous category, and one in ten was a professional but more than one-third were in unskilled white-collar jobs (clerical and sales, principally). Sons, slightly less than daughters, were concentrated in autonomous and routine white-collar positions. Their much higher employment rates in specialized manual work, however, approximate the pattern among male heads of household.

The relative monetary contribution of each individual worker to the household income is to a great extent determined by these differences in occupational distribution. The drastic differences in earning levels by sex, shown in Table 2, are largely a product of the "sex-typing" of occupations which allocates women workers to female-dominated jobs within each occupational category. They also reflect a greater tendency among women in certain occupations to work less than full time. This pattern is particularly frequent among school directors and teachers (who dominate the manager and professional categories for women) and autonomous workers--the three categories showing the lowest average income levels in relation to men's. Male workers' earning patterns are generally compatible with the expected differences between occupational groups. For women, however, earning levels are not significantly affected by occupational differences. Other studies in Brazil have also found that women's earnings are lower than men's in every category. Furthermore, since women's earnings also rise much less with education than do men's, salary differences between the sexes increase systematically with women's educational levels (Abreu 1977:17; Barrera 1978; Barroso 1982; Rato 1978; Saffioti 1969).

The comparison of mean earnings in Table 2 allows us to roughly characterize the potential financial contributions of workers in different categories. The highest earnings level, almost in a class by itself, is that of managers (who are male household heads). A second level is the exclusive domain of male household heads (owners and supervisors) and sons (professionals and technical). Average earnings for autonomous male workers are intermediate between these higher levels and the remaining categories. Slightly below the mean for autonomous males, average earnings for men in unskilled manual and nonmanual work and in specialized manual jobs were still well above the 1976 minimum wage. Female professionals and school directors finally entered the earnings hierarchy at this lowest level for males. Women workers in the remaining occupational categories averaged less than Cr$1,000 per month (roughly U.S.$70) in earnings. Given the uniformly low average earnings for women workers, it is not surprising that they constitute less than one-quarter of the neighborhood's labor force. Although their job options are both limited and low-paying, women nevertheless commonly work on an intermittent basis in response to fluctuating needs of the household.

Income-generating strategies among working class households are often characterized by the combination of different kinds of activities by different household members. In the neighborhood studied more than one-third (36.8 percent or 110 cases) of all domestic groups had more than one income earner. Nearly half of these multiple-earner households were composed of workers in at least two distinct occupational categories, and approximately one-third combined *more* than two categories (of the eight groups listed in Table 2). The occupational heterogeneity of households with two income earners is displayed in Table 3. Nearly half the households with white-collar heads have secondary workers in blue collar jobs. This figure is similar to findings for working class households in Mexico City (Garcia et al. 1982:141) but much higher than the proportion of such mixes found in an interior town of Sao Paulo (Bilac 1978:105). Even more common (83 percent) was the pattern of blue-collar heads with white-collar secondary workers (compared to less than 20 percent reported for the Mexico case by Garcia et al. 1982:148-51). In general terms, blue collar workers are relatively underrepresented in two-occupation households, when compared with the overall distribution of workers. This is because of the predominance of nonmanual and autonomous occupations for secondary workers, especially females. Autonomous occupations are particularly important in contributing to household heterogeneity; nearly one-half of all households with occupational mixes (including those with *more* than two distinct categories) had at least one autonomous worker.

These findings confirm the notion that self-employment, particularly among women, is best explained as part of a household-level strategy to supplement monetary income. Insufficient income or inadequate pooling of available income induce an intensification of household economic strategies, including the multiplication of remunerated workers. This in turn increases the likelihood of occupational heterogeneity within the household. More specifically, it increase the probability of self-employment. Both the number of earners and specifically of autonomous workers increase in households facing greater financial stress. Women play an important role in this secondary, autonomous income generation.

This prediction can be further examined by comparing the findings from the industrial community with patterns of female work participation in an adjacent neighborhood. The two neighborhoods share a common history and location and are primarily working-class communities but also differ in some aspects. The industrial neighborhood studied by the author has been favored by the concentration of public and private investments (such as the multinational steel plant and related infrastructural works), which have made it an emerging commercial and administrative subcenter characterized by higher property values and cost of living. On a number of measures it stands out from adjacent working-class neighborhoods as relatively well-off (Schmink 1979:Chaper 4).

In contrast, the adjacent neighborhood studied by Fausto Neto (192:32-43) lacks most basic services. The relatively precarious nature of land tenure and the lack of services have kept land prices low enough to permit low income populations to purchase lots there, whereas in the industrial neighborhood these are now out of reach. This "dormitory" community is probably more typical of working-class neighborhoods in metropolitan Latin America, consisting primarily of residences and small-scale commerce. Households in both the "industrial" and the "dormitory" communities chose these locations primarily for one of two reasons: proximity to employment or housing needs. But in the former, job-related reasons were given by about half the households surveyed, and housing issues were mentioned by less then 10 percent. In the dormitory community, by contrast, 63 percent claimed housing as their motive and only 19 percent mentioned employment opportunities (Fausto Neto 1982:42; Schmink 1979:263).

Some interesting patterns emerge from the comparison of household characteristics in the two neighborhoods. Table 4 shows that participation rates for both men and women are significantly higher in the less prosperous dormitory community. Despite their proximity to identical job opportunities, potential workers in the dormitory neighborhood are *twice* as likely to be economically active as those in the adjacent industrial neighborhood. Their higher number of workers per household reflects these differences (Table 5).

Women's economic participation rates in the industrial neighborhood are low, particularly after the age of twenty, although younger women often work in salaried jobs in teaching, sales, and office work. They do not begin working before the age of fifteen, when secondary schooling is normally completed (Table 6). In the dormitory community, women begin working earlier and continue later in life.

About half the households in the industrial neighborhood receive their income from only one income earner. By contrast, more than two-thirds of households in the dormitory community have two workers or more, and the *average* number of workers is also greater than two (Table 5). In comparing sources of household income, Table 7 reveals that households in the industrial neighborhood have much greater ties to the *formal* labor market, sufficient to support their consumption needs in two-thirds of the population. While both neighborhoods have a similar proportion of households supported by autonomous workers alone, nearly half of the dormitory community's households piece together their subsistence from some *combination* of salaried and autonomous employment. The corresponding proportion in the industrial neighborhood is only 15.2 percent. Thus, not only were households in the dormitory community more likely to have additional income earners, but at least one was more likely to be an autonomous worker.

THE HOUSEHOLD FOCUS: DISCUSSION

The Brazilian case study material presented above illustrates the utility of a focus on the household as a mediating unit that influences the decision of women to work for monetary earnings outside the home. Despite their limited labor-market opportunities, women in low-income families continue to play an important role in the strategies by which household maintenance is assured. One of their responsibilities is generating income, often on an irregular, intermittent basis. Economic stress at the household level can outweigh other variables that impede women's entry into the labor force (Birdsall and McGreevey 1983:7). This pattern is more evident in the less prosperous "dormitory" community. Furthermore, women and girls in low-income households are also allocated to domestic chores and to the "rearguard" tasks related to other household members' extra-domestic activities, such as meals and lunch boxes, clothing and uniforms, and scheduling (Fausto Neto 1982; Machado Neto 1978; Rodrigues 1978). It is these multiple responsibilities that overlap and accumulate to make up the double work burden of poor working women (Buvinic 1983:19-20).

The focus on household mediation should not, however, imply exclusive attention to variables at the level of the domestic unit. Rather, analysis moves from macrosocial to individual levels, passing through levels of social class and family determinations at different analytical moments. A comparative approach is also important in illuminating the degree of variability present within different segments of the Brazilian industrial working class with respect to patterns of household income-generating strategies. Mechanistic associations of social class with family structures must therefore give way to a more textured understanding.

The presentation of the case study was intended to illustrate the insights to be gained from a household-level focus, as well as the practical and conceptual difficulties such an approach presents. The latter have been treated in more detail elsewhere (Schmink 1984). Certain central issues, particularly related to women's work behavior, will nevertheless be mentioned here. During the past decade, a growing body of research has been devoted to the analysis of "family survival strategies" in Latin America. Many studies, including this one, focus only on the outcome of behavior. This presumes that the logic motivating household decisions is revealed by the results of those decisions (Borsotti 1981:183; Segura de Camacho 1982:87; Torrado 1981). Despite the usefulness of this approach for some purposes, it leaves aside important questions about the meaning of social behavior and the internal workings of domestic units.

A basic problem is that of conceptualizing the boundaries and functions of the domestic unit. It was noted earlier that households are usually defined in primarily economic or mateiral terms, as analytically distinct from the sets of social relations that constitute families. But since domestic units can rarely be reduced to their purely economic functions, this abstraction is not altogther satisfactory. In most cases the primary basis for the cohesion of the household unit is in fact a set of social relations and mutual obligations that are defined by kinship or other reciprocal relationships (Borsotti 1981:179-80). A focus only on the economic aspect of these relationships is misleading to the extent that behavior, including the division of labor within the household, is determined not just by economic, but also by social factors (Bach and Schraml 1982:328-29). Attention to strictly economic elements of domestic units ignores ideological and subjective determinants of behavior, factors particularly important in understanding patterns of women's behavior (Anderson 1983; Rodriguez 1981:249; Segura de Camacho 1982). Several authors stress the importance of the world now held by social actors in defining the meaning of social processes (Balan and Jelin 1980; Leite 1982; Macedo 1979; Merrick 1983; Segura de Camacho 1982; SSRC 1982).

Similar problems arise with the definition of household income and of standard of living. Despite apparently objective determinants, the concepts of "needs" and of "survival" are meaningful only in a particular social and historical context (Jelin 1983; Jelin et al. 1982: Jelin and Feijoo 1980:8-9; Merrick 1983). Since historical changes and experiences of social mobility shape both material conditions and perceptions of them (Jelin 1983; Jelin et al. 1982; Jelin and Feijoo 1980; Macedo 1979), it follows that the definition of minimal basic needs will vary over time both within and between societies (Borsotti 1981: 169). Comparisons of household strategies must therefore take as their empirical referent particular historical and social situations (Saenz and DiPaula 1981:156-57).

In considering the specifically economic aspects of household behavior, there is the danger or reifying the household unit and ignoring other pertinent organizational forms. Especially in studies of migration decisions, nonresident family members should be included in the analysis (Wood 1981). Similarly, the appropriate unit of analysis for some forms of consumption may be a noncoresident group (Bolles 1981:93; Jelin 1982). In consumption of collective services, for example, broader forms of collective political organization--i.e., at the community level--may be more important (Bach and Schraml 1982; Rodriguez 1981:243; Valdes and Acuna 1981:236). There may even be contradictions between goals of families (i.e., savings) and of other units like the wider kin network that exerts pressure for a "leveling" of resources (Anderson 1983:19; Lomnitz 1977). The most appropriate unit of analysis will depend on the particular object of study (Arguello 1981:201; Bender 1967; Borsotti 1981:174-75; Jelin 1982). Jelin (1982:14) suggests beginning with a provisional defintion of the unit, which is then disaggregated and analyzed in relation to the activities in question and finally reconstituted analytically. This critique, like the "life course" approach used by Hareven (1978:1) and others, emphasizes the fluid interaction of "individual time," "family time," and "historical time."

The assumptions underlying the decision rules imputed to household strategies have also been carefully scrutinized. A "veneer of free choice" is often implied by the concept of strategies, especially as used in neoclassical economic models of household decision making (Wood 1982:11). Household decisions are made within the confines of limiting structural constraints (Balan and Jelin 1980:15; Torrado 1981:206), although families nevertheless operate with a degree of "relative autonomy" (Humphries 1982). Second, to what extent does the concept of "strategy" imply conscious, rational behavior? Without necessarily adopting the assumptions of neoclassical analysis, the household-strategy approach presumes that domestic units pursue rational economic behavior (Folbre 1982:321). Whether or not explicit goals exist, their content and changing form over time are questions for empirical research (Anderson 1983; Bach and Schraml 1982; Fausto Neto 1982; Jelin 1983; Macedo 1979; Merrick 1983; SSRC 1982; Torredo 1981:206). Prevailing definitions of social roles, especially in a patriarchal social system, may undermine the presumed economic rationality of household strategies and, in particular, constrain women's behavior (Anderson 1983).

Finally, the internal process of decision making is relatively neglected in studies of household strategies. How are decisions made vis-a-vis different aspects of household welfare (Barlett 1980; Borsotti 1981:174; SSRC 1982)? The impact of authority structures and of internal power differentials deserves greater attention (Balan and Jelin 1980:13; Buvinic 1983:18; Fausto Neto 1982:chapter2; Folbre 1982; Jelin 1982:25; Macedo 1979:40-41; Merrick 1983; Torrado 1981:206), In the absence of more precise information about these internal processes, the concept of household strategies runs the risk of implying harmony of objectives within that unit (Balan and Jelin 1980:13; Dwyer 1983:2; Garcia et al. 1982:22; Jelin 1982). While some agreement on general goals (i.e., survival) is probable, conflict and tension between household members can also be expected, especially between generations and between the sexes (Anderson 1983; Balan and Jelin 1980; Dwyer 1983:8; Jelin 1982). Some studies have focused attention on these tensions (Banck 1980; Fausto Neto 1982; Folbre 1982, 1983; Jelin 1982, 1983; Macedo 1979:113-15; Segura de Camacho 1982:87-88), but more systematic information is needed in order to understand in which spheres and at what moments the decision-making process becomes fragmented into individual goals. Put in the language of neoclassical economics, preferences of individuals in a family may not be sufficiently consistent to constitute a single "utility function" (Arthur 1982:394). Some studies have focused not on one but on multiple parallel strategies followed by different household members (Anderson 1983; Dwyer 1983:3-5; Jelin 1982:14).

The study of hosuehold mediation is to be encouraged because of its methodological potential for linking different levels of analysis. It has been demonstrated to be particularly useful in illuminating the complex factors that condition women's productive behavior. Future research should help to reveal more about the specific position women occupy in the adaptive behavior of domestic units, and their active role in contributing to their own survival and that of their families.

NOTES

Field research on which this analysis is based was supported by grants from Fulbright-Hays and Social Science Research Council and the American Council of Learned Societies. The author is indebted to Judith Bruce, Mary Garcia Castro, Elisabeth Jelin, Thomas W. Merrick, and Charles H. Wood for useful discussions of some of the issues treated in this chapter.

[1] For recent studies of Brazilian women in particular occupational groups, see Abreu 1980; Leite 1982; Rodrigues 1979; Saffioti 1978; Spindel 1983; and Teixeira et al. 1983.

REFERENCES

Abreu, Alice de Paiva. 1977. Mao-de obra feminina e mercado de trabalho no Brasil. SENAC, Boletim Tecnico 3:1 (Jan/April):5-19.

_____. 1980. O Trabalho Industrial a Domicilio na Industria de Confeccao. Ph. D. dissertation, University of Sao Paulo.

Arguello, Omar. 1981. "Estrategias de supervivencia: un concepto en busca de su contenido." Demografia y Economia XV: 2:190-203.

Anderson, Jeanine. 1983. Redes y Estrategias. Un estudio de mujeres de barrios pobres limenos. Lima: unpublished manuscript.

Aramburu, Carlos E. 1981. Organizacion Socio-Economica de la Familia Campesina y Migracion en Tres Regiones del Peru. Lima: INANDEP.

Arizpe, Lourdes. 1977. "Women in the informal labor sector: the case of Mexico City." Signs 3:1 (Autumn):25-37.

Arthur, W. Brian. 1982. "Review of Gary S. Becker, A Treatise on the Family." Population and Development Review 8:2 (June:393-97.

Bach, Robert L. and Lisa A. Schraml. 1982. "Migration, crisis and theoretical conflict." International Migration Review 16:2 (Summer):320-41.

Balan, Jorge and Elisabeth Jelin. 1980. Taller sobre las condiciones de vida de los sectores populares urbanos: informe sobre sus resultados. Mexico City: The Population Council, Documento de Trabajo, No. 5.

Banck, Geert A. 1980. "Survival strategies of low-income urban households in Brazil." Urban Anthropology 9:2:227-42.

Barlett, Peggy F. (ed.). 1980. Agricultural Decision Making: Anthropological Contributions to Rural Development. New York: Academic Press.

Barrera, Manuel. 1978. "Diferencias salariales entre hombres y mujeres en America Latina." Presented at the IUPERJ seminar on "Women in the Labor Force in Latin America," Rio de Janeiro, November.

Barroso, Carmen. 1978. "Sozinhas on mal acompanhadas - a situacao de mulher chefe de familia." Anais: Primeiro Encontro Nacional de Estudos Populacionais. Rio de Janeiro: Associacao Brasileira de Estudos Populacionais.

Bender, D. R. 1967. "A refinement of the concept of household: families, coresidence, and domestic functions." American Anthropologist 69:493-504.

Ben-Porath, Yoram (ed.). 1982. "Income Distribution and the Family." Population and Development Review, Supplement to Volume 8.

Bilac, Elizabete Doria. 1978. Familias de Trabalhadores: Estrategias de Sobrevivencia. A organizacao de Vida Familiar em uma Cidade Paulista. Sao Paulo: Simbolo.

Birdsall, Nancy and William Paul McGreevey. 1983. "Women, poverty, and development." Pp. 3-13 in Mayra Buvinic, Margaret A. Lycette and William Paul McGreevey (eds.), Women and Poverty in the Third World. Baltimore: Johns Hopkins University Press.

Bolles A. Lynn. 1981. "Household economic strategies in Kingston, Jamaica." Pp. 83-96 in Naomi Black and Ann Baker Cottrell (eds.), Women and Social Change: Equity Issues in Development. Beverly Hills and London: Sage.

Borsotti, Carlos. 1977. "Notas sobre la familia como unidad socio-economica." Presented at the V. meeting of the Working Group on the Process of Reproduction of the Population and Development Commission of CLACSO, April 1976.

_____. 1981. "La organizacion social de la reproduccion de los agentes sociales, las unidades familiares y sus estrategias." Demografia y Economia XV:2:164-89.

Bruschini, Maria Christina A. 1978. "Sexualizacao das ocupacoes: o caso brasileiro." Presented at IUPERJ seminar on "Women in the Labor Force in Latin America,: Rio de Janeiro, November.

Buvinic, Mayra. 1983. "Women's issues in Third World Poverty: a policy analysis." Pp. 14-31 in Mayra Buvinic, Margaret A. Lycette, and William Paul McGreevy (eds.), Women and Poverty in the Third World. Baltimore: Johns Hopkins University Press.

Buvinic, Mayra and Nadya Youssef. 1978. "Women-Headed Households: The Ignored Factor in Development." Report submitted to AID/WID.

Deere, Carmen Diana, Jane Humphries and Magdalena Leon de Leal. 1978. "Class and Historical Analysis for the Study of Women and Economic Change." Paper prepared for The Role of Women and Demographic Change Research Program, I.L.O., Geneva.

Dinerman, Ina R. 1978. "Patterns of adaptation among households of U.S.-bound migrants from Michoacan, Mexico." International Migration Review 12:4:485-501.

Dwyer, Daisy Hilse. 1983. "Women and income in the Third World: Implications for policy." New York: The Population Council, International Programs Working Paper No. 18.

Fausto Neto, Ana Maria Q. 1982. Familia Operaria e Reproducao da Forca de Trabalho. Petropolis: Vozes.

Folbre, Nancy. 1982. "Exploitation comes home: a critique of the Marxian theory of family labour." Cambridge Journal of Economics 6:317-29.

______. 1983. "Household production in the Philippines: a non-neoclassical approach." Economic Development and Cultural Change, 32:2(January):303-330.

Garcia, Brigida, Humberto Munoz, and Orlandina de Oliveira. 1979. "Migracion, familia y fuerza de trabajo en la ciudad de Mexico." Cuadernos del Centro de Estudios Sociologicos No. 26, Colegio de Mexico.

______. 1982. Hogares y Trabajadores en la Ciudad de Mexico. Mexico City: El Colegio de Mexico/U.N.A.M.

GETEC (Grupo de Estudos e Trabalho em Educacao Comunitaria). 1978. Mutirao. Belo Horizonte: Cadernos GETEC, mimeo.

Hareven, Tamara K. 1978. Transitions: The Family and the Life Course in Historical Perspective. New York: Academic Press.

Humphries, Jane. 1982. "The family and economy: Notes toward a relative autonomy approach." Presented at the Social Science Research Council-sponsored Conference on Demographic Research in Latin America: Linking Individual, Household and Societal Variables, Ixtapan de la Sal, Mexico, August 23-27.

Humphrey, John. 1983. "The growth of female employment in Brazilian manufacturing industry in the 1970s." Mimeo.

Ianni, Octavio. 1977. Estado e Planejamento Economico no Brasil (1930-1970). Rio: Civilizacao Brasileira.

Jelin, Elisabeth. 1974. "Formas de organizacao da atividade economica e estrutura ocupacional." Estudos CEBRAP 9 (July-Aug.): 51-78.

______. 1982. "Pan y afectos: la organizacion domestica en la produccion y la reproduccion." Buenos Aires: CEDES, mimeo.

______. 1983. "A microsocial processing of a life style: The organization of expenditures among domestic units of the popular sectors." Presented at the Social Science Research Council-sponsored Conference on Demographic Research in Latin America: Linking Individual, Household and Societal Variables, Ixtapan de la Sal, Mexico, August 23-27.

Jelin, Elisabeth and Maria del Carmen Feijoo. 1980. "Trabajo y Familia en el Ciclo de Vida Feminino: el Caso de los Sectores Populares de Buenos Aires." Buenos Aires: Estudios CEDES 3:8-9.

Jelin, Elisabeth with Maria del Carmen Feijoo, Juan Jose Llovet, and Silvina Ramos. 1982. Las relaciones sociales del consumo: organizacion del gasto de las unidades domesticas de sectores populares. Buenos Aires: CEDES, mimeo.

Kuznesof, Elizabeth. 1980. "The role of the female-headed hosehold in Brazilian modernization: Sao Paulo 1765-1836." Journal of Social History 13:4:589-613.

Kuznets, Simon. 1976. "Demographic aspects of the size distribution of income: an exploratory essay." Economic Development and Cultural Change 25 (October):1-94.

Leeds, Anthony. 1964. "Brazilian careers and social structure: an evolutionary model and a case history." American Anthropologist 66:1321-47.

Leite, Rosalina de Santa Cruz. 1982. A Operaria Metalurgica. Estudo sobre as condicoes de vida e trabalho de operarias metalurgicas na cidade de Sao Paulo. Sao Paulo: Semente.

Lewin, Helena, Jaqueline Pitanguy and Carlos Manuel Romani. 1977. Mao-de-Obra no Brasil: Um Inventario Critico. Petropolis: Vozes/PUC/OIT.

Lomnitz, Larissa. 1971. "Reciprocity of favors in the urban middle class of Chile." Pp. 93-106 in George Dalton (ed.), Studies in Economic Anthropology. Anthopological Studies No. 7. Washington, D.C.: American Anthopological Association.

_____. 1977. Networks and Marginality. New York: Academic Press.

Macedo, Carmen Cinira. 1979. A Reproducao da Desigualdade. O Projeto de Vida Familiar de um Grupo Operario. Sao Paulo: Editora Hucitec.

Machado Neto, Zahide. 1978. "As meninas - sobre o trabalho da crianca e da adolescente na familia proletaria." Presented at the IUPERJ seminar on "Women in the Labor Force in Latin America," Rio de Janeiro, November.

Madeira, Felicia Reicher. 1979. As Condicoes do Trabalho de Mulhe e as Condicoes de Vida da Familia. Master's Thesis, Universidade de Sao Paulo.

Madeira, Felicia and Paul A. Singer. 1973. "Estrutura do Emprego e Trabalho Feminino no Brasil: 1920-1970." CEBRAP Caderno 13.

Margulis, Mario. 1980. "Reproduccion social de la vida y reproduccion del capital." Nueva Antropologia IV:13-14:47-64.

Margulis, Mario, Teresa Rendon and Mercedes Pedrero. 1981. "Fuerza de trabajo y estrategias de supervivencia en una poblacion de origen migratorio: Colonias populares de Reynosa." Demografia y Economia XV:3(47):265-311.

Martinez-Alier, Verena. 1975. "As mulheres do caminhao de turma. Debate & Critica 5 (March):59-85.

Meillassoux, Claude. 1981. Maidens, Meal, and Money. Capitalism and the Domestic Community. Cambridge: Cambridge University Press.

Merrick, Thomas W. 1983. "Perspectives on demographic research on Latin America." Social Science Research Council ITEMS (March).

Merrick, Thomas W. and Marianne Schmink. 1983. "Households headed by women and urban poverty in Brazil." Pp. 244-271 in Mayra Buvinic, Margaret A. Lycette, and William Paul McGreevey (eds.), Women and Poverty in the Third World. Baltimore: Johns Hopkins University Press.

Miller, Charlotte Ingrid. 1976. Middle Class Kinship Networks in Belo Horizonte, Minas Gerais, Brazil: The Functions of the Urban Parentela. Ph.D. Dissertation, University of Florida.

Moser, Caroline O. N. 1978. "Informal sector or petty commodity production: dualism or dependence in urban development." World Development 6:9-10:1041-64.

Moura, Esmeraldo Blanco B. de. 1982. Mulheres e Menores no Trabalho Industrial: Os Factores Sexo e Idade na Dinamica do Capital. Petropolis: Vozes.

Oliveira, Francisco de. 1975. "A economia Brasileira: Critica a razao dualista." Sao Paulo: Selecoes CEBRAP 1:5-78.

Oliveira, Maria Coleta F. A. 1978. A individualizacao da forca de trabalho e o trabalho feminino em Pederneiras-SP. Presented at IUPERJ seminar on "Women in the Labor Force in Latin America," Rio de Janeiro, November.

Pereira, L. C. Bresser. 1962. "The rise of middle class and middle management in Brazil." Journal of Inter-American Studies 4:313-20.

Perlman, Janice. 1969. The Myth of Marginality. Berkeley: University of California Press.

Pessar, Patricia R. 1982. "The role of households in international migration and the case of U.S.-bound migration from the Domincan Republic." International Migration Review XVI:342-64.

Rapp, Rayna. 1978. "Family and class in contemporary America: notes toward an understanding of ideology." Science and Society 42(Fall):278-300.

Rato, Maria Helena de Cunha. 1978. "A participacao feminina na populacao ativa frente as necessidades do sistema produtivo no Brazil." Presented at the IUPERJ seminar on "Women in the Labor Force in Latin America," Rio de Janeiro, November.

Rey de Marulanda, Nohra. 1982. "La unidad produccion-reproduccion en las mujeres del sector urbano en Colombia." Pp. 56-71 in Magdalena Leon (ed.), Debate Sobre la Mujer en America Latina y el Caribe: Discusion acerca de la unidad produccion-reproduccion, Vol. I, La Realidad Colombiana. Bogota: ACEP.

Rodrigues, Arakcy Martins. 1978. O padrao de distribuicao de papeis em familias operarias. Presented at the IUPERJ seminar on "Women in the Labor Force in Latin America," Rio de Janeiro, November.

Rodrigues, Jessita Martins. 1979. A Mulher Operaria. Un Estudo Sobre Tecelas. Sao Paulo: Hucitec.

Rodrigues, Leoncio Martins. 1970. Industrializacao e Atitudes Operarias (Estudo de um Grupo de Trabalhadores). Sao Paulo: Brasiliense.

Rodriguez, Daniel. 1981. "Discusiones en torno al concepto de estrategias de superviviencia." Demografia y Economia XV:2:238-52.

Saenz, Alvaro and Jorge DiPaula. 1981. "Precisiones teorico - metodologicos sobre la nocion de estrategias de existencia." Demografia y Economia XV: 2:149-63.

Saffioti, Heleith I. B. 1969. A Mulher na Sociedade de Classes, Mito e Realidade. Sao Paulo: Quatro Artes.

_____. 1978. Emprego Domestico e Capitalismo. Petropolis: Vozes.

Sant'Anna, Anna M., Thomas W. Merrick and Dipak Mazumbar. 1976. "Income Distribution and the Economy of the Urban Household: The Case of Belo Horizonte." Washington, D.C.: The World Bank, Working Paper No. 236.

Schmink, Marianne. 1979. *Community in Ascendance: Urban Industrial Growth and Household Income Strategies in Belo Horizonte, Brazil.* Ph.D. Dissertation, University of Texas at Austin.

_____. 1982. "Women in the Urban Economy in Latin America." Women, Low-Income Households and Urban Services Working Paper No. 1. New York: The Population Council. (Published in Spanish as "La Mujer en la Economia en America Latina," Documento de Trabajo No. 11, 1982. Mexico: The Population Council.)

_____. 1984. Household economic strategies: a review and research agenda. *Latin American Research Review* 19:3, 87-101.

Scott, Alison MacEwen. 1981. "Job differentiation and mobility amongst manual workers in Lima, Peru." Report submitted to the World Bank, May.

_____. 1983. "Economic development and urban women's work: the case of Lima, Peru." Unpublished.

Scott, Parry. 1979. "A producao domestica e a mulher no Recife." Presented at the meeting of the Associacao Nacional de Pos-Graduacao e Pesquisa nas Ciencias Sociais, Belo Horizonte, October.

Segura de Camacho, Nohra. 1982. "La reproduccion social, familia y trabajo." Pp. 84-98 in Magdalena Leon (ed.), *Debate Sobre la Mujer en America Latina y el Caribe: Discusion acerca de la unidad produccion-reproduccion, Vol. I, La Realidad Colombiana.* Bogota: ACEP.

Selby, Henry A. and Arthur D. Murphy. 1982. "The Mexican urban household and the decision to migrate to the United States." Philadelphia: ISHI Occasional Papers in Social Change, No. 4.

Singer, Paul. 1977. *Economia Politica de Trabalho.* Sao Paulo: Hucitec.

Soares, Glaucio A. D. 1968. "The new industrialization and the Brazilian political system." Pp. 186-201 in James Petras and Maurice Zeitlen (eds.), *Latin America: Reform or Revolution?* Greenwich, Conn.: Fawcett.

Social Science Research Council (SSRC). 1982. Notes from the meeting on "Demographic Research in Latin America: Linking Individual, Household, and the Societal Variables: sponsored by Social Science Research Council, Ixtapan de la Sal, Mexico, August 23-27, 1982. Unpublished.

Spindel, Cheywa R. 1983. "O 'uso' de trabalho da mulher na industria do vestuario." Pp. 89-113 in Carmen Barroso and Albertina Oliveira Costa (eds.), Mulher, Mulheres. Sao Paulo: Cortez Editora/Fundacao Carlos Chagas.

Teixeira, Amelia Rosa Sa B., Ana Clara T. Ribeiro, Filippina Chinelli and Roseli Elias. 1983. "O trabalho e a trabalhadora fabril a domicilio." Pp. 115-33 in Carmen Barroso and Albertina Oliveira Costa (eds.), Mulher, Mulheres. Sao Paulo: Cortez Editora/ Fundacao Carlos Chages.

Tilly, Lousie A. and Joan W. Scott. 1978. Women, Work and Family. New York: Holt, Rinehart and Winston.

Torrado, Susana. 1981. "Sobre los conceptos de 'estrategias familiares de vida' y 'processo de reproduccion de la fuerza de trabajo': notas teorico - metodologicas." Demografia y Economia XV: 2:204-33.

Valdes, Ximena and Miguel Acuna. 1981. "Precisiones metodologicas sobre las 'estrategias de supervivencia." Demografia y Economia XV: 2:234-37.

Vaneck, Joann. 1974. "Time spent in housework." Scientific American 233:5:116-20.

Wainerman, Catalina H. and Zulma Recchini de Lattes. 1981. El Trabajo Femenino en el Banquillo de los Acusados. La Medicion Censal en America Latina. Mexico: The Population Council/ Editorial Terra Nova.

Wood, Charles H. 1981. "Structural changes and household strategies: A conceptual framework for the study of rural migration." Human Organization 40 (Winter):338-44.

_____. 1982. "Equilibrium and historical-structural perspectives on migration: a comparative critique with implications for future research." International Migration Review 16:2 (Summer):298-319.

TABLE 1

Occupational Distribution by Position in Households, Below Horizonte Industrial Community, 1976

Occupation	Male Heads	Female Heads	Wives	Sons	Daugh- ters	Others
Owners	0.5	--	--	--	--	--
Managers	4.9	--	2.1	--	2.4	--
Professional and Technical	6.3	16.7	33.3	7.8	9.8	13.6
White collar	13.6	8.3	8.3	27.0	36.6	13.6
Supervision	10.2	--	--	--	--	--
Specialized	37.4	--	--	29.6	4.9	13.6
Unskilled	7.3	25.0	10.4	12.1	12.2	36.4
Autonomous	19.9	50.0	45.8	23.5	34.1	22.7
Total	100.0	100.0	99.9	100.0	100.0	99.9
N	(206)	(12)	(48)	(115)	(41)	(22)
% of Total Workers	46.4	2.7	10.8	25.9	9.2	5.0

Source: Survey by the author.

TABLE 2

Mean Earnings by Occupation, for Both Sexes
Belo Horizonte Industrial Community, 1976

	Mean Earnings (in cruzeiros)		
Occupation	Male	Female	Female/ Male
Owners	4000	--	--
Managers	7409	1640	.22
Professional and Technical	4195	1007	.24
White collar	1942	863	.44
Supervisors	4294	--	--
Specialized	1719	767	.45
Unskilled	1061	673	.63
Autonomous	2818	688	.24
Total	2366	812	.34
N	(285)	(86)	

Source: Survey by the author.

TABLE 3

Occupation of Household Head and Non-Head Workers in Two-Occupation[1] Households, 1976 (Percent of households in each cell)

	Non-Heads[2]					
Heads	Prof./ Tech.	White Collar	Speci- alized	Un- Skilled	Auto- nomous	Total
Owners	--	--	--	1.5	--	1.5
Managers	--	4.5	--	--	--	4.5
Professional and Technical	--	--	--	1.5	4.5	6.1
White collar	6.1	--	--	1.5	3.0	10.6
Supervision	4.5	3.0	--	--	3.0	10.6
Specialized	7.6	6.1	--	12.1	12.1	37.9
Unskilled	--	3.0	4.5	--	3.0	10.6
Autonomous	3.0	6.1	4.5	4.5	--	18.2
Total	21.2	22.7	9.1	21.2	25.8	100.0
N	(14)	(15)	(6)	(14)	(17)	(66)

[1] Includes only those households with two or more different occupations.

[2] There were no cases of non-head workers in the owners, managers, or supervision categories.

Source: Survey by the author.

TABLE 4

Participation Rates for Females and Males
In Two Belo Horizonte Neighborhoods,
1976-1977

	Dormitory Community	Industrial Community
Females	31.6	12.6
Males	69.7	35.0
Total	51.0	23.7

Sources: For dormitory community, Fausto Neto 1982:64, Quadro VIII; for industrial community, survey by the author.

TABLE 5

Number of Workers per Household
In Two Belo Horizonte Neighborhoods, 1977

	Industrial Neighborhood	Dormitory Neighborhood
0	13.9	2.3
1	49.3	32.6
2	20.7	25.8
3	7.3	15.2
4	5.7	12.9
5	2.0	5.3
6 or more	1.4	6.1
Total	100.1	100.2
N	(300)	(132)
Mean	1.54	2.57

Sources: Fausto Neto 1982:122, Quadro XVII; and survey by the author.

TABLE 6

Female Participation Rates by Age Groups
In Two Belo Horizonte Neighborhoods, 1977

Industrial Neighborhood	Age Groups	Dormitory Neighborhood	Age Groups
--	Under 15	6.2	Under 15
46.9	15-20	47.4	15-25
24.2	21-30	37.7	26-35
28.9	Over 30	39.5	Over 35
12.6	Total	31.6	Total
(126)	N	(103)	N

Sources: Fausto Neto 1982:64, Quadro VIII; survey by the author.

TABLE 7

Source of Household Income
In Two Belo Horizonte Neighborhoods, 1977

	Industrial Neighborhood	Dormitory Neighborhood
Salaried workers	68.2	37.2
Autonomous workers	16.6	16.3
Salaried and autonomous workers	15.2	46.5
Total	100.0	100.0
N	(211)	(129)

Source: For dormitory neighborhood, Fausto Neto 1982:125; for the industrial neighborhood, survey by the author.

9 Women in Petty Commodity Production in La Paz, Bolivia

Judith-Maria Beuchler

INTRODUCTION

Small scale production continues to play an important role in manufacturing and in the employment of women both in the Third World and in some highly industrialized areas of the First World (Eckstein 1983; Goddard 1978; Scott 1979 1981; Steel 1981). In Bolivia, small-scale production has grown in part because of, and in part in spite of, the uneven development of its large-scale export oriented extraction industry, inadequate communication and transportation facilities, underdeveloped infrastructure and political instability. It has been estimated that in the late 1970s, "approximately two thirds of all manufacturing output, and about 80 percent of all new firms still were artisan operations" (Eckstein 1983:8). In 1981, the author and Hans Buechler conducted a study of such enterprises in La Paz, Bolivia, and the effects the wider economic, social, and political conditions have had on them.

BACKGROUND: THE ECONOMIC FISCAL AND POLITICAL CRISIS

It has been estimated that activity in manufacturing, construction, and the oil industry had decreased more than 50 percent between 1980 and 1981 alone, and the mines were also working at less than half capacity. Exports dropped 19 percent and the formal trade deficit amounted to over $500 million. Bank accounts were at an all-time low, and the foreign debt at an all-time high: over $4 billion, with $460 million to be repaid by the end of 1981. The black market exchange rate rose from 25 to over 37 pesos per U.S. dollar, and inflation was calculated to be above 50 percent. The state had not paid its employees for several months, wages were frozen, and many subsidies for a wide range of basic necessities had been removed. International Monetary Fund standby loans were uncertain (Dunkerley 1982:32-33). For small-scale production, these economic crises meant unpredictable and scarce supplies of raw materials, capital, credit, and markets, both internal and external.

This economic crisis of major proportions was accompanied by a deep political crisis. In the last five years Bolivia has had three elections, ten presidents, at least eight attempted and successful coups, and general, factorywide, regional, miner and women's strikes. The short democratic experiment under the presidency of Lidia Gueiler (16 November 1979 to 17 July 1980) was followed by a series of military regimes that increased the use of paramilitary forces, which arrested and harassed countless persons and implemented a night curfew, suppressed all labor rights, and closed the university and intimidated the church (Dunkerley 1982). Such economic and political chaos contributed to further undermining the state's promotion of industry. Bolivian postrevolutionary governments (i.e., after 1952) "have been too internally divided to implement a unified policy in support of private sector development, too poor to finance projects on their own, and too weak to impose their investment priorities on local and foreign capital" (Eckstein 1983:35).

THE RESEARCH

The study was concerned with the organization and development of small-scale enterprises in La Paz, Bolivia, over time and the relationship between these firms and the processes of rural-urban migration,[1] industrialization and capitalization. The focus was on the relationship of small firms to one another and to larger firms both within the nation and abroad. These industries were geographically dispersed in the city, and ranged in size from single artisan workshops, through family firms, to modern factories with fifty employees with a capitalization of a few hundred dollars or less to a few with several million.

The sample of 196 persons in these industries included long-term urban residents and recent arrivals who produced traditional and modern goods for local, regional, national, and international markets.

In this chapter I shall concentrate primarily on the female members in these enterprises. I wish to explore the means whereby women as members of households, owners of enterprises, and workers control, or seek to control, the conditions and products of their labor. The analysis is based on work histories gathered in conjunction with female life histories. The women ranged in age from their early teens to their sixties. Some of them were recent migrants from the altiplano; others were urban born and bred. Some were illiterate, although most had enjoyed some primary education and at least a few had attended secondary school. Most, but not all, were bilingual, Aymara-Spanish speakers. The majority were married mothers with as many as six children. The most "successful" were widowed older women.

In general these women were found in industries that could be seen as extensions of "traditional" female domestic tasks, i.e., in the provision of food, clothing, and adornments. They baked bread, cakes, pastries, and savories, formed candies and chocolates, selected coffee, and catered cooked food. They knit, spun, wove, cut, sewed, embroidered and decorated traditional and modern clothing by hand and machine for daily wear and festive occasions, both for internal consumption and for export. In addition, they made rubber and leather shoes and other leather articles: belts, bags, wallets, eyeglass and other cases, jackets, and other leather articles. They tanned, cut, stitched, and carded alpaca garments, rugs, wall hangings, and coverlets. And they were heavily engaged in the manufacture of fiesta paraphernalia and tourist goods. These involved such items as miniatures (houses, trucks, clothing, home furnishings, etc.) made for and sold in the Alasitas fair in January--a fair held in honor of Ekeko, the god of plenty; costumes, masks, rattles, and float adornments for fiestas such as carnival, and palm-frond pins for Palm Sunday. Tourist items such as bayeta (Indian homespun) wall hangings, small weavings, dolls, and reed boats were also often made and sold by women. A few women are now engaged in "male" trades: tinsmithery, jewelry, furniture making, and printing. (However, in the nineteenth century tinsmithery was predominantly a female trade.). Although women are not actively engaged in production in machine shops, metalworks, foundries, sawmills, carpentry workshops, or plastic factories, they oversee and cook for male apprentices and employees in these enterprises and sell the goods produced in markets and to shops.

MODELS OF FEMALE LABOR-FORCE PARTICIPATION

Sokoloff's (1980) and Kelly's (1979) critique of the status-attainment, dual-market, and Marxist feminist models of female labor-force participation is essential to our understanding of the role of women in petty commodity production in late capitalism in Bolivia. Their work indicates the ways in which these women try to accommodate and attempt to resolve the tensions of sex, class, and race or ethnicity.

In particular, their emphasis on the political economy of women's labor-force participation, the interdependence of primary and secondary labor markets, and the relation of patriarchy to capitalism, derived from data on women in core countries, also serves to highlight the dilemmas of those in peripheral ones. My analysis puts even greater stress on the socioeconomic constraints on women's labor force participation, the two-way interdependence of capitalism on petty commodity production, and the priority of capitalism in the relation of capitalism to patriarchy. Further, the Bolivian case presents special contradictions. The conditions there are unattractive to the large-scale capitalist penetration in manufacturing and at the same time provide special opportunities for women in petty commodity production and in political expression. In this chapter I shall assess each model and determine the extent to which it serves to deepen my interpretation of the field data.

THE STATUS-ATTAINMENT MODEL

The status-attainment model is a version of the human capital theory held by economists and the individual deficit model espoused by psychologists; both claim that aspirations, motivations, values, and attitudes account for the distribution of women in the labor force. Competing in the same job market as men, women are seen as less desirable due to their education, marital status, motherhood, and work experience, and this attitude predisposes them to care less about status attainment through work achievement, their position in the market place becoming a matter of "choice" (Sokoloff 1980:1-34; Blau and Jusenius 1976:185-88; Nieva and Gutek 1981:116; Nash 1981:493). The life histories of Bolivian female petty-commodity producers refute this interpretation. They are proud of their activities, possess a positive self-image, and have high aspirations. Repeatedly, they voice pride and satisfaction in creating innovative jewelry, lovely spun cloth, tastefully designed cards, delicious food, and novel fiesta and tourist goods.

Virginia, a twenty-three year old mother with three preschool children, the wife of a medical student, and daughter of a tailor and long-distance trader, operates a jewelry store on a busy corner near a central marketplace in La Paz. Following her husband's family profession, with money from her mother-in-law and a rent-free shop provided by an uncle, she looks forward to learning all aspects of the business: buying materials, putting out work to other jewelers, repairing, and creating up-to-date, fashionable earrings to lure the "cholitas" (young women in traditional Indian dress) who pass by the store window. "This profession is for persons who possess a great deal of patience and are highly imaginative," she claims. Each establishment vies with others to introduce new styles. Her latest two creations were earrings in the form of a flower basket and a flowering branch.

Not only are Bolivian Aymara and mestizo women highly motivated, but they also conceive of themselves as hard-working, responsible individuals whose work is central and essential to the economic well-being of the whole family. It is they, the women, who appropriately control the accounts and purse. They share this view of themselves with independent traders, peasant women, and factory workers (Buechler 1976a, 1976b, 1978; Estes 1982).

Dona Flora, who owns and operates a family firm that manufactures alpaca cloth and clothing, exemplifies the woman who cannot even imagine what it might be like to "sit at home with one's arms crossed." She is the daughter of a weaver-peasant mother from the altiplano and a miner who later migrated to La Paz to work in a beer factory before retiring to his natal community on Lake Titicaca. When Dona Flora's husband, a truck driver, died in an accident, she was left with five minor children to support. Her parents supplied her with food from the countryside, and she began to spin, weave, sew, and knit garments, which she sold on the street with the aid of her children. Later, she sold in the market and retailed to a local exporter trained in America, until importers from abroad sought her out directly. Thereupon she began to employ close kin and to "put out" different tasks to some twenty-five unrelated individuals. Since then she has enlarged her home to house her married children and built a workshop, equipped with a weaving loom and sewing and knitting machines, where two persons work permanently. Spinning, knitting, and weaving are also "put out" to peasants near Lake Titicaca, a dairy farm family fifteen kilometers from La Paz, and artisans in Cochabamba. She now fills orders from abroad, sells on the street, and, with the aid of a brother, sells to the artisan market in Cochabamba.

Although her son-in-law, a former dispatching agent with some university education, ostensibly handles shipping, accounting, public relations, and legal matters, it is the illiterate Dona Flora who really organizes the work, has perfect recall of finances, and represents the firm to clients and government agencies. She hopes to expand her enterprise by setting up a permanent stall in the artisan market in Cochabamba, establishing a store in Australia, where one of her sons is currently working for an Ecuadorian client, and perhaps arranging for another outlet in the United States. Values, attitudes, and aspirations, then, are in no way lacking in this sample of women in small-scale enterprises.

The status-attainment model also attributes female labor-force participation to factors such as education, marital status, motherhood, and work experience. In Bolivia, it is true that in the past, and even to some extent today, women enjoy less formal education and fewer opportunities for apprenticeships. The 1976 census of the city of La Paz illustrates major discrepancies in the education of men and women. Out of 227,790 men between the ages of 10 and 70, 10,658, or 4 percent, were illiterate as against 52,057, or 21 percent, of the 245,560 women in the same age range (Republica de Boliva 1976:208-10).[2] School-attendance figures corroborate this discrepancy. Between the ages of five and forty and above, 40 percent of the men but only 31 percent of the women attend school. Moreover, the percentage of women drops sharply after the age of twelve. More women were monolingual Aymara or Quechua and bilingual than men, while more men were monolingual

Spanish speakers (Republica de Bolivia 1976:211-29 252-53).[3] Less schooling and inability to speak Spanish would be disadvantages for certain jobs but, as in the case of Dona Flora, need not be insuperable hindrances. The fact that a few women are able to overcome these disadvantages, however, is not to underestimate them. Rather, we must probe the reasons for these discrepancies.

The field observations corroborated the general statistics. Girls were and still are taken out of school early to help at home. Both mothers and fathers support the education of their children of both sexes. They decry their own deficiencies in this regard. But at the same time, they depend more heavily on their school-age daughters and other female relatives for domestic and other work.

Thus Juana, a migrant from the altiplano, who puts in sixteen-hour days in housework and *pollera*, or skirt making, points with considerable pride to the skills of her ten-year-old daughter, who can manage to clean, launder, market, cook, and care for her two younger siblings, unassisted if necessary. Juana's husband, a factory worker, puts in forty-eight hours a week and walks another six hours a week to get to his job, because of the lack of public transportation. Although he does not even "help" with the housework, he can be relied on to watch the children occasionally and to lend a hand in cutting and sewing the *polleras*.

In a similar fashion, Virginia (introduced earlier), who at twenty-three established a jewelry business with the financial aid of her mother-in-law (a jeweler too), works eight hours a day making, repairing, and selling jewelry and at least five hours in domestic duties. The care of her three children under five is primarily in the hands of her twelve-year-old sister-in-law, with the occasional assistance of her husband, a medical student who is at home, unable to complete his studies because of the forced closing of the university by the military government.[4]

This use of child labor, especially female child labor, must be seen in the context of the rising standards of housekeeping, food preparation and childcare. Domestic work in Bolivia has become even more arduous and time-consuming than before, especially since there are very few, if any, reasonably priced conveniences, appliances or services available. For parents who work in factories the hours are long and transportation inadequate, or very time consuming. As in the second case, interrupted careers prevent the employment of household help. Childcare facilities are scarce and expensive. Mandatory school attendance thus puts increased pressure on parents, especially on mothers who are thus deprived of their main labor resources, their children. We found that in general they supported education, and sent children of both sexes to school as long as pos- sible, at the cost of being doubly and triply burdened. When choices had to be made, parents and schools discriminated in favor of boys.

Supervised formal training and apprenticeships in skilled trades like construction, mechanics, draftsmanship, etc., are open primarily to young men. FOMO (Fomento De Mano de Obra), an organization supported by the Bolivian government, private industry, and the World Bank, offers technical training mostly to men, with the sole exception of a few women in agriculture in Santa Cruz.

Women tend to learn their crafts informally from relatives or neighbors. In the few instances where private, church, or international agencies offered training in artisanry, women were eager to attend. For example, CESEP (Centro Socio-economico de Estudio y Promociones), a private agency founded and directed by a woman lawyer with governmental and international experience, offered courses in weaving, jewelry making, and wood working, funded by the Central Bank. The courses include technical, artistic, financial, and organizational aspects of these industries and are open to only a handful of both women and men. However, in the sessions observed, women attended only wood working and textile courses, but not jewelry making. Such individual improvement programs and training sessions certainly provide useful services but, as Nieva and Gutek (1981:121) suggest, they may also prevent the examination and challenge or change of the status quo. In Bolivia, equalizing educational opportunities is very necessary but would require the restructuring of the economy dependent on female child, adolescent, and adult labor in the home. My research also suggests that entry into this sector requires social contacts in addition to technical education and skills.

Inadequate work experience has also been cited as a major influence in female labor-force participation. I found, however, that the Bolivian women studied bring to their productive activities a very broad range of past work experience and skills. They enter petty-commodity production from a variety of past experiences in farming, dairying, domestic service, marketing or trading, and factory and office work. They move between different kinds of work and tend to them simultaneously. Many combine production with supervision, food service, and sales, both in the market and in stores.

Saturnina, an older widow with five children, four of whom are adopted, illustrates the multifaceted nature of work experience and skills particularly well. The urban-born daughter of a mechanic and housewife, she began working as a domestic for a European family. At one time, she owned a store. Today, she runs her own bakery, where she adapts European recipes. Pastry making is her "passion." But, with the aid of her children, she also cooks lunch for the laborers in the sawmill next door, caters parties, sells ice cream from her rented freezer, and occasionally machine-knits sweaters, in addition to aiding her siblings in dressmaking and tailoring. One son is studying to be a doctor. A daughter works as a teacher. Both were helping the mother since their careers were interrupted by the political turmoil. Saturnina had the option of using her broad background to work for a large factory but chose not to abandon her enterprises. Like others in our study, she preferred "independent" work.

It remains for me to ask whether parental origins (the influence of father's and then mothers' occupations), individual mobility, marital status, and motherhood measurably affect the labor-force participation of our informants. As elsewhere, most of the literature on Bolivia refers to the social mobility of males with reference to their fathers (Kelley, Klein, and Robinson 1977). The persons involved in these firms come from families with long histories in particular artisanry and manufacturing and from families engaged in a wide range of different activities, one of which led to the present enterprise. Individual careers do not follow simple trajectories from unskilled worker, farmer, or domestic to professional (Buechler and Buechler 1982a). The more successful of these firms were headed by men from middle-class backgrounds who had had experience in civil service or the professions, European and Latin American migrants, and widowed women from a wide range of backgrounds, who continued the firms established in association with their husbands.

In Bolivia, marital status does not affect the percentage of women defined as economically active. According to national statistics, about 30 percent of all women--single, married, living in consensual unions, widowed, and divorced--work (Republica de Bolivia 1976:203-56). Since these statistics include only women working for regular wages, we would expect the true percentage to be higher. In my sample only a very small percentage of wives did not work in nondomestic labor. Upon marriage, both women and men often changed their activities, entering the enterprise that seemed to provide greater opportunities.

Motherhood is also no impediment to work.[5] Home and workplace are often one and the same place, so child care can be adjusted to work schedules and vice versa. Furthermore, infant and child care is often in the hands of a number of related persons in three generations, in addition to the mother. It is also facilitated by the fact that preschool children are commonly taken along to places of work, markets, workshops, or stores.

The Bolivian material, then, belies many aspects of the status-attainment model, particularly its stress on values, work experience, and marriage and motherhood. It is particularly inappropriate because it neglects the wider economic, social, and political context.

THE DUAL MARKET MODEL

Applying the dual-market model of economists or the structural model of psychologists (Sokoloff 1980; Blau and Jusenius 1976; Nieva and Gutek 1981) leads away from "blaming the victim" to other foci. The model maintains that there is a primary or core market for men providing stable employment, a career ladder, and on-the-job training and another, secondary or peripheral one, for women characterized by temporary work, low wages, high turnover, little possibility for advancement, and few means for union or other control. The socialization of women becomes, then, an adjustment to the structure of the labor market.

Such a model is difficult to apply to Bolivia since the "modern" core market is small and the numbers involved in petty-commodity production uncertain. Within this sector, however, women do tend to be clustered in piecework and putting out systems. But for the self-employed, wages compare favorably with other sectors, and the benefits of working at home are manifold. Further, the control they have over their work is no more curtailed than in the core market.

A very small percentage of the total labor force, 20 percent at most, enjoy the benefits described for the primary market. In professions and more highly mechanized, capitalized firms with more stable employment, better pay, and benefits, men predominate. The number of percentage of women and men involved in small-scale enterprises is difficult to ascertain exactly. I arrived at a number of approximations based on census figures, municipal tax records, earlier surveys, and registration figures in the *Instituto Boliviano de Pequenas Industrias y Artesanias* (the Bolivian Institute for Small Scale Industries and Artisans). One approximation would be that in 1976, out of a total population of 635,283, of whom 221,685 were economically active, 72,525 men and 6,818 women, or 35 percent, were engaged in small-scale industries. So a large percentage of all workers is involved in small-scale production. The percentage of women is probably underestimated.

In both areas, women are often subcontracted, temporarily, in a variety of piecework and putting-out systems. One modern, highly capitalized and mechanized coffee-exporting firm relied on this form of labor. Managed by a male owner and his son-in-law, this firm employs four salaried males, but it maintains its competitive edge not because of the newly imported machinery, but because of the fifty neighborhood women who are hired seasonally to select the coffee beans. It appears that even the most sophisticated electronic selectors are inferior to culling by eye and hand. The owner claims that such piecework "suits" the women because it allows them to comply with their familial chores and because they can also continue to trade in the market. Similarly, a modern shirt factory relies on a few permanently employed men and female piecework during periods of high demand. The women, after all, do not have to be paid social benefits and can be released at will.

Conditions in small-scale enterprises may not be better for some women, the younger, poorer relatives who work at piecework. One such family firm specializes in minutely detailed Bolivian miniature hat reproductions representing models of each fiesta dance group, all major cities, departments, and provinces.

This large assortment of miniature "collector" hats is exhibited and sold in the artisan's market in La Paz and the Alasitas fair in the capital, as well as in Cochabamba, Tarija, Santa Cruz, Sucre, and Potosi. Senor Camba recently also visited Los Angeles, accompanied by 14 other artisans, to attend an international craft fair. Although wife and husband are engaged in most of the intricate, time-consuming tasks of designing, cutting, shaping, sewing, and decorating the models, they are aided at night by their daughter, who works in a factory, and two of the wife's sisters, who make tassels and embroider at a piece rate. Yet another relative, a niece, sells their wares in the market. Thus for women work in a modern factory may not be any different than in a traditional firm. It is the placc within the firm and the relations of production that are essential.

Unlike the wages for persons who work on a temporary basis in piecework or in putting-out systems, earnings in petty-commodity production for the self-employed compare favorably with wage work in larger factories and some white-collar work. They are often much higher than in domestic service. But then Bolivian wages in all sectors are low, the workweek long, and benefits poor. Self-employed women and those who do piecework and other subsidiary tasks (cooking, trading, taking in boarders, etc.) in addition to their regular work cite independence, flexibility, and working at home as added benefits. Women are also *not* eager to work for wages in factories because their location is often at some distance, requiring long journeys by bus and on foot, poor and dangerous conditions, and long, defined shifts.

As Hartmann and Markusen (1980) aptly write, "a deeper understanding of women's roles in the labor force goes beyond a 'reserve army' argument to explore real constraints on women's labor time outside the home and an accompanying ideolgy that prescribes women's work, both of which are aspects of male domination" (89). The intermittent participation of women in wage work, in addition to self-employment and other "extraneous occupations," allow Bolivian women to "mesh" infant care and domestic labor with their other duties. It is similar to the arrangements described by Sen for the division of labor in early capitalist industrialization elsewhere (1980). In Bolivia, then, core and peripheral markets overlap in terms of work relations, wages, and conditions, with the latter having benefits for women that should not be overlooked.

Similarly, since during the military regimes union activities were severely curtailed and/or abolished for all sectors and are only now beginning to be reestablished,[6] women in petty commodity production sought, in a number of ways, to control the conditions of their work. They joined associations or clubs for women, organized by the Roman Catholic Church and International Agencies. They organized craft cooperatives, and supported private and government institutions established to provide technical assistance, education, and credit facilities, and also supported exhibits and fairs that sought to promote small-scale industries and artisanry. Of the first variety were mothers' clubs, supported by United Nations funds, organized as barrio-based artisan weaving and knitting cooperatives with an average of thirty-eight members. Financed by the sale of UN-donated staples to neighborhood families, clubs invest their capital in wool bought at wholesale prices and sold directly to the members, who then knit and weave sweaters, scarves, ponchos, and shawls for sale. The members learn the technical and financial aspects of weaving and also exhibit their wares. Perhaps the most important lesson learnt, according to the technician in charge, is the 'value of women's work." The class base for these clubs was broad but separate from the ones on the Alto, the new working-class neighborhood on the fringe of the city, involving primarily newly arrived migrant women and those in Sopocachi, a more central residential district associated with more middle-class members.

Groups of fifty weavers or so are in various stages of creating legal cooperatives in working-class neighborhoods in the Alto La Paz and Villa Ballivian. One such group, composed of women and men most of whom have migrated from an altiplano community with a long tradition of weaving, are trying to form a purchasing and sales cooperative in order to circumvent middlemen.

There are also loose associations of female artisans who try to purchase raw materials, accumulate merchandise, and arrange for commercialization of goods to competing exporters. Some of these were originally formed by missionaries, exporters, and other entrepreneurs to meet the growing demand for tourist goods, both locally and abroad. They range from simple bazaars and workshops to elaborately designed offices that cater to the cheap wholesale trade.

Female artisans are also trying to put some pressure on various governmental and private agencies to protect their working conditions and to further their cause. A female jeweler is in charge of the section devoted to artisanry at a city museum. She is very active in organizing courses and exhibits and in procuring mayoral support for credit. She is also working with a group of artisans who hope to buy a centrally located building that would serve as a permanent sales and exhibit hall. The artisan fairs in neighborhood parks and in the museum are also under her jurisdiction.

So far, they have been less effective in putting pressure on the governmental agency INBOPIA, which channels foreign contracts to this sector. They complain of the mismanagement of funds and contracts and delays in payment. The eagerly awaited producers' fair that was supposed to be sponsored by this institute never materialized, in part because of the political turmoil occasioned by the frequent coups, or attempted coups, during our research.

A series of problems plague these organizations. The production and marketing cooperatives suffer from ineffective organization, distrust and competition among members, poor quality control, and inadequate credit and marketing. However, the major problem is that different branches of federal, state, municipal, and private institutions vie with one another for the revenue from this sector, attempting to monopolize the raw materials, labor, and sales. Further, the size of the work force and the dispersion and location of workplaces hinders effective political action, even if legal restrictions were lifted.

Social historians, describing some women's trades in the transition to capitalism in Europe and America, suggest that these were more difficult to organize into strong guilds because they could not be easily monopolized. "All women as part of their home duties knew the arts of textile manufacturing, sewing, food processing and to some extent trading" (Hartmann 1976:151). In our opinion, this may be true for Bolivian women's trades, but the advent of military governments is certainly more significant. Also, at a time when all-male union activity was severely curtailed, these women met and tried to organize the "unorganized." Their limited success must be attributed to political conditions in general, the rise of the paramilitary, the curfew, and the general disorganization of governmental bureaucracy.

Thus, the major features of the core and peripheral labor markets cannot be distinguished with ease. The separation of the two, as posited by the dual-market model, is warranted neither in theory nor in practice. Sokoloff has argued cogently for the interdependence of these spheres (1980). In another paper we have argued against the separation of petty commodity production from capitalist production in Bolivia and for a model that includes the two-way flow of personnel, capital, and skills (Buechler and Buechler 1982b). One or more of the owner-operators of these firms often worked for more highly capitalized firms in the modern sector prior to establishing the "traditional" firm. Start-up capital and equipment may also derive from prior employment in larger concerns. But as we have seen, the articulation of the two modes of production is particularly evident in the relations of production. Putting out is commonplace in the clothing, furniture, and shoe industries of all sizes, as well as in tourist manufactures. In addition, employees in factories and larger firms work in family firms at night and in their spare time. Furthermore, modern and traditional firms use a wide variety of commercial outlets.

Separating the core from the peripheral labor market also obscures the extent to which men and the larger-scale international capitalist firms supported by the Bolivian government and by international financiers and agencies, benefit from women's work. These issues are addressed more fully by Marxist and Marxist feminist analyses.

MARXIST AND MARXIST FEMINIST ANALYSES

Marxist analysts accept the premises of the dual-market system but claim that it is only one of several ways in which women are oppressed under capitalism. They try to demonstrate the manner that capitalism divides working-class women from men. And they claim that women's labor in the home, domestic labor (whether defined as productive or not) serves to reproduce and maintain the labor force (Dalla Costa and James 1972). This interpretation shows the extent to which female labor helps to maintain low wages and high profits by "providing free or cheap cost of the reproduction of the labor force for the capitalist and by expanding goods and services during crises. Women's super exploitation as wage workers is also sustained by capitalism" (Holstrom 1981).[7]

According to Holstrom, the family benefits capitalism in manifold ways: the family is used as an ideological justification for discrimination in the work force; the family hides the unemployment and underemployment of half the population; and the family limits women's equal participation in the work force in both objective and psychological ways, including the formation of personality structures appropriate to "male" and "female" jobs (1981:197).

The Bolivian data demonstrate the ways in which female work and the family benefit capitalism both directly and indirectly. Firms can continue to pay both women and men low wages, maintain long hours, and offer poor working conditions since they are assured a captive male and female work force with few sources of alternative employment and/or governmental subsidies. The following example may serve to illuminate the complex issues involved. Senora Patricia lost two good executive secretarial jobs: one when the medical supply importers went bankrupt, and the other at a university that closed during the various periods of political strife. Then she decided to establish a printing firm for cards, letterheads, and calendars. Her husband works as a skilled supervisor and mechanic for a large printing press during the day and exchanges his expertise in repairing machinery for the use of a photocopier for their own firm. They bought a used printing press with a U.S. dollar loan at an interest rate of 5 percent *per month*. They are also dependent on a private semimonopoly for imported paper that is constantly going up in price.

In addition to providing "free domestic services" (cooking, cleaning, and the care of two children), Senora Patricia solicits clients in the neighborhood and from offices, banks, and associations, as well as from among acquaintances, and she designs, prints, loads, and delivers the stationery. In a good month, with many subcontracts from larger firms and orders from private individuals, she can earn as much as U.S.$240. But in a poor month, her earnings may fall as low as U.S.$6. Not only does demand vary, but payments are often delayed for as much as six months, especially for government contracts.

To understand this woman's work, family resources in terms of labor and capital need to be explored. Patricia's husband earns U.S.$250 a month as a printer on a large printing press and helps her at night and during the weekend. They live in two rooms in her parents' home "practically rent free." Her father is an inspector for Bolivian Power, in a grueling twelve-hour day job checking meters. Her father doesn't help her with her printing since he is exhausted when he comes home at night, but he does solicit clients. Her mother rents out a room as storage space for electric stoves. She also works at home, cares for her grandchildren, and assists in loading and delivering the heavy stacks of printed materials to their destination.

This example shows very clearly how the family, by pooling its resources, provided a cheap source of shelter and maintenance, expanded its services to cover the unemployment of the wife and the husband, and made it possible to live on low wages. By filling subcontracts, this small firm also serves as a crisis buffer for larger firms at the same time that it suffers from an inability to obtain reasonable credit, inflationary prices for its raw materials, and long bureaucratic delays in payments.

The pooling of resources among family members benefits capitalism, but also women. In this we follow Sen in her insistence that "women also, like men, benefit from resource pooling that goes on in working-class households and from the support and solidarity provided by kin networks" (1980:79). Similar, too, is our acknowledgment that these benefits should not be romanticized. They should be viewed in relation to their subordination within these selfsame families.

RADICAL MARXIST FEMINISTS

Does Western patriarchal capitalism benefit primarily men as the more radical Marxist feminists like Hartmann and Markusen (1976, 1980) claim? Do male workers play and "continue to play a crucial role in maintaining sexual divisions in the labor process" (Hartmann 1976:139)? Hartmann chides Engels, Zaretsky, and Dalla Costa, among others, for failing to analyze the labor process within the family sufficiently, particularly men's control over women's labor power, i.e., the material bases of patriarchy, the mechanisms that support the hierarchy and solidarity among men (1981). Hierarchical relations within the family further female dependence. "Hierarchy within the family is not based on the amount of work done or on productivity, but on the nature of one's claim on means of subsistence. . . . To ignore the fact that the basis of hierarchy is *dependence* and not the amount of work done, is to leave unused one of the most crucial insights of the analysis of class relations. Such an omission conceals the basis of women's oppression within working class families" (Sen 1980:78). Wages and money income develop as the main claim on subsistence.

It is *not* difficult to find support for the erosion of a traditionally more egalitarian division of labor within the family in the Andes (Bourque and Warren 1981; Buechler 1976a, 1976b). Since the conquest, both the Spanish and other neocolonialists (European and North American missionaries, both Roman Catholic and Protestant, development projects, etc.) have attempted to impose sex role models on Aymara women, who have not always been subject, dependent, or oppressed persons without resources or decision-making powers. Today, in this sector, they enjoy less control over resources than one might wish.

In my study I encountered numerous cases where both employed and self-employed males neglected their basic obligations to provide food, shelter, and school fees to wives and children, as well as other kin. They squandered hard-earned cash, earned by both, in drinking bouts with male cronies and left the supervision of enterprises, even in "male trades" like mechanic workshops and carpentry, in the hands of their wives and mothers.

Fiscal neglect and irresponsibility is sometimes compounded by physical abuse and/or abandonment, or the threat of abandonment. For example, the wife of one of the most successful migrants from a Lake Titicaca community, who established a flourishing aluminum factory in the Alto, is regularly beaten by her husband. Similarly, Inez, a handsome young woman from the same community, was beaten by her father when at sixteen she did not wish to accept her husband's proposal of marriage. She is now living in one room with her husband and five children, sewing skirts to feed them because her mechanic husband wastes his money on alcohol and beats her in his frequent drunken bouts of groundless jealousy. In another case, a woman with two young children was abandoned by her husband, who took up with another woman, who now has borne him two more children. His legal wife manages to keep afloat by selling potatoes in the market and by making palm-frond ornaments for Palm Sunday. She also occasionally fills a commission for a new skirt, but no one has money for new clothes these days. She is fortunate that she inherited a large compound in La Paz and has a few extra rooms to let.

It would, however, be misleading if one analyzed the subordination and dependence of women in the Bolivian families engaged in petty-commodity production from the perspective of marital relationships alone. The women described above are also daughters, sisters, and mothers. Thus Inez, who suffered at the hands of her father and her husband, enjoys the warm support of her godfather, brother, and oldest son. Her godfather wishes her to leave her husband and come to run a hotel in the Yungas, the semi-tropical valleys south of La Paz. She subcontracts work to her teenage brother so that he can earn a bit of money and he, in turn, helps her when she is overwhelmed with work. Her oldest son is also very close to his mother and tries to protect her from the father's physical abuse. Thus Inez's subordination and dependence on her husband is tempered by other male relationships that are warm, understanding, and supportive.

The economic dependence of wives on their husbands, and women on men generally, is also moderated by the fact that they may control their own earnings and inheritance. This is nothing new sin traditionally, women were supposed to handle money and, in many rural communities, inheritance of land and other valuables was supposed to be divided in an egalitarian fashion. Women engaged in marketing and trade, both in rural areas and in the city, enjoyed greater economic independence as well (Buechler 1976a, 1976b, 1978). In general, the women studied tried to control at least some income (even if that income was seen as peripheral and meager), gained in activities from catering food for apprentices and renting rooms to boarders to selling "occasionally" on the market.

The economic control of men over women lessens, to some extent, with time. Older widowed women continue to run businesses and enjoy considerable economic influence and security. Contrary to appearances, they often still claim that the accounts and financial arrangements are in the hands of their sons (who work in different professions). Nonethless, they seem perfectly aware of every aspect of the management and work process of the enterprise. When asked whether people took advantage of widows, one, Senora Elvira, who ran a family furniture factory, quickly denied any such suggestion: "It depends on your character. I don't let anyone get the better of me."

The women studied also have access to the support of an extended family and through *compadrazgo*, fictive kin who mediate disputes and may offer support in the form of housing, food, investment capital, and labor. It gives some of them the option of not marrying at all, or entering into consensual unions. As Sen has written, "the claim that the working class family has beneficial aspects for women does not contradict the view that women are indeed subordinate to men within the same family. What is contradictory is not the analysis but rather the position of women" (1980:85).

We need, then, to focus on the different relationships within the family over time, evaluating the positive ones without losing sight of the conflictful ones. In the Bolivian case, the family sustains a mutually inconsistent ideology of male superiority and female subordination at the same time that it provides the major source of social, economic, and psychological support for all members.

DIALECTICS, OR THE DOUBLE VISION

The understanding of social change in the position of women in the West and social feminist and Marxist social theories has led Joan Kelly to write:

> In thought and practice, neat distinctions we once made between sex and class, family and society, reproduction and production, even between women and men seem not to fit the social reality with which we are coping. . . . Experiences such as these increasingly make us aware that women's place

> is not a separate sphere or domain of existence but a position within social existence generally. It is a subordinate position, and it supports our social institutions at the same time that it serves and services men. Woman's place is to do women's work--at home and in the labor force. And it is to experience sex hierarchy in work relations and personal ones, in our public and private lives. Hence our analyses, regardless of the tradition they originate in, increasingly treat the family in relation to society; treat sexual and reproductive experience in terms of political economy; and treat productive relations of class in connection with sex hierarchy (1979:220, 221).

Similarly, Sokoloff concludes that it is "essential that one understands how the home and market continually interreact within the context of the dynamic relationship between patriarchy and capitalism" (1980:203). This is as true in an underdeveloped country such as Bolivia, as it is in core industrial countries.

THE POLITICAL ECONOMY OF WOMAN'S WORK IN BOLIVIA

In the case under examination, woman's place is to do women's work in the home, which is often also her place of work. Our informants themselves contextualize their concerns. They relate their personal woes, the difficulties of establishing and operating small-scale industries, to the political-economic turmoil that besets La Paz and Bolivia. For our present purpose, to understand the role of woman in the total labor power of the household in petty-commodity production, we need to see the historical process or conditions that impede the producer's access to just three central aspects of production: raw materials, capital, and markets.

Persistent shortages of both nationally produced and imported raw materials plague small-scale production. The supply of such raw materials as wool, leather, or wood is curtailed by poor and costly communication and transportation and by government monopolies. In the case of alpaca wool, the government monopolizes the machine spinning of wool in a factory financed by international capital. The monopoly sets limits on quantity and price. To gain access, members of families in small-scale industries who have migrated from herding communities try to collect wool or establish contacts with traders from those communities and from others who sell in adjacent locations at the large fair on the Alto and then put the raw wool out for poor female migrants to spin by hand.

Access to leather and high-grade wood for furniture is also scarce, for the government monopolizes the trade in semiprocessed hides and fine woods, leaving only poor and expensive materials for local production. Access to imported raw materials is hindered by difficulties of communication and transportation, exacerbated by shortages of foreign exchange and complicated banking regulations. Foreign exchange shortages became particularly acute during our stay due to Bolivia's default on its massive foreign debt.

The supply of capital and credit for other purposes was limited.[8] Start-up capital is often based on personal savings from wages or severance pay from another firm, and loans from kin and friends.

Since the class background of these family firms is varied, private sources of capital are often available. Similarly, one's ability to save is an expression of household resource pooling and multiple sources of income. One family firm regularly used capital gained from the proceeds of a business to invest in materials for an enterprise involving the seasonal manufacture of women's shoes for fiestas, which peaked in July and August.

Loans and credit from national and international banks are biased toward large-scale production. Funds are also earmarked for those smaller-scale producers who can provide real estate collateral, demonstrate cash flow through a bank account, and enjoy contacts based on social class. Such loans entail long delays. Some private and public agencies are attempting to provide the information and mediation necessary for credit. But government enterprises and those that supply the government seem particularly privileged. Money that is available is at high interest for short terms.

The supply and use of capital is also influenced adversely by persistent inflation and periodic devaluations. Since the profit margin is often small, the producers can rarely buy sufficient stock as a hedge against inflation. This is particularly true for imported goods, which are, of course, also subject to higher prices due to periodic devaluations.[9] When surplus cash is available, it is usually converted immediately into tangible--physical or social--assets: real estate, machinery and tools or stock, or a family or community fiesta.

The tax levy on smaller enterprises is complicated but relatively low. Compliance, however, entails an inordinate amount of time and energy devoted to paying numerous levies in multiple locations to competing agencies at regular and irregular intervals. Thus the complicatons involved, rather than the amount, seem to prevent adherence to law. The onerous dealing with the intricacies of governmental bureaucracies is considered a male job since it requires facility in Spanish, education, and prior expierence with formal legal entities. It also requires contact and communication with a predominantly male population. Women attend to these affairs reluctantly but they tend to rely on male relatives, if possible. In sum, access to raw materials, capital, and credit for small-scale producers is imbedded in social, class, and political constraints.

The linkage of women's roles in family and work to the political economy of markets for the goods produced by these industries also warrants our attention. Establishing commercial outlets is affected by competition from state enterprises, the proliferation of small firms, the penetration of foreign wares through contraband, and the establishment of rural enterprises by non-Bolivians (Buechler and Buechler 1982). As we have seen, women have tried to form associations and cooperatives to seek further outlets, and they participate in local and international fairs. They find, however, that the local market is overcrowded and the international one demanding in terms of low price and high volume. So they seek to find specialized niches in the local artisan markets in Bolivian cities and personal contacts with particular foreign and native exporters.

Thus Dona Flora, the textile entrepreneur we introduced earlier, sells in the local market herself, caters to a few importers from Germany and Australia by inviting them to family feasts, and seeks to establish further outlets by encouraging her brother to set up a stall in Cochabamba and her son to establish a store in Australia. She also encourages her daughter to attend the section on artisanry at a municipal museum. And lastly, she has traveled to trade fairs in neighboring countries, accompanied by her son-in-law. When lamenting the decline in sales, she relates the demise of consumer demand at home to inflation, the competition from cheap, partially synthetic contraband from Peru, and the decline in tourism associated with the recent series of governmental coups. This political instability has also affected importers who, fearing delays or noncompliance of contracts in Bolivia, seek sources in neighboring Andean countries. They, too, seem as fickle as tourists but, just like tourists, return relatively rapidly when economic and political conditions readjust.

It is no wonder then that women working in petty-commodity production do not place their concerns or organize their protests in feminist or class terms *per se*. In the context of Bolivia in the 1980s, they express the hope for a better life for their children and their families in a more stable Bolivia or elsewhere.

To conclude, case materials of work and life histories of Bolivian women in petty-commodity production have served as a way to evaluate current models for women's labor-force participation that derive mainly from the experience of women in highly industrialized North American and European settings. We have attempted to assess these in terms of the subjective experience of particular women. We then placed and interpreted their accounts and observed behaviors within the framework of individual situations, familial and work structures, and the conditions of the political economy. This unified approach allows us to appreciate the complex nature of the role of women in small-scale production in one urban area within a less developed country and adds to the growing literature on the conditions of female labor-force participation under industrialization and capitalism.

NOTES

I acknowledge the financial assistance of the National Science Foundation (BNS 80-24513) that made possible the research in La Paz in 1981 for the data presented in this chapter and the sabbatical leave from Hobart and William Smith Colleges.

[1] In 1980, 50 percent of the La Paz population and 60 percent of the economically active population were migrants. They represented 56.9 percent of the persons engaged in industry (Pabon and Maletta 1980).

[2] For the nation as a whole 48 percent of the women and 29 percent of the men are classified as illiterate (Gonzalez 1979:180).

[3] The 1976 census illustrates the major discrepancy in literacy in the department of La Paz. Out of a total of 510,175 males between the ages of 10 and 70 and censused 78,785 or 15 percent were illiterate, whereas for women of the same age range the percentage was 38 percent of 213,997 out of a total of 538,307 (Republica de Bolivia 1976 Census, pp. 41-42). However, for both sexes the percentage of literacy shows considerable improvement in the last sixty years. A similar difference shows up in school attendance with 34.3 percent of all males five through forty and above in school in contrast to 24.7 percent of the females, with the difference becoming more marked after the age of eleven. The percentage of women who speak only Aymara is almost three times that of males (Republica de Bolivia 1976:43-61).

[4] The universities were closed for nine months following the Mesa coup. "On August 18, 1980 the universities were formally suspended for complete reorganization. . . . The majority of their staff were purged and replaced. . . . The impact was felt at all levels of the middle class for many students were expelled under the new statutes that replaced the universities' traditional autonomous status, placed them under the direct control of military appointees, led to massive increases in fees and dismantled many areas of the curriculum, particularly in the humanities: (Dunkerley 1982:42, 21).

[5] Valerie Estes found that preliminary data showed that women working in a factory in La Paz, regardless of their marital status, were all financially and socially responsible for children (1982:20).

[6] In 1980 all labor rights were suppressed and all independent labor unions, except for those in transportation, were outlawed. Government-appointed representatives were to take the role of syndicate leaders (Dunkerley 1982:19).

[7] For an excellent understanding of the method and theory necessary to analyze the family in the transition to capitalism in Europe, c.f. Vogel 1978.

[8] An excellent analysis of the bias of international finance and credit with respect to the underdevelopment of Bolivian industrialization is offered by Eckstein (1983).

[9] On 30 November 1979, the peso was devalued 25 percent. On 5 February 1982, the peso was furthered devalued by 76 percent (Dunkerley 1982:41, 48).

REFERENCES

Beneria, Lourdes and Gita Sen. 1981. "Accumulation, Reproduction, and Women's Role in Economic Development: Boserup Revisited." Signs 7(2):279-99.

Blaxall, Martha and Barbara Reagan. 1976. Women and the Workplace. Chicago: University of Chicago Press.

Blau, Francine and Carol Jusenius. 1976. "Economists' Approaches to Sex Segregation in the Labor Market: An Appraisal." In Women and the Workplace. Martha Blaxall and Barbara Reagan, eds., pp. 181-201. Chicago: University of Chicago Press.

Bourque, Susan and Kay Warren. 1981. Women of the Andes. Ann Arbor: The University of Michigan Press.

Bromley, Ray and Chris Gerry, eds. 1979. Casual Work and Poverty in Third World Cities. New York: Wiley and Sons.

Buechler, Judith-Maria. 1976a. "Negociantes Contratistas en los Mercados Bolivianos." Estudios Andinos V(1):57-77.

_____. 1976b. "Something Funny Happened on the Way to the Agora: A Comparison of Bolivian and Spanish Galician Migrants." Anthropological Quarterly 49(1):62-69.

_____. 1978. "The Dynamics of the Market in La Paz, Bolivia." Urban Anthropology 7(4):343-59.

Buechler, Judith-Maria and Hans C. Buechler. 1981. "Government Policies and Small Scale Firms." Paper delivered at the American Anthropological Association meeting, Cincinnati.

_____. 1982a. "Small Scale Production and Late Capitalism in La Paz, Bolivia." Paper delivered at the Interational Congress of Americanists: Manchester, England.

_____. 1982b. "Small Trades Do Better in Bolivia." The Geographical Magazine. Vol. LIV (9):518-20.

Dalla Costa, Mariarosa and Selma James. 1972. Women and the Subversion of the Community. Bristol: Falling Wall Press.

Dunkerley, James. 1982. "Bolivia 1980-1981: The Political System in Crisis." University of London Institute of Latin American Studies. Working Papers 8: London.

Eckstein, Susan. 1983. "Transformation of a 'Revolution from Below' -- Bolivia and International Capital." Comparative Studies in History and Society 25:105-35.

_____ and Frances Hagopian. 1983. "The Limits of Industrialization in the Less Developed World: Bolivia." Economic Devlopment and Cultural Change 32(1 Oct):63-95.

Eisenstein, Zellak, ed. 1979a. Capitalist Patriarchy and the Case for Socialist Feminism. New York: Monthly Review Press.

_____. 1979b. "Developing a Theory of Capitalist Patriarchy and Socialist Feminism." In Capitalist Patriarchy and the Case for Socialist Feminism. Zellak Eisenstein, ed. pp. 5-41.

Estes, Valerie. 1982. "Factories and Families: Urban Working Women in La Paz, Bolivia." Mimeo.

Ferber, Marianne. 1982. "Women and Work: Issues of the 1980s." Signs 8(2):273-94.

Goddard, Victoria. 1978. Domestic Industry in Naples. Critique of Anthropology. London: Wiley.

Gonzalez, Rene. 1979. Informativo Economico de Bolivia. La Paz: Los Amigos Del Libro.

Hareven, Tamara. 1982. Family Time and Industrial Time. Cambridge: Cambridge University Press.

Hartmann, Heidi. 1976. "Capitalism, Patriarchy and Job Segregation by Sex." Signs. (Spring, pt. 2):137-69.

_____. 1981. "The Unhappy Marriage of Marxism and Feminism:

Towards a more progressive union." In Women and Revolution. Lydia Sargent, ed. pp. 1-43. Boston: South End Press.

_____ and Ann Markusen. 1980. "Contemporary Marxist Theory and Practice: A Feminist Critique." The Review of Radical Political Economics 12:2:87-94.

Holstrom, Nancy. 1981. "'Womens Work,' The Family and Capitalism." Science and Society 45:186-211.

Kelley, Jonathan, Herbert Klein, and Robert Robinson. 1977. "Mobilidad Social en Bolivia Rural: Comparacion con los Estados Unidos." Estudios Andinos 13:183-93.

Kelly, Joan. 1979. "The Doubled Vision of Feminist Theory: A postscript to the Women and Power Conference." Feminist Studies 5(1):216-27.

Leacock, Eleanor. 1981. "History, Development, and the Division of Labor by Sex: Implications for Organization." Signs 7(1):474-92.

Nash, June. 1981. Review of N. Sokoloff. "Between Love and Money." Signs 7(2):492-99.

Nieva, Veronica and Barbara Gutek. 1981. Women and Work: A Psychological Perspective. New York: Praeger.

Pabon, Escobar and H. Maletta. 1980. "Poblacion, migraciones y empleo: resultados preliminares." La Paz: Mimeo.

Republica de Bolivia. 1976. Resultados del Censo National de Poblacion y Vivienda. Vol. 2.

Sargent, Lydia, ed. 1981. Women and Revolution. Boston: South End Press.

Scott, Alison MacEwen. 1979. "Who are the self employed? In Casual Work and Poverty in Third World Cities. Ray Bromley and Chris Gerry, eds. pp. 105-33. New York: Wiley and Sons.

_____. 1981. "Job Differentiation and Mobility Amongst Manual Workers in Lima, Peru." Report submitted to the World Bank. Mimeo.

_____. 1982. "Changes in the Structure of Child Labour Under Conditions of Dualistic Economic Growth." Development and Change 13(4):537-550.

Sen, Gita. 1980. "The Sexual Division of Labor and the Working-class Family: Towards a Conceptual Synthesis of Class Relations and the Subordination of Women." Review of Radical Political Economics 12(2):76-85.

Sokoloff, Natalie J. 1980. Between Money and Love: The Dialectics of Women's Home and Market Work. New York: Praeger.

Steel, William. 1981. "Female and Small Scale Employment Under Modernization in Ghana." Economic Development and Cultural Change. 30(1):153-67.

Vogel, Lise. 1978. "The Contested Domain: A Note on the Family in the Transition to Capitalism." Marxist Perspectives :50-73.

______. 1981. "Marxism and Feminism: Unhappy Marriage, Trial Separation or Something Else." In Women and Revolution. Lydia Sargent, ed. pp. 195-219. Boston: South End Press.

Young, Iris. 1981. "Beyond the Unhappy Marriage: A Critique of the Dual Systems Theory." In Women and Revolution. Lydia Sargent, ed. pp. 43-71. Boston: South End Press.

10 Rural Women and Agrarian Reform in Peru, Chile, and Cuba

Carmen Diana Deere

The participation of rural women in the Latin American agrarian reform process of the last two decades has had mixed results. In this comparative analysis of Latin American agrarian reforms it will be shown that the Peruvian and Chilean reforms failed to incorporate a significant number of rural women into the agrarian reform process. In contrast, the Cuban agrarian reform, particularly during the 1970s, was considerably more successful.

It was found that in the Peruvian and Chilean cases, the specific criteria used to define the agrarian reform beneficiaries was the singular most important factor in limiting rural women's participation within the process. In the Cuban case, not only were the criteria different, but the incorporation of rural women into the agrarian reform was an explicit goal of state policy.

The first section of this chapter briefly compares redistributionary impact on the three agrarian reforms. Then, since the Peruvian and Chilean reforms offer similar experiences with regard to rural women, these two reform processes are analyzed jointly. The beneficiary criteria are considered first, followed by the economic and social costs of excluding women from the agrarian reform. This section concludes with a discussion of the problems of ensuring women's effective participation within the new agrarian structures. In the subsequent section, the elements that contributed to a more positive experience for rural women in Cuba are analyzed. The concluding section summarizes the relevant policy considerations for incorporating rural women into processes of agrarian reform.

THE THREE CASES

The three agrarian reform experiences analyzed here cover the 1968 to 1978 period of military government in Peru, the years between 1965 and 1973 during the Frei and Allende administrations in Chile, and the post-1959 agrarian reform era in Cuba. Since there is a bevy of literature on each of these agrarian reforms, only the most relevant redistributive aspects of each will be reviewed.[1]

The redistributionary impact of an agrarian reform largely reflects the political project that the reform represents. That is, its specific class base and the agrarian classes which it is designed to benefit. In the first instance, the impact of an agrarian reform upon rural women depends upon the class position of each woman's household, and whether that class, or segment of class, is a beneficiary of the reform. Thus, we must first consider the breadth of each of the reforms in terms of which social groups were beneficiaries, and of the relative impact on rural households.

The Chilean and Peruvian agrarian reforms were designed to eliminate both the traditional hacienda and the very large, modern commercial farms. The primary beneficiaries of these reforms were meant to be those peasants that worked lands in precapitalist forms of tenancy, as well as the permanent wage labor force on the estates. At the time of these agrarian reforms in Chile and Peru only a small percentage of the rural population resided on the estates. The great majority of rural households were found on small holdings outside the domain of the estates, and hence were excluded from the reform process. Neither reform was successful in incorporating as beneficiaries the estates' seasonal agricultural labor force, who resided on these small holdings or were landless workers. As a result, neither reform had as broad a redistributionary impact as might have been possible.

In the Chilean case, 58,170 families, or 20 percent of the rural labor force, were incorporated into the reform sector between 1965 and 1973 (Cifuentes 1975). In the Peruvian case, taking the broadest definition of beneficiaries, some 359,600 families were benefitted, representing 37.4 percent of all Peruvian rural households (Caballero and Alvarex 1980).[2] While in neither case was the reform insignificant, neither did a majority of the rural population benefit from the reform. Consequently, most rural women were in households that were automatically excluded from the benefits of reform.

The Cuban agrarian reform process had a more significant redistributionary impact. Every tenant, sharecropper, and squatter was given ownership of the land they cultivated. In addition, the creation of a state agricultural sector, through the expropriation of all farms over 67 hectares in size, created permanent employment opportunities for the largest group of the agricultural work force, the landless proletarians. After the implementation of the 1973 agrarian reform law, 63 percent of Cuba's cultivable land was within the state sector, and 37 percent within the private sector (MacEwan 1981: ch. 6 and 8).[3] According to one estimate, approximately 70 percent of all rural households were benefited either through land transfers or access to increased employment opportunities created by the agrarian reform. Given its broader redistributionary impact, a significantly higher percentage of Cuban women lived in households which were positively effected by the agrarian reform as compared to the Peruvian or Chilean processes.

While in the first instance, the impact of an agrarian reform on rural women may be measured through the reform's redistributionary impact upon rural households, it cannot be assumed that this effect is gender neutral. An increase in the household's access to land or in its level of income is not necessarily equivalent to a positive change in a woman's socioeconomic position. Processes of social change have complex economic, political, and ideological impacts, all of which may have an impact upon rural women's position relative to men's.

A central thesis of this chapter is that designating households as beneficiaries of an agrarian reform process, and then incorporating only male heads of household into the new agrarian reform structures, has significant negative economic, political, and ideological effects upon the position of rural women. A necessary, but not sufficient condition, for rural women to be benefitted equal with men, is that they too must be designated as beneficiaries and be given the opportunity to participate within the new agrarian cooperatives or state farms promoted by an agrarian reform.

THE PERUVIAN AND CHILEAN AGRARIAN REFORMS

Underlying both the Peruvian and Chilean agrarian reforms was the assumption that the primary social unit to be benefitted was the rural household. But for purposes of implementation, only one member of the household was officially designated the beneficiary. Hence, only the head of the household had the right of membership in the production cooperatives or credit and service cooperatives which constituted the reformed sector.[4]

Official data on the distribution of beneficiaries according to sex is unavailable, since data collection on beneficiaries was based on the household as a unit. The available estimates suggest that the overwhelming majority of cooperative members resulting from these agrarian reforms were men. In a 1971 survey of eighty-three Peruvian cooperatives it was found that of 724 members interviewed, approximately 5 percent were women (Buchler 1975). As a national estimate even this figure may be high, for the survey excluded the coastal agro-industrial sugar cooperatives where membership was exclusively male. In a study of the northern cotton producing cooperatives in Piura, Fernandez (1982) found that women comprised only 2 percent of the membership. Similarly, this author found that in 1976, women made up only 2 percent of the cooperative membership in the department of Cajamarca. Peasant women's participation in the cooperatives was perhaps greater in the southern highland region of Peru. A case study of a Cuzco department cooperative reports that women initially represented 7 percent of the membership (Chambeu 1981). In the Chilean case, Garrett (1982) infers that, as in the Peruvian agrarian reform, the majority of beneficiaries were men.

The argument that will be developed here is that this sexual imbalance in the composition of the agrarian reform beneficiaries was the result of the criteria utilized to determine beneficiary status. Moreover, that it not only had significantly negative repercussions for rural women but for the ultimate success of the agrarian reforms.

The Beneficiary Criteria

According to Article 84 of the 1969 Peruvian Agrarian Reform Law, in order to be designated as a beneficiary of the agrarian reform, one must have met the following criteria.:

1. Be over 18 years of age.
2. Be the head of a household that includes dependents.
3. Be dedicated exclusively to agriculture.
4. Not own more land than the regionally defined family unit.
5. Have worked as a *feudatario* on an estate (i.e., have worked under precapitalist forms of tenancy on a hacienda).

The beneficiary criteria in the Chilean case under the Frei administration's agrarian reform were almost identical with the exception of the fifth point, because Chile had experienced a greater degree of capitalist development in agriculture. One other criterion was substituted in its place: to have an aptitude for agriculture (Garrett 1982).

The most discriminatory criterion in terms of rural women is that of designating only the head of household as the beneficiary. Due to social custom, if both an adult man and woman reside in the same household the man is automatically considered its head. As a result, the vast majority of women who might have otherwise qualified as beneficiaries, were automatically excluded from participating in the agrarian reform Generally, only men became members of the production cooperatives or *asentamientos*, and in the Peruvian case, only men received title to individual land parcels which were distributed.

In both the Peruvian and Chilean agrarian reforms, the primary beneficiaries were the permanent agricultural wage workers who were employed on the estates at the moment of expropriation. In both countries, the permanent agricultural wage workers were generally men, although women were often an important component of the seasonal agricultural labor force, particularly for cotton and rice cultivation. For example, in the Peruvian case, Fernandez (1982) shows that on the northern cotton plantations women represented up to 40 percent of the temporary labor, but few women held permanent jobs on the plantations, and as a result women constituted only 2 percent of the cooperative membership.

In the Chilean case, Garrett's (1976) analysis demonstrates how the modernization process of Chilean agriculture over the course of the twentieth century resulted in a sharp decrease in the number of permanent agricultural workers. But women were displaced disproportionately from the labor force of estates as compared to men when these estates became mechanized. As a result, the beneficiaries of the reform were overwhelmingly men (Garrett 1982).

The inability of these agrarian reforms to benefit all seasonal agricultural workers certainly was detrimental to both men and women. But whereas men were found in both categories of workers, permanent and seasonal, women composed only a part of the seasonal work force, and were thus excluded as a social group. In order to become cooperative members and thus potential beneficiaries of the reform, the few women that were permanent workers on the estates were subject to the requirement that they also be household heads. This, of course, reduced their participation still further.

The differential impact of the head of household criteria is clearly seen in the case of those agricultural enterprises where both men and women were employed on a permanent basis. For example in the dairy region of northern Peru women made up from 30 percent to 50 percent of the permanent workers on the dairy farms, since milking was still done by hand and was considered a female occupation in the region (Deere 1977). But of the fifteen cooperatives in the region, it was found that in only five were there female members, and overall, women constituted only two percent of the cooperative membership.

Interviews revealed that the women workers had been excluded as cooperative members for the following reasons:

1. When as a wife, she and her husband worked on the same farm and he had already been designated as a beneficiary.
2. For not being a head of household, even though her husband was not employed on the farm.
3. For being the daughter of a male wage worker on the farm who was a beneficiary, even though the woman was over eighteen and a single mother.
4. For not being a head of household, even though over eighteen and a single mother, because the woman lived with her parents, even though she and her father were not employed on the farm.
5. For not having children. Though some women who lived alone or with their elderly parents were considered households heads.

The Costs of Excluding Women

The question may arise as to how important it is that women as well as men be included among the beneficiaries of an agrarian reform. If the goal of an agrarian reform is to foster a process of social transformation, as was considered to be the case in both the Peruvian and Chilean reforms, then the exclusion of one social group on the basis of family position or sex certainly limits the breadth and depth of such a reform process.

Social equity criteria are particularly relevant in the cases where both men and women are permanent agricultural workers. If the goal of state policy in creating production cooperatives is to allow the participation of workers in the decisions concerning their labor and in the allocation of the surplus that they produce, the exclusion of one social group on the basis of sex and kinship, is at best, discriminatory. At worst, it creates conditions in the cooperative for the exploitation of one social group by another.

This is also the case in terms of the relationship between permanent workers (the cooperative members) and temporary workers. In the Peruvian reform process, few temporary workers were incorporated into the cooperatives; neither were they covered by social benefits, and their wages were usually lower than those of the cooperative members. Fernandez (1982) and Chambeu (1981) report that in the cases of the cooperatives in Pirua and Cuzco which they studied, the majority of temporary workers were female and earned wages lower than those of the male temporary workers. Moreover, women's wages relative to both male temporary workers and the cooperative members declined over the reform period. In the case of the Piura cotton cooperatives, work opportunities for women also declined over the reform period (Fernandez 1982). It could be concluded then that the welfare of women workers deteriorated due to the reform process.

It is also important to know that it cannot be assumed that by benefitting the male head of a household, all household members will be benefitted as well. As was mentioned previously, the household is not gender neutral. Nor are the effects of a process of state intervention. To the extent that an agrarian reform directs state efforts and resources to benefit one group of the population, through access to land, credit, technical assistance, and marketing channels, it is concentrating resources on one specific group within the population, creating serious socioeconomic consequences for those who are excluded.

In most highland areas of Peru, inheritance of land has been bilateral. Even when women are not the principal agriculturalists of the family unit, their access to land through inheritance has been important in assuring their participation in agricultural decision-making, household income allocation, and in giving women a modicum of material security. They have not been totally dependent on a man, and if abandoned or separated, owning land has been central to their ability to maintain their family as single women. Ownership of land by women has thus been linked both to family stability, and to women's status within the household and community.

Data for the province of Cajamarca illustrates the importance placed by women on owning land. In this area, many of the large estates were subdivided by the landlord class in the 1950s and 1960s when the estates were converted into modern enterprises (Deere 1977). Peasant households were given the opportunity of purchasing the more marginal portions of hacienda lands. Through an analysis of the property registers of the province, it was found that 40 percent of these land sales to the peasantry were made to households where the land was registered in the name of both husband and wife. In the remaining 60 percent of the cases, land was registered only in the name of one person, but just as many women as men purchased land in their own name. In this sense, the agrarian reform process represents a real setback for rural women. Since generally only male heads of household have been designated the beneficiaries, the land titles issued by the reform agency have been given only to men.

It also cannot be assumed that indirect participation in a reform process (through the head of household) is the equivalent of direct participation. The organization of credit and service cooperatives among male household heads may have important consequences for women's agricultural productivity. Introducing technical information exclusively to men will not necessarily result in women gaining access to the information or putting it into practice. If women, for example, are traditionally charged with seed selection in the peasant household, they will not necessarily accept the second-hand advice of men.

An example from the Cajamarcan dairy cooperatives illustrates how the exclusion of women from cooperative membership can have an injurious effect on their productivity as wage workers. In one of the recently constituted dairy cooperatives, the members of the new cooperative decided that it would be more convenient if the cows were milked in the fields rather than in the rudimentary stable near the cooperative office since much time was lost by the members in walking the cows to and from the stables. What the members did not take into account was that the milkmaids would have to spend at least an additional half hour walking to and from their homes to milk the cows twice a day. These additional two hours were not going to be remunerated; since the milkmaids were not cooperative members, they did not have the right to voice their complaints to the membership. They complained, of course, each to their respective husband or father who were cooperative members. But their complaints were not taken seriously.

The practice of milking in the fields eventually had grave consequences. It subjected the milkmaids to the rains, which occurred in the region for a period of four to six months out of the year. The conditions discouraged the women from taking care that no milk remained in the cow's udder. The cows began developing infections and productivity fell. Almost a full year passed before one of the technicians realized the source of the problem.

The Problem of Assuring Effective Participation

Structural or legal limitations were the most important factors preventing women's participation in the Peruvian and Chilean agrarian reforms. Nonetheless, cooperative membership constitutes only a necessary and not a sufficient condition to assure women's effective participation in the reformed sector. This is clearly seen in the Chilean case.

Upon taking office the Allende government broadened the criteria for defining beneficiaries of the agrarian reform, since redistribution of access to resources as well as the generation of increased employment opportunities in the countryside were explicit policy goals of the Popular Unity government. The imbalance between the situation of permanent and temporary workers on the *asentamientos* was seen to be particularly problematic, so the *asentamientos* were reorganized in order to facilitate the incorporation of temporary workers. In this broadening of the potential beneficiaries of the reform, the legal/structural impediments to women's participation within the new agrarian reform structures were eliminated (Garrett 1982): neither sex nor marital status could constitute criteria for membership, and all individuals over eighteen were eligible to become members of the general assembly of the new Centers of Agrarian Reform (CERAs). Garrett argues that theoretically the conditions were in place for women to be able to participate in the agrarian reform, due to the state policy seeking to broaden the definition of beneficiary. The CERAs were short-lived due to the coup against Allende in September of 1973, but the new agrarian reform structure proved of little success in terms of incorporating women.

Garrett points out that women's participation in the CERAs was resisted by both men and women. The opposition of men (both peasant men and the male technicians) was largely due to the lack of clarity within the Popular Unity government as to what the role of women should be within the agrarian reform. In other words, the absence of a state policy vis-a-vis women's participation in the agrarian reform, was a source of confusion and acted as a barrier to the effective incorporation of women.

Ideological reasons were the basis for women's resistance to participate in the CERAs. Garrett points to the conservative influence of the strongest women's organization in the countryside at the time, the *Centros de Madres* (mothers' centers), organized by the Christian Democratic party under the Frei administration. The focus of the *Centros de Madres* had been on the domestic role of women, so they gave little attention to women's role in work and production.

Moreover, they were not concerned with social problems since these were considered inappropriate matters for women. But they did provide rural women with a form of social participation which drew them out of their homes into a forum where they could discuss ordinary problems. At their height, the *Centros* had some 10,500 members in the countryside.

Under the agrarian reform of the Frei government social problems on the *asentamientos* were largely ignored. Garrett proposes that this was partly due to the fact that women were excluded from membership in the *asentamientos*. The members were so concerned with the technical problems of running the farms, that social services such as schools, housing, and health care suffered from lack of attention at membership meetings. The people who could have given attention to these problems, women, were structurally excluded from being able to consider their solutions. The *Centros de Madres* were apparently never integrated into the structure of the *asentamientos.* The Popular Unity government apparently recognized this as a problem and proposed to organize rural women into Social Welfare Committees linked to each CERA.

The Social Welfare Committees were intended to find collective solutions to social problems. But as Garrett illustrates, neither sex was in agreement that women should be concerned with problems that went beyond their domestic units. Few rural women joined the Social Welfare Committees of their own volition, and the Allende government did not have the human resources required to organize rural women along lines different from those that had been traditionally successful. This was partly due to the difficult political conjuncture the Allende government faced by 1973, but also reflects the lack of a clear state policy in terms of the incorporation of women.

The Peruvian experience demonstrates a somewhat different problem in terms of the effective participation of rural women within agrarian reforms. Unfortunately, those women that did become cooperative members rarely exercised their right of membership. The trend in the postreform period has been for women that initially were members to drop out of the cooperatives. Female members usually attended cooperative meetings, but in few cases did they actually speak out at these meetings (Deere 1977; Fernandez 1982; Chambeu 1981). Buchler (1975:50) describes women's participation as follows: "At the cooperative meetings the woman member is expected to be more reserved than the men. She usually sits on the floor in peasant society while the men take up any of the chairs available. Nevertheless, she can speak up when her interests are endangered. Her opinion will be listened to, but she seldom has much effect unless seconded by some important male leader."

Fernandez (1982) reports that women (as well as men) view women's lack of education as the basis for their inability to participate as effective cooperative members. In rural Peru, the rate of illiteracy is disproportionately high among women. Men view this as the principal reason why women are unqualified to participate in the cooperative, and why women believe that men show little respect for female members. It is also important to consider that since women constituted such a minority of the membership, their lack of numbers is an important explanation for women's reluctance to participate. Another reason was the absence of any support structure or organization specifically directed at rural women to encourage their effective participation.

Women's lack of authority over men, as well as their lack of education, are among the principal reasons why women are not elected to leadership positions within the cooperatives. Buchler (1975) observes that the Peruvian male ego would be wounded if women held directive office. Only one case has been reported, in Cuzco, of a cooperative that elected a woman to such a position. Chambeu (1981) reports that the Cuzco experience was short-lived and quite negative. Due to family responsiblities, the woman was unable to effectively carry out the work she had been assigned, confirming the belief among the majority of men that women are not suited for leadership positions. But in fact, what this experience suggests is that women's reproductive responsibilities within the household do constitute a barrier to their effective participaton, and that this problem must be directly addressed.

In those Peruvian cooperatives where women were initially accepted as members, the trend over the last five years has been that women have gradually been displaced as members. For instance, what characterized the large female membership of one Cajamarcan dairy cooperative in 1976 was the fact that most of the women were single. Many of them subsequently married between the period 1976 and 1981. Because cooperative laws dictated that only the head of the household could become a member of the cooperative, these young women surrendered their membership positions to their husbands when they married. Marriage was also a means by which their husbands could obtain full-time employment in the countryside. Chambeu (1981) reports a similar phenomenon in the Cuzco region. On one cooperative, half of the original eight women members had resigned by 1979, being replaced by their husbands.

In both of these cooperatives, the male members viewed as problematic women's participation as members. The male leaders of the Cajamarcan cooperative explained to me that "women simply were not productive" (no rinden en el trabajo). Particularly at issue for them was a case in which one of the female members had become pregnant and demanded her legal right to a paid maternity leave. The male members felt that it was unjust for the cooperative to bear such a cost, and their pressure was instrumental in forcing the woman to resign. She was replaced in the cooperative by her husband.

Chambeu reports that in the Cuzco cooperative she studied, the male membership felt that women were not serious about their work because they often could not work a full day due to family problems. As the members put it, "women abandon work." And in fact, if the children get sick, it is the women who must abandon work to care for them, due to their overriding responsibility for both child care and domestic work. Rather than understand this was a social problem, the response in the Cuzco cooperative was to vote in 1980 not to accept any more women as members. The cooperative had already lowered the relative wages of women members as compared to men's, contrary to Peruvian minimum wage provisions. This denial of membership was not entirely unexpected.

Ultimately the experience of rural women in the Peruvian and Chilean agrarian reforms illustrates both the problems of excluding women from the process of agrarian transformation, as well as the problems of translating nominal membership into effective participation. At the heart of both problems was the lack of an explicit state policy with regard to women's role in the agrarian reform, as well as the lack of an effective women's organization to provide the mechanism to translate macro policy into effective local participation. Related to these, was the absence of policies designed to provide the support structures needed by women, either to voice their concerns at meetings, or to help them become more effective workers by alleviating some of their domestic responsibilities. The importance of these factors to the successful incorporation of women into an agrarian reform is made all the clearer by an analysis of the Cuban experience.

WOMEN IN THE CUBAN AGRARIAN REFORM

The Cuban agrarian reform process commenced along a similar road to the Peruvian and Chilean processes just described in terms of rural women's participation. The important small farm sector created through the first 1959 agrarian reform law was conceived to benefit household units. The National Association of Small Producers (ANAP), the principal organization charged with developing credit and service cooperatives among private producers, was composed of heads of households, who were primarily men. Within the state sector, the agricultural unions that were formed were also overwhelmingly male because they organized the permanent workers on the former sugar and cattle estates. Although the number of permanent workers in the state sector had steadily increased, particularly after the 1963 agrarian reform law was promulgated, few women were employed on a permanent basis until the mid 1960s.

The development of an explicit state policy with regard to the incorporation of rural women into the agrarian reform process was a product of both ideological and material necessities. As the Cuban revolution developed its socialist character, the issue of equality, not just between social classes, but between men and women had to be addressed. Drawing on the Marxist classics, the Cubans accepted the theoretical premise that women's equality with men required the incorporation of women into the social labor force (Engles 1975). The participation of women in productive labor was seen not only as a necessary step for women's own social development, but for the transformation of the social relations of Cuban society (Castro 1981; PCC 1976).

This theoretical position was complemented in the late 1960s by the economic necessity of increasing rural women's agricultural participation. Due to the expansion of sugar cane production during those years the demand for temporary labor increased significantly. It was at this time that a concrete policy to integrate rural women into the labor force took form, and it was largely the result of the joint efforts of ANAP and the Cuban Women's Federation (FMC). In 1966 these two organizations joined to promote what are known as the FMC/ANAP brigades of rural women (FMC 1975). Consisting at first of volunteer labor, they provided the mechanism by which thousands of rural women could participate in social production for the first time (Bengelsdorf and Hageman 1977).

These female brigades were responsible for solving the seasonal agricultural labor shortages in both the state sector and on private farms. It is estimated that by the mid-1970s women constituted over half of the seasonal labor force for the sugar cane, coffee, tobacco, and fruit harvests (FMC 1975). An important change which explains the steady increase in women's agricultural participation was that by the mid-1970s brigade work was no longer unremunerated. The FMC was successful in guaranteeing that women be paid for their work, and paid a wage equal to that of their male counterparts. Moreover, in order to encourage women's participation in the brigades as wage workers, it became imperative to recognize women's domestic needs. The FMC played a key role in promoting the development of child care centers in the countryside, as well as the expansion of communal eating facilities at rural work centers.

The organization of rural women by FMC/ANAP was not limited to women and their role in the seasonal labor reserve. The inclusion of women both as permanent workers on the state farms and as members of the credit and service cooperatives of private producers was also promoted. By the mid-1970s, women represented 53 percent of the permanent workers in the state tobacco industry, 41 percent in the dairy industry, 19 percent in food processing, and 7 percent in the sugar industry (FMC 1975:19),[5] Although the available data do not indicate the specific occupations in which women are employed within the state sectors, considerable state attention has been given to training women, particularly at the intermediate technician level.[6]

The criteria for cooperative membership was also changed in the 1970s, from one based on heads of households, to one that explicitly gave membership status to all adults within the farm household.[7] The FMC/ANAP brigades were organized on each of the credit and service cooperatives, not only to recruit women for temporary agricultural work, but to provide the support structure to gradually increase their participation in both the household farming operation and in cooperative decision-making. The FMC/ANAP brigades became the channel which provided technical assistance specifically to women to help them develop the general agronomic and veterinary knowledge required for modern farming, as well as specific skills to use in developing their own income-generating projects (FMC 1975).

The important role of the FMC/ANAP brigades as a method of organizing rural women can be seen in terms of their role in the promotion of production cooperatives. The development of production cooperatives, based on the collective use of land and other means of production, collective labor, and collective decision-making, became a goal of Cuban policy makers following the First Congress of the Communist Party in 1975. Up until 1975 specific incentives had been given to encourage private farmers to voluntarily contribute their land to the state farms. The result was that between 1968 ad 1978, some 30,000 peasant households did turn in their private parcels voluntarily in return for the guarantee of permanent employment on the state farms and the opportunity to live in the new agrarian communities. At the party congress, the constitution of private production cooperatives was officially recognized as contributing to the socialist construction of agriculture. So incentives were given to farmers to voluntarily pull down their fences and produce collectively, although working in the private sector.

Women have been an important force behind this process of voluntary collectivization (FMC 1975). In just four years, from 1976 to 1980, some 900 of these production cooperatives were organized, all with the visible participation of rural women. Analysis of the factors encouraging such voluntary collectivization suggests that they are strongly related to the direct material benefits offered women.

Up through the 1970s, Cuban policy greatly favored workers on state farms by the development of agricultural communities. These are a form of social organization linked to a production center, in essence were planned towns. These communities offered modern housing, guaranteed the provision of water, sanitation and electricity. Morover, they offered health centers, schools, day care centers, communal eating facilities, and stores provisioned with basic necessities. The principal change in policy with respect to the formation of production cooperatives, was that for the first time, the facilities for the construction of an agricultural community would be offered to farmers that pooled their land to form such a cooperative. The state would provide the materials and technical assistance, if the new cooperative members provided the labor.

The rural women interviewed were quite clear as to the benefits offered them by the new agricultural communities. What they all stressed was the benefit to their family's standard of living and well-being. Also important to them were the possibilities for child care and improved housework conditions. One woman recounted how difficult it had been to take her three small children from her countryside home to the district child care center whenever she worked in the brigade. With the child care center located in the agricultural community and with a nurse always stationed at the health center, she no longer worried as much leaving her children while she worked in the fields all day. But in addition, the improved housing greatly reduced the drudgery of housework. The majority of these women had previously lived in homes without running water or electricity, so just having running water significantly reduced the time previously spent on household chores.

It is clear that women's enthusiasm for the new agricultural communities has been an important factor in the successful development of production cooperatives. The production cooperatives also offered women important changes with respect to both their productive and reproductive roles.

Women's participation in the production cooperatives is significantly greater than in the previous credit and service cooperatives. In 1983 women constituted 26 percent of the 78,000 members of the country's 1,400 production cooperatives (Benjamin et al. 1984: ch. 13). The impact of women's incorporation into the production cooperatives is also reflected in the composition of the leadership of the small farmer organization, ANAP. By the mid-1970s, ANAP had one of the highest proportions of women in local leadership positions of all of the Cuban mass organizations, 16 percent (PCC 1976:30).

While impressive gains have been made towards incorporating women into the new agrarian reform structures, women still do not participate in production on equal terms with men (Croll 1979). Men are given preference in terms of the permanent work opportunities in the cooperative, and women are overrepresented within the seasonal labor force. What this means in terms of women's independent income-generating possibilities, their technical preparation, and employment opportunities, certainly requires further research.

It also appears as if women's incorporation into the rural labor force has increased their work load, creating a double workday. Women still carry the load of household responsibilities. The Cuban state has recently made important policy changes designed to alleviate this stituation. The new Family Law, promulgated in 1975, requires men to share equally in child rearing, and in domestic maintenance tasks when the wife works in social production (see Stone 1981: Appendix 2). This is a most innovative step in terms of social policy. In many ways it reflects recognition of the fact that domestic labor in an underdeveloped economy cannot be fully socialized. Its importance lies in state recognition of the fact that women's participation in social production alone cannot constitute the basis for women's equality with men. The traditional reproductive responsibility of women, and the burden that it places upon women, must also be recognized. If domestic labor cannot be socialized, the only alternative is for men to share the reproductive burden. While Cuban society has not yet eradicated the subordination of women, the important legal and economic preconditions necessary to achieve social equality are in place. The incorporation of rural women into the agrarian reform process is one such precondition.

CONCLUSION

The comparative analysis of the Peruvian, Chilean, and Cuban agrarian reform processes demonstrates that processes of socioeconomic change are not gender blind. It cannot be assumed that state policies designed to benefit a specific group of rural households will necessarily benefit the women within them. Lack of attention to the participation of women can result in women losing access to resources or being displaced from productive activities and decision-making. The consequences of this are economic (leading to lower female productivity or income) and social (leading to a lowering of female status and well-being). Additionally, lack of attention to the incorporation of women into new agrarian reform structures creates new barriers to achieving male-female equality, barriers which serve to reproduce women's subordination. Moreover, the lack of female participation may also lead to a less successful process of cooperative development, agrarian reform, and social transformation.

This comparative analysis of agrarian reform processes suggests that the status of rural women in an agrarian reform is directly tied to state policy. The incorporation of women into a process of social change does not happen automatically. As a start, it requires state attention to the structural and legal barriers that may preclude female participation. It has been shown that the criteria for selection of agrarian reform beneficiaries is most important in this regard. One crucial precondition for the incorporation of women into processes of agrarian reform is that all adults be legally entitled to participate.

The right of women to participate in agrarian reform cooperatives or state farms is crucial, but it is not enough. State policy must also be directed towards creating incentives and support structures for women. It is hoped that women will want to participate, will overcome the possible resistance of men, and have the ability to participate effectively. The Cuban experience suggests that if women receive equal pay for equal work and attention to their reproductive responsibilities within the household, and these are made compatible with productive work, that these elements will serve as incentive and support. Other policies relevant to assuring that women participate effectively within the new agrarian structures include agricultural and leadership training courses for women, as well as adult literacy programs.

The comparative analysis of the three agrarian reform experiences also suggests the important role that rural organizations can play in either promoting or discouraging women's participation within agrarian reforms. In the Cuban case, the mass organizations provided the crucial mechanism to link macro policy with local processes of change. The coordination between the women's organizations and the small farmers' organizations effectively integrated women into the overall process of agrarian reform while paying specific attention to the needs of women as women.

NOTES

An earlier version of this paper was published in UNESCO, Women on the Move: Contemporary Changes in Family and Society (Paris: UNESCO, 1985), and was presented to the Second Annual Women, Work, and Public Policy Workshop, Harvard University, April 1982.

1. For more on the Peruvian agrarian reform see Caballero and Alvarex (1980); on the Chilean, see Barraclough and Fernandez (1974); on the Cuban, see Aranda (1968) and MacEwan (1981).

2. As Caballero and Alvarez (1980) point out, the Peruvian calculation of beneficiaries of the reform is a bit deceptive because it includes all of the households belonging to the officially recognized peasant communities that were adjudicated some land. Peasant communities most often got access to grazing land through the reform and these households comprise 38.3 percent of the total number of beneficiary households.

3. Interview with ANAP officials, Havana, June 1980. Data in Aranda (1968:142-43) suggest that in the prerevoluntionary period, approximately two-thirds of all farms were worked in indirect forms of tenancy. This group constituted the principle beneficiary group within the private sector. MacEwan reports (1981:56) that 110,000 peasants became property owners as a result of the 1959 reform law. Mesa-Lago (1972:49) reports a somewhat higher figure of 200,000 beneficiary households. In addition, permanent employment in the state sector increased from approximately 50,000 in 1959 to 150,000 by 1962 (MacEwan 1981:53).

4. In the Chilean case, the reformed sector consisted of the *asentamientos*. These functioned in a manner similar to production cooperatives, but with considerable state direction and supervision. The production cooperatives in the Peruvian case were called *Cooperativas Agrarias de Produccion* (CAPs). The credit and service

cooperatives were denoted as *Cooperativas Agrarias de Servicio* (CAS). See sources in the first note for a more detailed description of the reformed sector in each case. Not discussed in this chapter is the role of women in the officially recognized peasant communities of Peru. See Bourque and Warren (1981) for a case study.

5. In 1970, women workers constituted 7.9 percent of the Cuban agricultural labor force (Pavon 1977: Table 18). According to the 1953 census, women represented 5.7 percent of the agricultural labor force. According to Pavon (1977), a comparison of these two figures is deceptive since in 1953 the majority of women enumerated as agricultural workers were unpaid family members. Those included in the 1970 estimates are apparently permanent agricultural workers.

6. Considerable effort has gone into promoting women in the agricultural sciences at the university level. In 1971, women represented 26.5 percent of the students enrolled (Pavon 1977: Table 22).

7. Interviews with ANAP and FMC, Havana, June, 1980.

REFERENCES

Aranda, S. 1968. La Revolucion Agraria en Cuba. Mexico: Siglo Veintiuno.

Barraclough, S. and J. A. Ferandez. 1974. Diagnostico de la Reforma Agraria Chilena. Mexico: Siglo Veintiuno.

Benglesdorf, C. and A. Hageman. 1977. "Emerging from Underdevelopment: Women and Work in Cuba." In Capitalist Patriarchy and the Case for Socialist Feminism, edited by A. Eisenstein. New York: Monthly Review Press.

Benjamin M., J. Collins and M. Scott. 1984. No Free Lunch: Food and Revolution in Cuba Today. San Francisco: Institute for Food and Development Policy.

Bourque, S. and K. Warren. 1981. Women of the Andes: Patriarchy and Social Change in two Peruvian Towns. Ann Arbor: University of Michigan Press.

Buchler, P. 1975. Agrarian Cooperatives in Peru. Berne: Sociological Institute.

Caballero, J. M. and E. Alvarex. 1980. Aspectos Cuantitativos de la Reforma Agraria (1969-79). Lima: Instituto de Estudios Peruanos.

Castro, F. 1981. "The Revolution within the Revolution." In Women and the Cuban Revolution, edited by E. Stone. New York: Pathfinder Press.

Chambeu, F. 1981. "Participacion de la Mujer Rural en Acciones y Cambios Ideologicos en un Contexto de Reforma Agraria." Unpublished research report, Lima.

Cifuentes, E. 1975. "Land Reform in Chile." Background Paper, Studies in Employment and Rural Development, No. 15. International Bank for Reconstruction and Development, Washington, D.C.

Croll, E. 1979. "Socialist Development Experience: Women in Rural Production and Reproduction in the Soviet Union, China, Cuba, and Tanzania." Discussion paper, Institute of Development Studies, Sussex University, England.

Deere, C. D. 1977. "Changing Social Relations of Production and Peruvian Peasant Women's Work." Latin American Perspectives 4, nos. 1 & 2:48-69.

Engles, F. 1975. The Origins of Private Property, the Family and the State. New York: International Publishers.

Federacion de Mujeres Cubanas (FMC). 1975. Memories: Second Congress of Cuban Women's Federation. La Habana: Editorial Orbit.

Fernandez, B. 1982. "Reforma Agraria y Condicion Socio-Economica de la Mujer: El Caso de dos Cooperativas Agrarias de Produccion Peruana." In Las Trabajadoras del Agro, edited by M. Leon. Bogota: ACEP.

Garrett, P. 1976. "Some Structural Constraints on the Agricultural Activity of Women: the Chilean Hacienda." Land Tenure Center Paper No. 70. Madison: University of Wisconsin.

Garrett, P. 1982. "La Reforma Agraria, Organizacion Popular, y Participacion de la Mujer en Chile." In Las Trabajadoras del Agro, edited by M. Leon.

Lafosse de Vega-Centeno, V. 1969. "La Ley de Reforma Agraria y sus Implicancias en la Estructura Familiar." Serie Documentos de Trabajo, No. 3. Lima: Pontificia Universidad Catolica del Peru.

MacEwan, A. 1981. Revolution and Economic Development in Cuba. London: MacMillan.

Mesa-Lago, C. 1972. The Labor Force, Employment, Unemployment and Underemployment in Cuba: 1899-1970. Beverly Hills, Calif.: Sage Publications Professional Paper.

Pavon Gonzalez, R. 1977. El Empleo Femenino en Cuba. La Habana: Ed. de Ciencias Sociales.

PCC, Comite Central de Partido Cumunista de Cuba. 1976. Sobre el Pleno Ejercicio de la Iqualdad de la Mujer. Tesis y Resolucion. La Habana.

Stone, E., ed. 1976. Women and the Cuban Revolution. New York: Pathfinder Press.

Villalobos, G. 1978. "La Mujer Campesina: su Aporte a la Economia Familiar y su Participacion Social." America Indigena 38.

11 Women in Farming Systems in Latin America

Cornelia Butler Flora and Blas Santos

Few studies have been done on women in agriculture in Latin America, although this is currently changing rapidly, particularly in Brazil and Chile. The assumption is that agriculture in Latin America is a male sphere (Boserup 1970:30). The latest census data from most Latin American countries lists between 3 and 11 percent of the female labor force as employed in agriculture (CEPAL 1982). But measuring women's input into agriculture is exceedingly difficult (Deere and Leon de Leal 1982; D'Souza 1978), and women's agricultural labor-force participation tends to be underenumerated.

Rural development efforts that ignore the hidden female components in agricultural production and in semiproletarianized family survival strategies will fail in the long-term goals of increasing family and national welfare. Ignorance of women's complementary roles in production and ignorance of the complex interactions of women's productive and reproductive roles both contribute to project failure measured by production and welfare outcomes. Initially, technology that does not take into account the sex of the person performing the task it is aimed to help will not be adopted. And if a technology is adopted that interferes with the existing balance of resources within the family, including both money and labor use, family welfare declines and social disorganization increases (Nash 1983). This chapter attempts to show how a holistic analysis of existing farming systems, undertaken with an understanding of the containing social and economic conjunctural situation, can influence the development of programs in which women participate, thereby facilitating the achievement of project goals and assuring that women are not negatively affected by the project.

Most research on agriculture in Latin America, particularly on women in agriculture, has been from the perspective of critical sociology, Thus, it tends to focus on two components of the farming system: land and labor. Latin American research on agriculture focuses first on land and who owns it and then on labor, who provides it through what kinds of social relations. That focus has related the division of labor by sex in agriculture and to the international division of labor in agriculture (Leon de Leal 1980).

The focus of agricultural research in Latin America on land and labor, rather than technology and production as in the United States, stems from the history of agricultural development in Latin America, which differs sharply in many ways from that in North America, Africa, and Asia. This chapter attempts to draw on the strengths of the Latin American intellectual tradition, feminist theory, and farming systems research tools to examine the role of women in Latin America farming systems in general and the roles of women in semiproletarian peasant households in the Dominican Republic in particular.

UNIT OF ANALYSIS

In looking at agricultural production and farming systems, the results obtained depend on the definition of the unit of analysis. Frequently the unit of analysis is defined geographically: the farm. Starting from the physical farm in the United States, agricultural research has led to a focus on output per acre and a technological emphasis, aimed at increasing that output. Technology was assumed to be a male domain. In Latin America, starting with the geographic unit of analysis has led to emphasis on who owns the land. Land ownership tends to be male in Latin America.

A second way that the unit of analysis has been formulated is as the farmer. Farmers are assumed to be men, therefore the farming system is made up of what the males do. In contrast, women in Latin America who study women in agriculture insist that the *family*, not the individual or geographic locale, is the correct production unit. Thus one has to look at a farming system in terms of family inputs and intrafamily relations to the factors of production, as well as at the family production itself. Ignoring the family as the unit of production makes it difficult to understand the dynamics of production, particularly how various kinds of farming systems can survive.

The farm family as the unit of analysis is the basis of a definition of farming systems research that allows us to link the entire rural household with its physical, biological, economic, and political environment.

Farming systems research is aimed at increasing the agricultural welfare of the farm family by understanding the whole farm in a comprehensive manner. The integrated demands of the unit of production/reproduction for alternative sources and uses of land, labor, and capital in production are related. The totality of crops and animals, and their by-products, for both subsistence use and for market, as well as temporary off-farm employment, are included. Farming systems research involves formal, interdisciplinary problem identification in participation with the farm family, taking into account the needs of society as a whole. In collaboration with farm families, appropriate technology is determined (usually from available technology) and evaluated on their fields under their constraints. Farming systems research implies a two-way flow of knowledge between farm families and researchers. (See Shaner, Phillips and Schmehl 1982 for an extensive development of this definition.)

FACTORS OF PRODUCTION

Land

Alternative uses of factors of production must take into account differences by sex and age within the family. Access to land varies by class and gender. Does the family have title to the land, do they sharecrop the land, or do they rent the land? How does access to land and use of land differ by sex? What are the alternative demands for land use at different time periods? When do male uses of the land conflict with female uses of the land, and what is the impact of the different uses for family welfare?

Ecological zone is a basic constraining determinant of land use. In the area of the Andes where most of small-holder farming takes place, there is a short growing season and limited soil and water resources. Crops tend to be limited to potatoes and wheat or barley. Land use in such zones is highly determined by the environment. Water availability, climate, slope, and soil condition are basic limitations. Irrigation, soil conservation, and fertilization can overcome some of these limits, but require capital resources. The more resources, the greater the alternatives. Alternative uses of land and how those alternative uses affect different members of the family unit by sex must be considered.

An example of shifting land use in a farming system disadvantaging women is drawn from southern Chile (interview with Grupo de Estudios Agrarios, December 1980). Southern Chile is relatively arid and cold. It is populated by the Mapuche Indians, who traditionally had complementary division of agricultural labor by sex. Women have been herders, primarily of sheep, and men have produced grains, primarily for subsistence. A new development project brought in dairy cattle, which took over the women's grazing lands. The women had used land for grazing sheep, whose wool they processed on the farm and then sold, providing an important source of female cash income. When the land was converted from sheep to cattle grazing, the women were deprived of their sole source of income. When resources shifted away from women, women's traditional use of money in the household, which was different from and complementary to that of men, suffered. In particular, family food consumption shifted, despite the milk production.

Labor

Labor is the second factor of production most examined in Latin American research on the role of women in agriculture. Traditional complementary division of labor by sex means that labor is not totally interchangeable. According to Max Weber ([1925] 1978), capitalist (modern economy) development demands interchangeable, highly mobile labor, suggesting that increased participation in a market economy would decrease division of labor by sex. In Latin America, the greater the capitalist penetration in an area and the more a farming unit is integrated into a market system the less segregated is the division of labor by sex, the more interchangeable those units are, and the more likely women are to do male tasks (Deere 1976; Deere and Leon de Leal 1982). Yet both men and women assume that men cannot do women's jobs. Women still cook and haul water. Women and children still gather wood. But women also sell their labor to pick cotton and coffee, and due to temporary male migration, they are also involved in subsistence production on the small plots. The poorer they are, the more likely they are to be doing this (Leon de Leal 1980; Deere 1977; Deere and Leon de Leal 1982).

The division of labor by sex and the use of female labor varies by degree of capitalist penetration. Capitalist penetration occurs through linkage to markets, either through the sale of products or the sale of labor. (Credit also links a family household to the capitalist system, but it presupposes the sale of goods or labor.)

Peasant farm households are more likely to be linked to markets by the sale of labor rather than the sale of products. Small farms are important sources of labor in Latin America, with dependence on seasonal labor demand leading to a semiproletarianization of many family households. While in traditional *hacienda* systems peasant agriculture coexisted with semifeudal labor arrangements in the same geographic locale, land reform, which has forced much of large-scale agriculture in Latin America to become more efficient, and the introduction of export agriculture have severed the relationship of peasant to land (de Janvry 1981). Temporary migration at times of peak labor demand has increased, providing cash inputs for the peasant household and resulting in labor shortages for domestic production. That temporary migration from one rural area to another tends to be male.

Control over capital as a factor of production also must be considered by sex. How does credit accessibility differ by sex? Do women have access to credit? Generally, women in Latin America have formal rights to credit, but in fact do not receive it. The institutions that give credit, particularly agricultural credit, deal only with men, even though there is no rule saying women should not have access to credit. Capital includes capital investment in a farming system--infrastructure, animals and machinery. These tend to be divided according to sex in many limited resource farming systems. Both formal and informal sources of credit need to be examined. Women often have primary linkage to informal credit markets.

How does access to marketing vary by sex? What are the complex marketing-capital linkages and how are they differentially controlled? What are the capital demands by sex during each stage of the harvest cycle? Division of labor by sex is reflected in differential use of income by sex. Female income is considered to be reproductive income. Income that a woman generates is controlled by her and used to maintain the household. Male income in these cases is seen as discretionary income--the men can take any surplus to the local *cantina* and drink it up if he so chooses. Thus peasant women often struggle to maintain their separate source of income because the use of the captial, as well as its source, varies by sex.

AGRICULTURAL STRUCTURE IN LATIN AMERICA

The Spanish conquest drastically affected land and labor in much of Latin America. The most productive land was ceded by the Spanish crown as large *latifundios*, resulting in the *hacienda* system. *Haciendas* were self-sufficient large farms based on semifeudal labor relations, in contrast to the other large landholding pattern, the plantation, that was linked to the world market and initially used slave labor. The economic arrangement of the *hacienda* maintained the status of the *hacendado* and maintained rural families in agriculture through customary land use. On the *hacienda*, to which peasants were bound by debt peonage, peasants had access to land on which family subsistence production took place. Both male and female labor was utilized (Carrion 1983). At the same time, a small independent peasantry arose in various Latin American countries, generally on less productive land. Although in some situations, such as in Colombia and Costa Rica, some peasants produced coffee for export, their primary product was basic foods for local markets.

The early pattern of land concentration--and the concentration of political power it represents--continues in most Latin American countries despite a much-heralded land reform. Potentially productive flat land has been shifted from extensive grazing to intensive use for export crops. The steep, less productive, harder-to-farm land continues in subsistence agriculture, producing the majority of the locally consumed foods.

The land reforms instituted in most of Latin America were oriented toward increasing productivity. Generally, land reform was engineered by modernizing elites seeking new sources of foreign exchange to finance import substitution (Barsky and Cosse 1981; de Janvry 1981). Although peasant movements and international pressures helped consolidate land reform legislation (Redclift 1978), the actual implementation did not change the internal balance of power within most nations. But it did change the major farming systems, imposing new constraints on peasant agriculture. Labor requirements became more seasonal, resulting in increasing semiproletarianization of the peasantry, who supplemented wages with subsistence production. Limited access to land and low prices for basic foods required a multifaceted survival strategy for capital accumulation. Increasing efficiency of large export agriculture and a peasantry whose primary income was derived from wage labor did not produce the basic grain requirments for most Latin American countries. Food imports grew at an alarming rate, and food tastes changed accordingly.

Despite increasing agricultural production, most large land holdings are not producing for domestic consumption. Many Latin American countries are net importers of food grains. Some countries have instituted massive programs aimed at small farmers, who are the primary wage food producers. SAM, *Sistema Alimenticia Mexicana*, in Mexico attempted to address small farmer productivity, but has recently been discontinued. PAN-DRI (*Plan Alimenticio Nacional-Desarrollo Rural Integrado*) in Colombia is aimed at trying to get small farmers to produce more wage foods in order to keep food prices down. Other integrated rural development projects in other Latin American countries are aimed at increased small-holder food production. In general, however, such projects have ignored women's contributions to the farming system and have had limited impact on productivity.

The international division of labor increases dependency on world markets for the sale of export crops, needed to generate foreign exchange not only to buy machinery but also subsistence foods. Those shifts in use of land and labor are reflected in the problems facing peasant agriculture and the division of labor by gender within it, as the domestic economy becomes more dependent on cash inputs. The crucial, although hidden, role of peasant women in the complex farming systems that have emerged in the face of increasing export production will be examined for limited resource farming systems in the Dominican Republic. Understanding women's contribution to those farming systems can in turn continue to influence an integrated rural development project the government of the Dominican Republic has under way in the area under study.

AGRICULTURAL STRUCTURE IN THE DOMINICAN REPUBLIC

The Dominican Republic was early tied into the world economy through the production and export of sugar. As in other places in Latin America, sugar and cattle raising took up the best land and was in the hands of either local elites or foreign firms. The flat land in the Dominican Republic that was not used for growing sugar in a plantation system developed into large, semiautonomous cattle haciendas, with semifeudal labor relationships. The peasants employed on the haciendas had small, shifting subsistence plots, but were mainly engaged in extensive cattle production.

As the need for foreign exchange increased, particularly under the ironhanded modernization of the Dominican economy under Rafael Trujillo between 1930 and 1961, land use shifted from cattle to sugar cane. Peasants previously farming and herding on the cattle haciendas were pushed into the mountains, bringing with them their extensive farming practices. The mountain slopes, initially heavily forested, were clear-cut by timber companies seeking quick profits and by peasants using slash-and-burn agricultural techniques for their subsistence crops. Peasants also used the initial land clearing to gain cash income by selling the trees to the timber industry that quickly grew up in the areas, supporting at one time as many as thirty sawmills. The peasants were not particularly concerned about the growing number of denuded mountain hectares, as the cleared area provided pasture for their small cattle herds. They followed many of the same practices that the large landowners used in cattle raising and sugar cane production that led to natural resource degradation in the more productive flat areas of the country (Hartshorn et al. 1981:86). On the small holders' lands, timber rights were often bought for a song, and no reforestation took place, On land that belonged to large landholders--and during the Trujillo era, more and more land became concentrated in fewer and fewer hands--some reforestation took place, as their legal titles and highly placed friends allowed them to take a longer view of the timber business.

Despite isolated attempts at reforestation, deforestation continued apace. Erosion became a severe problem and was intensified as more and more semiproletarian peasants moved to the mountains.

With the Cuban revolution, the United States Cuban sugar quota was allocated in part to the Dominican Republic. That increased assured market, plus the entrance of Gulf and Western as a major Dominican sugar producer, forced more land into sugar production--and more peasants into the mountains. Population pressure on the fragile soils increased through in-migration and natural increase.

The Dominican Republic, despite the large proportion of the economy devoted to agriculture, is a net importer of foodstuffs, spending over $100 million (U.S.) a year on food imports (Crawley 1980:207). There is also total dependence on imports for fossil fuel, a dependence felt even more keenly with the increase in fuel prices in 1973. Although dependence on sugar as a generator of foreign exchange has declined slightly in recent years (tourism, also a Gulf and Western product, contributes an ever-growing amount), sugar is still the major agricultural crop. The emphasis on sugar remains even though the world market for sugar is glutted and chances of reversing that glut in the near future are small. The United States, the prime market for Dominican sugar, is unlikely to increase the Dominican Republic's sugar quota. Europe, which in 1970 was a net importer of sugar, by 1980 became a net exporter of sugar, closing off markets there. Other developing countries have been putting more land into sugar, holding the world price of sugar well below the Dominican costs of production. Sugar employment is seasonal, usually provided by Haitians, migrating from the other end of the island of Hispaniola for the annual sugar harvest. The Dominican population forced off the land as sugar was planted over their grazing areas to urban areas. The Dominican sugar strategy, with its internal and external implications, has been criticized nationally and internationally but remains in place (NACLA 1982).

Populaton pressure in the mountains from that "sugar displacement" was felt in a number of ways. First was environmental degradation. The trees were gone. The soil eroded, which had an impact on the entire watershed. Dams constructed to help the cash-crop agriculture in the valleys began silting up much more rapdily than predicted. Indeed, the erosion from the hillsides began to endanger the whole large farm economy. Further, the poverty of the area tended to expel peasants both to the capital city of Santo Domingo and to New York as they sought a better way of life while still hanging onto their rural roots. In response, businessmen in the local trade center, Santiago de los Caballeros, got together with concerned church leaders to form a development project that dealt with the two problems of soil erosion and poverty. It was clear that people were part of the problems, and, while one could imagine simply taking everyone off the land in order to stop soil erosion and preserve the watershed, this was seen as neither politically nor humanistically desirable.

PLAN SIERRA

Recognition by regional elites of the problems of environmental degradation and poverty led to organization to solve them. A dual program aimed at stopping soil erosion and raising the standard of living in this very poor area was designed and ultimately became institutionalized as an integrated rural development project called Plan Sierra, under the leadership of Blas Santos. This project has sought to devise optimal land use that will not further impoverish the peasants, who are asked to make the short-term individual family sacrifices for the long-term greater good of the Dominican Republic.

The project defined two major problems that it is organized to solve. The first is environmental degradation of the upland watershed, as the erosion caused by poor soil management is resulting in declining water availability for valley agriculture. The second is family poverty among the residents of the mountain area, which Plan Sierra is designed to influence. Plan Sierra attempts to simultaneously solve both these problems by transforming the families residing in the region into efficient producers so they can produce what they need and at the same time conserve the soil.

During the first two years of the project, begun in April 1979, the project team identified two major constraints, which served as a starting point for their program strategy. The first was land tenure and the second was unequal exchange.

Unequal land distribution has resulted in most of the farm families having access to little land. Much of the land is in the hands of absentee landlords interested in neither production nor conservation. Thus the project sees as a first step the need to acquire land and to distribute it to farm families in the area. Negotiation for a portion of the land needed is already under way, as the Dominican Republic has a land reform law that allows the state to take over land that is underutilized, provided adequate compensation is made.

A large tract of Plan Sierra is in the hands of the Mera family. One member of this elite family is the wife of the current president, Jorge Blanco. They acquired this land during the Trujillo dictatorship. While they steadily increased their holdings, these absentee owners did manage to replant many of the trees that were previously logged. The land, which is a very large tract, is being negotiated for, and money has been set aside to purchase it.

A portion of the Mera land is called LaCelestina and is targeted as the first area to be redistributed. It is being defined as the part of the Mera land that belongs to the first lady directly, although this attribution is complicated by the fact that the land is held as a corporation rather than in individual parcels. This land, in the most arid part of Plan Sierra, is relatively scarcely populated at this point. Almost everyone living there is a squatter.

The second major constraint identified by Plan Sierra is unequal exchange between the people of the mountain region, a very underdeveloped area, and the rest of the country and the world economy. This has resulted in a long history of surplus extraction that has systematically disadvantaged the small producers of the area. The second strategy for developing the farming systems and the support project for them is to increase self-sufficiency through a diversified production strategy that includes considerations of both production and household needs of the farm families. Thus, the farming system to be implemented on the redistributed land includes small and large animals, basic grains and other carbohydrate crops, especially cassava and plantains, vegetable gardens, fruit trees, firewood plantations, timber production, and cash-crop trees, especially coffee. It also includes consideration of family off-farm labor in forestry and other enterprises on government-held land.

Plan Sierra recognizes that it is working with semiproletarianized peasants and attempts to increase their welfare without radically changing their life-style. The most radical thing to be changed are cultivation practices, which means shifting from a slash-and-burn agriculture of the *conuco*, where subsistence crops are raised, to a more stable cultivation arrangement. It also means taking a large area from grazing to tree and other permanent crop production as soil conservation and soil enrichment measures.

Current farming systems in the Sierra have evolved a mixed system of slash-and-burn agriculture that includes grazing, subsistence crops, crafts, and selling labor. A few individuals who sell their labor work on the land of larger farmers, while a majority work seasonally in coffee harvest in other parts of the Sierra. The local craft, particularly in La Celestina, involves weaving a palm leaf called *guineo* into coarse strips that are then sewn together either to form *esteras* that can be used as mats or light building material or to form bags or pouches that are used for tobacco after the harvest. The weaving, in which many women are engaged, takes place in the kitchens, which are buildings set aside from the main houses. Women and female children sit for long hours on the floor weaving and sewing the woven pieces together. They gather the raw materials, often walking many hours a day to find the proper leaves. Weaving is articulated with other women's work, which includes fixing three distinct meals per day and clearing up after them, husking coffee, milling coffee, carrying water, looking for wood, carrying wood, shopping for the few articles that are purchased, and, when the men are working in the fields, bringing them a hot meal at lunchtime in the fields. Children help out with some of these chores, but as children's schooling increases, their labor around the house decreases. Once a week, the women wash, which means carrying wood and water, boiling clothes, scrubbing them, and laying them out to dry.

Before 1979 women had a variety of small animals that ranged around the yard, including chickens, swine, and some goats. A few had a single, free-ranging milk cow. In 1978, swine fever hit the entire island of Hispaniola--both the nations of Haiti and the Dominican Republic. It was necessary to eradicate all hogs on the island, although Haiti began its program much later than did the Dominican Republic. Thus a major source of savings for women, the hogs that roamed the farmyard, were bought by the government and slaughtered. As replacement takes place, larger, more intensive operations acquire more highly bred swine that need higher nutritional levels for maintenance and growth, although, of course, they also yield much better if high-protein feed and confined conditions are provided.

Some of the households have substituted goats for pigs, but they do not provide the same flexible source of savings as hogs. This has undercut some of the women's sources of income.

Animals still play a major part in the farming systems. Important animals, besides goats, include *criolla*, or creole, chickens, which are birds that are able to fend for themselves, guinea hens, and pigeons. All these fowl belong to the women. Men have fighting cocks in order to participate in a major sport in the Sierra.

Men's contribution to the household is from the *conuco* (subsistence plots) and from selling their labor. There was no tradition of family gardens in the Sierra, although the women tended to raise flowers around their houses. Early consultants who visited the project, particularly Martha Lewis and Elsa Chaney (Chaney and Lewis 1980), noted the potentiality for gardens and worked with Plan Sierra to develop a land- and labor-intensive package of family gardens. Already organized Women's Clubs were used to introduce the gardens (see Flora, 1982, for a discussion of the development of women's groups in the Dominican Republic). The gardens took hold much more strongly than did the production changes required of the men. Possibly this is true because the male-oriented changes were much more radical, requiring more land for the male agriculture. Other reasons were the good prior organization of the women's groups and the women's strong desire to maintain a separate, complementary source of income and subsistence for their families.

In the area of La Celestina, there are no organized groups and no attempt has been made to introduce gardens. Yet there are gardens there that have been recently adopted by La Celestina women who had seen them in other parts of the Sierra. The crops in the gardens, which include tomatoes, carrots, leaf lettuce, cabbage, beets, onions, radishes--primarily salad vegetables--are distinct from those in the *conuco* subsistence plots. The subsistence plots produce yucca or cassava, some corn, beans, and pigeon peas. However, pigeon peas are also grown in the garden, so pigeon peas are either a male or a female crop (depending where grown), whereas cassava and beans tend to be male crops.

Plan Sierra covers an area of 1,682 square kilometers, which is 3.5 percent of the country. The total population covered by Plan Sierra is 105,000, of whom 95,000 live in rural areas. The development plan estimates that there are 16,000 families in rural areas, with an average of six persons per family. Plan Sierra intends to solve the problems of the limited-resource semiproletarian producers by maintaining a mix of off-farm labor and on-farm production. However, the goal is to make the on-farm production more steady. The off-farm labor planned includes working on government wood-production projects or in cooperative ventures involving either industrialization of local products or selected production of goods for market.

Plan Sierra has been funded primarily by Dominican Republic sources. Up to the end of 1982, a total of a little over twelve million Dominican Republic pesos have been used in the project. Officially, the conversion between Dominican pesos and the U.S. dollar is one to one. The Dominican Republic's government has been the source of the vast portion of the funds, although a major grant came from the Kellogg Foundation for health programs. Loans amounting to about $1 million have come from a variety of Dominican private and semipublic financial enterprises. The desire to base the program on local participation means it will be labor intensive, so staff expenses are relatively high. The next largest category of expenditure is credit. More than $1.5 million of credit has been expended. There was an additional half a million dollars in credit waiting to be disbursed at the end of 1982. The vast portion of credit has gone to agriculture production, trying to influence a shift in cultivation practices to those that conserve the soil and allow a higher standard of living for the peasants involved.

The projects aimed at the male members of the peasant household include reforestation of pines on the land of large landowners, the establishment of coffee, fruit trees, and sisal as permanent crops on small holdings, and annual crops, such as corn and beans. These projects require considerable initial investment of labor to reform the land through soil conservation technologies, which include terracing and other physical barriers to stop the soil erosion that occurs in this highly sloping area.

That infrastructure, which requires commitment to a different form of agriculture as well as relatively large investments with relatively long-term payoffs, has limited the speed at which the agronomic portion of the project has progressed. At the end of 1982, the project listed nearly 3,000 beneficiaries of coffee plants, nearly 2,000 for fruit trees, and about 400 for sisal, giving a total of around 5,000 different beneficiaries. Some received both fruit trees and coffee trees, so it is difficult to know the exact number of families affected by these projects. All projects generally involve credit, seedling distribution, and help improving the land. The male beneficiaries of these programs have responded relatively slowly, compared to the women in the smaller, women related programs, and only when inducements such as low-interest credit or free fruit or coffee trees have accompanied technological innovation. The complicated farming systems actually in process may explain this relatively low rate of adoption of male-oriented change.

THE SAMPLE

Data on existing farming systems were gathered from the area where the first land reform in Plan Sierra will take place, La Celestina. An attempt by the management of Plan Sierra was made to census all the families living in the area in order to then relocate them on appropriate farms. Data were gathered about the number of people in the immediate household, the number of people in the extended household who might be living elsewhere, the amount of land a family had access to, its location and the family's access rights, crops grown, credit received, livestock, household quality, household services, and sources of income for the family. The data were gathered as part of Plan Sierra's implementation of its program.

The initial questionnaire involved interviews with sixty families by social workers connected with Plan Sierra. Fifty-seven of the households included women and were analyzed for this chapter. The analysis was carried out to (1) begin to understand the role of women in the farming systems of the semiproletarian peasants who are the residents of the land-reform area, (2) provide a baseline against which to measure the potential benefits of the integrated rural development project, and (3) attempt to modify and perfect the questionnaire to better provide feedback for policy.

The analysis attempted to enumerate different contributions of women to the total peasant household economy. Women's artisan activity seemed to be the major female input by which to divide the population studied in terms of women's production. There were 15 households of eighty-eight people where adult females did not work or claim a skill. There were sixteen households of 105 people where the adult female did not participate in the family income in any way but claimed knowledge of palm-leaf weaving or other skills. These two types of households were very similar and were combined in data analysis. The last category involved twenty-six households of 157 people where the women actually contributed to the family income through craft work or other economic activity. Fifty percent of the households had no income from female artisan activities. Eight percent of the households had 10 percent of their income from artisan activities, 3 percent had 25 percent of their income from artisan activities, 10 percent had 33 percent of their income from artisan activities, 7 percent had half their income and 5 percent had three-quarters of their income from these activities. The analysis attempted to show the impact of this differential participation of women in the household economy on other production activities.

Generation of cash income through artisan work is indicative of a gamut of family survival strategies based on female production activity. Although La Celestina had not yet been organized by Plan Sierra, and although there were no on-going women's projects established in that area, nine home gardens had been established. All of those gardens were in households where women also participated in artisan activities, whereas none of the other women had home gardens. See Table 1.

Artisan activity is also related to the presence of poultry, a female responsibility, but not to cattle, beasts of burden (burros, mules, and horses), or goats.

One of the faults of the initial survey is that it did not distinguish between milk cows, dual purpose cattle, and beef cattle. (The introduction of tethered milk cows is one of the innovations Plan Sierra is planning for the land-reform area.) The end use of an animal would indicate whether it was a male or female activity.

When cows are used for milk, they are solely a female responsibility. When a woman is temporarily absent, instead of having her husband or sons do the milking, she asks a trusted female neighbor.

Burros, mules, and horses are cared for by all family members, particularly children. Oxen, which are male property and used for draft, were owned by only three households; all of those households had women engaged in artisan work.

The overwhelming majority of the households gained cash income from selling their labor. The households that did not have any family members selling their labor were older households, where no one could work. There was no difference in degree of semiproletarianization by female artisan activity.

Cash aid from relatives was received by nearly a quarter of the households. Half that aid was received from relatives in the Dominican Republic and half was received from relatives in the United States, primarily New York City. These remittances are very important in family maintenance. Although the amount received is small, it is a large portion of the total household cash income. Farming-systems research often ignores the impact of remittances in the farming system.

Most (70 percent) of the households reported little or no cash income from their own agricultural production. La Celestina is a particularly arid area of the Sierra, and cultivation is difficult due to low and unreliable rainfall and depleted soils. However, agricultural ac- tivities are important in providing food for the family as well as for grazing small animals and cattle. Agricultural income for a small portion of the sample was from the sale of crops from the *conuco*: cassava and beans. Some families sold wood, sugar cane, and cut fodder, a few sold cattle or goats, and several sold oregano. Those that sold oregano may have had this source of income cultivated by women.

Officially, all the land in the area surveyed belongs to the Mera family, but the families that had squatted on the land had been there for up to forty years. Most of them considered themselves to be owners, despite the legal niceties. The amounts of land that the families had varied from nearly 1,500 tareas to only the land on which their house was located. The largest landholders generally had coffee lands in other parts of Plan Sierra. Some of the households had title to land outside La Celestina, but were squatting on the property where their house was located.

Landholding is generally greater for households with women engaged in handicrafts. Nearly one-fifth of the households where the women did not participate in handicrafts claimed no land, whereas only one of the households where the women did handicrafts work had no land. The better-off peasant households are households with multiple survival strategies based on female activity. One could anticipate that these household will be innovators in other technology adoption as well, if that does not interfere with women's independent income generation.

While the cash income of most households is low, their expenditures also are kept low. Purchases are moderated through the use of credit, usually obtained informally. The majority of the credit that the households owed was to the *pulperia* (neighborhood store). Women negotiate much of this credit, allowing cash to be used for agricultural inputs when necessary. The second important source of credit was private individuals, often relatives, either blood or fictive kin. Only a few (those with the largest land holdings) had debts to the bank. Only one of the households had credit from Plan Sierra. Women's role in provision of credit would be totally ignored if only formal credit sources were examined.

WOMEN IN PLAN SIERRA

Peasant households can be differentiated--divided into domains, in farming systems terms--according to women's participation in generating cash and in-kind consumption items. The more innovative households are more likely to have a high degree of female participation in a wide number of areas.

Plan Sierra was initially designed on the assumption that women in the area were involved only in household reproductive activities. Women's activities to maintain their separate source of income, their important subsistence production, and their role in the provision of credit were essentially hidden. Objectively, these activities can be classified as agricultural, as they involve growing grains and vegetables, as well as the "husbandry" of small animals. However, in terms of the normative division of labor in the Sierra, they are labeled nonagricultural because women do them. Women are not supposed to engage in agriculture.

Once project personnel began to realize the importance of women's activities, primarily through the enthusiasm women showed for their grassroots homemakers' organizations, as well as their quick adoption of offered technology, the plan shifted to an overt attempt to design and implement projects for women. The gardens are the most successful.

The garden project, which was initiated two years after the plan was under way and received much less financial support than the agronomic project, has spread much more rapidly. By January 1983 there were 6,000 household gardens. Their cultivation involves the use of some of the same methods of soil conservation suggested for other crops. Other production projects for women include a poultry project and a milk cow project.

The chicken project attempts to increase the quality of the chickens raised on the farmstead. Chickens are an excellent small animal for household production. They are able to forage, requiring little care, and produce high-quality protein with minimal inputs (Bishop 1984). Rhode Island Red baby chicks were distributed to women in Plan Sierra in large numbers. Although initial instruction was given, few chicks survived to produce either eggs or meat. The tradition of ranging (nonconfined) poultry production in the Sierra favored the heartier, if less meaty, native breeds. Further, cool Sierra nights favored a variety of chicken diseases. At first, no preventative vaccination programs were taught. Some women invested in expensive antibiotics once the chickens were sick, but the chickens continued to die. The improved breed of chicken requires high-protein feed for maintenance-level growth. Often that feed has to be purchased, whereas previously the chickens foraged in the farmyard. Although the production potential is higher, so is the investment necessary to reach that potential. The chickens, bred for production conditions in developed countries, are not resistant to tropical poultry diseases.

Plan Sierra is currently trying to adapt the chickens to the climate by raising them to semimaturity in large aviaries before distributing them to the women. However, physical adaptation of the chicks will not deal with the problem of genetic maladaptation. Further, the adapted chicks are raised in confinement, whereas the tradition of the Sierra, with chickens as with all livestock, is to let them forage freely. There are other poultry projects in the Dominican Republic that are developing crossbred chickens. Plan Sierra may follow that direction.

Another women's project involves credit in kind. Women receive a milk cow after undergoing training in tethered-cow raising. Such confinement is a new practice for the Sierra. The confined method requires that land be put into improved pasture for grazing, with other grasses and fodder hand-carried to the animal each day. That increases the labor requirement, as well as the need for purchased inputs.

The crossbred cows are pregnant when they are delivered to the women. Each woman repays her load by delivering the offspring to Plan Sierra, who give the calf to another peasant woman. By January 1983, more than seventy cows had been "loaned." However, only three calves have been paid back to the project. There have been several deaths of cows strangled on their tethers. A number of offspring have been reported as born dead. It is too soon to tell if the payback rate will improve.

When a woman receives a cow, she signs a contract stating that she will not sell the whole milk produced. She can sell milk products, such as cheese and a milk-based sweet. Such sales are likely to occur, given the peasant women's desire to maintain their own cash-income source within the peasant household.

CONCLUSION

Women's participation in limited resource-farming systems in Latin America depends greatly on the physical and economic location of those farming systems. They will have lesser roles in direct traditional agricultural production, although they may be important in certain aspects such as weeding, seed selection, organizing labor exchanges, and cooking for field hands.

Instead, their contributions to the peasant economy may be in efforts to generate household income that can be combined with their other household duties. Those include the task of gathering water and fuel, as well as cooking meals. Projects that have ignored women in introducing new technological advances have disadvantaged women and at times have disadvantaged entire families because of shifts in the division of income within the household.

The semiproletarian families in the first land-reform area in Plan Sierra demonstrate the complex nature of the peasant economy and the separate but highly complementary inputs of males and females. There are "his" crops and "her" crops, "his" animals and "her" animals, his ways of gaining cash and her ways of gaining cash. Clearly any analysis of a farming system must take into account those two methods of production and those two intertwined uses of the basic factors of production, land, labor, and capital, and must make sure that the factors of production are available to both sexes through different channels. Traditionally, increased factors of production channeled to peasant families have gone to peasant men, without a realization that they will not necessarily be equally divided within the family or even divided at all.

Delivery systems must be aimed specifically at women and must take into account the heavy tasks of household reproduction women have at the same time as they take into account women's crucial productive activities.

Effective programs will allow women to organize, help women to carry out their basic reproductive household functions, and provide them with increased opportunities for effectively providing subsistence products and cash income for their families. To do this, a recognition of women's worth, both by the project and by the women themselves, is necessary. Organization perhaps is the crucial variable in setting up development projects that truly meet the needs of limited resource farmers. Only if women are organized can they begin to see and recognize the contributions they make to the peasant households--contributions that they took for granted.

REFERENCES

Arauz, Jose Roman and Juan Carlos Martinez. 1983. "Institutional Innovation in National Agricultural Research: On Farm Research with IDIAP, Panama." In Farming Systems in the Field. Cornelia Butler Flora, ed. pp. 99-125. Manhattan, Kansas: Farming Systems Research Paper Series Number 5, Kansas State University.

Baez Evertsz, Franc. 1978. Azucar y dependencia en la Republica Dominicana. Santo Domingo: Editora de la Universidad Autonoma de Santo Domingo.

Barsky, Osvaldo and Gustavo Cosse. 1981. Tecnologia y cambio social: Las haciendas lecheras del Ecuador. Quito, Educador: Facultad Latinoamericana de Ciencias Sociales.

Berrios Martinez, Ruben. 1983. "Dependent Capitalism and Prospects for Democracy in Puerto Rico and the Dominican Republic." In The Newer Caribbean: Decolonization, Democracy and Development. Paget Henry and Carl Stone, eds. pp. 327-39. Philadelphia: ISHI.

Bishop, John P. 1984. "Backyard Animal Production in the Humid Tropics." In Animals in Farming Systems. Cornelia Butler Flora, ed. pp. 135-44. Kansas: Farming Systems Research Paper Number 6, Kansas State University.

Boserup, Ester. 1970. Women's Role in Economic Development. New York: St. Martin's Press.

Carrion, Lucia. 1983. "Modernizacion agraria y cambio en el rol de la mujer." Paper presented at the Conference on The Impact of Modernization on Women's Roles in Latin American Agriculture, Atibaia, Brazil, September.

CEPAL. 1982. Cinco estudios sobre la situacion de la mujer en America Latina. Santiago de Chile: Naciones Unidas.

Chaney, Elsa, and Martha Lewis. 1980. "Planning a Family Food Production Program: Some Alternatives and Suggestions for Plan Sierra." Unpublished paper, San Jose de las Matas, Dominican Republic.

Crawley, Eduardo (editor). 1980. Latin America and Caribbean, 1980. Essex, England: World of Information, 1980.

Deere, Carmen Diana. 1976. "Rural Women's Subsistence Production in the Capitalist Periphery." Review of Radical Political Economy 8: 9-17.

_____. 1977. "Changing Social Relations of Production and Peruvian Peasant Women's Work." Latin American Perspectives IV (Winter and Spring): 48-69.

_____ and Magdalena Leon de Leal. 1982. Women in Andean Agriculture: Peasant Production and Rural Wage Employment in Colombia and Peru. Washington, D.C.: International Labor Office.

de Janvry, Alain. 1981. The Agrarian Question and Reformism in Latin America. Baltimore: Johns Hopkins University Press.

D'Souza, Stanislas. 1978. "Sex-Based Stereotypes, Sex Biases and National Data Systems." Unpublished paper, Seminario a Mulher no Forca de Trabalho na America Latina, Rio de Janeiro, Brazil.

Flora, Cornelia Butler. 1982. "Socialist Feminism in Latin America." East Lansing, Michigan: Women in International Development Working Paper No. 14.

Hartshorn, Gary, Gustavo Antonini, Random DuBois, David Harcharik, Stanley Heckadon, Harvey Newton, Carlos Quesada, John Shores and George Staples. 1981. "The Dominican Republic: Country Environmental Profile." A Field Study. McLean, Virginia JRB Associates.

Leon de Leal, Magdalena. 1980. Mujer y capitalismo agrario: Estudio de cuatro regiones Colombianas. Bogota: ACEP.

Nash, June. 1983. "Implications of Technological Change for Household Level and Rural Development." Michigan State University: Women in International Development Working Paper No. 37 (October).

North American Congress on Latin America (NACLA). 1982. "Dominican Republic: The Launching of Democracy?" NACLA Report on the Americas 16, No. 6.

Redclift, M. R. 1978. Agrarian Reform and Peasant Organization on the Ecuadorian Coast. University of London: The Athlone Press.

Shaner, W. W., P. F. Philipp and W. R. Schmehl. 1982. Farming Systems Research and Development: Guidelines for Developing Countries. Boulder, Colorado: Westview Press.

Weber, Max. 1978. Economy and Society. Berkeley: University of California Press.

Wiarda, Howard J. and Michael J. Kryzanek. 1982. The Dominican Republic: A Caribbean Crucible. Boulder, Colorado: Westview Press.

Zandstra, Hubert, Kenneth Swanberg, Carlos Zulberti, and Barry Nestel. 1978. Caqueza: Experiencias en desarrollo rural. Bogota: CIID.

TABLE 1

Presence of Survival Strategies by
Women's Participation in Handicrafts

Survival Strategy Present	Women's Participation in Handicrafts		
	No	Yes	Total
Home garden*	0%	32%	16%
Grazing animals:			
Goats	19%	21%	20%
Poultry**	19%	50%	35%
Cattle	30%	32%	31%
Burros, mules or horses	59%	57%	58%
Oxen	0%	11%	5%
Income from selling labor	74%	81%	75%
Income from agriculture	33%	25%	29%
Income from livestock	0%	11%	5%
Cash from relatives	26%	25%	25%
Number of household	27	28	55

* Chi-square significant at the .01 level, which means that the differences between the percentages have only a 1% (or 5%) probability of being due to chance.

** Chi-square significant at the .05 level

IV Migration, Social Reproduction, and Production

Some of the interconnections developed in the preceeding sections between social and biological reproduction and production in the market are further specified for migrant populations. The importance of gender disaggregation of data is especially important in studies of migrants because of the wide variation in motives and strategies of behavior between male and female migrants. Mary Garcia Castro shows significant divergences between men and women in the level of consciousness and patterns of behavior in the case of Columbian women in New York. The conflict between these divergent goals of male and female migrants is further analyzed by Patricia Pessar in the case of Dominicans in the United States. Margalit Berlin's study of Columbian women migrants in a Venezuelan garment factory highlights the many contradictions involved in the entry of migrant workers in marginalized industries in the host country.

12 Work Versus Life: *Colombian Women in New York*

Mary Garcia Castro

GENERAL QUESTIONS

Most authors, using a structural framework, consider migration as a process of labor-force mobility or, as Gaudemar (1978) claims, a natural component of the sale of the labor force in capital accumulation with migrant's social realization as that of "persons of capital". But it must also be realized that migrants are social beings with flesh, minds, and cultures, and not just factors as is suggested by the partial manipulation of such macrocategories as class, capital, international division of labor, and so on.

Specific preoccupations stimulated me to design an exploratory study on Colombian women migrants:

1. How do women react to and participate in a given structural situation?
2. What is the specificity of women's participation in the migratory process vis-a-vis men?
3. What is migrant women's participation in social reproduction?

Reproduction is understood to be related to a labor force that circulates in a "sex-gender system"[1] supported by objective situations, cultural arrangements, and ideologies--interdependent, but with a certain degree of autonomy (Althusser 1978).

The Althusserian consideration that ideology should be understood not as a reflection of reality but as an idealization with existential bases in a lived reality has been influencing my thoughts about women's types of consciousness (Garcia Castro 1979, 1980, 1982). However, I should clarify that now the "bottom line" of these preoccupations--my own "value premises" on these themes--is influenced by Gramsci's and Rowbotham's perspectives: ideologies are linked to domination and not to an imaginary process although individuals are not passive objects in this process (Rouanet 1978; Gramsci 1977; Rowbotham 1977)[2].

The specificity of Colombian women in the host society, New York, and its labor market is examined according to the assumption that there is internal differentiation in the so-called segmented market (Piore 1980). So, Colombian women are expected to be recruited in a particular way and have lower positions than Colombian men in the labor market because of a combination of factors involving the organization of the market as well as women's participation in the process of reproduction. Consciousness is considered an important element of this process.

Some authors refer to the same level of consciousness with the following terms: "intuitive" (Lenin, cited by Althusser 1978) "real" (Goldmann 1978), and "cognitive stage" (Leggett, cited in Safa 1976). With some simplification, this level of consciousness could be understood as the way reality is perceived. This perception could be a critical or uncritical one, but, for those authors, this level of consciouness would not guarantee action to change the perceived reality, even in the personal sphere.

Another level of consciousness often referred to is that of the social consciousness, related to stimuli for change. For some Marxists, the emphasis in the formation of this type of consciousness should be on class; for some radical feminists, it should be on sex; whereas for some materialist feminists, class and sex or patriarchal oppression and capitalist exploitation should be basic, integrated references. Family and market force should be analyzed in an integrated way.

In the discussion of linkages and passages from real to social consciousness, Goldmann provides another concept, the Marxist one of "possible consciousness." This concept is related to the question of the point at which people could in actual conditions change their way of thinking and how these changes might stimulate their participation in social transformation movements:

> Every group tends, de facto, to know reality in some way, but its knowledge cannot go beyond a maximum limit compatible with its existence. . . . to be scientific, the sociologist should not ask him/herself what a certain member of a social group thinks today about a refrigerator and comfort, about marriage and sexual life, but rather what the level of consciousness is within which this or that group of men [and, I add, women] can without modifying his/her structure vary his/her thinking about all these problems and in sum, what are the limits which his/her consciousness of reality cannot go beyond, without previously undergoing a profound social transformation? (Goldmann 1978:43, 49. My translation).

Goldmann's observation suggests that some kind of identification of structures should be tried in order to understand the way Colombian migrant women refer to their realities.

For the discussion of levels of consciousness, the articulation of three intimately related structures--class, sex-gender, nationality or ethnicity (Safa 1976)--are proposed. The way a migrant moves in these structures is basic to the configuration of his or her identity. If the reference is female sex-gender, then family should be considered. But family is not just as a type of relation or a type of coexistence; it is also as a way of thinking about reality.

A discussion of familial orientations in the case of migrant women must consider that they may leave a specific family arrangement but carry with them notions and behaviors concerning families and themselves. Naturally, these factors are not deterministic ones, but they must be taken into account. Yet many studies on relations between migration and changes in personal lives do not consider that social space does not necessarily vary with change of physical economic space.

In summary, the analysis develops along the following lines: Colombian women migrants' levels of consciousness regarding their actual situation in the labor market and in the family are formed by the way they live and have lived their experiences as women, as Hispanics in the North American society, and as members of specific socioeconomic classes in that society as well as in Colombia.

I am limiting my study to the identification of levels of consciousness, without necessarily legitimating a priori definite levels. Also, social consciousness, including what Rowbatham calls "female consciousness," is not my prime concern in analytical terms, although this concern is one of the basic stimuli of my studies of women. My ultimate concern is to identifiy some of the constraints to reaching that level of consciousness.

Methodological Procedures

The analysis is based on survey data (ninety-eight cases) and in-depth interviews (twelve cases). Survey data were collected by the Hispanic Research Center, Fordham University, under the direction of Douglas Gurak, and details about the sampling techniques are available from his project (1981). This chapter focuses on the subsample of Colombians living in Queens, New York, in December 1981.[3] Interviews were also conducted with women living in different areas of Queens. This phase of the research lasted until March 1982.

Interviews with twelve women living in different areas of the borough of Queens were carried out over a five-month period.

WHERE COLOMBIAN WOMEN COME FROM

According to an earlier study of Colombian migration (Cardona

et al. 1980), there is information by sex for the Colombian stream to the United States only from 1960 onward. Since that time, the sex ratio has been more favorable to women.[4] Urrea offers the following figures on the actual volume of these migrants.

> New York City has received about 36 percent of the Colombian migrants legally admitted to the United States during the years 1966-79 (CCRP 1980, for 1966-76). . . . Within New York City, the Colombian immigrant population has traditionally been concentrated in the borough of Queens. . . . and according to the calculations of the Departments of City Planning of the City of New York, between 60 percent and 65 percent of the city's Colombian population was concentrated in this borough. (Urrea 1982:2).

For 1980, he estimates that the Colombian population in Queens is 32,000-42,000 in New York, 50,000-65,000; and the United States as a whole, 125,000-160,000.

In th CCRP study in 1975, the participation of middle-class individuals in the Columbian stream was stressed. The study called attention to the cases of secretaries and schoolteachers who migrated by saying they were domestic servants. The study also documented the case of nurses who migrate without changing occupations. Within our sample, few Colombian nurses were found, perhaps reflecting the presumption that more recent streams were composed of a higher presence of lower-middle-class people.

According to a study of unemployment and poverty (*empleo y pobreza*) developed by the University of Los Andes in 1977, about 50 percent of the families in four principal Colombian cities (Bogota, Cali, Medellin and Barranguilla) generated household incomes insufficient for covering the minimal costs of nutrition--1,340 Colombian pesos (Rey de Marulanda y Ayala 1979, cited in Garcia Castro 1982) In 1977, in these same four cities, about 42 percent of the economically active women (census definition) were in the so-called informal, or nonprotected, sector; among men, 35.1 percent were in that same sector. A Colombian government report analyzes the relationship between economic growth and labor-force absorption as follows:

> The labor force offer has surpassed the demand. The results are unemployment indexes of 13.5 percent, 11.4 percent and 16.3 percent respectively, for each census year (1951, 1964, and 1973). . . . In the period 1974-73, although the annual average growth of the Gross Domestic Product was 5.9 percent higher than that registered for the previous period, unemployment was five times higher in relation to the previous census period (1951-64), when unemployment was 1.1 percent. (DNP 1980:59; NY translation)

Recently, along with their discussions of poverty issues, Colombian economists have been focusing their attention on another issue, the so-called middle class proletarianization:

> When a dynamic perspective is adopted, considering the time, it is clear that beyond not being able to maintain its status, the middle class is also proletarianizing itself. Indeed, between 1976 and 1979, the proportion of the population in the middle class decreased from 19 percent to 16 percent. In that period there was an increase of almost 80 percent in the number of persons who did not earn the minimum income (by governmental standard) necessary for supporting a worker's family in Colombia. . . . employers' income in the past decade suffered a deterioration twice that of the deterioration suffered by workers' income. (Pinzano, Samper cited in Garcia Castro 1981)

So it would seem that Colombian international migration is highly associated with this process of "proletarianization." Indeed, in the interviews there are constant references to economic problems faced in Colombia, particularly those caused by monetary or salary devaluations.[5]

The different receptions given to Colombian men and to Colombian women as they enter the New York labor market will be discussed in this chapter. The difference is the same one that women encounter when they enter the Colombian market. For instance, in the more urbanized Colombian labor market Bogota, Cali, Medellin and Barranquilla.

> Women who work in industry are concentrated in less capital-intensive sectors, which generate a lower proportion of total production and possibly are in the less dynamic sectors and those which require an artisanal type of production. (Rey de Marulanda 1981:16, Author's translation)

The inter-sex differential ratio among Colombians is weighted in favor of women, especially in the lowest-paid, less protected, and typically patriarchal-oriented jobs such as domestic service, and other traditional female jobs such as office work (secretaries, typists, clerks, etc.), saleswomen in stores, and home workers (or "artisans"--within this group the highest proportion of women are seamstresses). It should be observed that women are also crowded in just those occupations that can be performed at or near the home. Colombian migrant women generally have had their work experience in those occupations in which women predominate in Colombia. Salary differentials in Colombia are also pointed out in different studies (Rey de Marulanda 1981; Garcia Castro 1979, 1981, 1982).

Women also face norms that "put them in their place" and shape their ideological worlds. Colombia is a social category with special characteristics and families presenting special internal organizational patterns. In each subculture, there are specific results of the interactions among the colonial heritage, e.g., the Roman Catholic Church (imposed by Spain), recent Western political and economic influence, and the resistance of the pre-Colombian cultures.

In 1969 anthropologist Gutierrez de Pineda referred to the following subcultures in Colombia: (1) Andean, or American complex; (2) Santander or new-Hispanic; (3) Antioquian, or mountain; and (4) Negro "fluvio minero" complex. Of course, in the urban areas, these subcultures blend with each other and with external influences. With all this complexity, I must make some simplifications when trying to present family and sex orientations in the "lower middle class".

There are rigid internal hierarchies, and the father, or pater familias, is respected, but he has many family responsibilities, including that of the economic sustenance of the family. Women are supposed to command the domestic sphere in terms of housework, children's education, etc., but generally decisions concerning investments or other expenditures are made by the "man of the house." Visits and strong relationships with other members of the extended family are cultivated. There is relatively strong vigilance by mothers over their daughters' behavior, and virginity, fidelity, and marriage in the Roman Catholic Church are cultivated values.

Not only do women have a double burden of work, but they also live surrounded by a sexual double standard, since virginity, fidelity, and homosocial linkages (friends of the same sex) are generally values imposed only on women. Naturally, reality is more complex than these general remarks, and intrafamilial and intergenerational conflicts are constantly found by sociological researchers.

Living conditions in the "place of origin" is a common reference in interviews with Colombian migrant women in New York. They stress different factors influencing their decision to migrate and to stay according to their age, conjugal status, and other family-cycle characteristics. Younger single women are more critical of their family's internal relationships and the repression of their sexuality, such as restrictions on their going out with either male or female friends, difficulties related to the Colombian educational system (economic constraints faced when trying to get into the universities, political or military repression of students, and the quality of education or its lack of relevance to the labor market), as well as problems of being hired in a society where there is a strong need to know influential people in order to get good jobs. Married women who came with their husbands stress the educational opportunities for their children in the United States. These women also seem to be more influenced by the "typical American" consumption patterns not available to their social group in Colombia. Single older women are more apt to combine economic reasons, such as better earnings, with a search for sexual and affective realization. Female heads of household frequently refer to economic considerations and to the desire for a "better education" for their children.

THE VICIOUS CIRCLE OF INEQUALITIES

The majority of people included in the Fordham survey (Gurak, 1981) arrived in New York between 1970 and 1973 (27.4 percent of the men; 33.3 percent of the women) and 1974 and 1979 (46.2 percent of the men; 34.6 percent of the women). In terms of age at arrival and time of residence, men and women had a similar migratory experience. Men on the average arrived when they were twenty-three years old, while women averaged twenty-five years of age.

Women predominate in the thirty to thirty-nine age group, while men present a bi-modal distribution[6]--they predominate in the twenty-five to twenty-nine age group, an early stage in one's economically active life,--and also in the forty-five to forty-nine age group. But both sexes have similar average ages, women averaging thirty-three while men average thirty-one.

Differences of age between Colombian men and women and differences according to civil status, e.g., a larger predominance of single people among men than among women, probably influence the way both subpopulations compete in the labor market. (But as we can observe from the survey data, women with different characteristics in terms of age, civil status, and scholarship occupy similar positions in the labor market, so we cannot attribute their position in the labor market solely to these factors).

Women are in more unfavorable situations in a number of categories, such as:

1. lower level of formal education.
2. courses now being taken in the United States.
3. no knowledge of English.
4. more limitations to jobs near or in the home.
5. more employed by small firms.

See Table 1 for more details.

The average weekly earnings of Colombian women are $174, while men averaged $266.61. In the case of women, the extremes range from $50.00 to $300.00, and the median is $169.00. For men, it runs from $60.00 to $800.00, with a median of $249.00. The majority of Colombian men and women are in the group that earns from $141.00 to $250.00, but while 51.9 percent of the men earn more than this amount, just 11.3 percent of the women do.

In any event, it is relative and circular to explain the lower position of women in the labor market by using indicators of scholarship, for instance. Women with higher education were found in the garment industry or as blue-collar workers. Single women are not in better jobs, and a high proportion of married women with small children work full-time.

Both male and female interviewees noted that a lack of knowledge of English also limits their possibilities of employment, but women generally would add that they did not study English for reasons related to their working conditions (tiring work, long distances to travel, housework, complex scheduling, etc.), their double burden, complaints about the poor quality of English courses available near their homes, etc. So a vicious circle is reinforced, and more women remain in their first jobs or in the same occupational sphere in which they first entered the labor market.

From the outset, they are more restricted in the labor market by the way they were first recruited. It is more likely that Colombian women will have less turnover or job changes and will stay longer in their first jobs than men. ("Once you get into the garment industry, it is difficult to get out, because I only know people who work there, and sewing is the only skill I have developed."--Mary, a married interviewee.)

Within the Colombian community in New York, women's incomes are necessary both for household maintenance and for remittances. At the same time, the salary in New York allows some potential autonomy to women-("At least if I want to, I can live alone here with the money I make; in Colombia, I could not afford to live alone.") In any event, at the household level, because of her lower income, the Colombian woman is still considered a supplementary breadwinner.

SEGMENTATION WITHIN SEGMENTATION

The data presented highlight that while it can be confirmed that there is a high rate of occupational segregation based on sex, women do not necessarily predominate in all activities regarded as "women's work" in terms of the reproduction of domestic activities. For example, sewing is an activity where one finds only women, regardless of the degree of institutionalization or legality of the workplace, be it at home or in the factory. Women also predominate in activities such as pressing clothes and operating sewing machines (specializing in producing the final product for market). Women also predominate in the category of personal domestic services (maid services, baby-sitting). However, when it comes to cooking, if it occurs in a restaurant, we find men. The same holds true of waiting on tables and washing dishes. Maintenance work, both in the public sector and that which is provided by service enterprises, is carried out by men and women.

In summary, the only categories that just barely qualify as exclusive fields for women are those of domestic personal services and sewing. Men already predominate in the majority of the other occupations.

Men not only have more diversified alternatives, but they also participate in some occupations that historically have been dominated by women, like cleaning, and of course, men are more highly represented in activities that have traditionally been "masculine"--for instance, the "30s group" is weighted toward the mechanics and repair categories.

It appears that the "masculinization" of some feminine activities is related to the dynamics of the economy. As overall demand contracts, in relation to economic cycles, the migrant male labor force has to engage in what, in Colombia, would have been 'women's work." But this invasion of spheres is relative. The social characteristics of work are not determined by what one does as much as by how one does it. Thus, we find that activities related to personal consumption, with the family as its locus, such as making clothes at home or working as maids, continue to be women's work.

Women make up a higher proportion of the total only in the activity/occupation of housewife (24.7 percent), pressing and sewing clothes in the garment industry (12.9 percent), and as unskilled labor in factories producing nondurable goods (10.8 percent). Only men have a concentration of over 10 percent in the occupational categories of mechanics/repairmen (14.9 percent) and workers in building maintenance (12.5 percent).

The validity of the concept of segmentation within segmentation is thus demonstrated by the fact that Colombian women are found in the least attractive activities within the labor market. This analysis seeks to underscore the relationship between the two dimensions of segmentation, ethnicity and sex.

According to the theory of dual labor markets, men and women are recruited in different ways. The labor market is structured to the disadvantage of women (Sokoloff 1981). Several studies undertaken by North American researchers demonstrate that North American women are also found in occupations characterized by instability, lack of possibilities for promotions ("dead-end" jobs, or jobs held by "target earners"), poorer working conditions than men, lack of social security coverage, part-time employment, etc.--in short, jobs within the secondary market. In the case of women, Sokoloff's basic tenet is that the duality, or multiplicity, of job markets emphasizes the absence of competition between men and women as workers. "Instead, they are paid to work in separate jobs, separate industries, and separate labor markets. In each case, women are paid less than men" (Sokoloff 1981:130).

LEVELS OF CONSCIOUSNESS AND SOCIAL REPRODUCTION

This chapter makes the following inferences about women's social reproduction:

1. The importance of differentiating among women and paying attention to their positions in the family structure. For instance, for single women, for married women with or without children, for separated women with children, and for others migration has different meanings. I have been concerned with some but not all of these types

of women, and with a migrant stream that, simplifying somewhat, belongs to a specific class background--another basic factor giving comprehensive strength to the concept of "migrant."

2. The importance of linking the perception of the present situation to a combination of previous and present experiences. In the case of women, beyond analyzing the class positions, attention should be given to characteristics of the "sex-gender" societies in which they have been living. The women migrants I interviewed never "lived" entirely in the host society, and their comments about their present situations were commonly based on comparisons between New York and Colombia.

3. The importance of considering how experiences in the family and at work reinforce each other, without necessarily leading to ruptures or changes in the familial ideology or in the family as an organization, depending on a series of social factors. On the other hand, the patriarchal ideology of women's subordination is not restricted to certain organizations, such as the family. The rules of segmentation in the labor market incorporates this, and, for instance, income differences at the conjugal level are not questioned but assumed as natural. The idea that women's salary is complementary, oriented to child rearing, consumption at home, and help for the family abroad, allows no criticism of those differences in income, so that the husband continues to be considered the principal breadwinner.

4. If, in some way, the rules of the labor market reinforce family stability, they also allow for changes in the intrafamilial balance of power. Women's income, as pointed out in other studies, indeed allows women workers a broader potential or real autonomy. The way this autonomy will be used is related to other intrafamilial alliances, such as the goal of improving the family's consumption level, or of obtaining better education for the children. The use of autonomy will also depend on points of conflict, such as the intention to use the income for the woman's personal project, e.g., studies. So in the relationship of family and work, attention must be given not only to the dynamics of conflicts and alliances inside the family, but also to the dynamics of conflicts and alliances inside institutions. The now old-fashioned idea of the family as a refuge from the outside world, and especially from working conditions, is still a basic tenet of the women interviewed during the course of the research in New York, who say that only in the family is "creativity" or "autonomy" allowed.

ETHNICITY AND CONSCIOUSNESS LEVELS

Although discussions about why migrants do not return to their home countries often refer to the living situation and to economic and cultural constraints in Colombian society, our evidence supports Piore's thesis that those who stay do not necessarily believe that they have already become successful in the United States (Piore 1980).

The lack of viable alternatives and inertia also reinforce the decision to stay. Another observation by Piore is also pertinent: that the migrant's common plans for a return at a future date are not always carried out. Few admit that they will not go back, or that they intend to remain in the United States forever. Few do not have links with Colombian society. But what kinds of linkages do they have and with what Colombian society?

Colombian newspapers were not commonly read by the women I interviewed.[7] Few were interested in, or knew anything about, the presidential campaign, which was under way in Colombia during the period of these interviews. They talk about violence, political and police repression, and guerrillas, but most often, they just talk about the "deteriorating" situation in Colombia in general terms.

At the same time, all of them maintain constant contact by mail and by telephone with their relatives and closest friends who have remained there: "I am here, but I live there since I am always thinking about them" (her children, who remained in Colombia)--Mary, a married interviewee.

Those who admit that they do not intend to go back are generally eager to bring family members and to encourage their friends to migrate here. This orientation is not always shared by husband and wife, and it can become a point of conflict.

Indeed, since lower-middle-class people--especially women--are restricted to concerns about "their world," it is natural that the Colombian society of reference is the one in which their relatives and friends live. It is natural that their national roots and ethnic identity are narrowly based. Music, food, memories of the Colombian landscape, and regional character, for instance, are a strong material basis for their feelings of belonging to a specific ethnic group.

When we analyze the meanings of "we Colombians are different" or "we used to be. . . ." and so on, the parameter is commonly one region or one specific social group.

> The "rollos" [a regional expression for people from Bogota] are rather metaphysical. Colombian men are phonies ["mamadores de gallo"], and they like to talk without compromise about their existence. No, these gringos are very serious and objective. Yes, Colombian men are very "macho" but I miss the relationship with them. (Maria Fernandez--a married interviewee)

> In Bogota, people have culture. . . . People from La Costa are lazy. . . . We "paisas" (from Antioquia region) are used to working hard. (Maria Ana--a married interviewee)

> We don't have friends here. These Colombians who live here, you don't know where they come from. (Helena--a married interviewee)

The work situation and its rules of competition endanger ethnic solidarity, but I must note that even in the original country this ethnic identity was influenced by class differences. Although they are now blue-collar or service workers, the women interviewed still see themselves as members of the middle class. Their ideological references are based on this idealized class position. Elitism is a common feature of this self-image, and it clearly interferes with their perceptions of their situation in the American society in which they live. The following dialogue illustrates this point.

> *Question*: Do you think there is discrimination against Colombians in New York?
>
> *Julio* (24 year-old Colombian student): The "gringos" dont' pay attention to Latins. They despise us, but I think few Colombians perceive it. Colombians who live in Queens are conservative. I know few Colombians here who have Puerto Rican or black friends.
>
> I'm studying at Queens College. Few of my Colombian friends have Puerto Rican or black girlfriends. . . . I used to have a black girlfriend, and my friends said that I'd turned into an African. . . .
>
> At school, my Latin friends say that it's great ("una berraquera") to have a North American girlfriend. But this isn't common. American girls like another kind of music. They have their own customs, and they come from a society in which status is very important, and we Latins have a lower ("mas bajito") status.
>
> Hispanics feel they are inferior. Among them, there are mutual recriminations, such as comments that Puerto Ricans live on welfare. That Colombians are involved in drugs.
>
> *Maria Ana* (a Colombian married woman): I don't think there is discrimination. Americans treat Hispanics well. I don't know anyone in this borough. We've lived here for six years. . . . It's just a hello, a scale in the fruit store. . . . In this borough, there are Chinese, Cubans, Irish, and Colombians. The people who live here are decent. Here, in this neighborhood, there are no robberies. When a black person is hanging around the supermarket, they tell you to be careful. . . .
>
> At work (a sweatshop in the garment district) there are only Hispanic women, but I don't talk freely with them. Perhaps because we are from different countries. They're different. They're more used to that work. . . . An although the place is small, there's a lot of disagreements among the workers. People fight for work--we do piece work. You want to work faster than

the others. They tell jokes about your country. Maybe in a bigger factory things would be worse. I don't know. . . .

Eve (a single, twenty-four-year-old Colombian woman): I have no Colombian friends. This area has more Americans and Jews.

Of course Americans discriminate against Hispanics. Look, in the subway they don't even look at you. I don't believe people are reading, they are just hiding. . . . They don't like you to bump into them. . . . Oh, all those "excuse me's" and "I'm sorry's" are just ways they keep their distance. . . . You simply don't exist for them. They ignore you.

I live all alone. At work people are so vulgar and the men don't respect the women. They are Puerto Ricans and Dominicans, and they say vulgar things to you. I try to keep away from them. I know this isn't their fault they come from poorer backgrounds. But it's hard to get along with them on a day-to-day basis. . . .

My friends are from other parts of the city. I seem to live in two worlds. My friends are students, artists. . . .

Lina (a single, twenty-three-year-old Colombian woman): I have a lot of Colombian friends. Well, not necessarily friends, where you can't trust people like you do in Colombia. No American friends, because of my poor English. I know them at high school. They are workers, accountants. . . . It's not fair to treat Colombians as if they were all involved with drugs. It's discrimination. But all the Americans I know, like for instance my employers (she is a domestic worker), they treat me very well.

SEX-GENDER AND CONSCIOUSNESS LEVELS

As we have noted, migration is commonly evaluated positively as a way of making some money, at least enough to help support the family in the United States and abroad, to be able to buy what they want for their homes, and to pay for their children's future education, according to married women. Single women praised migration for bringing greater autonomy or the possibility of leading their sexual and personal lives away from the control of their families. Married women also believe that their lives with their husbands have improved, since the men's social spheres have been reduced.

Let us first analyze the case of married women.

The common inference that migrant women gain self-esteem and autonomy in relation to their spouses because they begin to earn more money is not completely supported in the cases of the Colombian women interviewed. It is possible that my findings result from the conjunction of unique factors, such as the fact that most of the Colombian wives in New York worked in Colombia. Of course, they earn more money now, comparatively, and they know this. But they look down upon their social position as workers, and, since at the intrafamilial level they are still in inferior positions, earning less than their husbands, the sexual division of power is reinforced. This reinforcement comes from the sexual division of work in the labor market.

Mothers' and wives' migratory plans are generally not individual ones. It is common to hear them say: "I came/I stay for better educational opportunities for my children" or "to improve 'our' [the family's] level of living."

Analysis confirms a common observation of migration studies that the concept of family should not be restricted to the residential unit (Urrea 1979). About 13 percent of the women interviewed in the Fordham survey had children in Colombia, and 38 percent of these were less than six years of age. Many Colombians in Queens send money to their relatives. For these people, migration is a strategy of family support, and they evaluate it as such. Personal exhaustion is compensated by the feeling that it serves the family, and discrimination against women in the labor market is disguised by "total family salary." Many separations were related to the husband's refusal to perform his economic role for the family, but it should not be inferred that his failure is the only factor that "destabilizes" a family.

Indicators of change in the intersexual relations of the family pointed out by Colombian wives usually focused on changes in the husband's behavior--often changes forced by outside restrictions, such as exhaustion in the workplace, the weather (it is said that in the winter, people do not even go out on weekends), and social isolation (few friends or relatives--"he helps me here because his friends can't see him"). My observations are restricted to a point in time in the life histories of Colombian migrant women. Thus it is difficult to say that these women's intrafamilial changes are structural ones.

Isolation is commonly used to define their present situation. This isolation leads to the reflection that although "the Big Apple" was their goal Colombian women migrants live in only a part of it, a very restricted part, at that.

In terms of intrafamilial relations, if married Colombian women are optimistic about the effects of immigration on their husbands' behavior, they also worry about their children's outside socialization. Findings similar to those reported by Chaney (1980) were observed in my interviews with Colombian women. Mothers commonly worry about changes in their children's behavior and values because of their school contacts with American and other Hispanic children. Since in the cases I investigated, women generally had few contacts with the North American part of New York society, many of their parameters must be based on stereotypes. Common value judgments about the North American family were used to express their fears about their children's socialization: "excessive freedom allowed by American parents," "lack of commitment to the family," "no respect for tradition," and "lack of respect and affection for their parents."

We have been discussing the formation of consciousness among married Colombian women migrants. What about the women who migrate alone? In terms of their gender identity, for these women migration itself formed part of a process of reaction against or a level of female consciousness about, their oppression at the cognitive level. As the comments of Lina, Maria Fernandez, and Eve, among others indicate, they came because of economic pressures, but it was also important for them to get away from direct family control and community censure. These women are generally more concerned with individual plans when they discuss the meanings of migration. They are more critical of their working conditions in the garment industry, in domestic services, etc. They agree that they need money to maintain their sexual autonomy, and their life-style in general, but they question the price they have to pay for this autonomy--the exhausting and draining conditions of the workplace.

So according to each woman's perspective, gains or "autonomy" here can be measured in terms of optimism or reservations.

Lina is a domestic worker. She is finishing her high school equivalency degree and has made a lot of Hispanic friends. She had many plans and intends to study interior decoration. According to her, this will be easy (she has not yet looked into admissions procedure and the cost of tuition) if she can get her permanent resident visa, for she is still undocumented.

> *Lina*: Perhaps in Colombia things would be better. But many changes would have to occur. And how? My family is poor. The schools there are not any good. I want to study, but I don't know how to manage it. Education is a myth in this country. Tuition is very high. How can a person who works in a factory afford schooling? I need a scholarship, but to get one, I have to be legal. . . .
>
> Here I am freer. There everyone in my family used to pressure me. Where are you going? Why are you coming back so late? And so on. . . . When you move away, you have to be responsible for your things. This is good, but life here is very hard.
>
> I send money to my family in Colombia. I don't earn much where I work. No friends where I live, no friends at work. I used to go out on the weekends, to Soho, to Manhattan. . . . I made friends with students, artists. . . . I used to feel I was going stupid in those factories. Now I am taking a dance class and an English class. . . . I try. . . . I don't want to live with my sister, and I don't want to live like her and other Colombian women I know. *They don't live. They just work.*

> Relationships between women and men are very difficult here. I've never had North American friends because I don't speak much English. . . . I don't know. . . . Hispanic men are so "macho." They're still looking for women either as future wives or to take to bed. . . . Perhaps the problem is mine. They only respect their mothers and their wives.
>
> *Question*: Like Mary's and Eve's, right?
>
> From the interview with Eve: Yes, that's it. *They really do continue to look at women as either sinful Eves or holy Marys. . . .*

WORK VERSUS LIFE: FINAL REMARKS

I must emphasize that there is no basis upon which to evaluate changes observed in intrafamilial relationships (in the case of married women), such as gains stimulated by women's consciousness about their rights and the activities that force less asymmetrical relations. According to one married interviewee, Mary, "There is no time to waste. We don't have relatives here. Weekends are for cleaning, washing, and going out with the children and going to Mass. My husband and I are more together here. *We live for work and for our family.*"

Married women's spheres of activity are still limited. Married women are not used to going out alone or with their female friends, to using their time to study, or to filling it with activities other than housework. In general, their values about sexuality are still very similar to those found among Colombian women in Colombia (Garcia Castro 1979, 1981, 1982), as is shown by these comments from interviews with married women:

> When he wants sex, it's okay. I don't care one way or another about it. . . .
>
> I just go out alone to go shopping or to go to work. . . .
>
> I grew up "knowing" that women belong to their homes. . . .
>
> American women seem to like to stay out. Children don't obey their parents. We're different. We're Colombians, people concerned with our families.
>
> Sure I like it here, but I want my children to grow up in the Colombian style. . . .

Changes observed by me, as well as those mentioned by married women migrants in intrafamilial relationships, are not necessarily a result of women's struggle for less subordination and more autonomy. To some extent, these changes have been caused by the prevailing conditions of migrant labor-force exploitation and the reification of personal relations. These relationships are mediated by the goal of working more to make more money and by the isolation of the wife and husband reinforced by elitist ideology, strongly reminiscent of their middle-class position in Colombia.

Married women came with crystallized values and in most cases live in Colombian family style and in a social environment that favors segregation. Contacts between women are generally limited to their countrywomen, most of whom they already knew in Colombia.

Even single women had few contacts with North Americans. The lack of English and the social and cultural differences between Colombian women and their coworkers concur to isolate Colombian women from other women, from Americans, from Hispanics, and even from Colombians. Competition, distance, life-styles, and work burdens (including the double burden) are other factors that reinforce this isolation.

Given these objective constraints, especially when reinforced by the women's ideological heritage, it would be difficult to expect Colombian migrant women to overlap the cognitive level of their consciousness with their actual situation. Generally, even the critical commentaries on their daily lives are mixed with rationalizations that "things in Colombia would be worse." Although in a different form, proper to the new context, the identities of these women are socially reproduced.

Although single women were in general more critical about their living conditions, including their work life, actions for changing it were not so common. To a great extent, migrants' living conditions are accepted because of their expectations for the future, because of the ideology of accessibility or the belief that consumption goods are easily attained with hard work. Obstacles to personal mobility goals are the visa, learning English, and getting some skills. The structural constraints that these obstacles disguise are not recognized.

Migration itself contributed to changes in ways of living and was part of a movement toward change. But there are many more questions than simple answers in the process of woman's liberation, and not just in Latin America. Class exploitation and sex oppression are connected. "Possible consciouness" for women migrants is made more complex by the heritage of their experiences in Colombia. This is true for all women, no matter what their marital status. "Possible consciousness" is also limited by the solitude, the isolation, of these women, regardless of their marital state.

This isolation is partially reinforced by the ideology of elitism that they developed in Colombia. They look down on their female Hispanic coworkers, and even among Colombians, their social relations are restricted.

The spreading of stigma of Colombians being involved in the drug trade contributes to segregation within the Colombian community. This stereotype is reinforced by the North American mass media. Competition for jobs and fear of getting involved with undocumented aliens, or having their status as illegals used against them (since the immigration laws encourage informing on illegal aliens) are other factors that contribute to their self-imposed isolation. Although they do not say this in so many words, there is a feeling that even with legal residence, they are foreigners and, some think, outcasts. Americans are doing them a favor by allowing them to stay here, and in order to secure the situation they have obtained, they must respect the law and should distrust other Colombians since they are potential competitors. The literature on migration stresses networks and mutual aid among migrants and my interviews confirmed their existence, but that is just one side of the coin. The wider society demands competition, and conflicts are part of the dynamics of social life.

This research project did not have enough resources to allow an in-depth investigation of one basic theme, that of internal solidarity among Colombians. My hypothesis is that more reflections are necessary before talking about a "Colombian community" (Chaney 1980).

I hypothesized that Colombian women's perceptions of their actual conditions are mediated by their past experiences in Colombia in such a way that their "possible consciousness" is limited to their consciousness level about women's situations in the United States and in Colombia, and their related specificities. Their past experience as "middle class", and their stereotypes on "American women" are references that limit their analyses on their present situation.

With this logic, I argued that differences in salary or in the "value" of money between the two countries and the greater restriction of the husband to the family sphere, as well as the less direct family control of women's behavior (i.e., single or separated women),[8] contribute to a positive evaluation of the migratory experience. But when the women talk about themselves, their comments contain both criticism of working conditions and a recognition of linkages among these working conditions, other societal barriers, and their daily living condition as social limits on their ability to enter certain spheres, groups of friends, and so on. At a certain level, life and work are separated, or as Mercedes, a head of household interviewee, pointed out, "Here it's good for work, to earn money. There, it's good to live. I miss my friends."[9]

Yet complaints about changes in human relationships, growing lack of free time, and affective arrangements suggest a beginning toward a reunification of these images, and for some women the life they endure is conditioned by the situation in which they work.

Women are usually considered to be more consumption-oriented than men, and in truth, many of our interviewees praised American society for the diversity of things available and the ease of buying these products. This is a significant parameter that fits their middle-class ideology, but instead of "blaming the victim" for this orientation, we should place it in the context of culturally structured gender. Woman's objectification and object orientation are not separated. It is not by chance that women, more restricted to the home, are more concerned with supporting a higher consumption level. But their references to the "dehumanization" of their relationships here, the lack of intimate contacts among friends--primary colloquial relations are replaced by instrumental ones--indicates that they are becoming conscious of their self-consumption.

What do critical perceptions mean, in terms of stimulating "rebellion," or, in other words, where are these women in terms of social consciousness?

The actual conditions I observed do not support optimistic inferences. In addition, in this project there have been many issues that have not been discussed. We need more studies about existing associations, and the potential of new organizations concerned with Hispanic people in New York: better identification of points of resistance to the placement of Hispanics in the North American society; unions' and civic associations' policies and practices regarding migrants--specifically women migrants; more long-term observations of women in other situations, such as the "head of households" role, and of the mother-child relationship.

At this stage of knowledge, my general impression is that the women I interviewed are to a great extent involved in an individual processes of "female consciousness formation" (Rowbotham 1977),[10] which criticizes but does not try to alter their present condition. This is intimately articulated with their lower-middle-class identities, which still persist in spite of their new class position. In that process of "consciousness formation," some went as far as the possible alternatives allow, while others stayed where they were. The case of women alone (single and separated women) suggests that women less involved in familial relations have more probability to go further in their criticisms and rebellion. This point deserves more study. Anyhow, the involvement of the interviewed Colombian Marys and Eves in expanding the possible alternatives goes beyond their isolated efforts.

Discussions of Colombian migrant women's social reproduction as workers and as women in New York requires more consideration about the host society itself, such as the life conditions of women and workers. As demonstrated, Colombian migrant women are largely restricted to Hispanic environments and a reduced labor market, or to a very limited part of the "Big Apple," and the influences of American women's way of living are not easily perceived. But the expression "North American women" is also an abstraction, and more qualifications about it are needed.

Migration itself is insufficient to stimulate changes in the process of women's social reproduction. At one level, familial ideology and traditional familial organization are still present in this first migrant wave. Their original social position influences these women. At another level, some single women who try to get away from those familial parameters are usually faced with fighting a lonely struggle. There were changes, but as Rowbotham points out, "The point is to change those conditions, not to make a virtue out of small personal triumphs over adversity" (1977:xiv).

NOTES

This chapter is a partial reproduction of a study titled "Mary and Eve's Social Reproduction in the 'Big Apple': Colombian Voices," published by the Center for Latin American and Caribbean Studies, New York Unversity, New York 1982.

1 "Every society has some form of organized economic activity. Sex is sex, but what counts as sex is equally culturally determined and obtained. Every society also has a sex/gender system--a set of arrangements by which the biological raw material of human sex and procreation is shaped by human, social intervention and satisfied in a conventional manner" (Rubin 1979:157).

2 "There are three main theses which Althusser used to explain the nature of ideology in general. First, ideology is a 'representation' of the imaginary relationship of individuals to their real conditions of existence: This thesis implies a definite break with all conceptualizations of ideology as false consciousness or as a distorted representation of reality. Ideology is not a representation of reality at all. What ideology represents is men's lived relations with reality: it is a relation of the second degree. Althusser insists that this lived relation is necessarily an imaginary one. Ideology then is not a representation of real conditions of existence (that is, the existing relations of production and other relations that derive from them) but a representation of an imaginary relationship of individuals to the real conditions of existence. Second, ideology has a material existence. . . Any analysis of ideology is an analysis of social relations themselves, not a reflection of social relations in the world ideas. Third, ideology interpellates individuals as subjects" (McDonough and Harrison 1978:17).

3 Fernando Urrea and I were responsible for the codification and processing of survey data in December 1981, with support from New York University's Computer Center (with the fine assistance of George Sharrard). Dr. Gurak's total sample includes Colombians and Dominicans in Queens and in some parts of Manhattan. We just used

the part of the sample referring to Colombians in Queens.

4 In 1960, there were 1,286 Colombian migrant men in the United States, and 1,703 women. In 1976, there 2,514 legal Colombian migrant men and 3,228 women (data from INS). The 1970 census gives a similar picture: for the total New York population, the ratio of women to men was 10:9, but among Colombians it was 10:8.

5 Chaney (1980) distinguished some cohorts in Colombian migration to New York; first, from 1918-48, basically composed of some college-educated and middle-level technicians; second, from 1948-62, with a large percentage of people indirectly fleeing the effects of the Colombian civil war, know as "la Violencia" and third, post-1962, whom she calls "economic exiles." Chaney calls attention to the responsibilities of rearing children (providing education, etc.). These last factors are also constantly mentioned by those who arrived in the 1970s.

6 The Fordham survey just chose persons eighteen years of age or older, so these data do not refer to the possible age distribution of the total Colombian population in Queens.

7 Interviewees said they watch American TV stations in order to learn English. They listen to Spanish-language radio stations and read Mexican women's magazines.

8 Separation is a theme not studied in this project. Most of the cases I found in my direct interviews were related to women who were separated from their husbands before migrating to the United States.

9 The Queens social structure and community life also deserve more space than I have given them. According to persons who live there and to researchers who know the area, Jackson Heights, where many of the interviewees live, and some other parts of Queens are old, structured communities, strongly influenced by European and Asian immigrants. European immigrants and Americans of European ancestry hold important roles in community life, directing local civic organizations and participating in local politics. (I am especially indebted to Catherine Benamou for her observations on this topic.) Conservative patterns predominate. Few interviewees have friends in the borough where they live.

10 "I do not believe that women or men are determined either by anatomy or economics, though I do think both contribute to a definition of what we can be and what we have to struggle to go beyond. An emergent female consciousness is part of the specific sexual and social conjuncture, which it seeks to control and transform. But its

very formation serves to change its own situation" (Rowbotham 1977:x).

REFERENCES

Cardona, Ramiro, Carmen Ines Cruz, and Juanita Castano. 1980. "El proceso migratorio en Colombia: el flujo a los Estados Unidos." In Cardona et. al., El exodo de Colombianos: un estudio de la corriente migratoria a los Estados Unidos y un intento para propiciar el retorno. Bogota: Editoral Tercer Mundo.

Chaney, Elsa. 1980. "America Latina en los Estados Unidos." In Cardona et. al., El exodo de Colombianos: un estudio de la corriente migratoria a los Estados Unidos y un intento para propiciar el retorno. Bogota: Editoral Tercer Mundo.

DNP Departamento Nacional de Planificacion. 1979. Plan De Integracion Nacional: 1979-1982. Bogota: Colombian Government.

DNP Departamento Nacional de Planificacion. 1980. El mercado laboral en Colombia - Bogota. Documento DNP, Division de Precios Salarios. Bogota.

Duhran, Eunice. 1979. Introduction. In Macedo. A Reproducao das Desigualidades: O Projeto de Vida Familiar de um Grupo Operario. Sao Paulo: Editora Hucitec.

Eisenstein, Zillah. 1979. Capitalist Patriarchy and the Case for Socialist Feminism. New York: Monthly Review Press.

Garcia Castro, Mary. 1979. Migracion laboral feminina en Colombia. Bogota: International Labour Organization.

______. 1980. "A Questao da Mulher na Reproducao da Forca De Trabalho." Revista Civilizacao Brasileira. Rio de Janeiro.

______. 1981. "Empleo domestico, sector informal, migracion y movilidad ocupacional en areas urbanas en Colombia." Bogota: PNUD-OIT Project (COL 72-0L7).

______. 1982. "El trabajo de las Mujeres pobres, jefes de hogar y esposas, en Bogota, Colombia." Preliminary report to the International Labour Organization, Women's Roles and Demographic Changes Project. Geneva. (mimeo)

Gaudemar, Jean Paul de. 1978. Mobilite du Travail et Accumulation du Capital. Paris: Francois Maspero.

Goldman, Lucien. 1978. "Importancia do Conceito de Consciencia Possivel para a Cumunicacao." Paris: Ecole Parctique des Hautes Etudes. (Translation without bibliographical reference.)

Gramsci, Antonio. 1977. Il materialismo historico. Rome: Ed. Riunite.

Gurak, Douglas. 1981. "Hispanic Migrants in New York: Work, Settlement, Adjustment," Research proposal, Hispanic Research Center, Fordham University. New York.

Gutierrez de Pineda, Virginia. 1968. Familia y cultura en Colombia. Bogota: Editora Tercer Mundo and The Department of Sociology, National University.

Hartman, Heidi I. 1981. "The Family as a Locus of Gender, Class, and Political Struggle: The Example of Housework." Signs 6, 3.

Jelin, Elizabeth and Maria del Carmen Feijo. 1980. Trabajo y familia en el ciclo de vida feminino: El caso de los subsectores populares de Buenos Aires. Buenos Aires: Ed. Cedes.

Kuhn, Annette and Anne Marie Wolpe. 1978. Feminism and Materialism. Boston: Routledge and Kegan Paul.

Lefebvre, Henry. 1969. O Direito a Cidade. Sao Paulo: Ed. Documentos.

Leon de Leal, Magdalena, Ed. 1977. La mujer y el desarrollo en Colombia. Bogota: ACEP.

Marx, Karl. 1946. Cap. XXI. Reproduccion simple en el capital: Critica de la economia politica. Buenos Aires: Nueva Editora.

Oakley, Ann. 1974. The Sociology of Housework. New York: Pantheon Books.

Ordonez Gomez, Myriam. 1981. "La poblacion de Colombia en 1980." Bogota: DANE. (mimeo).

Piore, Michael. 1980. Birds of Passage: Migrant Labor and Industrial Societies. Cambridge: Cambridge University Press.

Rapp, Reyna. 1982. "Family and Class in Contemporary America: Notes toward an Understanding of Ideology." In Thorne and Yalom (eds.), Rethinking the Family: Some Feminist Questions. New York: Longman.

Rey de Marulanda, Nohra. 1981. "El trabajo de la mujer." Document 063. Bogota: Uniandes, CEDE.

Roberts, Helen. 1981. Doing Feminist Research. London: Routledge and Kegan Paul.

Rouanet, Sergio Paulo. 1978. "Imaginario e Dominacao, Diagrama." Tempos Brasileiros 9.

Rowbatham, Sheila. 1977. Woman's Consciousness, Man's World. New York: Penguin Books.

Rubin, Gary. 1981. "The Reagan Administration's Immigration Proposals--A Background Memorandum." New York: American Jewish Committee, Institute on Pluralism and Group Identity. (mimeo)

Rubin, Gayle. 1979. "The Traffic in Women: Notes on the Political Economy of Sex." In Reiter, Rayna R. (ed.), Toward an Anthropolgy of Women. New York: Monthly Review Press.

Safa, Helen Icken. 1976. "Class Consciousness Among Working Class Women in Latin America: Puerto Rico." In Nash and Safa (eds.), Sex and Class In Latin America. New York: Praeger Publishers.

Sassen-Koob, Saskia. 1979. "Formal and Informal Associations: Dominicans and Colombians in New York." International Migration Review (special issue on Caribbean Migration) 15, Summer.

Schmukler, Beatriz. 1982. Family and Patriarchal Domination in Capitalism. New Haven: Yale University Press.

Sokoloff, Natalie. 1981. Between Money and Love: The Dialectics of Women's Home and Market Work. New York: Praeger Special Studies.

Stanton, Morris. 1981. "Hispanic Women's Center Newsletter." 2. New York.

Stuart, Joanna Gould. 1981. "The Use of State Services by Latin American Immigrant Women in New York City." Ph.D. dissertation, City University of New York.

Thorne, Barrie and Marilyn Yalon, eds. 1982. Rethinking the Family: Some Feminist Questions. New York: Longman.

Urrea Giraldo, Fernando. 1979. Plan piloto para regulacion de los flujos migratorios. Bogota OIT:PNUD (Mimeo)

Urrea Giraldo, Fernando. 1982. Life Strategies and the Labor Market: Colombians in New York in the 1970s. New York: Occasional Paper No. 34, Center for Latin American and Caribbean Studies.

TABLE 1

Distribution and Dissimilarities Between Colombian Men and Women in Queens, New York, 1981

Category	Men	Women	Sex Differential Ratio
Residence in the United States			
Less than 1 year	6.5%	6.5%	-4.6%
1-5 years	40.0%	36.8%	8.7%
6-10 years	26.2%	25.8%	1.6%
11-15 years	20.0%	22.6%	-11.5%
16-25 years	6.3%	6.5%	-3.0%
Distribution by Age			
Average age	31	34	
Age range	20-47	20-47	
Median age	29	33	
Mode	35-29 years	30-34 years	
25-29	31.1%	11.9%	158.3%
30-34	16.1%	30.2%	-46.7%
Distribution by Civil Status			
Single	26.2%	16.1%	62.7%
Married	60.0%	65.6%	-8.5%
Common-law marriage	6.3%	4.3%	46.5%
Widow/widower	0	1.1%	just women
Separated/divorced	7.5%	12.9%	-41.8%
Educational Level			
Primary school--complete	6.3%	26.9%	-76.5%
Primary school--incomplete	1.2%	5.4%	-77.7%
Secondary school--complete	53.7%	35.5%	51.3%
Secondary school--incomplete	16.2%	19.4%	-16.5%
Associate/technical degree	10.0%	8.6%	16.3%
Bachelor's degree	6.3%	3.2%	96.9%
Study in the United States			
Never studied in the United States	67.5%	79.6%	-15.2%

TABLE 1 (Continued)

Distribution and Dissimilarities Between Colombian Men and Women in Queens, New York, 1981

Category	Men	Women	Sex Differential Ratio
Economically Active Life (Paid Labor)			
Number of Jobs			
1	21.2%	25.8%	-17.8%
2	38.7%	31.2%	24.0%
3-5	33.7%	29.0%	16.2%
6-8	5.0%	2.2%	127.3%
9 or more	0	8.6%	just women
Student only	0	1.1%	just women
Length of Time in Labor Market			
0-2 years	14.9%	22.6%	-34.1%
3-5 years	23.7%	22.6%	4.9%
6-10 years	35.0%	24.7%	41.7%
11-15 years	20.0%	16.1%	24.2%
Duration of First Job			
Less than 1 year	41.0%	22.0%	86.4%
More than 3 years	27.0%	44.2%	-38.9%
Majority of Coworkers Are Hispanic	46.0%	62.8%	-26.8%
First Occupation in the United States			
Unskilled blue-collar	39.8%	41.4%	-3.9%
Service workers	37.5%	15.1%	148.3%
Garment industry	2.5%	23.7%	89.5%
Present Occupation			
Blue-collar	37.4%	48.9%	-23.5%
Domestic servants	0	4.3%	just women
Nondomestic service workers	26.1%	14.0%	88.4%
White-collar	31.0%	8.0%	287.5%
Unemployed People-Reasons for Not Looking for Work			
Pregnancy	0	5.9%	just women
Family Responsibilities	0	64.7	just women
Will look after finding place to live	100.0%	0	just men

TABLE 1 (Continued)

Distribution and Dissimilarities Between Colombian Men and Women in Queens, New York, 1981

Category	Men	Women	Sex Differential Ratio
Location of Work Place			
Own home or building	1.4%	8.3%	-83.1%
Own neighborhood	6.8%	6.7%	1.5%
Other areas in Queens	28.4%	33.3%	-14.7%
Manhattan	45.9%	36.7%	25.1%
Other areas of New York City	4.1%	5.0%	18.0%
Occupational Mobility-First and Present Occupations in United States the Same	44.4%	56.0%	-20.7%
Size of Firms Employing Colombians			
1-10 employees	21.3%	35.7%	-40.3%
51-100 employees	22.7%	16.1%	41.0%
Income--Weekly			
Average	$266.61	$174.00	
Range	$60-800.00	$50-300.00	
Median	$249.00	$169.00	
Mode	$141-250.00	$141-250.00	
Above the mode	51.9%	11.3%	359.3%
Friends' Ethnicity			
Majority not Hispanic	5.0%	5.4%	-7.4%
At least half not Hispanic	6.3%	2.2%	186.4%
Few are not Hispanic	68.8%	58.1%	18.4%
None is not Hispanic	18.8%	32.3%	-41.8%
Knowledge of English			
No knowledge of English	18.8%	46.2%	-59.3%

TABLE 1 (Continued)

Distribution and Dissimilarities Between Colombian Men and Women in Queens, New York, 1981

Category	Men	Women	Sex Differential Ratio
Knowledge of English (Continued)			
Total Comprehension--oral and written	55.0%	31.2%	76.3%
Remittance to Colombia--Money/Goods			
Nothing	37.5%	48.4%	-22.5%
Relatives in United States			
None at time of arrival	31.1%	14.0%	122.1%
Spouse already here	2.7%	16.1%	-83.2%
Spouse and others already here	21.5%	32.3%	-33.4%
Help Received Upon Arrival			
None	46.2%	34.4%	34.3%
Way of Getting Present Job			
Through friends or relatives	70.7%	75.4%	-6.2%

Source: Fordham Survey

For more details on the complete distribution in some of these categories, see Urrea, 1982.

13 Migrant Female Labor in the Venezuelan Garment Industry

Margalit Berlin

Women's adaptation to urban life and to the changing division of labor takes into account their marital and reproductive situation. Black women in the United States develop networks of cooperation to adapt to urban economic conditions such as low incomes, the meager economic contribution of males, and welfare laws (Stack 1974). Portuguese working women in the United States do very much the same: Their networks act as a mode of adaptation, and tend to inhibit the loss of male or female partners through marriage or long-term relationships when they are crucial to the community (Lamphere 1974). To cope with the absence of a male provider and with a number of children to support, Mexican women at the United States border work at various illegal occupations until they are evicted or get a more stable job at a *maquiladora* (Fernandez-Kelly 1983). This chapter will show that Colombian migrant women's special mode of adaptation to the changing division of labor entails adjusting to a specific set of job opportunities, migration policies, housing conditions, availability of health services, as well as their marital and reproductive situation.

This situation varies according to the individual migrant. It is dependent on the number of children or siblings to be supported, who takes care of them and of the household chores, and whether or not she has family in the host country. The migrant's family or extended kin helps her to fulfill her responsibilities as a woman. Thus what she does with her savings and with her time inside and outside the factory will depend very much on this reproductive situation. This chapter is based on participant observation and extensive interviews with five women met during fieldwork in a Venezuelan garment factory where the author worked as a seamstress helper for three months.

In order to understand how the changing division of labor influences these migrant women, this chapter will discuss the employment strategies of the Coro factory (fictitious name) and how the labor process there was organized. First, employment strategy and the elements included in it will be defined. Second, will be to locate the different employment strategies in a typology constructed on the basis of the characteristics that production and employment take in three different industries: the industrial system of the fashion manufacturer, the oil industry, and Coro. Third, the organization of work within Coro wil be described: the training process, how wages are set, and the role of management. Then the strategies migrant workers develop in order to cope with what Coro offers them, and with their individual (marital and reproductive) circumstances will be dealt with. This part wil include a qualitative description of the relations developed among co-workers and management, as well as the factors impinging on them (visa or temporary contracts, remittances, housing arrangements). How migrant workers' behavior affects management decision regarding the allocation of personnel and task assignment will also be studied.

WHAT IS AN EMPLOYENT STRATEGY?

The term employment strategy refers to a time-horizon an employer is able to offer a worker, and has to do with the degree of job stability guaranteed to the worker. Arthur Okun (1981) explains that this time-horizon is associated with the wage the worker is paid. Thus, a longer time-horizon is realized with a higher number of incentives. For instance, a career strategy is gained by incentives geared at caring for the workers' needs over a long period, such as the education of his or her children. A shorter time-horizon is attained because of the lack of incentives offered to workers, such as low wages and little or no hope for job promotion.

The exchange that takes place when a worker is hired, i.e., between the industry and the worker, is expressed in the job contract. Okun explains that there are two kinds of contracts: explicit and implicit. Explicit contracts are binding obligations to some rate of pay, some length of employment or both. These have costs in the lack of flexibility and in the rigidity that may bring loss of motivation on the part of both employers and employees. Implicit contracts are statements about the future that are not binding (Okun 1982). With these the firm can wait to evaluate the behavior of the worker and then decide whether to fulfill the contract statements or not, thus gaining control and a more flexible labor force. The worker may or may not consider these statements nonbinding depending on both the situation in the labor market and his or her personal situation.[1] Firms assert the right to reject noncooperative or unnecessary workers because they must invest an initial amount of money for each new employee, which Okun calls the "toll costs" (Okun, 1982).

Whether the workers are needed by the firm for a long or brief period of time will depend on the specific industrial structure, which is defined according to five characteristics: nature of training, time required to obtain it, stability of sales, stability of production and stability of employment.

TYPOLOGY OF EMPLOYMENT STRATEGIES

Coro lies in the middle of a threefold typology of employment strategies constructed on the characteristics mentioned in the former section. They shall be repeated as the typology is discussed.

First, there is the putting-out system which characterizes the fashion industry in the Sentier of Paris. Much of the work in the Sentier is done by Vietnamese migrant families living in La Place D'Italie. The training is easy to obtain and it is short in duration since sales are fickle and seasonal. Given the variable nature of women's fashions, production is unstable and inventories become unsaleable. Because employment is erratic and subject to production flows, the strategy of employment taken by industries of this type is to minimize the linkages between worker and industry. What the industry does is offer piecework jobs to finish at home and be delivered back to the factory upon completion. New fashion waves will demand different kinds of garments, and so new lots will be assigned to these domestic workers. Families of seamstresses can sustain this system because they have the flexibility and unconditional support of every member, which is required to devote hours of cutting and sewing at peak times. In the same way families are able to stretch meager resources when there are no sewing jobs.

In the oil industry, the employment strategies are opposite to the putting-out system. The training required in this industry is very specific: it covers a long period of time and does not exist outside the plant since it can only be acquired by hands on experience. Sales are generally stable and when unstable, can be adjusted through inventories. Unlike the garment industry, inventories can be used since products are not subject to fashion trends as in the putting-out system. Thus production is stable and can be programmed for a full year. The strategy of employment in industries such as oil production and refining is to maximize linkages betwen the factory and its workers. In other words, to offer longer time-horizons.[2]

Coro's employment strategies lie in the middle of these two extremes: training is acquired in the homes of workers, because women often learn to sew from their mothers, grandmothers, or sisters. Adjustment to the assembly line or group work is important, and acquisition of the specific movements and skills takes from six to twelve weeks of training. This is much shorter than the case of the oil industry, but since learning the specific characteristics of the assembly line is valuable to the factory, management guarantees an apprenticeship wage as an incentive for the worker to learn and stay in Coro. However, it will not go out of its way to encourage the worker to remain for very long as does the oil industry. Sales are seasonally unstable. Coro sells more during Christmas and Easter than during the rest of the year. Men's fashions are not as unstable as women's fashions in the Sentier, so inventories can be adjusted to periods of unstable sales.

Hence the employment strategy at Coro is stable, but also sensitive to the level of production, which may vary from year to year. For Coro, the flexibility of the labor force is of crucial importance in helping them adapt to these variations in the level of production. Herein lies the importance of the female migrant worker, whose economic need may provide sufficient incentives to make her want to stay when the wage incentives are lacking. Coro does not need a labor force as flexible as the putting-out system, but it does require workers who are ready to operate different machines and are easily adaptable to changes in management. The flexibility is present in the migrant worker who develops meaningful relations in the factory, and is willing to do anything to keep them since through them she can obtain what she would not get otherwise.

THE ORGANIZATION OF WORK IN CORO

The work process in this factory is not as automated as in many textile and electronics factories, but it is sufficiently fragmented that many different workers complete the various operations. The production line is divided such that one worker sews sleeves, another buttons, still another zippers, and so on. Each worker is responsible for her small part, and thus must wait for the preceding worker to fulfill her task and deliver it to the seamstress helper, who hands it to the seamstress in charge of the next step. The worker has little control over the product since she usually does not understand its origin or destiny. Only the seamstress helper, who could go from one floor to the other carrying threads and fabrics from the deposit to the operation room, was able to understand the stages of the factory. This division of work is essential for implementation of the piecework wage system.

The rhythm of production is ensured through the piecework wage system. Behind this system lies the principle of Taylorism, based on the idea that the tendency of an unsupervised worker is to slow down the work process. The industrial engineer intervenes to evaluate the output per hour in order to inhibit this tendency. According to this wage system, seamstresses are paid by the number of pieces they finish in a day. In order to earn more in wages the worker must hurry to finish a higher number of pieces. To do that, she hurries the worker in charge of the operation preceding hers, and sometimes impatience with the inexperience of workmates can develop. Hence there is a built-in conflict in the production process between the interdependent nature of the factory or industrial work process and the individualistic nature of the piecework system. As a result, the possibilites of establishing friendship or cooperation with fellow workers on the basis of common tasks are reduced, but the development of special ties with managers who can help the worker get higher piecework wages are increased.[3] In their need to establish relationships with management as a means of gaining job security, obtaining housing, and extending their stay in the country, migrant women made the levels of production higher, therefore making it more difficult for other workers to fulfill the basic quotas.

Besides piecework wages there are also apprenticeship wages. These are wages the factory gives employees as incentives to continue with their work while learning to finish a high number of pieces per day. Coro pays beginners according to a base quantity, if and when they learn to complete the minimum rate of pieces. If the worker does not finish the specified quantity by the second week, the factory demotes her to the minimum piecework wage, which is less than she would be paid if she finished the maximum number of pieces per day. This payment serves as an incentive to make workers adjust to the specific requirements and characteristics of the assembly line. The apprenticeship period takes from six to twelve weeks. After that, workers in these positions can quickly receive the minimum wage for a seamstress, Bs. 42 ($9.80) per day, rather than Bs. 32 ($7.40) per day, the apprenticeship wage.[4]

The main garment union, headed by the leading political party, AD (Accion Democratica), through collective contracts signed every three years, increases the base salary wage for both apprentices and regular seamstresses. Union leaders are in conflict with industrial engineers regarding the issue of wages. The former argue that the wage of the worker must be set independently of productivity, emphasizing that the worker has needs independent of the results of time and motion studies performed by engineers. There is little possibility that workers can encourage the consideration of engineers during their time and motion studies, so workers will have to wait for union increases.

MANAGERIAL CONTROL

Middle management plays a vital role in organizing production. Several types of managers are involved in the production process: The floor manager, the personnel manager, the supervisor of each section, and the chief of quality control.[5] During my work at Coro, the floor manager was responsible for assigning personnel to each position and thus integrating the production process with the management of personnel. In order to do that, he had to be aware of each woman's work performance, and how each responded to the part for which she was responsible, particularly in the case of new procedures. He also had to intervene whenever there was a discontinuity in the production process, for example when fabrics were not ready to be used by the seamstress, or when they came in nonmatching colors.

The supervisor had to keep the assembly line together and to deliver the final product. At the end of the day, the supervisor collected and checked production sheets from each worker, specifying the number of pieces each had completed that day. In effect, it was her responsibility to check the workers' performance.

The chief of quality control trained seamstresses to do their job better. When quality standards were not met, he made them redo their work. He used to sit ten minutes at each seamstress's machine, demonstrating to her how to sew better and more efficiently. Thus, he was an important person to whom the workers went for help to get higher piecework wages.

The personnel manager was responsible for the selection and hiring process. He often worked as a pair with the social worker, who was aware of personal problems such as housing and the health of workers. The personnel manager kept a file on each worker in his office, and the file was checked whenever any decision had to be made about the workers' situation in the factory. He too was an important figure in the eyes of the migrant worker, whose job contract was temporary, usually limited to one year. For those workers who had a large number of dependents, the possibilty of losing their jobs and having to return to their country was completely undesirable. The chief of personnel would often complain that migrant workers were dependent on him and the social worker for matters such as health, saying "Colombian women are unable to go to the doctor without the social worker." This manager is probably unaware of the difficulties migrant workers have in getting health services.[6] Once the role of management is clarified, the significance of the relations developed by migrant workers as survival strategies can be understood.

RELATIONS DEVELOPED BY MIGRANT WORKERS AS STRATEGIES OF SURVIVAL

The employment strategy of Coro, which was shown above, is characterized by stability but is also responsive to annual variation in demand. Migrant workers too, develop strategies to cope with cyclical production demand and the family situation at home. These strategies consist mainly in developing relations among co-workers and with supervisors and managers.

Prominent among the survival relationships of migrant workers is the patron-client or clientelist, relationship between the worker and management. These are marked by lowered degrees of cooperation and friendship with co-workers, both Venezuelan and Colombian. Clientelist relations are asymmetrical, since one side has more power than the other, but both do gain from the relationship.[7] In the context of the factory, these relations were demonstrated by the repeated number of times the workers went to the supervisor seeking their approval or advice on how to proceed in the sewing process, or in personal matters such as housing or remittances. In return, management gained a wider sphere of influence to implement orders. Migrant workers would seek advice from the supervisor who could help them to get the specific things they needed. Thus, if they needed to stay in Coro and get higher piecework wages, they would try to become utility workers, those who know how to operate several machines and can fill in at any point of the assembly line. In interviews with management I learned that these workers were treated preferentially, but the details were kept secret. Women who wanted to assume these work roles sought the help of the chief of quality control to get instructions as to how to sew better and faster. For example, when the chief of quality control, Alonso, was hired by Coro to check the quality of a new product, Cilia, a migrant worker with a temporary visa and huge family responsibilities, would call him many times to ask him for instructions to work better and more efficiently. While Cilia and Omaira (another immigrant) occupied the chief's time, Venezuelan workers would complain about their fellow employees and supervisors. Of course, they never sought help and tried to avoid these co-workers and managers.

The different behavior of Colombian and Venezuelan workers indicate the strategy of migrant workers to learn from Alonso to get higher wages and visa renewal. Venezuelan workers looked for such help from their extended kin group. For example. Aida counted on the help of her stepfather and mother to feed and house her three children.

If migrant workers needed a visa, they tried to gain help from the chief of quality control, by ingratiating themselves to the floor manager who was responsible for the organization and the allocation of personnel. When there was a break in the assembly line, due for instance, to the reorganization of products, migrant workers would go to this floor manager rather than to the supervisor of their section since it was the floor manager who decided, about the contract renewal. Migrants would also utilize opportunities such as asking where the new fabrics were stored to make themselves visible to the floor manager. For instance, when Omaira, a former maid who came from Colombia through the *caminos verdes* (clandestine way), did not know what to sew next, she called the floor manager and expressed her doubts to him rather than to Enriqueta, the Colombia supervisor in her section. Omaira already had her resident visa but since she wanted to stay in Coro and make a higher wage, she did everything she could in order to make herself indispensable to the factory. Her hope was to become a utility worker.

When workers needed help in more personal issues such as aid in getting housing arrangements, they went to the personnel manager.

He was only indirectly involved in the decisions regarding contract renewal of workers, although in moments of conflict, when opinions about workers differed among managers, he would be consulted since he had met the workers during their recruitment in Colombia. Both the personnel manager and the social worker made contacts with the pension owners to house the recruited Colombian workers. In order to move to a different house it was necessary to mobilize this linkage with the personnel office since *pension* owners preferred to rent rooms to workers with management recommendations. For example, when Cilia came from her country as one of the two workers with a one-year contract she was unhappy with the *pension* that the factory placed her in. To get a room in another pension; she had to wait to get introduced to a new pension owner by the social worker. Cilia cultivated her relationship with the latter by visiting her, helping her do housework, and taking care of her adolescent child. Gladiola, the other Colombian worker with a one-year contract, was able to move from a *rancho* to the same pension as Cilia by using similar channels. Gladiola had thought several times of changing jobs because she was not satisfied with her wage, but she learned after searching a long time for housing that without factory contacts it would be impossible to move in to a better arrangement.

Pressure to develop clientelist relations can come from not having relatives to depend on. Consequently, the migrant in this situation is cautious in every move and careful with every penny in order to build a future in the host country. This was the case with Enriqueta, the supervisor. She developed a high degree of clientelism with the floor manager. She tried to show him that she was tough with her countrywomen by making them work extra hard and not giving them any breaks or special consideration when she collected their production sheets at the end of the day. At the same time; she would favor Aida, a Venezuelan worker, through whom she was introduced to a follower of the Maria Lionza cult who told her ideas about the future.[8] Enriqueta helped Aida to leave her job earlier by completing her production sheets. This behavior made Enriqueta suspicious in the eyes of most Colombian workers, who did not go to her for advice on job matters as a result.

When Gladiola's one-year contract ended, she was offered a renewal for six months but at the base salary (Bs. 42 per day) and with no piecework wage. She would be making less per week for those six months than she was making during the contract period (Bs. 280, rather than Bs. 360 per week). Gladiola blamed this on the supervisor Enriqueta, whom she viewed as arbitrary in her behavior with the seamstresses. The decrease in wage was due to a reorganization of the sections caused by the shift in production from an elegant suit which did not sell during the recession of 1980 to a sport pant. This change required workers to be flexible enough to adapt to the new product and wait for an increase in demand for it. Such an increase in demand might bring the possibility of higher quotas for the number of pieces finished. The conflicts over layoffs were often interpreted in personal terms such as jealousies and rivalries and were probably a result of the way things were obtained at Coro by the cultivation of favoritism. This was illustrated above by the case of Aida, the Venezuelan worker, who was favored by the Colom- bian supervisor through the cultivation of clientelism and special ties.

A high degree of clientelism is usually associated with little sharing among co-workers at the worksite. Deference to authority and cultivating ties with management, negated friendship and cooperation among co-workers. Thus, Cilia, the more clientelist worker, did not interact much with her co-workers. She would often sit alone if her only friend, Gladiola, was busy talking with other workers.

In the factory, friendship ties were developed in the locker room and not in the operation room since employees were not allowed to talk during hours except to communicate specifically about work. Friendships were also formed in the cafeteria, on the stairs, and in Coro's bus. In the locker room, workers had the opportunity to talk while they changed uniforms or while they ate their snacks. During meals, workers would look for their favorite workmates and so groups were formed and maintained daily. Colombians would tend to sit with Colombians and Venezuelans with Venezuelans. Conversation among Colombians and Venezuelans was not different since all workers talked about relatives, friends, managers, work, food, wages, and prices. But the interests of migrant and native workers were quite different. Remittances were a main concern among Colombians, while Venezuelans had more immediate obligations to friends and family because they paid visits and shared household tasks with them. Migrants would show one another pictures of the things their relatives had purchased with their remittances: new electric appliances, new wall hanging, toys or clothes for the children.

Food habits also differed between the two groups. Lunch in Coro's cafeteria cost Bs. 10 for a warm meal consisting of meat, salad, and *arepa* (a corn meal bread). Among migrant workers, Bs. 10 was too much to spend daily for lunch so they brought food from home. This meal would consist of rice and beans, fried bananas, salad, and occasionally there would be shredded meat or chicken. At noon they would eat at the dining room tables, though some of them preferred to use the thirty minutes allowed for lunch to relax and did not bother to go down five floors, to eat in the dining room. Instead they would sit on the stairs right next to the fifth floor. Some others would use lunch time to write letters or to iron some of their clothes with the factory's iron. It was interesting to note that the migrant workers who lived with their relatives ate on the stairs, while the migrant workers who lived in pensiones ate in the dining room. The latter had a greater need for a relaxed and harmonious meal, because the former had warm meals and a family waiting for them at dinner.

Enriqueta, the supervisor, sat on the stairs. She lived an austere life and, as was mentioned earlier, did not interact with workers outside the factory. She used her free time at the factory to write letters to her sister and make some arrangements on the phone, such as helping her boyfriend get a taxicab license.

Attitudes about money influenced group formation, providing a common base of interest among workers. Since most native workers would allow themselves to spend a bit more on food, they criticized Colombian women for being so *pichirre* or stingy. Mary, a Venezuelan worker, said she despised Colombians for that reason. She often ate in a restaurant outside the factory where she paid Bs. 15 (3.60), more than it would cost at Coro, for a better meal than was offered at the factory. At the same time, Colombian women would claim that Venezuelans were careless about their families, that they did not save, and preferred to spend their money carelessly. These monetary beliefs, based on different consumption goals, made group formation on the basis of nationality almost inevitable both inside and outside the factory.

Coro provided migrant workers with a base to develop ties for entrepreneurial activities. For instance, Marina, a Colombian worker who traveled back and forth between Colombia and Venezuela, would bring cloth, dresses, pants, and shirts from her mother's boutique to sell to her workmates. Marina modeled some of the items she sold by wearing them in the factory. Also, a group of Colombians joined a *san*, a rotating credit association. Each of the ten workers constituting the membership gave Bs. 20 ($5) each week in order to receive Bs. 2.000 ($ 465) at the end of the ten weeks as a loan to purchase anything they needed. This informal association was an important form of saving since it was very hard for migrants with temporary visas and difficulties in getting sponsors to bank effectively. All these entrepreneurial activities were a base for stronger ties among Colombians.

Strategies developed by migrant workers changed according to the migrant's legal status and their family situation. Clientelist and friendship relations developed in the factory were forces that encouraged migrants to stay in Coro. The factory offered the worker some stability of employment through explicit and implicit incentives. For native workers, these incentives were money. The migrants had other needs such as visa renewals or better housing arrangements. To meet these needs, they looked beyond the economic incentive and developed clientelist relations.

The attitudes of management were influenced by the survival strategies which Colombian workers adopted. Task assignment decisions were made according to the behavior of Colombian and Venezuelan employees. The floor manager preferred to assign unskilled positions, such as jacket cleaner or seamstress helper to Venezuelans, while he placed Colombian workers in apprenticeship positions because they showed more willingness to adapt to specific factory requirements.[9]

CONCLUSIONS

Given the constraints presented by the marital and reproductive situation of migrants, their special mode of adaptation shows a remarkable degree of flexibility.

Their legal status, the number of dependents, the location of their families, all these factors influenced the relationships they developed in and out of the factory. Dependence on management was greater when legal and housing pressures were stronger, and thus clientelist relations with managers developed. These tend to inhibit the formation of cooperative ties among co-workers. Friendship and cooperation ties developed in the factory served as networks to get jobs, housing, send remittances, participation in entrepreneurial activities, and were an incentive for migrants to stay in a factory even when the economic gain was not altogether satisfactory.

NOTES

I wish to thank Ricardo Hausmann for his help and advice.

1 Implicit contracts gain special significance in the discussion of Coro's employment strategies and their migrant workers, since they implicitly offer the migrant worker visa renewal if and when they cooperate with the factory.

2 Benjamin Coriat (1976) reports much the same type of training in the case of cement workers.

3 In more automated industries this conflict between the interdependent nature of the assembly line and the individualistic nature of the piecework wage system is solved by using machines which produce a fixed number of pieces without affecting the worker's wage. But this does not increase the possibilities of cooperation between workers. Michael Burawoy (1979) found in a participant observation study of a railroad pieces industry that workers engage in small competitive games among themselves such as the game of *making out*. That is, they try to be the worker who finished the highest number of pieces per day. These games help the worker survive and adapt to a routinized type of work, and develop camaraderie, as well as consent, within the factory.

4 The figures in dollars are calculated according to the currency exchange for 1980, that is $1.00 U.S. = Bs. 4.30 Bs. Bolivares.

5 The owners and main managers are involved in the buying of

materials, distribution, sales, and publicity. They are not directly involved in the production.

6 It is hard enough for a native worker to be attended at the Public Health Services, even more than it is for foreign workers. The newspapers publicize the lack of public services as a result of the thousands of illegal immigrants in the country. These news articles function to stereotype the Colombians as an unwanted population, which often results in their mistreatment. For a detailed discussion of the stereotypes of Colombians, see Ralph Van Roy's "Los Colombianos en la Prensa y Television Venezolana," a paper presented at the Seminar on Selective Migration Policies, Caracas, October 1980.

7 They have been noticed in the agricultural sector by Eric Wolf in Mexico, by Sydel Silverman in the Italian Mezzogiorno, and in the Brazilian urban sector, by William Norris, (in Salvador, Bahia). These authors describe such relations as asymmetrical in character, note that the exchanged products are material objects, such as land and fruits. In the urban area there is a specialization or a distribution of dependence. Thus there may develop a patron client relationship with a bureaucrat who can help one get medical service, but cannot also get one work, or a spot in school for one's child. In the city each resource tends to have a different person controlling it. In the case of this factory, the distribution of dependence is among the different managers and supervisors who control different things.

8 For more information on this cult see Magia y Religion in Venezuela, by Gustavo Martin, Ediciones Universidad Central de Venezuela.

9 In a recent interview with Coro's management, I could see that this attitude has changed in the last years because there are no more Colombians with temporary visas since selective migration policies have ended. An analysis of this change is beyond the scope of this work since the fieldwork was done in the years 1979 and 1980.

REFERENCES

Burawoy, Michael. 1979. Manufacturing Consent: The Labor Process in Monopoly Capitalism. Chicago: University of Chicago Press.

Coriat, Benjamin. 1976. Ciencia, Tecnica y Capital. Herman Blume Ediciones.

Fernandez-Kelly, Maria Patricia, ed. 1984. "Mexican Border Industrializaiton, Female Labor Force Participation and Migration." In Women, Men and the International Division of Labor, edited by June Nash and Maria Patricia Fernandez-Kelly. Albany: State University of New York Press.

______. 1983. For We are Sold, I and My People. Albany: State University of New York Press.

Lamphere, Louise, ed. 1974. "Strategies, Cooperation, and Conflict among Women In Domestic Groups." In Women, Culture, and Society, edited by Michelle A. Rosaldo and Louise Lamphere. Stanford, Calif.: Stanford University Press.

Norris, William. 1984. "Patron-Client Relationships in the Urban Social Structure: A Brazilian Case Study." Human Organization 43, No. 1.

Okun, Arthur. 1981. Prices and Quantities: A Macroeconomic Analysis. Washington, D.C.: The Brookings Insitute.

Silverman, Sydel. 1981. "Rituals of Inequality: Stratification and Symbol in Central Italy." In Social Inequality: Comparative and Developmental Approaches, edited by G. Berreman and K. Zaretsky. New York: Academic Press.

Stack, Carol. 1974. All Our Kin: Strategies for Survival in a Black Community. New York: Harper & Row.

Van Roy, Ralph. 1980. "Los Colombianos en la Presa y Television Venezolana." Paper presented at the seminar on Selective Migration Policies. Caracas, October.

Wolf, Eric. 1977. "Kinship, Friendship and Patron-Client Relationships in Complex Societies." In Friends, Followers and Factions, edited by Steffen W. Schmidt, James Scott, Carl Lande, and Laura Gausti. Berkeley: University of California Press.

14 The Role of Gender in Dominican Settlement in the United States

Patricia Pessar

Until recently the term "migrant" suffered from the same gender stereotyping found in the riddles about the big indian and the little indian, and the surgeon and the son. In each case the term carried a masculine connotation, unless otherwise specified. While this perception makes for amusing riddles, the assumption that the "true" migrant is male has limited the possibility for generalization from empirical research and produced misleading theoretical premises. This chapter will briefly speculate upon the epistemological origins of this serious omission before turning to a discussion of the gaps in our understanding of migration caused by the failure to include gender within theoretical frameworks.

AN EXPLORATION INTO WHY WOMEN WERE EXCLUDED FROM MIGRATION RESEARCH

Until the late 1970s, most researchers excluded women from their studies of migrant populations.[1] This omission can be related to two central premises of modernization theory, which was the epistemological framework for most research on population movement. First, migration was viewed as a matter of individual choice whereby people relocated from backward rural areas to modern, urban locales. According to one popular variant of the modernization approach, those individuals with the ability to project themselves into the role of western man headed off to the cities where the benefits of modern life could be attained (Redfield 1955; Lewis 1959). Modernization theorists often assumed that a dichotomy existed between men and women. The former were allegedly more apt to be risk-takers and achievers, while the latter were portrayed as guardians of tradition and stability. On this premise, female migrants could be explained away as wives and mothers who were the passive followers of male pioneers. This misconception has only recently been corrected with the publication of studies describing a pattern in which women migrate first, and later may be joined by other family members (Abadan-Unat 1977; Smith 1980).

The second factor that contributed to the disregard for female immigrants was the common conflation of "migrant" with "waged laborer," and the misapprehension that women migrants do not work. Illustrative of this view of female migrants was the French government's classification of Algerians in official statistics as either "men" or "women and children under 16" (Morokvasic 1979). This system of classification stands as a metaphor for gender roles in capitalist societies wherein women are a priori assumed, along with children, to be dependents of men. In fact, when researchers have included women in their surveys, they have found a high proportion of employment. For example, 91.5 percent of all Dominican women surveyed in the New York metropolitan area in 1981 had been employed at least once since their emigration, and 49.7 percent were currently in the labor force (Gurak and Kritz 1982).

More recent accounts of migration acknowledge the productive role of women in the migration process. For example, several social scientists have noted that the women who remain behind in rural communities and participate in noncapitalist modes of production often subsidize the low, unsteady wages paid to other migrant household members (Meillassoux 1981; Chaney and Lewis 1980; Smale 1980). It has also been recognized that immigrant women's work in the household can help to stretch low family income (Pessar 1982b). Other researchers have documented the large supply of, and demand for, female immigrant labor in the secondary sector of advanced capitalist societies (Guhleman and Tienda 1981; Castro 1982; Sassen-Koob 1981).

The structuralist approach to migration has helped to remove women from obscurity. Nonetheless, its proponents commonly go too far by assuming that migrants can be treated as if they were genderless workers or do not proceed far enough by failing to differentiate among women. The remainder of this chapter, will explore both of these shortcomings in light of the ethnographic data collected in the Dominican Republic and United States.[2] In place of the prevailing, gender-free model of migrant settlement developed by Michael Piore (1979), an alternate scheme will be proposed that includes gender ideology and sex roles. This latter framework accounts for features of the immigrant experience that remain obscure or unexplored in previous works.

A GENDER-FREE MODEL OF THE SETTLEMENT PROCESS

One of the most elaborate models of migrant settlement within advanced industrial society has been developed by Michael Piore. His scheme is based on a two step process in which gender is entirely absent. He raises two central questions. Why is the migrant so well suited at first to the role he or she is assigned in the economy of the receiving society? And why does the migrant population begin to lose its "special" status and adopt orientations toward work that are congruent with the native-born working class?

According to Piore, the answer to the first question is based on the fact that the migrant arrives as a pure economic maximizer. He or she is willing to accept any job, no matter how demeaning, because the self-defined status of temporary worker promotes a sharp dichotomy between work and social identity. The social identity of migrants remains untouched by work experiences and is said to be rooted in their country of their origin: work is essentially asocial for the immigrant laborer (Piore 1979:54).

> Work performed in the receiving society is purely instrumental: a means to gather income, income that can be taken back to his or her home community and used to fulfill or enhance his or her role within that social structure. From the perspective of the immigrant, work is essentially asocial (Piore 1979:54).

His answer to the second query is that due to the general instability of jobs in which migrants are employed, they are unable to accumulate sufficient savings to return after a short period as they may have initially intended. As the migrants prolong their stay, social attachments develop and demands are made upon the individual from within the migrant community. In keeping with this argument, Piore advises the reader that in the second phase, "migration and settlement must be understood as processes relating to communities rather than individuals" (Ibid: 75). Piore's argument is grounded upon a phenomenological view of identity and motivation. The initial, anomic stage is purportedly a by-product of the social rootlessness of the migrant who has been removed from the community of origin in which identity and volition are forged and authenticated. The second stage is said to emerge once the migrant adopts a community of peers in the receiving society to act as his or her new social referent. Adopting conventional sociological terminology, we may say that within the host society the individual has made the transition from "immigrant" to "ethnic."

Unfortunately, this model is inadquate to account for several of the most important features of Dominican immigration, the most significant being the contrasting orientations of men and women to return migration. Ironically, its shortcoming lies, in large part, in Piore's failure to develop a truly phenomenological framework in which the gender-determined aspects of social identity and volition are included. This chapter with its analysis of Dominican migration sets out to accomplish this goal.[3]

THE ROLE OF GENDER IN THE PHENOMENOLOGY OF DOMINICAN IMMIGRATION

Taking Piore's model as a starting point, one can ask whether the community of origin is the primary social referent for Dominican male and female immigrants.[4] Interviews and participant observation have shown that in the case of male immigrants the two significant social arenas in which migrant status initially gains definition and purpose are the household in the host society and the home community. The meanings, values, and social relations associated with these two arenas may at times be contradictory and antithetical. For men the tension between these two domains must be managed throughout the period of migration. The salience attached to one or the other varies, and the manner in which the tension is resolved influences whether the migrant and his household settle permanently, semi-permanently, or return to the Dominican Republic.

By contrast, women's identity is firmly rooted in the household.[5] Even as a "bird of passage," the woman may be metaphorically compared to an actual bird which carries in its genetic makeup the capacity and proclivity to construct a nest wherever it goes. As part of her "cultural programming" the Dominican woman transports the values and roles associated with the home wherever she settles. The tension which migrant men experience between the demands and goals of his household in the United States on the one hand, and the meanings and values of the home community on the other, are much less pronounced for women. Further for a Dominican woman, there is far less discontinuity between her social identity as wife, mother and homemaker, on the one hand, and resident and worker in the United States, on the other. Contrary to Piore's depiction of work as asocial, the woman's contribution as a laborer permits her to more fully realize activities and values associated with her roles as wife and mother. In contrast to men, migration does not rupture the social sphere in which women are self-actualized. On the contrary, migration reinforces women's attachment to the household because it emerges as a more valued institution and becomes a social field for women to achieve greater autonomy and equity with their male partners. When conflict arises it is commonly between men who seek to return to their communities of origin and women who engage in strategies to prolong the household's stay in the United States.

The Social Construction of Male and Female Migrants Within the Household

Questions arise as to how Dominican male migrants are socially constructed in the immigrant household and what the limitations are to the social production of a new identity and role. Piore is correct when he observes that the immigrants' first jobs tend to be at the lowest rung of the prestige hierarchy, and that the meanings and values associated with these may contradict the identity and sense of worth which the migrant possesses. This is particularly true for Dominican men whose premigration employment placed them in the ranks of the lower middle class. (See Tables 1 and 2) Although men experience a personal decline in status, as measured against their premigration position, they are urged by others in the household and immigrant community to subsume their individual identities and goals within a larger sphere, the household. Herein lies the paradox and tension of the migrant experience for many Dominican men.

The purpose for migrating according to most Dominicans, economic and social progress, may not be realized at the level of the individual, but is often achieved collectively. The wages migrants receive and the level of consumption this income makes possible, permit the domestic unit to enjoy what is by its members' standards a middle-class life-style.[6] Not withstanding the social mobility realized at the household level, Dominican men in the United States, because of their low occupational status, may become frustrated by their inability to translate these household gains into publicly recognized prestige. This observation underscores what is for men an uneasy balance between becoming first among equals in the immigrant household, and the prevailing gender ideology and sex roles in the Dominican Republic that promote patriarchy in the home and prestige and privilege for men in the public sphere.

With this tension as a major catalyst, some men choose to pursue financial strategies in which frugal living and savings are emphasized to ensure that the household will eventually return to the Dominican Republic. Interviews with returned migrants and immigrants soon to depart for the Dominican Republic revealed that men anticipated not only a rise in occupational status, but equally important, the recognition of the man's social and material achievements among peers and others in the wider community. In fact, upon return to the Dominican Republic, the household and community become realigned from the man's perspective. It is his work in the Dominican Republic and the value it is accorded by the larger community that brings a higher status to the household which he represents and maintains.

For women the household was the locus of social identity prior to migration, and continues as such after migration by gaining salience in the United States for all members regardless of gender. These facts prove beneficial to women and have profound consequences for women's orientation to migration and settlement. In marked contrast to Piore's assertion that temporary migrants dichotomize between themselves as social beings on the one hand, and workers on the other, the data obtained for this chapter shows that very real negotiations over gender ideology and the sexual division of labor within the household are possible precisely because Dominican women do not dicthotomize between the home and the workplace. Consideration of how these negotiations affect Dominican settlement in the United States will follow a preliminary discussion of the three main domains in which social change has occurred. These are control over household budgeting, authority as the household head, and the sexual division of labor in housework.

CHANGES IN GENDER IDEOLOGY AND ROLES WITHIN IMMIGRANT HOUSEHOLDS

Income Allocation and Generation

There are three dominant modes of budgetary control characterizing Dominican households. These have been termed the traditional, patriarchal form; the household allowance; and pooled income. The first occurs when members give all or part of their wages to a senior male member. He is empowered with authority to decide income allocation and oversee the payment of household expenditures. If there are savings, the account bears only the man's name. The second mode, the household allowance, operates when a senior woman is given funds to cover basic expenditures such as food and clothing. Her responsibility is to manage these funds to ensure the daily maintenance of the domestic group. Her authority over decision-making and the management of income allocation exists within this very basic sphere. By contrast, the senior male is the principal decision-maker for long-term and costly expenditures and is at greater liberty to direct household income to personal items of consumption, such as entertainment. In the third mode, pooled income, all income-generating members donate a specific amount of their wages or profits to fixed household expenses, such as food, rent, electricity, and gas. The meeting of the daily needs of the unit becomes a more collective task entailing more or less equivalent contributions and greater shared responsiblitiy for activities such as shopping and paying bills. There are two major patterns of control over the remaining funds. In the first case, the senior members donate the surplus to a common kitty which is used for all other expenses and savings. In the second instance each member is at liberty to use the remaining funds according to his or her personal discretion.[7]

As Table 3 shows, for the fifty-five migrant households studied by this author, the dominant mode of budgetary control prior to emigration was as follows: ten were characterized by the traditional, patriarchal form: twenty-eight operated with the household allowance pattern; and seventeen pooled household income. Of this third group, fifteen of the fifty-five domestic units were matrifocal. In the households where men controlled the household revenue, (modes one and two) women, either as wives or daughters, contributed income on a regular or semiregular basis in sixteen of the thirty-eight cases. Among those units characterized by the household allowance mode, the woman's income was most commonly directed toward household, rather than personal items of consumption. Women tended to specialize in luxury items however, such as designer sheets and imported foods, rather than staples. Both objectively and symbolically, the direction of these savings to some nonessential prestige items for the household reinforced the image of the man as the breadwinner and the woman, at best, as the bestower of modern status goods, and at worst, as the purchaser of *tonterias* (frivolities).

There has been a profound change in budgetary allocation for Dominican hosuehold s in the United States after migration. The households in which the fifty-five informants are currently found can be characterized by the following forms of budgetary control. Two follow the traditional pattern. In fifteen households, which are characterized for the most part by the wife's nonemployment or participation in industrial homework, the women receive a household allowance. Thirty-eight households pool their income. Of this last group, twenty are nuclear and eighteen are female-headed domestic units, owing either to the absence of a senior male or to his irregular and limited financial contributions to the household as measured against those of the senior woman.

The predominant mode of budgetary control, income pooling within nuclear households, brings women advantages unknown in the three premigration patterns. Responsibility for meeting the basic needs of the domestic group are more equally distributed among members (regardless of gender), thus mitigating the invidious comparisons between "essential" male contributions and "supplementary" female inputs. According to informants, the greater participation by men in decision-making in strategies for stretching the household budget, and managing irregularities in income flow, has led them to appreciate more fully the experience and skills women bring to this task.

Household Authority

It remains to be seen how women have managed to gain greater respect for and control over the fruits of their labor. Conversations with women, as well as observations of conflict between partners, reveal that when equity in budgetary control has been elevated to a right it has occurred within the symbolic and behavioral domain of "household head." For most Dominicans the status of household head is equated with the notion of "defending the household" (*quien defiende la casa)*. This defense is largely conceived in material terms. As women demonstrate their capacity to share material responsibility with men on more or less equal terms, they begin to expect to be copartners in heading the household. In response to the question, who is the household head now, and who was the head previous to your emigration, many echoed the words of the following woman:

> We both are the heads. If both husband and wife are earning salaries then they should equally rule in the household. In the Dominican Republic it is always the husband who gives the orders in the household (*manda lo de la casa*). But here when the two are working, the woman feels herself the equal of the man in ruling the home (*se siente capacitada de mandar iqual al hombre*).

Interviews and participant observation reveal that women's claims to copartnership in heading the household have brought them increased authority in decision-making over budgeting, contraception, the discipline and education of children, and control over social life outside of the household. When asked to compare decision-making in these areas prior to migration and at present, 80 percent of the married immigrant women noted an improvement in the frequency in which the spouse solicited and adhered to the woman's advice. Observations of conflicts that arose over decision-making revealed that women most often advanced their claims in terms that distinguished their previous status as subordinates (*una nina*, a little girl, or *una esclava*, a slave) from their present position as partners with men.

The Double Burden

The problem of the double burden is an area in which immigrant women report significant changes in men's willingness to accept the need for change. Women complain to their husbands that they are being treated unjustly when they are forced to extend their workday by toiling in the home after work and on weekends. The compromise reached by the majority of the women interviewed involves the husband's minor participation in housework. The degree of participation usually varies according to the domestic cycle of the household and its gender composition. The man's contribution increases when the children are young and decreases once daughters are old enough to help their mothers. The most commonly shared domestic tasks are cooking and weekly shopping.

Women tend to view their husband's help in housework as a moral victory. That is, by his minor assistance the husband recognizes the value of women's domestic activities and acknowledges her sacrifices for the household. Women realize that their husbands do not, and perhaps should not, provide an equal contribution to household maintenance. The majority of the women interviewed expressed the belief that the man's equal participation in all phases of housework is emasculating. Proof of this came from stories about women who insisted that their sons and daughters share equally in household chores, only to discover later that their sons have become homosexuals. These beliefs emanate from a conceptual framework of the place of gender in the social universe. This cultural model ascribes men by nature to the public sphere and women to the domestic sphere. This view was repeatedly expressed by informants in their responses to the following question: "In some households the woman goes out and works for wages and the man remains behind and assumes the child care and housekeeping responsibilities. Do you think this is right, and do you think the man can do as good a job as a woman?" The following quote is representative:

> I know of such cases where the man assumes the housekeeping and child care responsibilities. But, I don't believe a man can be as good as a woman. This is something in the nature of a woman; she is made for the home and the man is made to work.

Economic necessity has often required Dominican immigrant women, at least temporarily, to leave the domestic sphere for part of the day. This practice has in turn tempered the patriarchal dichotomy concerning the natural place of men and women in the world. The workplace has become an ideological resource drawn upon by women to redefine and renegotiate certain features of the sexual division of labor within the household. For many working immigrant women, the workplace mediates between the public sphere and the domestic sphere. This new orientation to the workplace challenges the more traditional ascription of men to the public workplace and women to the private household. Work enhances women's self-esteem as wives and mothers, affords them an income to actualize these roles more fully, and provides them with heightened leverage to participate equally with men in household decision-making.

This finding adds to the growing body of literature on women, work and the household which challenges earlier functionalist dichotomies between the family and workplace. For example, Talcott Parsons (1956) promulgated the belief that women would experience profound role conflicts if they added the status of worker to their primary positions as housewife and mother. The facile nature of such thinking is attested to by the fact that the very same woman who claimed it was in the nature of the woman to do housework and for the man to labor outside of the home, also stated that the aspect of her life that most satisfied her was her role "as a worker, because I can buy things for my daughter that I could not afford in the Dominican Republic."

Work outside of the home has in many cases improved Do women's lot and satisfaction in the home, although it has not provided women with a new status that challenges or subordinates their primary identities as wives and mothers. Stated another way, in many cases work has reinforced these statuses because it has allowed women to redefine their roles as wives and mothers in a more satisfying manner than existed prior to their employment and residence in the United States.[8]

DOMINICAN WOMEN'S ORIENTATION TO RETURN MIGRATION

The data indicate that the modification in status for migrant women from temporary to semipermanent or permanent, migrant unfolds within the interdependent settings of the household and workplace where women experience an improvement in their roles as women, wives, and mothers. This requires further specification for there are several types of Dominican immigrant households and women toil in different work contexts. As shall be seen, a woman's job and the specific type of household in which she resides contribute to differences in the way women view settlement in the United States. Furthermore, despite women's common reluctance to return to the Dominican Republic, many households do eventually relocate. This phenomenon also requires explanation.[9]

Two major household forms exist within the Dominican migrant community. These are the nuclear and female-headed household. A survey of Dominicans residing in New York revealed that 48 percent of the Dominican households were nuclear and 37 percent were female-headed (Archdiocese of New York 1983:117). Four different household types can be distinguished within the nuclear and female-headed forms. The nuclear form can be broken down into those units in which the wife engages in both wage work and housework (type 1), and those in which she works solely in the home or in a family business (type 2). The female-headed household can be divided into those units where the majority of income comes from wages (type 3), and households which subsist mainly on public assistance payments (type 4).

The research for this chapter on return migrant neighborhoods in the Dominican Republic and in migrant communities in the United States indicates that type 2 nuclear households are those most likely to return to the Dominican Republic. There are several factors that contribute to this development. Of the thirty-four return migrant households interviewed twenty owned their own business in the United States, and of these 80 percent of the wives were working full- or part-time in the business at least one year prior to the return. These households were characterized by the combination of sufficient savings, to establish a business and middle-class life-style in the Dominican Republic, with the wife's positive orientation toward relocating. The renegotiation of women's influence in the household, which informants who worked until their departure cited as one of the most feared aspects of readjustment, was already being confronted and managed by the first group of returnees while in the United States. They accepted the traditional bourgeois model in which the removal of the wife from the labor market symbolizes the household's material and social achievements. In most cases the wife's decision to return to the Dominican Republic was motivated by the desire to hire a domestic employee to relieve her of many housekeeping chores, to increase her social contacts, and to provide the children with a healthier (*mas sana*) social and home environment.

In cases of dual wage-earning households in which couples relocated to the Dominican Republic, all of the women expressed reservations about the return. In most cases the decision was the husband's, having convinced his wife that they had accumulated sufficient property and savings to replicate or improve their standard of living. The second, and often more powerful inducement from the wife's perspective was the husband's claim that the children would receive a better upbringing in the Dominican Republic. Reflected in women's acquiescence to these arguments is the tension that many women experience between their roles as wage-earners and as mothers. The critical question is whether they are most effectively meeting their children's needs by working to acquire necessary commodities and savings for a good education, or whether they are gambling with their children's futures by not remaining at home to oversee their socialization. When the wife's income is needed to sustain the household in the United States, this role conflict must be relegated to a secondary concern. However, if the savings realized from the couple's combined income do not make it necessary for the wife to work, she is often prodded by the husband to weigh the personal gains derived from her work and salary against her responsibilities as a mother. When the children actively oppose the return, this fortifies the woman's belief that she is being a good mother by working. In these instances, the weight of the wife-mother/child coalition diminishes the husband-father's ability to insist on the household's relocation.

In the other three variants of migrant households one finds an orientation on the part of women to postpone the family's return to the Dominican Republic. Let us consider the strategies by which women delay the return, and relate the motives behind this reorientation to the particular situation found in each household type. In the case of nuclear households where both wife and husband are employed, this author found that many women begin to use their income to create a household type that resembles, in several features, the domestic form that Tilly and Scott (1978) have termed "the family consumer economy." This domestic category refers to a change for working families from a previous state of acquiri⁻ sufficent income to subsist, to a condition in which members toil to meet new and increasing family consumption needs which are often defined and managed by the wife.

In the Dominican household context, this is manifested in women's insistence that part of the pooled household income be used to purchase expensive durable goods, such as new appliances and home furnishings, rather than deposited in a joint savings account. Such behavior can be attributed, in part, to women's greater identification with the household and their desire to have it represent the struggle of all members to acquire a middle-class life-style. There is, however, another fundamental issue operating, and it is captured in the common complaint by men that, "Five dollars wasted today means five more years of postponement of the return to the Dominican Republic." Most employed, married women who were interviewed sought to delay the family's return to the Dominican Republic. A common strategy is to spend money to root the family securely and comfortably in the United States, and to deplete the collective fund needed to relocate to the Dominican Republic. Women admit that what often underlies this strategy is their desire to postpone return to the Dominican Republic where the job market is unfavorable for them (Gurak and Kritz 1980; Pessar 1983). Women fear that the gains they have made in replacing patriarchal domestic relations with more egalitarian ones, and in providing for their children's welfare will be severely reduced if women return as dependents to a more male-dominated, Dominican society.[10]

Female heads of households were even more adamant in their interviews than were married women about the unlikelihood of their return to the Dominican Republic. One of the contrasts which helps to explain the difference between these two categories of female migrants is that female household heads do not have to contend with a husband's proclivities to return to the Dominican Republic. There is a second reason that reinforces women's desires to remain in the United States. For female-headed households the original motive for settling temporarily in the Untied States--to progress economically and socially--is rendered highly problematic by the fact that they are women. For example, the average Dominican woman earns approximately $2,500 less per year than a man. Furthermore, women are employed in segments of the economy, such as the garment industry, which experience tremendous instability in employment and sometimes operate illegally. This means that women may not have access to unemployment insurance when they are laid off, and must use their savings to sustain themselves and their families. When these funds are dissipated, women may be forced to obtain welfare. In many cases, then, the incomes of female heads of households are insufficient to permit a return to the Dominican Republic with adequate savings to sustain the quality of life associated with a successful migratory experience.

IMPLICATIONS OF PROLONGED MIGRATION

It remains to be seen what the consequences are of the prolongation of a household's stay in the United States. One has to acknowledge that the socioeconomic and language barriers of non-English speaking Hispanic migrants with limited education and skills, can limit their ability to find good jobs. But the work histories collected for the fifty-five Dominican women immigrants show a tendency over time for these individuals to seek and secure jobs which afforded higher pay, more security, better working conditions, and some career mobility. Interviews establish that these women became socialized by other workers and accumulated knowledge through their experiences in different workplaces. This rendered them less vulnerable to the illegal practices of some employers and less willing to remain in low-paying, deadend jobs.

Before generalizing about the changing role of immigrant women via-a-vis employers, it should be noted again that a worker's orientation to the workplace and her potential for reducing the employment costs of owners are mediated by the composition and organization of the household. Four subgroups are distinguishable among the fifty-five women who were the main informants of the households described in this chapter. The first segment (fifteen cases) consists of married women who view their work as supplementary rather than complementary to their husbands'. They commonly reside in homes where the household allowance mode operates. They are less committed to consumerism than other married women, and are least likely to change jobs for higher wages, increased benefits, and improved job mobility.[11] In contrast, the second group is comprised of employed female heads of households (sixteen cases). They tend to be more alert to opportunities for acquiring a higher paying job with increased benefits and security. When possible, they seek to gain access to new productive tasks to increase their versatility, visibility, and irreplaceability within the workplace. Many of these women actively pursue employment in union shops and tend to be more secure than the former group in their identity as workers, and more forthright in their condemnation of employers as exploitative. The third group (seven cases) comes closest to approximating the conventional function for employers associated with women and migrants. These are women who are receiving transfer payments while working anonymously (off the books) in sweatshops, or at home doing industrial homework. They are willing to accept wages far below the minimum wage ($1.50 to $2.50 per hour) in establishments that do not meet the minimum health and safety requirements. In this way they augment the income they receive from the state. The last group (seventeen cases) consists of married women who manage to use their access to the workplace and wages to gain greater equality with their husbands in the household. They are women engaged in creating the domestic type referred to as the "family consumer economy." These women actively pursue higher wages, benefits, and career mobility. For example, one woman rose from a factory operative to a supervisor in eleven years.

Due to the lack of randomness in the selection of these women, it would be inappropriate to use these findings as generalizations about the entire Dominican immigrant population. What these cases do clearly reveal, however, is that many female migrants operate in a fashion which challenges the requirements of a sector of the capitalist class for cheap, passive, and temporary workers.[12] Leaving aside the important question of duration of settlement, which all but five of the fifty-five women were actively seeking to prolong, a minority of the women (twenty-two) expressed beliefs and evinced behaviors that are congruent with a docile, inexpensive workforce. In contrast, thirty-three women aspired to, and pursued, improved working conditions and opportunities.

Finally, lest the capacity of female migrants to achieve improved wages, benefits, and career mobility be overstated, it must be stressed that there are gender-based structural and ideological factors that work together to constrain women's progress. While women's identities and orientations to migration and work are partly constructed in the household, these identities are shaped as well in the labor market with its own gender ideology and occupational segregation by gender. Furthermore, Dominican women are restricted by a set of beliefs that makes both Dominican males and females feel secure in relegating women to "protected" work spaces, such as garment shops. Such safe havens are characterized by jobs requiring limited training and little in the way of mental initiative. Furthermore, their workers receive low salaries, suffer job insecurity, and are offered few opportunities for mobility (Cf. Oakley 1981; Kessler-Harris 1981). The ideological defense for this segregation and discrimination is commonly found in the claim that because women are subsidized by men who are the primary wage earners they have a greater degree of security. These findings reveal a paradox. Women are usually the active agents in prolonging a household's stay, and this makes them and their household members less desirable workers for that economic sector that depends on a more temporary labor force. Yet, as women, they are less likely to reap the rewards of training and job mobility that are available over time to their male counterparts.

CONCLUSION

Using Dominican immigration as an illustrative case, this chapter has sought to demonstrate the necessity of including gender as a key variable in accounting for features of the migration experience, such as changes in immigrants orientation to settlement. A few researchers have explored objective aspects of gender and migration, such as how the demand for female immigrant labor is tied to occupational discrimination based on sex and the manner in which the secondary sector economy operates (Sassen-Koob 1981; Castro 1982). The other side of the equation--the subjective elements associated with gender and migration--has been far less explored. This chapter contributes to the latter perspective. While championing the study of women in migration, caution has been exercised against treating women as an undifferentiated social category. It has been shown that women's orientation to settlement and their role in reducing the costs for employers are not uniform. Rather they vary according to the organization of women's households.

NOTES

[1] For collections of studies on women and migration, or annotated bibliographies see Buechler 1976; Castro, et al. 1983; Migration Today 1982; Mortimer and Laporte 1981.

[2] The data and analysis found in the following sections are by-products of three years of ethnographic fieldwork (1980-1983) conducted in rural communities in the Cibao region of the Dominican Republic, in return migrant neighborhoods in the city of Santiago, and in Dominican neighborhoods in the New York metropolitan area.

The study was funded by the National Institutes of Health, the National Science Foundation, and New York University's New York Research Program in Inter-American Affairs. Much of the data presented in this chapter was collected by my research assistants, Catherine Benamou, Nancy Clark, Anneris Goris, and Julia Tavares. I would like to thank them for their help and acknowledge, as well, the continuing intellectual and personal support I have received from my research collaborator, Dr. Sherri Grasmuck, and from the staff and visiting scholars at New York University's Center for Latin American and Caribbean Studies.

[3] Data for the analysis of gender differences in the migration process come from fieldwork conducted in the United States and the Dominican Republic. The generalizations that are made about experiences in the United States are based on structured interviews and casual conversation with several hundred Dominican immigrants as well as participant observation in households, workplaces, and social gatherings. There are clearly problems inherent in generalizing about such a large population when people are not chosen on some sort of random basis to ensure a representative sample. Particularly in the New York phase of the study, a process of self-selection operated which was based on people's willingness to participate over time in a series of visits and interviews, often in their homes.

Three principal groups form the basis for much of the data and analysis presented below: members of fifty-five immigrant households who provided information over a year's period (1981 to 1982) on topics such as social networks, decision-making, income generation, control over budgeting, and beliefs about sex roles; twenty garment workers who were queried (1982 to 1983) about the above topics as well as the nature of their workplace and beliefs about their role as workers; and members of thirty-four return migrant households (1982) whose readjustment to life in the Dominican Republic was studied.

These informants were obtained through various means, such as introductions by community leaders in the churches, schools or local associations. Previous contact with an individual or family members and friends in the Dominican Republic proved extremely useful for making initial contacts in New York. Interviews with undocumented immigrants and with people who were involved in illegal economic activities produced the most reliable data when an assistant or myself was either personally known prior to the research or had gained the deep trust of a close family member or friend. Finally, to explore the veracity and significance of patterns in beliefs and behavior that emerged in interviews and participant observations, key informants were relied upon extensively.

[4] Estimates of the number of Dominicans residing in the United States (as both documented and undocumented immigrants) range from 500,000 to 800,000. The majority of this population has arrived since 1961, and approximately 90 percent reside in the New York metropolitan area. Most come from urban, lower middle-class backgrounds, and 60.4 percent of the Dominicans residing in New York are women (Gurak and Kritz 1982; Ugalde et al. 1979).

According to a 1981 probability survey (the Hispanic Settlement in New York City Survey directed by Douglas Gurak, Fordham University) for this female population the average age of arrival was 22.2 years and the median level of education was 8.0 years. The majority of the women (53 percent) were married, another 12 percent had never married, and 35 percent were divorced or separated. While only 31 percent of the female population had been employed prior to emigration, 91.5 percent had worked for pay at some time since their emigration, and 49.7 percent were currently in the labor force (employed or seeking employment). The mean income in 1981 for female migrants was $6,884 as compared to $9,430 for males.

Of the 39.6 percent that were males, the average age of arrival was 22, and the median level of education was 9.4 years; 65 percent were married, 23 percent were never married, and 12 percent were divorced or separated. The majority of the men (64 percent) had been employed prior to migration, 91.3 percent had worked for wages at some time during their residence in the United States, and 87.6 percent were currently in the labor force.

[5] For other studies of Dominican immigrant women see

Gonzalez 1980, 1976; Gurak and Kritz 1982; and Pessar 1985

6 See Grant and Herbstein (1983) for a treatment of social mobility realized at the household level for several immigrant populations residing in New York.

7 For a discussion of the material underpinnings of these three modes of budgetary control see Pessar 1985.

8 Women also acknowledge that in instances of marital discord, wage work provides them with the material security to entertain a separation or divorce.

9 Findings from a national survey conducted in 1974 (Diagnos) indicate that approximately 39 percent of those who emigrated came back. This return rate seems high, and one of the factors accounting for this is the many return migrants who went to the United States to pursue their studies. Of the returnee population, one-fourth resettled after finishing their schooling. About 19 percent reported adjustment problems as motivating their return, while 7 percent returned after having saved the money to start a business (Ugalde et al. 1979:249)

10 In ten of the eighteen cases of divorce or separation among the fifty-five households studied, the woman and man had opposing financial strategies. That is, the man directed his own surplus income to savings and exhorted other household members to do the same. The woman, on the other hand, applied her earnings to commodities (often purchased on credit), and encouraged working children to invest their money in education or personal items of consumption. In five cases what actually precipitated the breakup was the man's return to the Dominican Republic with sufficient savings to reestablish himself while the woman elected to remain in the United States.

11 It is my impression that of all the household types, the women from type 1 households are most positively disposed to return migration. Unfortunately, the interviews in return migrant households were not structured in such a manner to allow for the testing of this proposition.

12 For a discussion of how the class background and identification of Dominican women affect their orientation to the workplace see Pessar 1985.

REFERENCES

Abadan-Unat, Nermin. 1977. "Implications of Migration on

Emancipation and Pseudo-Emancipation of Turkish Women." International Migration Review 11 No. 1:31-58.

Archdiocese of New York. 1982. Hispanics in New York: Religious, Cultural and Social Experiences. New York: Office of Pastoral Research.

Buechler, Judith. 1976. "Women and Migration." Anthropological Quarterly 49 no. 1-76.

Castro, Mary Garcia, Margaret Gill and Margaret Jean Gearing. 1983. Women in Migration. A Selective Annotated Bibliography. Occasional Paper 2. Gainesville, Fla.: Center for Latin American Studies, University of Florida.

Chaney, Elsa and Martha Lewis. 1980. "Women, Migration and the Decline of Smallholder Agriculture." Washington, D.C.: Report prepared for the Office of Women in Development. United States Agency for International Development.

Gonzalez, Nancie. 1970. "Peasants' Progress: Dominicans in New York." Caribbean Studies 10 No. 3:154-71.

_____. 1976. "Multiple Migratory Experiences of Dominican Women." Anthropological Quarterly 49 No. 1:36-43.

Grant, Geraldine and Judith Herbstein. 1983. "Immigrant Mobility: Upward, Downward or Outward?" Paper presented at the Society for Applied Anthropology Meetings, San Diego.

Guhleman, Patricia and Marta Tienda. 1981. "A Socioeconomic Profile of Hispanic American Female Workers: Perspectives on Labor Force Participation and Earnings." Center for Demography and Ecology Working Papers 81-87, University of Wisconsin, Madison.

Gurak, Douglas and Mary Kritz. 1982. "Settlement and Integration Processes of Dominicans and Colombians in New York City." Unpublished paper presented at the Annual Meetings of the American Sociological Association, New York.

_____. 1982. "Women in New York City: Household Structure and and Employment Patterns." Migration Today 10 No. 3 and 4:15-21.

Gurak, Douglas, Mary Kritz, Manuel Ortega and Brian Early. 1980. "Early Employment of Two Cohorts of Women in the Dominican Republic." Unpublished paper presented at the Annual

Meetings of the American Sociological Association, New York.

Kessler Harris, Alice. 1981. Women Have Always Worked. Old Westbury: Feminist Press.

Lewis, Oscar. 1959. Five Families: Mexican Case Studies in the Culture of Poverty. New York: Basic Books.

Meillassoux, Claude. 1981. Maidens, Meal, and Money: Capitalism and the Domestic Community. New York: Cambridge University Press.

Migration Today. 1982. "Women and Migration" (special issue). Vol. 10 nos. 3 and 4:6-51.

Morokvasic, Mirjana. 1979. "The Migration of Women in Europe." Paper presented at a Conference on the Continuing Subordination of Women in the Development Process. Institute for Development Studies, Sussex, England.

Mortimer, Dolores and Roy S. Bryce-Laporte. 1981. Female Immigrants to the United States: Caribbean, Latin American and African Experiences. RIIES Occasional Papers, No. 2. Washington, D.C.: Research Institute of Immigration and Ethnic Studies, Smithsonian Institution.

Oakley, Ann. 1981. Subject Women. New York: Pantheon Books.

Parsons, Talcott and R. Bales. 1956. Family, Socialization and Interaction Process. Glencoe, Illinois: Free Press.

Pessar, Patricia. 1982a. "The Role of Households in International Migration." International Migration Review 16 No. 2:324-64.

_____. 1982b. "Kinship Relations of Production in the Migration Process: The Case of Dominican Emigration to the United States." Occasional Paper 32. New York: Center for Latin American and Caribbean Studies, New York University.

_____. 1985. "The Constraints upon and Release of Female Labor Power: The Case of Dominican Migration to the United States." In Women, Income and Poverty (forthcoming), edited by Daisy Dwyer and Judith Bruce.

Piore, Michael. 1979. Birds of Passage: Migrant Labor and Industrial Societies. Cambridge: Cambridge University Press.

Redfield Robert. 1955. The Little Community. Chicago: University of Chicago Press.

Safa, Helen. n.d. "Work and Women's Liberation." In Urban Anthropology in the United States, edited by Leith Mullings. New York: Columbia University Press.

Sassen-Koob, Saskia. 1981. "Exporting Capital and Importing Labor: The Role of Women." In Female Immigrants to the United States, edited by Dolores Mortimer and Roy S. Bryce-Laporte. Washington. D.C.: Smithsonian Institution Press.

Smale, Melinda. 1980. "Women in Mauritania: The Effects of Drought and Migration on Their Economic Status and Implications for Development Programs." Washington, D.C.: United States Agency for International Development.

Smith, M. Estellie. 1980. "The Portuguese Female Immigrant: The Marginal Man." International Migration Review 14 No. 1:77-92.

Tilly, Lousie, and Joan Scott. 1978. Women, Work and Family. New York: Holt, Rinehart and Winston.

Ugalde, Antonio, Frank Bean, and Gil Cardenas. 1979. "International Migration from the Dominican Republic: Findings from a National Survey." International Migration Review 13 No. 2:235-54.

TABLE 1

Occupation of Employed Dominican Men in New York

Occupation	% of Males	
No Occupation	33	(14.8)
Professional Workers	11	(4.9)
Managers, Proprietors, Officials	14	(6.3)
Clerical Workers	11	(4.9)
Sales Workers	10	(4.5)
Domestic Services	0	
Other Service Workers	39	(17.5)
Farmers, Farm Laborers, Miners, etc.	0	
Skilled, Blue Collar, or Craft Workers	14	(6.3)
Semiskilled Operatives	68	(30.5)
Unskilled Nonfarm Laborers	23	(10.3)
Unknown	0	
(n)	223	

Source: The Hispanic Settlement in New York City Survey 1981

TABLE 2

Last Occupation Held by Immigrant Men Prior to Migration

Occupation	% of Males	
No Occupation	53	(23.8)
Professional Workers	20	(9.0)
Managers, Proprietors, Officials	12	(5.4)
Clerical Workers	24	(10.8)
Sales Workers	12	(5.4)
Domestic Services	0	
Other Service Workers	24	(10.8)
Farmers, Farm Laborers, Miners, etc.	14	(6.3)
Skilled, Blue Collar, or Craft Workers	17	(7.6)
Semiskilled Operatives	30	(13.5)
Unskilled Nonfarm Laborers	5	(2.2)
Unknown	12	(5.4)
(n)	223	

Source: The Hispanic Settlement in New York City Survey 1981

TABLE 3

Dominant Mode of Budgetary Control
in the Dominican Republic Prior to Emigration
and in Dominican Immigrant Households In New York

Mode of Budgetary Control	Prior to Migration	Subsequent to Migration
Traditional Patriarchal Form	10	2
Household Allowance	28	15
Pooled Income	17	38
(n)	55	55

V Political Action and the State

Since the first edition of our anthology, *Sex and Class in Latin America*, several Latin American countries have fallen under military regimes while others have turned to democratic and socialist states. How women have fared in the changing political climates is examined in chapters included in this section. Ximena Bunster-Burotto shows the extreme use of sexual sadism in the torture of women by the Chilean military regmine to enforce political conformity. Gloria Ardaya S. summarizes the resistance of Bolivian women to the miliary regime of Hugo Banzer. Isabel Larguia and John Dumoulin indicate the achievements of the Cuban government and the shortcomings in the goal of integrating women in the Cuban revolution.

Preparatory assembly for the fourth congress of the Federation of Cuban Women

15 Surviving Beyond Fear:
Women and Torture in Latin America

Ximena Bunster-Burotto

Military regimes in Latin America have developed patterns of punishments specifically designed for women who are perceived as actively fighting against or in any way resisting the oppression and exploitation visited upon their peoples by dictatorial governments. The attempts to dominate and coerce women through terrorism and torture have become organized and systematic--administered by the military state. The more generalized and diffused female sexual enslavement through the patriarchal state has been crystallized and physically literalized through the military state as torturer.

Punitive sexual enslavement of female political prisoners is found throughout Latin America. However, the armed, organized terrorizing of women may best be understood in the context of political, economic, and social forces present in a given historical-national situation. We, therefore, see a somewhat different profile in the victimization of women taking place in Nicaragua, Salvador, Guatemala, and Honduras than that which has become characteristic of the countries of the Southern Cone--Argentina, Chile, Uruguay, Paraguay, and Bolivia.

In the first cluster of countries--those forming part of Central America--political torture reaches women as daily terror. Women are most often injured or killed in contexts of generalized violence: in massacres, attacks on churches during mass, and the burning of villages. This generalized violence affects different segments of the population who happen to be present during the attacks--men, older people, children, and even domestic animals. By contrast, in the countries of the Southern Cone, where a military government or succession of military governments have been entrenched for decades, women are *systematically identified*--with names, address, and family composition--as "enemies" of the government. They are methodically tracked down and incarcerated. There are institutions within the military government dedicated specifically and exclusively to this task.

For the purposes of this chapter, I have concentrated an analysis of sexual torture of female political prisoners who are or have been citizens of Argentina, Chile, and Uruguay. The Argentinian state has been militarized on and off since 1930 and the Chilean and the Uruguayan states since 1973. I have selected these three countries for the following reasons:

1. Each at one time was a flourishing democratic government, later aborted by military takeover.

2. These nations have had years of military dictatorship during which torture as a method of "security" has become inistitutionalized. These institutions incorporate scientifically trained torture specialists, physicians, modern hardware, and "refined" methods in the systematic torturing of political prisoners.

3. Each of these countries had a highly organized, politically conscious urban proletariat from whose ranks prominent female union and community leaders emerged.

In her work *Female Sexual Slavery*, Kathleen Barry says:

> Female sexual slavery is present in ALL situations where women or girls cannot change the immediate conditions of their existence; where regardless of how they got into those conditions they cannot get out; and where they are subject to sexual violence and exploitation (1979:40).

My analysis of the nature of the torture endured by Latin American female political prisoners stems from Barry's groundbreaking work. For I believe--and this I have tried to document in the pages that follow--that once one has listened to firsthand and eyewitness accounts and has read and analyzed the written testimonies of how pain and suffering are inflicted on women prisoners, a distinctive pattern of torture emerges.

In the state torturers' efforts to force confessions, elicit information, or to punish, a pattern in structure and in content is clearly discernible. These common elements experienced by female political prisoners in violent sexual attacks upon her body and psyche are consciously designed to violate her sense of herself, her female human dignity. The combination of culturally defined moral debasement and physical battering is the demented scenario whereby the prisoner is to undergo a rapid metamorphosis from madonna-- "respectable woman and/or mother"--to whore. To women through processes of socialization, this violent sexual treatment administered by the state becomes most cruelly doubly disorienting; it exacerbates and magnifies the woman's already subservient, prescribed, passive, secondary position in Latin American society and culture.

In order to better understand--while maintaining an awareness of the pitfalls that cultural generalization entails--how societal archetypes and stereotypes are manipulated by the torturers, it is important to look briefly at the delicate balance and complementarity of the male and female roles and the culturally assigned gender differences in Latin American society.

Many authors have discussed the bipolar conception of *machismo/Marianismo* underlying the socialization of men and women in Latin America. *Machismo*, or the cult of virility, has been described as embracing an "exaggerated agressiveness and intransigence in male-to-male interpersonal relationships and arrogance and sexual aggression in male-to-female relationships"; *Marianismo*, as "the cult of feminine spiritual superiority which teaches that women are semi-divine, morally superior to and spiritually stronger than men" (Stevens 1973:91). Machismo and marianismo, are New World variations on Old World themes.

Machismo is obviously a Latin American manifestation of global patriarchy, whereby males enjoy special privileges within the society and within the family and are considered superior to women. "Marianismo, Mariology," or the cult of the Virgin Mother--she who embodies simultaneously the ideal of nurturance/motherhood and chastity--permeates the world view of Latin America and all aspects of its culture and institutions. Latin American women are supposed to pattern their role as women after this perfect model inspired through pervasive Catholicism. The patriarchal madonna/whore schema, too, is global.[1] Its particular manifestation in Latin America through the cult of the Virgin shows the extent to which Catholic ideology and the sexual stereotypes it introduced have been assimilated. Latin America has clearly absorbed the Spanish culture introduced by the conquistadores, itself marked by seven centuries of Arab-Muslim domination. The manipulation of these images proved useful to later waves of exploitation through capitalism.

Perhaps one example at this point will serve to bring home the fact of the double brutalization involved in socializing women in particular modes and then using that very socialization as a method of torture. One of the secret detention camps in Argentina, called Olimpo, was opened in the Western zone of Buenos Aires in August 1980. Testimony provided by Argentinians who were detained there describe how the torture of detainees involved icons of the Virgin Mary:

> In the very corridor leading to the torture rooms, along which new inmates had passed naked and in which they were beaten when they were first kidnapped, a small chapel was installed. It is a strange kind of Christianity these people have, enjoying punishing and beating until the victim loses consciousness--in front of the image of the Virgin Mary. (Amnesty International--U.S.A. 1980:10)

Two important characteristics, then, of Latin American culture are crucial to an understanding of the specific nature of female sexual torture in these countries. First, women are basically recognized and valued only as mothers, after the Blessed Virgin Mother. Second, women have adopted and internalized these patterns under the historical weight of Hispanic-Arab and Christian heritage and are now faced and overburdened by contemporary underdevelopment--a situation that must be felt and understood in its dailiness. Latin America has undergone conquest and colonization, and with these has seen Western values imposed over those autochthonic belief systems represented through high Indian civilizations at the time of the conquest. It is in this context that we hear the resonance of the Latin American/Caribbean Women's Collective in exile in Europe today: "domination in Latin America has been a prolongation of the history of man's exploitation of man and of men's domination of women." (Latin American and Caribbean Women's Collective 1980:8)

In view of this cultural heritage and the ways in which the cultural baggage affects patterned gender differences, it is important to ask whether it matters that the state as torturer is a military state. It seems clear, from the countries examined and the systematic, ordered processes of torture of female political prisoners that are evident, that it does, indeed, matter. The fact that these states where torture has become institutionalized are military states should be kept in mind. It seems that military regimes exhibit the impulse of the state to secure and defend the patriarchal structure and the privileged status of "masculinity" more blatantly than do other authoritarian states. The military state understands itself to be run for the perpetuation and extension of the values of the military, masculinity, power, and public authority to a greater extent than do other patriarchal states. It is founded on the assumption that women and notions of the "feminine" are tools to be used by men; simultaneously, militarism as an ideology purports that women are fearsome threats to public order, to the heriarchy defined and controlled by men. It is important to stress the fact that although other patriarchal states also torture women, militaristic states rely more than civilian states on the use of coercion to strengthen and perpetuate their public authority (Enloe 1983).

The military elites of Argentina, Chile, and Uruguay have brought internal police forces under their control and have strengthened and further entrenched the institutionalized torture machine through formal coordination of internal security bureaucracies and military bureaucracies. Thus, not only have the internal police come within the cloak of the military regimes but the military has also taken an active role in internal security matters. In Argentina, for example, one of the most infamous torture and detention centers is not run by the police, but by the navy. In Chile, separate torture centers are run by the air force, the navy, and the army. In attempts to unify and tighten their bureaucratic torture machines, the military regimes in both Argentina and Chile have brought in the internal intelligence agencies and "publicly employed" physicians, who supervise torture directly under their control.

The woman who is abducted is made to understand that she is under the control and at the mercy of a military state in every aspect of her life,--her socioeconomic future, her family life, her sexuality, her internal feelings and sense of herself. Torture is the chosen method to convince her of these "truths."

ARREST, INTIMIDATION AND BRUTALIZATION AS PUNISHMENT

It seems viable to use, as a point of orientation, the definition of torture--the "standard" definition--as adopted by the Inter-American Commission on Human Rights:

> Torture is understood to be the practice or instigation, by means of which physical or mental pain or suffering is intentionally inflicted upon a person, having taken into consideration the age, sex or condition of the person, for the purpose of intimidation, or in order to obtain a confession or information from the person or in order to punish the person for an act committed or which it is suspected that the person committed. (1982:91)

Although I have used this definition simply for the sake of clarity, and for consistency when using data gathered through various human rights agencies, it is important for us to realize this definition is itself limited and limiting when it comes to an understanding of the special nature of female sexual slavery and torture.

There is a distinctive pattern of torture when female political prisoners are involved. We must recognize and have recognized the fact that when the issue of torture of political prisoners is raised as a human rights issue it never deals with women. We must recognize that the physical and psychic torture of *women as women*--female sexual slavery in patriarchal societies reaching its "logical" extension and quintessential crystallization in the military state--is made invisible. As the military state so often tortures women as a mode of punishing their "man," so even to many human rights advocates the "desecration" of the female is processed as torture of the male.

In order to delineate specific phases and stages of the brutalization and attempted extinction of women as human beings, I have used both composites derived from the large number of recorded violations in Argentina, Chile, and Uruguay, and examples from personal interviews, conversations, and correspondence with women who have witnessed and survived the torture.

Due to common elements in their recent histories, a relatively large body of literature exists dealing with human rights violations in Argentina, Chile, and Uruguay. Free public primary, secondary, and university education has provided thousands of women with occupational and professional degrees. From the ranks of the working class and enlarged middle class, female members of the house of representatives (*diputadas*) and senators for the national congress (*senadoras*) emerged. Women committed to change and the abolishment of social injustice have been particularly active in these countries. Human rights organizations such as Amnesty International and the Inter-American Commission have, therefore, been able to amass evidence of the extent of institutionalized torture. These publications document organized phases of terror in the sexual enslavement and torture of female political prisoners.

I must at this point speak to the bravery of those women who have survived what is in fact unspeakable physical and psychological torment and have then come forth to bear witness. We know the psychic pain involved for each of us as we work with these issues; the survivors of these horrors relive their experiences in the telling--their courage and commitment to the rights of human beings must remain for us, here, the inspiration to continue. The bulk of the cases utilized in this study cover the period 1973-81, when the experiences of these women took place. I have been in touch with women who have survived torture since 1973; the most recent conversations and interviews have taken place in 1982-83.

It was not deemed necessary to identify the country in each of the cases that follow as my analysis is directed toward an understanding of the nature of the commonality of pattern of sexual slavery in torture--a pattern that typifies the experiences of all women political prisoners in the Southern Cone of Latin America.

The aim of the first phase in the psychological and physical maltreatment of female political prisoners staged by military, navy, air force or police torturers is to intimidate and create a sense of anxiety in their victims. Two categories of women are targeted for attention.

Captors representing the state as torturer direct their established institutions of violence at the many Latin American women whose political consciousness has spurred them into political activism on behalf of the establishment of a more just social order within their own countries. This has been the case of Chilean women who worked within the Allende government toward the construction of a more egalitarian socioeconomic order. This has also been the case of Argentinian, Uruguayan, and--following the coup--Chilean women who became active in the struggle to liberate their countries and peoples from repressive dictatorships and the complicity of those regimes with foreign interests exploiting the human and natural resources of their nations. This group of women, many with public roles--as union leaders, lawyers, doctors, professors--are targeted because of their commitment to a people's struggle.

Institutionalized violence, torture, is also aimed at a second category of women--women who do not have a publically recognized identity of their own, but, from the perspective of the state, derive their identity from their relationship to a male. These women are targeted because of the activism of a husband, lover, son, father, or brother. The "super-macho" military system brutalizes these women as an extension of the ego and as a possession of the male whom they consider the "enemy" in an "internal war." The women undergo imprisonment as hostages in this "internal war" and are then savagely tortured to get even with their men--the enemies of the military regime in power. The sexual enslavement of women belonging to this category is used to intimidate, emasculate, bring forth confessions from, and, in many cases, destroy the men to whom they are legally or emotionally attached.

Intimidation begins with the process of arrest. In the majority of cases, these women have been arrested at home or at their place of work. There are, however, a significant number of seizures in the streets, where women are taken on their way home from a day's work at a factory, office, hospital, school, store--a variety of work sites. A consistent modus operandi is used when making an arrest in the street. The woman's way is blocked by three to five men dressed in civilian clothing; only in a very rare instance do these men identify themselves in any way. The woman is grasped violently by the arm by one of the kidnappers while others flank her on each side with their bodies. She is then pushed into a waiting vehicle, handcuffed, and her eyes taped. Sunglasses are usually placed over the scotch or adhesive tape. She sits with eyes lowered and her body tensed with fear. The agents of the government try to use caution lest the fact of their taking a hostage be noted by onlookers. If there are passer-by in a highly congested city area or an oncoming car with passengers, the woman is rapidly thrown to the floor of the vehicle and slapped or beaten with the butt of a revolver.

Probably the most terrorizing arrest is that which takes place when the woman is at home with her family. This violent military operation--envisioned only for the most dangerous criminals in countries with stable democracies--is carried out by an *allanamiento*, a large group of soldiers who come in two or three vehicles and surround the house or building where the apartment of the woman is situated. They carry machine guns and an assortment of other weapons. If any resistance is offered, there is an official housebreaking and search of the home, accompanied by the destruction of furniture, the ripping of mattresses, and the armed intimidation of all the people who are in the house at the moment. This inhumane and cowardly action takes place at night--all reports place such action between midnight and 3:00.

Arresting a woman in the home, in front of her children, is doubly painful to the Latin American woman. The family is traditionally run by the mother. The main agent of socialization of children, who has the culturally prescribed role of guardian of the moral values of the society; it is she who must ensure that guidelines for the social and sexually accepted behavior of family members are adopted and absorbed. She represents the popularly accepted stereotype of the ideal woman exemplified in the Virgin Mother. This cultural pattern permeates all social classes and all adult women, be they mothers or childless. The women are to be morally superior and spiritually stronger than men, sexually pure as opposed to promiscuous, submissive and understanding of the frailties and patriarchal whims of their fathers, husbands, and sons, yet strong beneath that submissiveness. The identity of the Latin American woman is derived from her position in the family and especially from her "sacred" mothering role, where she is overprotective in her nurturing, absolutely devoted to her children, and willing to sacrifice her own desires to please her family--especially the male members. Her love is sacrifice and selflessness personified. It is crucial to understand the extent to which the conceptions are internalized; these attributes provide the foundation on which the edifice of the Latin American woman's self-perception and self-respect is built. These attributes also reflect upon the male members of her family, whose sense of personal honor and dignity is conceived as directly related to and dependent on the sense of moral propriety of the women in their family.

Given all these cultural antecedents, when a woman is imprisoned in her home, the protection and refuge of the home that she represents is shattered, and the control and coherence she maintained in the intimate sphere of the household is destroyed as well.

This assault on a woman's sense of self and the manipulation of her traditional role as wife and mother is used by the torturers to break, punish, and ultimately destroy her. During this violation of her human dignity, torture as intimidation and torture as punishment blend into the same criminal act. This is the stage in an enslaved woman's torment when *family torture* is enacted by her captors. The following cases exemplify this strategy of the state tortures:

> *N.N.*, forty-six-year-old widow, was imprisoned in her proletarian home and punished for not releasing the names of left-wing workers. She was beaten in front of her fourteen-year-old son. As she kept repeating that she was ignorant of the facts, the torturer beat her fourteen-year-old son in her presence, fracturing his jaw, breaking part of his rib cage, and infliciting pain on both arms.

> *V.L.*, a young married mother of three children was assaulted at one o'clock in the morning. Just she and her children were at home when three men in civilian clothing--

members of a military torturing squad broke in. They raped her repeatedly at gunpoint in front of her children, aged five, four, and two, while threatening to shoot her if she cried for help. This heinous act was repeated on six other occasions over a two-month period, creating a constant state of terror for V.L. and her children. Her husband had previously been detained by authorities; she was subjected to this repreated sexual torment in the state's effort to lower her defenses and obtain information concerning the husband's political activities.

V.P.R.'s apartment was broken into and the building surrounded by soldiers armed wih machine guns. Everyone was dragged from bed at gunpoint. She, her husband, their twelve-year-old son, and their maid were immobilized, guns aimed at their heads. The smaller children, a girl, aged seven and a boy, aged eight, awoke and, entering the living room, were confronted with the spectacle of their mother at gunpoint. Terrorized, the two children started shaking with violent convulsions and crying out loud. The captors cut off the electricity to the apartment and walked out with the mother, father, brother, and maid, leaving the two children huddled together in anguish and complete darkness within their own home. The father subsequently was executed, his skull broken with brutal beatings. The mother was subjected to further torture through beatings, massive rape and electricity applied to her genital area.

A.C. de R., a nineteen-year old woman, was sleeping with her husband. They were living at her parents' home at the time of the police operation. The household included A.C. de R.'s mother and two sisters, aged thirteen and fifteen; her father, a commercial pilot, was away. During the 3:30 arrest, the young husband was gunned down in the bedroom in his wife's presence; he died instantly. The young widow, her mother, and two sisters were blindfolded, hooded, and taken as hostages for interrogation. The mother and two younger daughters were eventually released; but A.C. de R. is one of the many persons "missing" in the Southern Cone of Latin America today.

After the terror of arrest, the hostage woman is forced to face a series of phases of torture through which her state torturers hope to destroy her psychically as well as physically. Again, it is to obtain a confession or information, or as authorized punishment that these "security" methods are applied.

Both male and female detainees are tortured; some methods are applied equally to both sexes: incommunicado detention, wall-standing, the electric prod, the electric grid, the submarine, the dry submarine, the *pau de arara*, and inventive variations of the theme of beating (see Appendix A).

The overall terrorizing environment of the detention centers should be understood as the backdrop for the torments particularly designed for women. From the institutional perspective, these are orderly affairs. The state's bureaucratic torturing system has incorporated doctors. Physicians are in charge of supervising the physical and psychological torment of prisoners--their scientific knowledge allows them to indicate when a given method of torture should be suspended if the death of the hostage is not desired.

Carefully designed mental torment is applied in counterpoint with the physical torture of detainees in a premeditated effort to increase the total feeling of powerlessness and pain. Simulated executions are staged in the middle of the night; captors threaten that a loved one will "disappear" or that a spouse, an aging parent, or small child will be tortured if cooperation and information are not forthcoming. Prisoners are forced to witness the torture and death of other detainees or are placed in rooms or cells where they must listen to the moaning of other hostages being beaten with the butts of machine guns, rifles, and revolver. Often, standing naked and blindfolded, survivors report having to listen to the screams and "almost animal howls of pain" of prisoners being tortured in the same room or an adjacent one. Blindfolds are removed, however, when the detainee is forced through buildings to encounter a flow of fellow prisoners who can hardly walk or talk following torture sessions.

This is a climate, a world, of mounting and disorienting fear. For the prisoner, this is a totally unstructured situation--with "reality" defined and composed by the torturers. Prisoners have no moment-to-moment, no daily control of their lives; they survive in a dim present with very little hope for the future.

TORTURE DESIGNED FOR FEMALE POLITICAL PRISONERS

Female and male prisoners, then, are subjected to many of the same torturing practices, whose aim is to inflict physical pain, mental distress, and general suffering. However, the torture of men, while horrible, has as its object something less then the extinction of their sexual, gender identity. The primary form of sexual torture of men is directed toward their sexual confidence; their humanity is debased by placing them in powerless situations, where they cannot defend a female political prisoner--usually a wife, daughter, mother, lover, or friend--from brutal sexual torture performed in their presence.

Women's torment is comparatively much worse than men's because it is painfully magnified a thousand times by the most inhuman, cruel, and degrading methods of torture consciously and systematically directed at her female sexual identity and female anatomy. The processes of imprisonment and torture of women political prisoners is female sexual slavery in its most hideous and blantantly obvious forms. It represents "macho" patriarchal contempt and misogyny crystallized and implemented through military-police structures of organized violence. These are not simply males "out of control with permission", with a demonic irony, the sexual torture of women is named "control" and is authorized state "security." This fact should not surprise us; the military is, by definition, the most sexist and patriarchal institution of the many institutions that reinforce ideological subordination of women in the family and in society at large (Chapkis 1981).

The sexual violence unleashed against women political prisoners is seen as the key in controlling them, through punishment and interrogations. Gang rape, massive rape becomes the standard torture mechanism for the social control of the imprisoned women. Politically commited, active women who have dared to take control of their own lives by struggling against an oppressive regime demand sexual torture--as do the women who have stood by their men in an organized poitical effort to liberate their country and themselves from a coercive military regime. One of the essential ideas behind the sexual slavery of a woman in torture is to teach her that she must retreat into the home and fulfill the traditional role of wife and mother. It is this role only that provides her with respect in a society where she is ideologically defined as inferior to the men from whom she derives her secondary identity--she is some male's mother, sister, wife, and *companera*. With a too usual contradiction and reversal, the method of the "lesson" forcing a return to the *marianissimo* ideal simultaneously violates that possibility. There seems to be not only a willingness to violate cultural notions of what the "natural" social order is, but in fact to direct torment with excruciating precision just to those areas of societal definition. We can only describe these patterns of state torture, we cannot make them rational.

Behind the sequence of brutal sexual acts committed on a woman's body and mind while she is in captivity lurks the criminal attempt to humiliate, degrade, and morally and physically destroy her through and within the social, cultural, and political environment that is familiar to her. It is, in an important sense, too distancing to speak of culturally accepted and defined gender distinctions. The ideological conceptions, the myths, and the realities of the paradigmatic vision of Woman, are much of the ground from which springs a woman's sense of herself and from which she derives the emotional needs and the gratifications that give meaning to her life--the love and respect of her family and the esteem and caring of her coworkers.

A woman's self-respect, sense of dignity, and physical integrity is shattered when at the hands of her captors she unwillingly becomes the participant-observer of the planned and enforced destruction of her culturally defined womanhood. In every sense of the word, in every level of her being, the torturers' invasion involves radical disorientation.

The sequence of types and examples of torture that follows is from cases of women in Argentina, Chile, and Uruguay. There is always a danger, when cases of the torture of people are summarized and then classified. As painful as it is we must not allow ourselves to forget, even for a moment, that we are speaking of pain and torment inflicted upon individuals. Even in the notions of selection of "evidence" of what is held to be a viable methodology we neutralize the FACT of the agony for these women, woman by woman.

The woman prisoner is brought blindfolded and hooded to one of the many *casas de tortura* (torture houses) administered by the security forces of these countries. They are most often established in regiments, police quarters, naval and air force bases, and academies, and in houses rented and equipped for purposes of torturing. The woman has already undergone the trauma of arrest and the geographical disorientation of being taken blindfolded to the torture house. She has been cut off from her family; or, if her arrest went unobserved by relatives, neighbors or passers-by, she has "disappeared"--she knows that no one knows where to look for her. Some victims captured on the streets start shouting their own names aloud so that the family will know they were dragged away.

While she is presumably at the information desk or in the "reception room" of the detention center--"presumably" because survivors report that it takes a while to look from under the blindfold without being discovered and beaten--her name and address are taken and entered into files with a number. While she is giving the information demanded, her body--especially her breasts, buttocks and entire genital area--is fingered and pawed by countless male hands. Her body is squeezed and explored producing in her a sense of outrage, sometimes physical pain, shame, and despair.

She is then taken to another room, where a group of men undress her, literally tear her clothing and start slapping and beating her up continuously. No sooner has she been able to get on her feet when she is again thrown to the floor or against a wall. Her nose starts bleeding and she aches all over. During the course of this brutal battering, she is given orders to sit down--there is never a chair--so she falls to the floor. She is then given contradictory orders to march in a given direction, obeying, hits herself against a wall, then she is told to kneel and squat because she has to go under a table. In the meantime she is the target of crude verbal abuse and vile ridicule of her naked body. She becomes the pathetic jester who amuses the torturers by her aimless movements directed to make her fall, roll on the floor, crawl on all fours, and jump over obstacles that are nonexistent. Fun is made of the shape of the woman's breasts, her birthmarks, or the scars left on her abdomen after a cesarean birth. This stage of torture is marked by the captors sadistic objectification of the women at their mercy.

Questions are interjected during the process of physical and verbal abuse. Depending on her presumed "profile," the woman is interrogated concerning the whereabouts of her husband, or a key male political figure who is in hiding, or about whether or not she is active in a specific political party. If the woman political prisoner claims ignorance or refuses to cooperate, the sexual violence of the torture escalates. She is thrown to the floor, splashed wih cold water all over her body, and the electric prod is applied to her eyelids, gums, nipples and genital area.

As interrogations continue, sexual torture is increased. Cigarettes are extinguished on the woman's breasts and nipples; her breasts are slashed with sharpened instruments; blades, hot irons and electrical surgical "pens" are used to brand different parts of her body.

> *R.B.* was detained because she had been the secretary of a prominent woman senator belonging to a leftist party. She was undressed, punched in the stomach with brass knuckles, and given systematic electric shocks. But her most excruciating pain was produced when the torturers tied her nipples with a cord and started pulling them with sadistic violence first forwardly and then in all directions as if intending to uproot them from her body. As a result of the prolonged sexual torture, she had a miscarriage and a stroke that paralyzed the left side of her body.

> *M.A.G.C.* was a professor of mathematics at the time of her arrest. She was accused of collaborating with "international Marxist forces"; she was considered a threat to the military state. M.A.G.C. was methodically immersed head down in the swimming pool of the Naval Academy in Valparaison, Chile, until she was on the verge of asphyxiation. This violence was alternated wth beatings and regular squeezing and biting of her breasts by her torturers.

> *V.L.M.*, a homemaker married to a politically active husband who was in hiding, had the Communist party symbol of the hammer and sickel branded with electricity--she describes it as "an electrical pen used on flesh" on her thigh. This was done, she was told, so that "she would stop being a Marxist."

Many women have had the words "Marxist" or "Mirista"--(Mir is a political party that the military junta in Chile calls the revolutionary leftist movement: its members have been systematically murdered), "extremist," and/or "dangerous" tattooed across their breasts. These words are often also imprinted on their foreheads. It must be understood that this organized political torture is not applied only to women thought to be Marxists. It is applied to women from a variety of political parties, to women who are active in center political parties, and to women who are not involved in politics at all. Women are branded if their captors believe them to be against the military government.

There is a male-bonding in the violence of massive criminal rape--performed in succession, by three to twenty-seven men in some cases--against women political prisoners. Rape is part of almost every torture sequence endured by a women, especially women from twelve to forty-nine years of age. Power and domination are exerted on the victims of sexual slavery in a torture situation where women cannot leave nor fight back. Testimonies of older women political prisoners who have survived correspond in their hair-raising accounts of massive rapes perpetrated on the younger women upon arrival at the "houses of torture." Following these vile sessions of rape and other forms of sexual abuse, many women suffered severe hemorrhaging for days with no medical attention.

The use of animals to physically and psychically torture women is yet another phase in this unutterable process. Women's mental stability and physical health have been seriously threatened, sometimes destroyed, by the introductoon of mice into their vaginas. Foreign objects, such as sticks and dull instruments, have also been introduced into the vagina and anus; but it is difficult to compare even such abuse with the psychological and physical suffering brought about by a scratching, biting, disoriented mouse forced into a female's genital region. Women, now in exile, who survived this torture, explain that they have not, nor do they believe they ever can, really recover from the trauma of this experience. Many of them developed ulcers within their vaginal walls as a result of the rodent's action inside them.

Many female political prisoners in Chile have been raped by trained dogs--usually boxers (Denuncia y Testimonio 1975:99). This is evidently one of the most brutalizing and traumatic experiences suffered by women in prison. The survivors of this torment find it very difficult to report their exposure to this extreme sexual debasement. With sickening canniness, the torturers traumatize their victims into feeling shame for their own bodies. The women who are able to do so are willing to recall these events in an effort to make known these atrocities although they suffer anew by speaking of them.

The military state--the patriarchal state in distillation--with its dependence on coercion to mold human beings to the ideology that will sustain its authority, uses the paradigm of female sexual enslavement, rape, in as many forms as it can imagine. Patriarchy under stress tends to reveal itself with contradictory zeal. The notion of Madonna/Whore in the context of male linearity of thinking (Barry 1979:262) as it melds with rape systematically applied to exert absolute control is illustrated through the case of A.N.M.R. This courageous young widow, whose husband had been assassinated during a "military" operation, was seized by the police and mercilessly tortured for long periods. As she refused to talk, she was given electric shocks, sent to her cell for a short while, and then dragged out again by the officer in charge of the supervision of her sexual torture. Officers would shout to groups of soldiers inviting them to rape her with the following order: "Come and have a good time with this whore, because she needs it!" They did rape her. She sums it up in her own words, "Thus I was debased and raped countless times." As if continual rape were not enough "control," her uterus was later ruptured by a high-voltage shock with an electric prod.

Rape is used during sessions of "family torture," usually to extract information from a noncooperative male prisoner. It is for this reason, for leverage in interrogations, that women in the family are kidnapped along with the male "subversive." Numerous wives and daughters of male prisoners have been sexually debased and massively raped in front of their husbands, lovers, or fathers. If a man is wanted and in hiding, his wife and female children are incarcerated in a manipulative attempt to extract information concerning his activities and hiding place. If the wife does not cooperate with her captors, she is raped. If this does not produce the desired information, she is threatened with the rape of her daughters. In addition to the physical suffering, the psychic strain of having to deal with such a confrontation of loyalties and the consequences of any so-called "decision" are devastating. Unfortunately, many threats are made good by the torturers, and mothers are forced to witness in shock and powerless pain violent sexual acts committed upon their innocent female youngsters. (See further discussion of this below.)

The case of L. de las N.A.M., single, is, unfortunately, a typical example of a most vile form of "family torture." At the time of the arrest she was twenty-three years old. She was imprisoned together with her father and fifteen-year-old brother. To extract information from the father and the daughter, the torturers first applied electricity to the father in front of her, she in turn was administered electricity in front of her father so that he would talk. Her fifteen-year-old brother was savagely tortured in her presence. Watching this suffering was the only time in her prolonged torture when her blindfold was removed. In order to psychologically and physically weaken her further, L. de las N.A.M. was battered and bruised all over her body; her breasts and other parts of her body was slashed with a blade and her nipples brutally squeezed and pulled while at the same time the torturers introduced their dirty hands into her vagina and stuck a variety of metal objects inside her. Later on she was submitted to electric shocks, then hung by the knees from a horizontal plank, with hands and ankles tied together (the dreaded pau de arara). She fainted, and when she recovered, her five tormentors started threatening her with rape. Her father and her brother were brought in and the captors started forcing the father and daughter into having intercourse. L. de las N.A.M., screaming in terror, fainted again. She was revived with slaps, thrown onto a mattress on the floor, and raped by many men--she cannot recall exactly how many they were. She describes herself (after the massive rape) as "waking up soiled ["impure," her chastity taken away from her by force] and bleeding." What she describes as "waking up" is the realizaton that the culturally defined dignity of her womanhood had been shattered; she had fought back so bravely, like a caged animal at the mercy of her executioners. Further suffering was inflicted on this brave woman by introducing mice into her vagina. She describes mice as "going berserk inside me and painfully inserting their paw nails in my flesh."

An extension of the notion of degradation of a woman in the "community" of her family is the forced abuse and humilation of a woman through her peers. As with 'family torture' this method produces pain and humiliation in all those forced to participate in this particular type of sexual torment. A naked woman political prisoner is placed in the middle of a human circle formed by her naked male coprisoners, many of whom know her. In cases where she is not known personally, she stands as the representative of "one of their own" ideologically. The men are forced at gunpoint to masturbate while looking at the naked body of the woman and having her as a target when they ejaculate. Once again the woman who finds herself in this type of situation, from which she cannot escape, is further degraded in a painfully debasing incident in which male domination not only increases her inferiority as a woman but robs her of her dignity and individuality as a person.

It should be noted that there appears to be a class element and racial component in the most extreme cases of sexual violence. Proletarian women and women with markedly *meztizo* features--the fusion of European and Indian admixtures--have been even more brutalized than their lighter sisters coming from bourgeois families. It is, however, also important to stress that the fact that in the highly class-conscious society of Latin America, the sexual torture of female political prisoners has cut across class lines. The common denominator has been the defintion as enemy by the fascist military governments whether the "security threat" comes directly through the woman's--real or supposed--political activism or through the identity she is seen to derive from a male who is politically active.

TORTURE OF THE FEMALE PSYCHE

Although, as is quite evident by now, it is impossible to separate, physical abuse from psychological abuse, the state torturers have designed methods specifically aimed at the mental torment of their prisoners--methods that underscore their domination and control. This harrowing of the psyche of these women is used by their tormentors as complement to the sexual violence that their bodies are undergoing. Psychological torture leaves scars that are almost impossible to heal. A woman's sympathy and empathy for others is played upon; her deep sense of herself as nurturer is manipulated and torn. The following situations and cases show different aspects of sexual/gender violence.

Many women have reported how painfully humiliating it is to have their physiological processes, basically elimination, controlled and observed by their torturers. They were not allowed to go to the bathroom when they needed to go but when their guard felt like taking them. Once in the bathroom, they had to eliminate in front of the torturer, who was aiming all the time at them with a shotgun. He would not even turn his head aside.

Many survivors of torture, while in sexual slavery at the mercy of their authoized torturers, describe the agonizing impact that the sobbing and crying of other women being raped in an adjacent room or a few feet away from them had on the moral integrity that they were trying to preserve, in order not to break down. Psychological torture is delivered with false news of the death of family members and/or by threats of having a loved one disappear. A woman professor of mathematics was thrown against a wall and, with a revolver against her forehead, her torturer--a marine--shouted, "Talk, talk, for once and for all, because you are going to be executed and you will never see your small daughter again."

Psychological suffering is also administered by purposely having female political prisoners become aware or witness the rape of women in advanced stages of pregnancy--seven to eight and a half months.

Infliction of extreme psychological cruelty is most often reserved for those women who have dared to take an active role, in their own right, toward the improvement of socioeconomic conditions in their countries. Women given this special attention include political leaders from now banned workers' unions, activists in syndicates and committees consisting of white-collar and professional workers in the fields of health, education, and community welfare, and women who have participated in key political movements.

Elba Vergara's case provides but an illustation of the kind of psychological brutalization female political prisoners are forced to endure (Denuncia 1975:167-69). A member of the Socialist party, Elba Vergara had been President Allende's secretary for many years. She was fifty-one years old at the time of her arrest, fifteen months after the Chilean military's bloody coup.

Upon her arrest, Elba was taken to a friend's home, a young woman with a three-year-old son. One of her captors took the child by the ankles and walked to the balcony of the nineteenth floor apartment, threatening to drop him head first if Elba did not give them the information they wanted. The mother of the boy shouted, "Throw him down! But we won't confess to anything!" This was Elba's introduction to what would be the special nature of her ordeal.

Taken to one of the "torture houses," Elba was interrogated for seven hours. This relentless interrogation continued for eight days. Still refusing to cooperate, Elba was forced to witness the sadistic murder of two young men she had known during the time Allende was in power. She was taken to a room called the little blue room, a small area lit by only two blue bulbs. Her blindfold was removed. Four hooded executioners broke into the room, shouting, "Bring in the actor!" A covered body was wheeled in on a stretcher. One of them, then turning to Elba, said, "Sit down. Here you are going to see the representation of a bad actor. You have to help him remember his lines."

They uncovered the naked body of a brutally disfigured young man. His torture had been so severe he could not speak. Elba was asked if she recognized him. She said, "No." She did, in fact, recognize the young man. He had been a chauffeur for a member of the Allende government.

"You are telling us that you don't know him. We shall see whether you know him or not." They took one of his hands and pulled out his fingernails. Elba continued to insist that she could not identify the man. They tore off the one ear he had left at that point. They cut his tongue out. They punctured and emptied one of his eyes. This ordeal lasted three hours. He died then.

A second man was now brought into the "little blue room." He, too, had already suffered horribly. This time the executioners took five hours to kill him in their efforts to force Elba to speak. She still would not give them the information they needed.

This exteme psychological torture was designed to torment, terrorize, and break Elba to annihilate her morally, through a sadistic attack on her humanity and the deep maternal aspect of her socialization as a Latin American woman. As the courageous Elba Vergara herself says, referring to the first young man tortured and killed before her,

> He could have been my son. The son of any mother in the world. Somebody with whom one had been twenty days before, when he was healthy, fine. . . . and then they kill him under your very eyes. It is probably worse than any physical torture aimed at oneself.

This kind of psychological torture, this torment through torture of another, involves both the immediate horror and the devastation wrought from helplessness and the long agony resulting fom the pretense of choice given a woman.

The use of children by these state torturers and the manipulation of the woman's caring and nurturing role takes many forms. As in the case of Elba Vergara, many women have had to endure having their own children or the children of female friends and political comrades tortured in their presence.

L.V., it is reprorted by a friend, had her four-and-a-half-year-old son tortured in front of her. She and her husband, both captured, were then further tortured and killed.

The young offspring of women and men who are sought by a dictatorial regime for their clandestine activities against the government and the children of women and men considered a threat to the "internal security" of the government have been kidnapped by force from their homes. These children are placed in so-called Homes for Children run by the armed forces; they are hostages used to exert pressure on their parents. Most often, a message will reach the mother of the child with an ultimatum--if she does not turn herself in to the security forces, the little girl or boy will remain in captivity and undergo torture or be placed "under the vigilance of sexual perverts who prefer children."

The bureaucratic torture machines of Argentina and Chile use both threats of the torture of children and the actual torture of children to further heighten a woman's suffering while still physically brutalizing her. Examples already on the record include.

Tamara, a child of three, was tortured in Chile. Her mother, now in exile, described the treatment her daughter received in detention:

> They undressed my little daughter and whipped her with a leather whip. They put her in a barrel with ice water and held her head under the water until she almost drowned. They threatened to rape her and whipped her again. This was repeated four times a day for four days. (Children 1979:15).

N.B.L., a young mother, was kidnapped by Argentinian Task Force No. 3, Military Personnel, November 1977. The task force made her son "Facundo cry in the operating theatre"-- torture chamber--next to the one in which she was being tortured.

Christina was abducted along with her mother, M. del C. J., by a special task force in October 1978. M., during her own interrogation, was forced to listen to her young daughter's screams. (Testimony 1980:18-19)

Evidence has been on the record and continues to mount showing that babies and children are not safeguarded from torture; their torment is sadistically aimed at their mothers.

Under the threat of having a child tortured or "disappear" altogether, mothers have sometimes confessed the hiding place of their husband or *companero*. Here again is a most diabolical form of psychological torture: The Latin American mother placed in a situation of conflict between her role as wife/lover and her role as mother will almost always opt for her "sacred" maternal duty of protecting the vulnerable child. In additon to living with the brutal assault her body has taken while under interrogation, she must live now, as well, with the "guilt" of having revealed the whereabouts or activities of her husband. There is shattering moral pain brought about by the disintegration of her family. This is the cruelest attack upon a woman's psyche; it shows us so clearly how the torture of these dictatorial military regimes pierces to the esssentials of female sexual slavery. The woman must not only suffer in every part of her being; she must also be faced with a shame that is called a "choice" and feel herself a "collaborator" with her torturer, no matter what she does or does not do (see Appendix B).

Kathy Barry, in exposing the pervasive patterns and practice of female sexual slavery, beings to weave those threads of connection showing how slavery extends beyond the individual and further enslaves her. We see this with shocking clarity in how the female is used in the selected ways in which she is tormented as a political prisoner. This is especially and painfully so when it affects and abuses a woman's nurturing role. The split consciousness of this cultural sadism not only tries to smash a woman in and through the center of her being but also zealously spans generations. We do not need to wait thirty years to test a hypothesis of possible damage to the children of V.L., who watched her repeatly raped, nor the children of V.P.R., left huddled in terror, nor the children who underwent the torment of the detention centers. We do not need to wait to ask about the unutterable complexities of damage done to those who both witnessed and served as examples.

The state torturers must spread their terror both throughout the community and across generations. The military state sadistically literalizes patterns of female sexual slavery. It is important to speak specifically to the facts of those women taken when pregnant.

When a pregnant political prisoner does not die on the torture table or lose her baby after beatings on the abdomen, being kicked, raped and tortured with electric shock--under the supervision of a doctor--she is returned to her cell, under the same conditions as the rest of the prisoners.

Following her subjection to the pattern of torture described, a young Argentinian woman gave birth to a son. She was tied to a bed by her hands and feet during a five-hour labor, receiving medical attention just as the baby was born; for the duration of their incarceration, the infant was made to sleep on the floor of the cell. Anmesty International doctors examined the woman and the child following their release from prison. Miraculously, the baby appears to show normal mental and physical development. The mother suffers from impaired memory, headaches, inability to concentrate, nervousness, and dizziness (Children 1979:19).

Amnesty International has documented numerous cases of the disappearance of mothers and children, where the child was either born in prison or abducted with the mother (1980, 1981). In Argentina, the greatest number of pregnant women and mothers of infants and schoolchildren "disappeared" between 1976 and 1980. During this period, pregnant women were taken to ESMA--the prinicpal Naval Training College in Buenos Aires--which was earmarked as the maternity unit for secret detention camps in the capital city district. All pregnant women who survived interrogation were attended at ESMA by a doctor from the naval hospital. After the birth, the mothers were usually "transferred" and the infants sent to official or clandestine orphanages or adopted by childless couples in the armed forces.

"Transfer," according to surviving witnesses, is the name given to massive assassination in Argentina. Guards tell prisoners at a detention camp that they are to be "transferred" to another place, to a location where they will not be allowed to take their few possessions or additional clothing as they will be issued uniforms at the next detention center. In actuality, they are all killed or become *desaparecidos*--missing--the word used to describe thousands of Argentinians who have never been heard from again, and whose bodies have not been returned to their families for burial.

Hundreds of Agentinian women have given birth and been "transferred." Their babies have been reported as "missing" by grandparents and surviving relatives. The toddlers and older children abducted with their mothers have never been seen again. The grandmothers of these missing babies and children, who have also lost their own daughters and sons, have formed an association *The Grandmothers of the Plaza de Mayo*--an offshoot of *The Mothers of the Plaza de Mayo*.[3]

Evidence and documentation concerning the *sale* of some of these children, both in Latin America and abroad is just surfacing.

Female sexual enslavement, one of its most hideous forms, is the most salient characteristic of the oppressive military dictatorships in many Latin American countries. It is one of the most difficult crimes against women to punish and eradicate because the oppressors, the torturers, the persecutors, and executioners of women are all members of the authoritarian state, the miliary state, that has done away with all the basic human rights to which individuals are entitled.

The military state depends on the oppression and exploitation of the poverty-sticken masses of Latin Americans; it is against the full participation of ethnic minorities in national affairs because it is racist. The military state is also the epitome of sexist patriarachal ideology and therefore against the largest minority, women, who have been made to retreat to their traditional role of reproducers and nurturers of the younger generations.

The military state endorses an economic exploitation of the bulk of the population and the natural resources of the country it purports to represent by protecting the economic interests of the wealthy families belonging to the upper-class and by serving as a watchdog for the investment of multinational corporations. Profits for some are reaped faster when the constitution of a country is ignored; when the congress that is to guarantee the democratic process is closed indefinitely, its politicians banned from participation in government affairs; and when strikes and criticisms of the government are made illegal, a cause for punishment and imprisonment.

If the segment of the population that dares criticize the totalitarian military state is female, the punishment is administered through female sexual slavery in torture. The subservient, dependent, passive, and unequal position in society that women experience as opposed to men in a "machista"-patriarchal society is exacerbated in torture. The courageous women who have managed to survive this brutual appropriation, colonization, and objectification of their bodies, as well as the psychological suffering derived from the cruelly premeditated deprivation of their human womanly dignity have set an example of bravery for us all. They have also handed us the banner of struggle by surviving, by not succumbing at the feet of their tormentors, by transcending their sense of shame and humiliation and offering their personal terstimonies to make known the criminal acts of the military state. Their cry is for justice, for the elimination of sexual slavery in torture, for the diffusion of the awareness of its existence and its monstrosity so that it may be stopped, so that it will never happen again.

Thousands of women in countries of the Southern Cone--Peru, Argentina, Chile, Uruguay, Bolivia, and Paraguay have dared struggle for a more just socieconomic order. Many of them have died. Thousands have disappeared and thousands are still fighting dictatorships. By so doing they have acquired an identity of their own; they have beome full persons in their own right and thus challenged the passive, submissive, dependent role assigned to women based on the conservative religious archetype of the Virgin Mother that the patriarchal institutions have imprinted through the socialization of all women. These are the women who, by their direct actions, are transforming the cultural content of *marianismo, Mariology*. They have contributed, and are contributing to rapid and radical changes in the societies to which they belong, they are also creating new female models for the younger generations to follow. *This* is the legacy of the women political prisoners who have survived sexual slavery in torture. It is also the example that has been presented to us by the women commanders of Nicaragua--Doris Tijerino and so many others--who played an instrumental role in ousting the Somoza regime and who are now involved in the reconstruction of their country. It is also the example set forth by many members of the new Catholic Church in Latin America, whose religious leaders have thrown in their lot with the poor, the persecuted, and the oppressed. The blueprint for the socialization of the traditionally passive Latin American female is changing rapidly. No one as yet has more eloquently described this root change than Sister Martha, who sees the sexism on which Nicaraguan society is found and speaks about it--about women looked upon as objects of sexual satisfaction, required to be submissive to their husbands, and to obligingly take care of houehold duties and the children.

But, Sister Martha says, Nicaraguan women now want to change this situation because

> they have taken an active part in the Revolution not only to achieve freedom for the people but also to achieve their own freedom as women. Today, Nicaraguan women hold Mary the Mother of God as their first model for promoting this Revolution. She too carried to the world a message of liberation. . . . Mary isn't the sugar-sweet stupid woman reactionary Christians so often make her out to be. At the age of fifteen--the same age as Doris Maria Tijerino--she took an active part in the liberation of her people. She doesn't speak to individual moralistic changes, but of the reorganization of the social order into one which there are no rich and poor, powerful and humble. And so, faced with this new dawn filled with great hopes and with Christian and revolutionary responsiblities, Nicaraguan women must follow the path begun by Mary of Nazareth and Doris Maria of Matagalpa. We have but one alternative: *To be women of hope working for the consolidation of our revolution.* (Randall 1981:162)

ADDENDUM

As one investigates the torture of female political prisoners in Latin American, many connections, sometimes enlightening, though also horrifying, and widespread both geographically and temporally come to mind.

While doing this very taxing analysis I have noted parallels between how women political prisoners have been brutalized in torture in the Southern Cone of Latin American and the black female experience in the United States before the Civil War. Slave masters on plantations terrorized and "tamed" their women slaves by subjecting them to sexual exploitation and oppression through rape, forced breeding, sadistic floggings during which black women were stripped naked and publicly whipped. Pregnant women were made to lie on the ground, over holes dug to receive an abdomen full with child, and were flogged with whips or beated with a paddle (see Davis 1971; Hooks 1982).

Written evidence and "graphics" surviving from the European Middle Ages also describe tortures of women strikingly similar--in fact, in many details identical--to those used by the state tortures in Latin America. The same parts of the body are attacked, in the same ways--technologies were simply somewhat different. Pregnant women met with special attention. The Virgin, here, too, was often mounted in torture chambers by the state torturers; "despite" the intimate relationships between church and state.

With the death throes of the European Medieval world view came a pervasive torture and murder of women. This time, we were called witches, and the church and state then defined witchcraft as a *crimen exceptum*, a crime distinct from all others, the rules of proof suspended, as were all holds on torture. These threats to the public security met with highly refined, highly similar torture techniques. Perhaps a most significant parallel here is the extension and perpetuation of female enslavement through torture. Young female children were threatened and/or tortured into confessing against their mothers; young girls were forced to watch their mothers tortured and then often burned at the stake without the usual dispatchment by an executioner. (Lois Brynes, of Clark University, drew my attention to these parallels.)

Women now working on issues and problems of women survivors of the Nazi holocaust, note many, too many, connections and particularly powerful ones with the situation of women in Latin America; gender defined issues--whether in hiding, underground actions, "passing," in interrogation, in camps. As males were in hiding, a mother and her children were often picked up for "interrogation"--a mother threatened with the murder of her daughter, the daughter threatened with being forced to watch the torture of her mother. "They seemed to have a sense of exactly what would terrorize you the most." (Tamar March, *Reflections from a Shattered Mirror*, w.i.p.). In these survivors we see clearly the long-term impact of heinous, authorized torment. We also see the psychic complexities of being one who survives--not only in terms of memory and of what is passed to and through the next generation--but of the subtle, insidious torture of "blaming the victim," for even the "sympathetic" analyzers use grounds for discussion that imply some ineffable sort of option. These modes of schematizing patriarchy, as it reveals itself under stress, only serve to perpetuate myth systems in their external manifestations and devastating internalization.

Related to what may be described as the final psychic torture through the theme of collaboration in one's family's, community's, or even one's own destruction is the "token torturer" (see, e.g., Mary Daly, *GynEcology*). My interviews reveal that there are women with the bureaucratic appraratus who have duties related to torture. A closer examination of their role reveals that they are in low-level, powerless positions. They are not in charge of ordering torture, when and how it should start, if and when it should end; they are not involved in developing the equipment that is used, nor in the apparently predictable, imaginative sessions that design torment for women. The women involved in these state institutions play supplementary roles to and for male officials. Therefore, it is important to learn more about how women are used by the military state for these supportive activities in torture, which women are selected, and the effect this subordinate collaboration has on these women.

Just as we should look twice, as feminists, at the shaven heads of so-called collaborators, we should strongly object to the common male stereotype of the Teutonic fascist woman guard in a concentration camp. She is most probably a figment of the patriarchal imagination as she certainly by no means devises and runs the state's torture machine.

NOTES

I wish to acknowledge the women who have survived sexual slavery in torture and have found the strength to bear witness, and the women who did not survive the torture but who did contribute and are contributing toward change for all of us. My special admiration and feeling of gratitude goes to my friend V. de N. or V.N. for her inestimable contribution to this chapter in sharing with me her painful experience in varius torture centers in her own country. Her courage and her strength not to give up, to continue living, as well as her efforts to adapt to a difficult situation in exile, supporting herself and her children, provided an inspiration for all of us. Perhaps her greatest contribution is the fact that she has not lost faith in her political ideas, which seek the liberation of her people. On the contrary, her horrendous experience of torture seems to have made her commitment even stronger.

I also wish to thank those persons active in and through human rights organizations who cannot be named out of concerns for repercussions.

Kathleen Barry's work on female sexual slavery allowed me to make coherent, if not rational, the patterns of torture designed for women political prisoners. I am particularly indebted to her for insights concerning expansion of the concept of political terror as torture and the extension of slavery beyond the individual, thereby further enslaving her.

I am grateful to Lois Brynes for lengthy discussions on the issues addressed through this chapter and for her theoretical insights--particularly on notions of "option" and collaboration and connections made with women to the Middle Ages and women who survived the Nazi holocaust. I am especially grateful for her labors as editorial consultant, which meant "diving into the wreck" of these horrors again and again.

I would also like to acknowledge the constructive criticisms of the draft of this chapter offered by Cynthia Enloe and her generosity in sharing with me her expertise on militaristic institutions, as well as her analyses of the effects of militarization in countries controlled by military elites.

Finally, I am grateful to Elizabeth Gervais who put this chapter into readable form under inordinate time pressures. She did not type as of "some distant tribe."

[1] Mariolatry, 'by any other name,' and its attendant conceptions of Madonna/Whore--Mors per Evam, Vita per Miriam--is indeed *global*, in the socialization of women, in the schematization of women in patriarchy. It is simply more superficially apparent in Latin America, through the entrenched dominance of Catholicism.

[2] A definition of torture may bring certain atrocities into relief, but at the same time, it keeps us from allowing other equally heinous facts from coming into focus. As feminists we must understand and make understood the political torture involved in living in a state of terror--and ask who the tormentor may be. As feminists we must refuse the neutralization of limitation by definition, we must ask if it is more a torment to have a torch held to your skin or to be covered by napalm.

[3] The Mothers of the Plaza de Mayo circle in silence for half an hour daily wearing white headscarves and bearing the photos of their "missing" ones. For Mother's Day of October 1981, over five thousand women filled the square. The Grandmothers of the Plaza de Mayo share a small office and their placards with the mothers' group but petition on their own for the approximately eight hundred missing children of missing parents. The grandmothers believe that their grandchildren are in offical and clandestine orphanages or that they have been adopted in Argentina and in neighboring countries. Some of Argentina's "missing children" have been found in Uruguay, Brazil, and Chile. Unfortunately, too few have been found--see Buenos Aires Herald, 11 July 1981; the Manchester Guardian, 28 November 1981; Connexions, An International Women's Quarterly Winter 1983, No. 7.

APPENDIX A

Information gathered through direct communication, reports quoted in the OAS Report on the Situation of Human Rights in Uruguay, and my own analysis of hundreds of recorded cases of human rights violations in Chile, Argentina, and Uruguay, show that all female and male detainees have been tortured with the different methods described below.

Incommunicado detention. This is a type of punishment where the prisoner is placed in isolation, usually hooded or with eyes closed by a blindfold, in a room with no light or ventilation. Women report having been isolated from ten days up to four months.

Wall-standing. The prisoner is ordered to remain standing in a fixed position, sometimes with arms upraised or holding weighty objects, with legs kept well apart, for hours or days. Sometimes wall-standing takes place nude and in the open air. Many women have been forced to stand, handcuffed and blindfolded for two to three consecutive days without food and without sleep. Sometimes they have been forbidden to go to the bathroom.

Beatings. There are a variety of ways in which prisoners are beaten: karate, with sticks, with iron objects, with rubber bludgeons, fistcuffs, brassknuckles, kicks, and so forth. Many prisoners have lost teeth and suffered fractured ribs and ruptured eardrums. Women prisoners are usually slapped on the face with open palms and punched in the stomach making them lose their balance and fall; they are kicked until they stand up again. It is common for women prisoners to faint under this agonizing treatment; they are "revived" by a cold shower, followed by electric shocks.

Electric prod. Electric current is applied to the most sensitive part of the prisoners' bodies--gums, lips, eyes, genital organs, breasts. If the torturers are careful and expert, 200 volts exactly are used as 220 volts are regarded as fatal.

Parrilla electrica (Electric grid). Here the prisoner is tied naked to a metallic bedlike frame with arms and legs open. This facilitates the application of electric shocks.

The submarine. The prisoner is repeatedly immersed upside down, in a tank of water--generally mixed with vomit, blood, or urine--until on the verge of asphyxiation. Many times the prisoner dies during this torture.

The dry submarine. This method of torture involves the slow asphyxiation of the prisoner by wrapping the head of the tortured person in a plastic bag or sack.

Stocks. The prisoner, generally nude, is tied to four stakes in the ground--always in the open air--so that arms and legs are completely separated.

The horse (This specific type of torture is designed for men). The nude prisoner is made to mount a sawhorse which keeps him from touching the ground. His arms are held open, and the sawhorse is moved backward and forward beneath him so that the individual being tortured feels as if he were being sawed in half. This results in serious injury to the genital organs.

Pau de arara. The person being tortured is hung by the knees from a horizontal plank, with hands and ankles tied together. This procedure cuts off the circulation of the blood; the body turns livid and the individual being tortured faints.

Drugs. Pentothal, especially, is administered to produce a relaxed semihypnotic state in the prisoner whereby he or she offers little resistance, and information is easily obtained.

Violent sexual acts. There are many and varied cases where torturers violate detainees and when mutilating devices are inserted in the vagina and anus. At times male detainees are sexually violated.

REFERENCES

Amnesty International. 1979. Children. London: Amnesty Publications.

Amnesty International. 1980. Testimony on secret detention camps in Argentina. U.S.A.: Amnesty International Publications.

Amnesty International. 1980. Amnesty International report 1980. London: Amnesty Publications.

Amnesty International. 1981. Amnesty International report 1981. London: Amnesty Publications.

Amnesty International. 1982. Amnesty International report 1982. London: Amnesty Publications.

Amnesty International. 1982. Matchbox. U.S.A.: Published by Amnesty International U.S.A.

Barry, Kathleen. 1979. Female sexual slavery. New York: Avon Books.

Comision Interamericana de Derechos Humanos. 1974. Informe Sobre la Situacion de los Derechos Humanos en Chile. Washington, D.C.: Secretaria General de los Estados Americanos.

Comision Internacional de Investigacion de los Crimenes de la Junta Militar en Chile. 1975. Denuncia y Testimonio. Helsinki: Comision Internacional de Investigacion de los Crimenes de la Junta Militar en Chile.

Comision Interamericana de Derechos Humanos. 1980. Informe Sobre la Situacion de los Derechos Humanos en Argentina. Washington, D.C.: CIDH. Secretaria General de los Estados Americanos.

Connexions/An International Woman's Quarterly. 1983. "Las Abuelas-Search for the Missing." From Connexions, An International Woman's Quareterly. Winter, No. 7.

Davis, Angela. 1971. "Reflections on the Black woman's role in the community of slaves." In The Black Scholar, Vol. 3. No. 4. December.

Elu de Lenero, Maria del Carmen, (Ed.). 1976. Perspectivas Femeninas en American Latina. Mexico: Sep-Setentas.

Enloe, Cynthia. 1981. "The Military Model," "Nato: What is it and why should women care?" and "Nato: The lesson machine, " in W. Chapkis (Ed.) Loaded Questions Women in the Military. Amsterdam/Washington, D.C.: Transnational Institute.

_____. 1983. Does Khaki become you? The militarization of women's lives. London: Pluto Press, (May) and Boston: South End Press (August).

Hooks, Bell. 1982. Ain't I a woman. Black Women and Feminism. Boston: South End Press.

Inter-American Commission on Human Rights. 1977. Third report on the situation of human rights in Chile. Washington, D.C.: General Secretariat of the Organization of American States.

_____. 1978. Report on the situation of human rights in Uruguay. Washington, D.C.: CIDH General Secretariat of the Organization of American States.

_____. 1982. Ten years of activities 1971-1981. Washington, D.C.: General Secretariat of the Organization of American States.

Latin American and Caribbean Women's Collective. 1980. Slaves of slaves, the challenge of Latin American women. London: Zed Press.

Lernoux, Penny. 1980. Cry of the people. New York: Doubleday and Company.

Nash, June and Helen I. Safa, (Eds.). 1976 Sex and class in Latin America. New York: Praeger Publishers.

Randall, Margaret. 1981. Sandino's daughters. Testimonies of Nicaraguan women in struggle. Vancouver: New Star Books Ltd.

Schoultz, Lars. 1981. Human rights and United States policy towards Latin America. Princeton, New Jersey: Princeton University Press.

Stevens, Evelyn P. 1973. "Marianismo: The other face of machismo in Latin America." In Ann Pescatello (Ed.) Female and male in Latin America. Pittsburgh: University of Pittsburgh Press.

16 The Barzolas and the Housewives Committee

Gloria Ardaya Salinas

INTRODUCTION

The study of women's political and social movements in Latin America is gaining importance after a long period during which the female question was considered, in every respect, to have little relevance. For several years, the dominating trends in the social sciences steered research in other directions, effectively blocking any real knowledge of this kind of political and social expression. Politically, too, women's participation received no encouragement from parties, whether on the left or the right. Nevertheless, at present there is apparently interest in explaining and motivating these essential aspects of social dynamics, and it is within that framework that women's social movements are being treated as important expressions of the class struggle and of our peoples' history. This interest is not accidental: It is due to the growing significance of these movements in Latin America, and particularly in Bolivia.

Within the Latin American context, Bolivia stands out as one of the few cases of an organized political experience involving women. The Female Commands of the Revolutionary Nationalist Movement (M.N.R.) constituted important bastions in the struggle against the oligarchy between 1946 and 1952. They represented the massive, organized response to women's groups, which integrated their own struggle and particular demands with the collective actions of the exploited classes that were seeking to bring about a new kind of social and national emancipation. And at times they were decisive. Almost parallel with these M.N.R. Commands, there appeared at the nationalized mines in 1961 another mass women's movement, the

"Housewives Committees," whose contrbution to the mining sector's struggle came in the form of new modes of political and union organization and participation for women miners. Both these movements attained national significance not only because of the style of their organization, but also, fundamentally, because of the contents of the restitutional struggle that they unleashed.

SOME CHARACTERISTICS OF BOLIVIAN SOCIETY

During the period in which the oligarchy ruled, the Bolivian social formation was unable to develop a bourgeoisie capable of bringing about industrialization. Nor could it build up an internal market or make any headway in terms of structural transformations. Out of necessity, therefore, there developed a system of domination in which representatives of mining interests joined hands with large landholding interests. It was a coalition which despite internal rifts, managed to maintain the system.

In the economic sphere, a weak type of capitalist development appeared alongside precapitalist forms of production, until the dominant capitalist sector definitively acquired the characteristics of a "mining town." The implantation of this "development" model greatly restricted the social and political participation of nearly the entire population.

This particular development model was incapable of promoting any sustained economic growth benefiting the population. Rather, it was a dependent, distorted form of development, and it brought on poverty, malnutrition and unemployment--conditions that had an especially strong effect on the female population.

The Women's Struggle as Part of the Popular National Movement

Today it can be stated that the most important political experiences for Bolivian women, and perhaps for Latin American women as a whole, were the popular movement that came to power following the 1952 uprising and, later, the events connected with the unions at the nationalized mines.

On 9 April 1952, a military-civilian coup became transformed into a mass insurrection. As a result of common interests and objectives, the uprising involved the proletariat, the peasantry, middle-level professionals, and the urban working class.

The M.N.R. shared the political leadership of the process with the powerful union organizations that made up the C.O.B. Both elements came to power concomitantly.

During all these developments, the participation by the female sectors was tremendously important and, in fact, at times decisive. Women were members of resistence groups, acted as agitators, circulated propaganda, and during the uprising itself fought in the streets. Women's participation was therefore a vital element of the

M.N.R., springing up, growing in strength, and then declining alongside it. On the other hand, the organization of women miners sprang up, grew in strength, and is of increasing significance to the miners' unions.

For the purposes of this chapter, we will refer only to these two mass women's movements, for they are the most consequential. We should nonetheless note the existence of other, less important, women's movements. The Union of Bolivian Women (UMBO), created in 1962, and the Democratic Federation of Bolivian Women (FDMB) were both promoted by the political left. In the latter, however, we have witnessed the creation of the "Bartolina Sisa" National Federation of Women Peasants, an organization associated with the United Confederation of Peasant Workers of Bolivia. Its objectives are to achieve peasant women's participation in political and union affairs on the national level, and it is rapidly gaining in strength.

WOMEN AND THE M.N.R.

The M.N.R. was the first political party to open its ranks to Bolivian women. Women enter and engage in politics through the M.N.R.

The M.N.R. is a party built basically around its critique of the mining and land-owning oligarchy, and thus of the existing state system; its aim was to destroy the ideological apparatus of the oligarchic state. Its criticisms were founded on a strong nationalist-indigenist current and on a thoroughly revised version of the country's main historical events. Another of its principal goals was to build national unity, and in this regard it relied on a strong ally, the militantly antiimperialist proletariat.

Although the M.N.R. had this ideological basis, its leaders were members of the petty bourgeoisie, bearers of the bourgeois revolution. All of their statements are, in effect, brilliant nationalistic invocations (Paz Estenssoro 1966). The workers movement, lacking a party of its own, accepted this M.N.R. leadership, despite being the main force in taking power and despite its political and military hegemony during the months following the uprising. The working class, almost in its entirety, took an active part within the M.N.R. at one time, although it was not their own party. This was because the M.N.R. did not belong to one class. It was an alliance of several classes, under the economic and political hegemony of the petty bourgeoisie. It was a genuine party of the masses. It gave the masses its nationalism and populism, and in return it received an impluse from them.

The predominance of petty bourgeois ideology within the party and within government would prove to be a determining factor for the political and institutional behavior directed at women and at their future political participation.

In effect, the tasks that the party assigned to women during the period of resistance of the "six-year reign"[1] were essentially typically female: court appeals, religious posts, clandestine messenger services, street marches, arms transportation, caring for the sick, visiting prisoners, hunger strikes--all an indication of the plans that the party had drawn up for them. It must be added here that in carrying out these assignments, the female activists always demonstrated strict standards of discipline. Unlike with other sectors (the proletariat, the peasantry, the midsection), the M.N.R. did not have a specific political platform that addressed demands unique to the country's female sector. Instead, it incorporated women into the party in massive numbers, and had them adopt and fight for the general demands determined by the party at each juncture. In fact, there is not one single political or ideological document belonging to the M.N.R. that addresses or proposes the matter of women's struggles within their given context. As a central theme in its messages to the female sector, women were repeatedly reminded that it had been the M.N.R. that had granted women political rights through universal suffrage.[2] Furthermore, there were no activist or intellectual women members within the party of the Female Commands (which was the internal channel created by the M.N.R.) who could assume or fight for a politically more prominent position, one that would allow them to perform a specific role in the struggle that women as a discriminated sector--even within the revolution and the party--had to carry on. Instead they waited, pacifically, for the party and party heads to decide the role they would play. This is confirmed by Lydia Gueiler, the party's principal female leader, who recalls, "My first disappointment was to realize that, in spite of our revolutionary development, and even with the undeniable aid of holding the power in one's hands, the executive leadership had done absolutely nothing to organize M.N.R. women in any responsible or serious manner. If this did not occur within the party, the vanguard of the revolution, we could scarcely demand it of working women or of women in general." Nor was this motivation forthcoming from the labor unions, members of the Movement almost every one of them: "there still hadn't appeared any pressing need to organize women so that they could overcome their backwardness or to help them surmount the traditional difficulties and prejudices lingering from the past, so we could scarcely demand it of the rank and file" (Gueiler 1959:149).

During the "hegemony of the masses" phase,[3] women's participation in general activities was effective and on a large scale. They worked virtually undifferentiated from the rest of the classes that made up the M.N.R. For the most part, however, the jobs assigned required no special skills; they were routine and mechanical, with certain risks and no political responsibility. Women who had been notable for their energetic militancy during the "six-year reign" were relegated to third or last rank after the revolution had succeeded. Thus, those who had had extensive political experience were given low-level administrative posts in the state bureaucracy and, what is more, took care of internal matters as assigned by the party. Lydia Gueiler, who skillfully occupied the party post of commander of the M.N.R. Armed Militias--militias with military experience, vital for the defense of the national revolution--was later employed as a secretary in a municipal division.

The early stages of the revolution were difficult in that it was then that the first disputes erupted over administrative positions and high-level political and state posts. This was because within the M.N.R. there coexisted vastly contrasting tendencies. The radical currents survived for a long time, until they finally took on the face of the predominant sector, the bourgeois leadership.

Throughout the entire process of the national revolution, the class struggle and the women's movement established a direct relationship with one another. This relationship was the nucleus from which the objectives of women's liberation were subsequently feebly posited within the ideocratic framework of national liberation, a struggle which initially won certain partial rights, such as women's franchise. Nevertheless, "commercial and finance capital" was, in the meantime, undermining the new foundations of the young state and ended up rupturing the state's political self-determination by splintering the national movement and hampering the popular--and more specifically, women's--movement within the party.

THE BARZOLAS

We should recall that the M.N.R. National Female Command was organized during the "six-year reign" with specific objectives and tasks related to antioligarchic resistance and struggle. During the early years of the revolution, too, the objectives and tasks were very limited. In fact, one of the women's main functions was to mobilize their own sector throughout the country for political events and shows of support for the M.N.R. government. This mobilization, while directed by the party, could in many respects be termed spontaneous.

The activities carried out by the women were initially one of the crucial factors for the revolution because of their connection with the masses of women and the national movement with which they maintained institutional ties. Later, this women's movement came to be utilized as a tool, in response to the necessities posed by the state's new relations with international capital and the ruling sectors.

The initial impulse of the women's movement was gradually lost, as was the ability to effect social change that it had acquired through close contact with the workers and popular urban masses. And this was because the women's movement that was organized around the M.N.R. was national, but essentially urban, in nature. Peasant women passively joined the M.N.R. They participated via the National Peasantry Command or through the peasant union. Their involvement was thus quite indirect, via their peasant husbands and companions. As a result, the women themselves were never able to articulate their own demands or link them to the general ones claimed by the peasants' movement as its own. It is highly probable that the fact that peasant women were not incorporated into the National Female Command of the Revolutionary Nationalist Movement diminished the latter's political and institutional power.

These and other factors, such as the lack of a coherent political and ideological platform put forth by women M.N.R. members, prevented them from gaining political autonomy or any real power within the party itself. The absence of such a platform concerning the role they were to play also prevented them from breaking relations with the state apparatus and the party, neither of which sought their liberation. On the contrary, neither of these institutions allowed the women's movement to genuinely generate social change; instead, it became an instrument for promoting social integration and dependence on the newly installed order.

We have already seen how, beginning in 1952, the Bolivian political process was marked by the masses, great ascendancy and subsequent hegemony. In 1954, however, when the crisis was expressed in terms of a real dearth of food products, constant internal strife, and so on, the labor movement broke the alliance that had been the key to the M.N.R.'s power. "As long as the co-government formula was efficacious, the bourgeois state of 1952 maintained its democratic character" (Zabaleta 1974). When its efficacy dwindled, however, the state was obliged to make a mass appeal to the peasantry, to women and, later, to the army.

Gueiler (1959) corroborates this observation when she writes, "Given these circumstances--and with more enthusiasm than awareness of the problem--a group of activists from the party's women's section banded together on a temporary basis. As always, unfortunately, with very precise, very concrete and particular objectives: the party needed a total mobilization of its forces to take up political positions against the opposition in what were to be the most democratic elections ever held in the country. For this, naturally, they remembered the women."

A women's preelectoral committee was therefore created, and contributed toward the M.N.R.'s electoral triumph in 1956. This was the first election in which women had the franchise. Despite their massive turnout in the election, however, we can attest only to the virtually total absence of women among those elected. In fact, "only three women were included, as Assistant Deputies, on the M.N.F.'s parliamentary candidate lists" (Gueiler 1959:150) that year.

With the idea of carrying out concrete, specific assignments, there arose within the National Female Command a group of women called the Barzolas.[4] This was the personal initiative of the women themselves, and it received strong support from the party chief, Victor Paz Estenssoro, who planned to make the group "a sort of women's secret police.[5] One member of the group writes, "This handful of selfless women, popularly known as 'Barzolas,' whose burning passion and boundless audacity quickly brought them fame both within and outside party ranks, was never accorded the seat of honor that belongs to the revolutionary woman. She adds, "the blame lay not with them, but with those whose mission it was to guide their struggle and direct their political work. Women's valor and sacrifice should never be utilized for sectarian purposes, much less for 'shock troops.' In every political party, this style of work belongs unquestionably to the male sector" (Gueiler 1959:155). Someone who did not belong to the party but observed what the Barzolas did comments:

> The M.N.R.'s Barzolas gave of themselves to serve the party's interests, and instead helped repress the people. They served as an instrument of repression. For this reason, there is still a feeling of animosity in Bolivia toward the Barzolas. In La Paz, for example, when a sector of the working class demanded something, the Barzolas would jump in front of them, brandishing razors, penknives, and whips, attacking the people who had gathered in a protest demonstration against harmful measures adopted by the goverment. In the parliament, too, the Barzolas would stand up and if someone spoke against the M.N.R., they were there with tomatoes and other things to throw at them and make them keep quiet (Viezzer 1978:78).

Characteristic of women M.N.R. members' political involvement during this period were its variations according to circumstances outside the women's movement itself; that is, it depended on party interests. During this time, for example, a vast contingent of women from the urban popular sector--more specifically, *cholas* from the cities--could be seen mobilizing around the National Congress, consitituting a virtual "cheering section" for M.N.R. delegates, greeting their remarks with loud shouts and applause. They would behave just the opposite, however, when it came to the parliamentary opposition, reaching the extreme of physically attacking them or preventing the congressional session from continuing. These women were so well known for the *waykillas* that they waged that whenever members of the oppositon left the congressional grounds, they did so under strong police protection. (*Waykilla* is a common term for ganging up on one person and physically assaulting him or her.)

Also typifying this women's group during this period was their performance as "shock troops" in street confrontations with demonstrators who opposed government policy. At the same time, these and other women took an active part in mass public events sponsored by the government and in the party's public gatherings. The distribution of food and drinks at these events was almost solely in the hands of the Barzolas. In Santa Cruz de la Sierra, the party sought to resolve the problem of low-income housing by handing out parcels of urban land that were directly occupied. The *tambos*, part of an exploitative system based on the monopoly of urban real estate, were thus distributed. And the Barzolas played a very important part in dividing these urban and suburban parcels and later distributing them among M.N.R. supporters and activists. Another tactic that M.N.R. women frequently resorted to was to pronounce their "unconditional support" for one party chief or leader or another. Through their "resolutions" and by using the mass media, they made known their acceptance or disapproval of this or that figure or of certain measures that had been or were about to be taken.

The "Communication" published in the newspaper *La Nacion* on 19 May 1964 serves as an example of this type of politicking. In its most noteworthy section, it says. "The Women's Coordinating Committee of the National Political Command, through this Resolution, expresses its unconditional suppprt for the Maximum Head of the National Revolution, Victor Paz Estenssoro, and appeals to the Unit of Bolivian Women to join the men of the M.N.R. in continuing the struggle for solidarity with the Party and the Revolutionary People."

Two fundamental factors influencing the movement's present and future actions were the use that was made of women in the party and the absence of party intellectuals. In spite of this, at one point the following reflection was made:

> A lack of direction among party leadership and a lack of political maturity among its members has meant that women have not yet been organized on a permanent basis in order to achieve the objectives of their own liberation. Shock troops and other forms of organized violence in the service of certain leaders or of sectarian, divisive groups, are not the way to organize revolutionary women. Despite universal suffrage and a very limited involvement in affairs of State, I can affirm, without fear of being wrong or unjust, that in actuality, the equal opportunity they require to fully develop their political abilities and social involvement has not yet been granted (Gueiler 1959:158).

These observations notwithstanding, women's involvement continued along the same path. This role taken on by women during the time of the national revolution came under sharp ideological attack from society in general (with the exception of certain party interests). In the first place, they did not accept women's unbridled participation in government politics. Nor did they accept the actual function that had been assigned to women. Rather, they sought to preserve women's traditional role. Every M.N.R. woman at that time was given the pejorative labor of "Barzola." As Gueiler tells us, "The bourgeois ladies of the old and new creole oligarchy were not the only ones to use this label. They regularly differentiate themselves from revolutionary women, hurling at them an epithet that is actually a glorious combat name that expresses the proud temperament of the revolutionary tradition of M.N.R. working-class women: "Barzola" (1959).

But who were these women whom "society" feared and scorned so? The Barzolas lived in primarily lower-class urban sections. The majority of them were illiterate, wives of "militia men" or simply of M.N.R. activists. Their main occupation was being "housewives." In other words, they were fundamentally in charge of the domestic reproduction of labor. This activity required that they additionally take on supplementary, income-producing employment, either at home or outside, since their companions' salaries were insufficient. The loyalty that a Barzola felt for the party or for a given leader was intense. Many of these women, in fact, being activists of proven loyalty, obtained various benefits that the party granted its militants, such as locations in municipal marketplaces as "regular vendors." This "autonomous" work, furthermore, allowed them to attend to their household chores or carry them on simultaneously, as well as to respond immediately to calls from the party or a local head to mobilize. In addition, as compensation for their loyalty, these women would receive rations and vouchers[6] from the party.

The Barzolas also assumed a significant role within the structure and operations of the provisioning system, and this, in turn, endowed them with importance in the overall political scene. Through state policy, another sector of the Barzolas succeeded in gaining access to economic surpluses and comprising an important commercial sector. In time, they developed close ties with a new urban social sector, linked to retail trade and contraband, two activities that attracted a large number of women.

Still another group of Barzolas worked as domestic servants for the Bolivian middle and upper classes. These women had the same characteristics as were mentioned earlier, but their activity was more limited in that they were involved in servile work relations. Nevertheless, they fulfilled a specific and very useful function for the party, which was to provide information on the political activities and thinking of the *patrones* in whose houses they worked--information that was highly valued by the party.

THE HOUSEWIVES COMMITTEES

It was between 1956 and 1964 that the working class disengaged itself from the M.N.R. "Imperialism has imposed its plans on the government," reads the treatise of the Federated Union of Mining Workers of Bolivia (FSTMB), dated Colquiri, 13 July 1958.

We have already examined how, in the absence of a truly revolutionary party, post-1952 Bolivian organized labor constituted a state organ with decision-making power. During this period, the labor unions tried to compensate for the inadequacies of political parties by advancing a political program of their own.[7] These efforts reached a peak in the Popular Assembly of 1971, for Bolivian workers almost never conceived of the labor union as merely a union, and on certain occasions such unions are a determining factor.

Thus the FSTMB, which is the most prestigious labor organization in the country, has demonstrated its outstanding qualities, not only in regard to its treatise, but also in relation to its leaders and its *decisive* presence in every important event that has taken place in the country in recent years.

In fact, its political radicalization, its aggressive cohesion, and its notable influence on popular movements situates mining unionism in a unique category. Its influence goes beyond the union model and marks it as one of the most energetic motivating forces in organizing and mobilizing the Bolivian masses. In this regard, Zabaleta (1974) claims FSTMB was always more important and more powerful than the very parties that its members belong to.

Following their decisive roles in the popular uprising of 1952, the Bolivian miners gained even more leverage in the class struggle. Besides the nationalization of the mines, the two most important achievements of the working class were: the popular militias made up of city, mining, and rural workers; and workers control, with the right to veto.

Workers control of the nationalized mines, with veto rights, was passed on 15 December 1952, becoming one of the greatest conquests for the country's working class--a conquest allowing them to take part in administration and security matters affecting nationalized mining. Workers' comanagement was based on three essential rights: the right to supervise in economic, administrative, and financial areas; the right to oversee all agreements and veto those which it deems contrary to the interests of underground workers or of the national economy; and the right to elect representatives to the local boards and to the Central Board of the Bolivian Mining Corporation (COMIBOL), the state-owned mining enterprise.

During this period, the unions at the mines of Catavi and Siglo XX (in the Department of Potosi) were the best organized and most politicized. It is with the imposition of the Stabilization Plan, promoted by the United States through John Jackson Eder that the unions began to oppose the M.N.R. regime. This marked the actual return of imperialism to the reins of Bolivian affairs. And unlike the peasant unions, the miners proclaim themselves unconnected to the government, and act accordingly (Garcia 1974).

It is during this confrontation between the miners' unions and the government that the first acts of political and economic repression against the miners were recorded. And it is within this context that, for the first time, there appeared a form of women's organization at the mines, the Housewives Committees. Their beginnings go back to

1960, when a group of sixty woman organized to obtain freedom for their companions, who, as leaders demanding better working conditions, had been imprisoned. The women won all their requests after having waged a hunger strike for ten days. And following this, they decided to organize into a coalition that they called "The Housewives Committee of Siglo XX (Viezzer 1978:42).

According to the same testimony, "from then on, the Committee was on a par with the labor unions and other working-class organizations, fighting for the same causes. We always make our voices heard, and we are always on the alert to carry out tasks that the working class sets before itself (Viezzer 1978).

The Housewives Committee of Siglo XX initially consisted of approximately sixty miners' wives. Their first leader was Norberta de Aguliar, also the wife of a miner. Later on, this same type of organization took shape at other mining centers. Its rise could be accounted for, as we have discussed, by the necessities imposed by the political struggle of the moment.

The objectives that the Housewives first set for themselves were concerned with improving living conditions for the workers and their families and with the partnership that the women would be forming in the struggle being waged by the workers, their husbands. To this end, they engaged in a series of actions that were politically supportive of the struggle being carried out by the labor union. They also undertook the task of demanding an improvement in public goods and services (good provisions, health, schooling, housing, sanitation, potable water, etc.), which the state mining enterprise provided in a manner that left much to be desired, as a form of indirect wages for the worker and their families.

The Housewives Committee's support and "partnership" activities included defending those who had been arrested because of their political and union activiites in the district; sending petitions and other documents to the government and the company; and giving the workers oral and written support. In addition, they vocally criticized the executive branch and the mining company; provided continual guard service for the union's prisoners and hostages; and supplied security measures for the union's assets (offices, library, radio transmitter, etc.).

Women also pursued actions aimed at pressuring the government or the company, among them hunger strikes, demonstrations, and protest marches, as well as street confrontations with the army and strikebreakers. They also organized themselves into shock troops against those reporting for work. One day, at about six o'clock in the morning, some women hurled stones at several vehicles at the Salvadora mining camp because they were transporting strikebreakers.

> Since the men could no longer do anything because they ran the certain risk of being caught and jailed, the women

> spontaneously organized, positioning themselves and their children in front of the work sites. . . . and the women would show harsh treatment towards anyone showing up for work: "Cowards" we have seven or eight children and still we're going on with the strike. How is it possible for you to sell out and go to work?" They would pelt them with stones and drag them away (Viezzer 1978:247).

At the same time, they were involved in demanding social improvements for the workers and their families. One issue was the cost of foodstuffs[8] and the quantity, quality, and regularity of rations (cupos) allotted to each family. Another area that the committee concentrated on was the hospital, demanding more and better medical and paramedical care, as well as more adequate provisions of medicines and surgical equipment and a better hospital infrastructure. They also turned their attention to education, the quality of teaching, school breakfasts, and teachers' treatment of students. The committee thus strictly regulated the areas of health and education, among others.

Parallel with these activities, during union or national emergencies the Housewives Committee would take on other responsibilities, such as transporting and caring for those injured during confrontations with the army, and preparing food and community meals. Also during emergency situations, they would attend wakes and funerals for those killed by the state's repressive machinery and visit political prisoners. Additionally, they would act as "letter carriers," connecting the mining union movement with other popular sectors.

All of this attests to the versatility displayed by the women's movement at the mines. The truth is, the activities of the Housewives Committee varied radically according to the political circumstances of the country at a given moment. As was described above, during periods when unionism was legal (although in confrontation with the government), the committee engaged in activities that supported and complemented those of the union. To some extent, the committee was undertaking and carrying out some of the functions that every union normally fulfills, but never did these include political and union leadership. At the last Mining Congress, held in 1982, the F.S.T.M.B. for the first time enumerated the functions of the Housewives Committee. Points 2, 3, and 4 of Resolution 5 read as follows:

> 2. To instruct all mining labor unions in the country, in both nationalized and private industry, to guide, support, provide motiviation, or initiate the organization and activity of Housewives Committees at every mining center. For this purpose, they are to hold assemblies or elections in order to constitute the respective governing boards (with the

indispensable number of portfolios, and in accordance with each union's needs) of the Housewives Committees, which will function as *auxiliaries* to the mining unions, *subordinate* to them.

3. To authorize all the Housewives Committees at the mines to attend and participate in the next Mining Congress (with voting privileges), through representation by their respective Secretary General and a local delegate elected in Assembly. Transportation and per diem expenses for both delegates will be paid through financial contributions of all the housewives and supplemented with funds from each union.

4. To charge the Executive Committee of the F.S.T.M.B. with designing a proposal for a Declaration of Principles and a Statute for the Housewives Committees, and presenting it at the next Congress. It is to define the organizations' objectives, functions, and internal operations, as well as their formal application and relations with the miners unions, the F.S.T.M.B. and the C.O.B.

During periods of political represssion and absence of political and union rights, the Housewives Committee has accepted every task assigned to it by the union and published documents under the union's clandestine direction, taking on in full the union's activities.

Throughout the existence of the Housewives Committee, the sole organized and continuous participation of women miners was instigated basically by the union itself. Despite various problems, the committee succeeded in mobilizing large masses of women around very concrete issues. The nucleus formed by the women in the committee demonstrated continuity in regard to the activities that they planned and conducted.

When the Housewives Committee joined the union's and workers' struggle, it took great pains to explicitly differentiate itself from present-day women's movements in Europe and the United States: "for us, the first and principal job does not consist of fighting with our *companeros*. It consists, rather, of working with them to change the system under which we live for another one--one in which men and women have the right to live, to work, and to organize. . . . In the task that the workers are laboring at, they receive collaboration from us, their *companeras*" (Viezzer 1978:44, 221).

At the beginning, the Houewives Committee's struggle was directed against United States imperialism, the second administration of Paz Estenssoro, and the state mining enterprise, COMIBOL. COMIBOL had by that time adopted almost purely capitalistic features, as a service to United State capital and to medium-scale mining interests, a new faction of the bourgeoisie that came into being under the auspices of COMIBOL. Later, their struggle was principally against the military dictatorships. Let us not forget the four mining women who, through their hunger strike, made the democratic overture of 1978 possible. Nor the battle that mining women effectively waged in resistance to the 17 July coup and the subsequent military governments. Their role in defending political and union rights and in restoring democracy on 10 October 1982 has been a crucial one.

The Housewives Committee was therefore organized, and acted, as an auxiliary association of the Mining Workers Union, adopting the union's demands and acting on them. In no instance did the committee propose relative autonomy for itself. Nor did it ever press for restitution as a sector of women who were being exploited both by the captialist system and indirectly by the state-owned mining company. The latter, by underpaying their husbands, obligated these women to provide part of the miners' subsistence through their own additional labor--this in addition to the oppression and discrimination they suffered due to the sexual division of labor. In this respect, the women of the Housewives Committee adopted the position of the Bolivian political left with regard to women's current situation: they do not deny that women are at a disadvantage compared to men, but consider this to be a result of the capitalist exploitation of their country and believe that the solution will come once the proletariat conquers its historic objectives. The entire struggle, therefore, should proceed in that direction. Any other suggestion is seen as an attempt, on the part of its class enemies, to divide the popular movement--especially "feminisit" proposals, which, in this case, are considered distortions.

The mining women's objective situation is similar to that of the Barzolas. They are women whose main activity is domestic labor,[9] that is, the production of use goods to be directly consumed by family members. The housewife receives help from her children, who, from a very early age, must assist with the housework and related activities. This work is indispensable for the reproduction of the capitalist system. It provides services that are essential to the reproduction of the labor force and for which neither capital nor the state offers any substitute--in Bolivia, neither is capable of achieving even minimally socialized domestic labor.

Given these conditions and the large number of children that Bolivian mining families have, the women spend long hours at home, their principal place of work and, on rare occasions, of leisure, too. Their work, according to the logic of capitalist accumulation, is not remunerated, and the amount of time it consumes depends on how the woman allocates it, the help that she gets from her children, and the other activities that she must undertake as a survival strategy, or in search of a partial--and necessary--income to offset the cost of reproducing the domestic labor force.

In general, there is no division, and certainly no socialization, of domestic activities. Nevertheless, at the mining centers and in popular urban neighborhoods, houewives do have occasion to be exposed to urban issues, either while shopping for household goods or while getting water at the public taps or fountains (mining and low-income housing is not equipped with indoor plumbing, making it necessary to attend to this need outside the home). In the long waiting lines, they discuss the issues of work, food supplies, and domestic and national issues.

Unlike their salaried husbands and companions, these women have no regular work hours, for once they have finished with their housework, they go on to other domestic activities, within the confines of their homes, selling their services to the outside at a set price. These "services" include preparing traditional regional or national foods; laundering and ironing; spinning and weaving; and sewing. In contrast, for salaried workers, as in the case of the male miners, the home is a place where they consume but do not work, and their time belongs wholly to themselves. Men in both bourgeois and popular Bolivian families do not assist with domestic chores, for during the process of their socialization, a rigid sexual division of labor is set down. In fact, when a man does share in the housework, he is harshly criticized by his peers and what is more, by his own wife and children, who do not approve of his help with "women's work." Under these circumstances, it is often the family itself that considers it normal for the "head of the family" to get drunk, or to carry on affairs, and sees his physical and verbal mistreatment of his family, and especially his wife, as "proof of his affection."

Domestic labor and the sale of certain services for cash are both forms of work that pass unnoticed by family members and even by the woman herself. This is because these services are consumed on a virtually continuous basis. The time that these chores require easily surpasses the value of the husband's salary because they are carried out by both the woman and her children. In this sense, women, while lacking control of the means of production, are actual, and very rarely potential, workers in the capitalist system. It is solely by recognizing women's dual role (real or potential) in production that one can analyze their class position and the tensions within it that lead to change.

SOME PROVISIONAL CONCLUSIONS

Based on what we have seen here, we can state that, within the context of Latin America, Bolivia represents one of the few cases of women's organized political experience, particularly within popular sectors. In fact, even before the establishment of a republic, women's political participation was both important and multi-faceted. And if in most instances their involvement was spontaneous in nature, this was due to the particular historical period of development of the popular classes, during which time their part in the struggle took on spontaneous, and at other times racial and/or regional, overtones.

Women were present in every social movement, their activities affecting many aspects of national life, and at times their participation was decisive. Nonetheless, we can speak of Bolivian women's organized political struggle only beginning with the M.N.R.'s Female Commands which, starting in 1946, constituted important bastions in the struggle against the oligarchy and against chaos. Later, parallel with the Barzolas' activities, we have the advent of the Housewives Committees as another form of women's organized efforts in the struggle--this time against the state-owned capitalist venture in which women are exploited not directly, but rather via the insufficient salaries that their husbands receive. In both cases, they are groups of women who linked their own struggle with the demands and collective actions of subordinate classes who sought to achieve a new kind of social and national emancipation.

Both forms of women's organization--the one that is created as an adjunct and subordinate to a party and later to the state apparatus and the one that arises as a subordinate arm of a labor union--share similar characteristics, although the contexts and objectives differ. In both cases we can speak of a mass movement in which there is extensive participation by women from low-income or urban sectors and from the mines. And both the M.N.R. Barzolas and the Housewives Committees are social movements that extend beyond local or regional boundaries to acquire national and popular importance.

While it is true that both the National Revolution of 1952 and the miners unions generated a broad system of political participation for women as well as greater opportunities for them to take part in other socioeconomic activities, it is less accurate to say that either the party or the labor union had any coherent politicoideological plan to pursue women's liberation as part of the more global struggle taking place within the context of the national and popular processes that the country was going through. On the contrary, both the party and the union subordinated the women's struggle to the interests of their institutions' upper echelons; at no time did they address demands specific to women as an exploited and discriminated sector. Such specific demands did not contradict any of the overall demands put forth by the party or the union; in fact, they tended to complement the restitutions called for by the popular movement. In this respect, the party that called itself nationalist and revolutionary and the union that called itself class conscious both fell under the influence of patriarchal capitalist society when it came to their conception of women's role in a society in which they are already active participants.

In both cases, it is regrettable that there were no intellectuals from the women's liberation movement, especially among the women themselves. Neither the party nor the union encouraged the growth of any internal politicoideological movement that would make it possible to come up with actions or goals differing from those they had been pursuing. The result of this new type of women's political involvement was the recreation of new mechanisms to subordinate and discriminate against women.

This is due to the fact that women's activities, within both the party and the labor union, are merely extensions of domestic chores carried out within the home, except that in this case, they are activities that are directed in an authoritarian and vertical fashion from the bureaucratic spheres of the organization. At no time has there been a suggestion that there be equal participation (except in dangerous situations, when women must "prove" their heroism and bravery) in political decision-making or in apportioning political power.

The women's struggle in Boliva can no longer restrict itself to searching for formal mechanisms of participation. Women effectively participate in other ways. Every possible legal restitution has been written into law, but in actual practice discrimination against women is still sanctioned in every sphere of Bolivian society.

NOTES

This chapter is a preliminary study based on research sponsored by the Latin American Social Science Council (CLASCO). The translation is by Annabelle Shirk.

1 The *sexenio* was the six-year period beginning in 1946 with the fall of the Villarroel government, of which the MNR was a part, and ending in 1952, the year of the Revolution.

2 According to the Decree of 21 July, 1952, women and all popular sectors are incorporated into political participation through universal suffrage.

3 The period from 1952 to 1956, see Rene Zabaleta, *El Poder Dual*.

4 Maria Barzola was a reknowned woman miner, who headed a march in defense of union rights and economic issues. She lost her life on 21 December, 1942 in what was later called the Catavi Massacre.

5 Interview with Ela Campero, La Paz, 1980.

6 In view of the crisis in production and the recent reordering of the economy, the MNR began distributing rations and vouchers (*cupos y bonos*) among its activists, as a way of providing them

with the basic household goods at subsidized prices. In many areas, this system generated intense speculation.

7 See the Federation of Bolivian Tin Miners Unions (FSTMB) The Pulacayo treatise, the Colquiri Treatise, and the Treatise of the Central Bolivian Workers Union (COB).

8 The food-provisioning system at the mines represents a victory for the workers. Certain food products are made available by the company at subsidized prices.

9 We understand domestic labor to be the production of use values under nonsalaried relations of production within the captialist mode of production (Cf. Gardiner, Hinmelwei, and Mackintosh 1980).

REFERENCES

Garcia, Antonio. 1974. Los sindicatos en el esquema de la revolucion nacional. Mexico, D. F.

Gardiner, J., S Hinmelwei, and A. Mackintosh. 1980. "El trabajo domestico de la mujer." In Teoria 4 (enero-marzo).

Gueiler, Lydia. 1959. La mujer y la revolucion. La Paz: Editorial Burillo.

Paz Estenssoro, Hugo. 1966. Presencia de la revolucion nacional. Lima.

Viezzer, Moema. 1978. Testimonio de Domitila. Mexico, D. F.: Editorial Siglo Veintiuno.

Zabaleta Mercado, Rene. 1974. El poder dual. Mexico, D. F.: Editorial Siglo Veintiuno.

17 Women's Equality and the Cuban Revolution

Isabel Larguia and John Dumoulin

The advances that have been made toward women's equality in Cuba are certainly worthy of study, as is the strategy that has been implemented. A first impression of the magnitude of progress can be gained from looking at one development index, the labor-force participation rate for women, and comparing the rapidity of the recent increase in Cuba with that of a similar rise in the United States in an earlier period: the increase observed in Cuba in nine years, 1970-79, took the United States from the late nineteenth century to the mid-twentieth to achieve.[1] Another example is the movement of women into qualified jobs: figures for 1975-79 show that women constituted 60 percent of new professionals and technicians during the period (Castro 1980b). Of course, these examples are taken out of context. In order to have a concrete idea of the strategy for women's equality in Cuba and what it has achieved, a complex analysis is required, going from the more general to the more specific.

The socialist world of today, with its achievements and prospects for development and with all its problems, is still a young and growing social organism. Much has yet to be consolidated, and much still bears the mark of the past. This holds also for the dynamics of the situation of women in present-day socialism.

The struggle for women's equality in Cuba is conceived to be an integral part of an overall process of social transformation, socialist revolution, and the building of a classless society. There is no conception of meaningful progress through the isolated struggle and independent action of intellectual elites.

The profound social inequality between men and women that was shaped in the conditions of backwardness and dependence is inseparable from the disparities and antagonisms prevalent in all relations, throughout the country, notably between the different classes, regions, branches of economic activity, ethnic groups, and between the city and countryside. Sex inequality could only be redressed through a process of change that would correct a whole system of violent contrast and disproportion. A process of economic expansion had to be set in motion whereby there would be a democratization of employment and all extradomestic life, higher productivity and skills, an improved standard of living, and more services made available. In order to achieve these goals, there had to be a break with the support structures of underdevelopment, chronic unemployment, a deformed structure of production, foreign dependence, an elite-oriented educational system, an agrarian structure based on latifundia, and, in the most general and essential features, private ownership of the basic means of production. It was only through revolution that the particular interests of women came into harmony with the general interests of the country. Both required the transformation of basic structures and overcoming underdevelopment in such a way as to further the interests of the great majority.

In general terms, the conditions are common to many underdeveloped countries. In order to understand the concrete issue of women in the context of the Cuban revolution, certain specific historical features that worsened their economic exploitation and sharpened patriarchal structures of subordination need to be taken into account. They are discussed briefly below.

The majority of Cuban women lived in the interior of the country. But the characteristic deformation of the Cuban economy and corresponding patriarchal tradition denied them direct agricultural work without offering any alternative sources of income. All but a few women were working full-time as housewives, i.e., in reproduction of their household labor power.[2] Women were reported to comprise only 1 percent of those engaged in agriculture as an occupation (TSE 1955:204). Although the limitations of this datum have yet to be studied systematically, it may be said that women's access to remunerative agricultural work was in general limited to short stints at very specific tasks in certain crops other than sugar cane. Very significantly, women were widely impeded even from working on subsistence plots, or, at least, if men were scarce, did so almost secretly, since women's extra domestic labor was seen by society as a whole as shameful for the male provider and head of household. It dishonored him socially.

The fact that rural women produced no *visible* product contributed to their having no access to trade. Since there was no rural cottage industry to speak of, neither was there a tradition of women's crafts. Unlike much of Latin America, rural women produced no local pottery, nor did they spin or weave, make basketry or do leatherwork. The fact that the Cuban woman, even in rural areas, did not customarily make any durable or salable, *visible* product (Larguia 1970)[3] contributed to her lack of awareness of her identity, her worth, and her human rights.

Unlike in other areas of Latin America, women did not work in agriculture alongside their husbands and sons. With rare exceptions, cane cutting was a seasonal, male occupation. There was chronic unemployment and underemployment. It was inconceivable for women to work in a sugar mill, even cleaning floors.

The lack of employment for women in rural areas perpetuated patriarchal behavior patterns. This situation, coupled with want, prompted women to migrate to urban areas, where low employment levels in industry and commerce, due to the country's overall stagnation, channeled them into domestic service or toward prostitution. The 13.7 percent of women fourteen and over classified as economically active in the 1953 census included 70,000 domestics, more than a quarter of the total (TSE 1955:183). There was a significant number of officially registered prostitutes, plus women who worked in the sales and service sectors and also engaged in a more disguised form of prostitution.

The tobacco and garment industries, where a certain number of women were employed, were mostly in small shops scattered throughout various locations, so that the conscious female proletariat, such as it was, could have no great influence on the 86 percent of women who were just housewives.

There was no electricity in the countryside; 87 percent of dwellings were lit by kerosene lamps; 63 percent were rustic homes with a dirt floor (TSE 1955:213); 42 percent of the rural population over the age of ten was illiterate (TSE 1955:143); and agricultural workers were found to have an average dietary deficiency of 1,000 calories a day, as a result of which 14 percent were tuberculosis victims, 13 percent had had typhoid fever and 36 percent had parasites (Agrupacion Catolica Universitaria 1972). Under these conditions of generalized poverty, the home was a school, a hospital, an old people's home, and a refuge for the unemployed.

The 1956-57 unemployment rate was measured at 16.4 percent, plus 10.1 percent "partially employed" (Pino Santos 1961:92). High male unemployment made less skilled and cheaper female labor a potential threat. Taboos based on the notion of women's physical and mental inferiority took extreme forms. The housewife's invisible labor, her wifely and motherly duties, were viewed with almost religious respect. The concept of the woman as an exclusively sexual, dehumanized biological being was reinforced by extensive prostitution. The combination of such adverse historical factors built up a patriarchal value structure that would prove very difficult to break down.

This was the situation in which the largest sectors of the female population found themselves on 2 January 1959, when the revolution came to power.

THE STRATEGY FOR WOMEN'S LIBERATION

A group of vanquard women had emerged in the course of the national liberation struggle. Together with the top revolutionary leadership they understood the need for--and women's interest in--taking an active part in the struggle that was opening up for the development of the country. They faced the difficult task of organizing a mass of women who had little notion of their basic human rights. However, Cuban women and the people as a whole had a sharp and rapidly developing understanding of the country's main problems at that stage, conceived in the aggregate as national liberation.

In August 1960 the Federation of Cuban Women (FMC) was founded, as a women's mass organization supporting the revolutionary transformation of the country. The first local branches spanned the length and breadth of the island, bringing together the most progressive women in each locale, along with a number of ex-combatants and revolutionary activists.

In posing the problem of women's equality, the revolutionary leadership in fact took account of two basic historical regularities:

1. It is only possible to achieve full and definitive emancipation on the basis of the interests and the awareness of all the different sectors of oppressed women. This consciousness must lead to the breakup and later elimination of the patriarchal ideology inherited from the previous society.

2. It is a historical regularity that the mass of women in the most exploited sectors, in order to become involved in the public sphere, first go through a stage of development of their so-called traditional tasks, before breaking into the fields from which they were previously barred, at least on any large scale, The main thrust of the initial organizing effort was in this direction, although from the early years of the revolution there were women of humble origin who were promoted to highly qualified posts of responsibility; the two processes took place simultaneously.

At first, even very cautious activism designed to draw women out of domestic seclusion and enlist their support could easily meet with strong reaction and create a climate of confusion in a given locality. The first FMC leaders in isolated areas had to face the hostitility and violent reaction of patriarchal consciousness, as well as the attacks of the counterrevolution. The first achievements in breaking with a tradition that kept women cloistered were very modest, seeking support in values and activities considered "proper" for women. The first step was to channel these activities so that they were not just for the benefit of an authoritarian head of household, but rather for the service of the community. Cuban women took as theirs the slogans of the revolution. They were ready to support and defend the decisive structural transformations of the early years without questioning the traditional role of women in society.

Women's labor power needed to be channeled to the community, and to produce visible objects, in order for them to realize themselves as human beings. Thus the first FMC gardens were set up, whose produce was for the consumption of the local FMC organizations.

Women were introduced into craftwork and took upon themselves the building and running of the first day-care centers (circulos infantiles). The home began to open up to community life, to lose its closed, stagnating existence; and women almost imperceptibly began to direct their activity toward the public sphere. Women's labor power was ceasing to be the property of fathers, husbands, or pimps. In turning their efforts to the service of the community, women started to become aware of their worth, and, fundamentally, of owning the product of their labor. In the consciousness of oppressed Cuban women, two concepts--for them inseparable--began to take shape: collectivity and personal identity or, as they would say, revolution and women's liberation.

To understand this formative period of the 1960s proves particularly difficult for those who defend women's rights with little knowledge of the inner linkages of revolutionary change. For example, one of the most successful measures of the early 1960s was the seamstress-training program, and this despite the fact that there is no export garment industry on the island. The Ana Betancourt Schools, as they were called, were named after a well-known figure of the first war of independence, in the nineteenth century, who very early spoke up for women's rights. These schools were set up to bring in young women from outlying rural areas, women whose parents would often frown on their even learning to read and write, let alone agree to their working outside the home for a wage, and by the same token would be against their participating in any women's organization. The nominal function of the Ana Betancourt schools was to teach young rural women to cut and sew, and for this they left their homes in remote rural areas to come to the city. At the same time they were given an elementary education and were exposed to the social and political ideas and motivations that were emerging with the revolution. They became conscious participants in the profound structural changes taking place in the country. They returned to their places of origin, committed to helping other young women out of patriarchal isolation and toward political awareness, thus becoming a bridge for the FMC to continue its work of emancipating the most oppressed sectors of women.

In 1961, the literacy campaign marked the start of a mass educational drive, particularly in the rural areas. As volunteer teachers, tens of thousands of young women left their cloistered homes in cities and towns and, together with the young men, went into rural and remote mountainous areas for months on end, living and working with poor families, and for the first time living a life of their own.

Voluntary work was seen as a socially useful activity supporting the achievements of the revolution. It attracted women because they saw themselves reflected in these achievements. It became a means of tradition whereby women came out of domestic stagnation, began to lose their fear of the outside world, and gained experience and confidence in themselves; they were gradually prepared to stabilize that condition by thereafter entering into wage work.

The struggle between the revolution and its internal and external enemies, in deciding the country's fate, made defense extraordinarily important. Both women and society in general become aware of this need. Women began to enlist in the militia and in the revolutionary police force, wearing uniforms and bearing arms for the first time. Some few trained in military schools and attained rank and command posts. One of the most formidable barriers in the division of labor by sex was thus broken down and an unprecedented number of women became engaged in military activity.

These early measures, very modest in themselves, had the great virtue of mobilizing millions of women to destroy the very bases of the patriarchal structure that was the heritage of colonialism and a plantation society led by slaveowners, and was reinforced in neocolonial society. Rehabilitation programs for prostitutes were introduced and within three years they were reabsorbed without stigma into normal social activity, work, and study. The same can be said of the 70,000 domestics. By 1970 the so-called informal sector had practically disappeared.

The breaking down of private ownership of women's labor power was perhaps the point of departure, the necessary precondition for large-scale participation in social production, scientific research, and political leadership. It was done in the collective interest, and it was in serving that collective interest that women grew aware of their independence and worth as human beings. It comes as no surprise, then that Cuban women in the 1980s cannot see their emancipation as women as divorced from structural change in the revolutionary process. For them private property and domestic slavery are practically synonymous--a part of a hated past. For them *women's liberation* and *social revolution* mean one and the same thing.

When the revolution struck at the anachronistic institutions that were blocking national development, it paved the way for an unprecedented expansion of employment. By the mid-1960s the great mass of unemployed, which a few years before made up at least 16.4 percent of the labor force (Pino Santos 1961:92), had been reabsorbed. From then on the expansion of the labor force was achieved funamentally with the incorporation of women, which for the first time became a necessity for national development. Women understood this need and throughout the 1960s entered the labor force with strong patriotic motivations. The Federation of Cuban Women made continous efforts to promote and facilitate the incorporation of women into social production.

By 1968 the number of women who were yearly joining the work force had increased greatly. With this, however, came considerable instability in female employment. This was due in large part to the lack of adequate support measures, needed because of the magnitude of change with respect to traditional usage. While large numbers of women were entering employment, many were also dropping out and going back to the home. Transitional measures were adopted in order to help women workers and to ensure that their extra-domestic activity would not result in a total breakdown in the mechanisms governing men and women's behavior, motiviation and self-image. These measures were also deeigned to assure the reproduction of labor power through domestic labor, which in the 1960s was still almost exclusively women's responsibility.

The process initiated by the FMC in the workplace had passed into the hands of the trade union organization, and in 1970 the Central Organization of Cuban Trade Unions set up its new Women's Affairs Department. This department is active on all levels, from the workplace right up to the national level, and sees to the particular needs of women workers. Administrators were instructed to make due provision for women's needs. Along with these measures, there were others designed to promote women to skilled jobs.

CUBAN WOMEN AND THE PRIVATE REPRODUCTION OF LABOR POWER

Real progress in development and in women's equality have been achieved together in the context of the revolutionary transformation of the country, the struggle against undervelopment, and against the anachronistic captialist society that underlay it. It was toward the end of the first decade that the patriarchal character of the family inherited from the previous society stood out as an obstacle of the country's progress and was added to the list of structures whose replacement was from the beginning the strategic objective. The need to change the relations between the sexes was proclaimed, seeking equality and greater freedom in the development of the individual personality.

The gradual extinction of the household in its function as a private economic cell, as a place of work where labor power is reproduced, is an irreversible tendency of social development. But the mass replacement of the tiny domestic sweatshop by an effective socialized productive system not only presupposes extraordinary development of the productive forces, but also requires the human habitat to be redesigned. And mentalities must develop enormously. Such progress can only be achieved on a global scale, once the immense waste of the arms race has ceased.

Despite the country's poverty, the FMC fought from the beginning for services that would alleviate the work of the second shift. The services created by the revolutionary regime had reached, by 1981, 92,000 places in day-care centers (CEE 1982:235), and 403,000 children on the all-day school plan (CEE1982:240) with school lunch, which are benefits reserved for working mothers. The number of scholarship students with full room and board at all levels reached 589,000 (CEE 1982:238, 240, 246). Lunchrooms for workers and students freed working women from a particularly troublesome burden. Participation of women in political and productive life increased by leaps and bounds. Nevertheless, the services set up by the revolutionary government, although a very significant help, could not supplant the direct reproduction of labor power in the home. This task continued to weigh on women.

Old strictures prohibited men from doing the smallest domestic chore and taking active part in the care of their children. The division of labor in the family projected--and still projects--its shadow on public life. If women had to work twelve hours a day, between their place of work and the domestic sphere, they tended to prefer jobs that were easier than men's and with less responsibility so as to have energy left over for the second shift at home. How could this situation be overcome? Customs change slowly; in this case there is a complex and contradictory process in which vigorous government measures mix with ideological struggle and the erosion of the old behavior patterns under the influence of great material change.

In the early 1970s a tendency was already underway in Cuba toward the social reorientation of domestic life, a tendency that had won ground in the mind of the average Cuban, especially in the homes of working women.

Th whole complex of motivations and needs of the new life, the revolutionary activities and ideals of social justice, bit by bit made their influence felt in the home and pushed toward its reorganization. This process gained strength in 1975 with two measures that reflected this tendency and stimulated it. The first congress of the party, held that year, adopted Thesis No. 3 on women's equality. The document was first discussed and voted on in the study circles in all local organizations and places of work, in which amendments were suggested. The thesis states that men should fully share domestic work with women. This principle acquired the force of law in the same year with the enactment of the Family Code, which renewed and systematized family-related legislation, establishing the sharing of domestic responsibilities. Its pertinent stipulations make up the new marriage oath, and they are explained and exemplified for the couple when they are about to take their vows. This Code was submitted to the same process of discussion and approval as Thesis 3.

A permanent ideological struggle is being waged within Cuban society to get men to share all domestic chores, as an immediate way of freeing women's creative capacities in a period of transition.

The results can be seen in Table 1: between 1970 and 1979 the labor-force participation rate for married women rose from 16.3

percent to 36.7 percent and for women in common-law unions the figure jumped from 9.2 percent to 24.8 percent. This means a national increase of 124.9 percent for the former and 169.0 percent for the latter in the nine-year period. These two groups of women with husbands made the greatest contribution to the rise in women's overall participation rate, given that they make up two-thirds of the female population aged over fourteen. The relatively low figure for single women reflects the large proportion of young people who are studying.

The years 1967-71, when the great surge in women's labor force participation was beginning, were the critical years for the growth and stability of women's employment, and we believe that they were also the critical years for marriage. In testing this, instead of using the more common gross rate of divorce, we found it preferable to calculate the frequency in relation to an estimate of the number of legally formalized unions existing in the given year. The data employed comes from tables assembled by the demography section of the State Committee for Statistics, and released in various publications (CEEDD 1981a, 1981b; Dumoulin 1977).

The annual divorce rate went up very steeply, from 0.4 percent of existing legal marriages in 1967 to 2.3 percent in 1971. The rate ceased to grow in the first half of the 1970s, as practical solutions were found for the problems of the moment; it dropped down to as little as 1.7 percent and leveled off, while large numbers of wives with husbands present continued to swell the ranks of the labor force. These figures attest to the profound restructuring of values that took place in the psychology of the broadest sectors of the population. No revolutionary change comes about without some measure of trial and tribulation (the more so, the more overdue these changes are), but in this case the transitional instability introduced long-term improvement. Whereas in 1960 a man would have felt dishonored if his wife went to work, today he is ashamed if she doesn't and tends to rationalize with explanations like these: "She isn't well," "She's having trouble with her nerves," "She has problems," "She's looking for something that would suit her".

Cuban women, for their part, in evaluating a prospective spouse, today give first place to the criterion of "understanding", (*que me comprenda*), that is, that he understands her need and right to have an active and diversified life, that he not expect to have a mere domestic slave, all of which presupposes that he share in the domestic labor.

The enactment of the Family Code is the center of a direct and massive confrontation with macho patterns and with the foundation of the division of labor between the sexes. Its objective is to free the Cuban women's energies for expansion in all areas of social activity, so that they can achieve the personal fulfillment which had always been denied them.

Along with this came the change in custom in the sphere of

sexual relations and biological reproduction. Varied contraceptive devices and abortion are freely available. The birth rate, and infant mortality as well, have gone down in two decades to levels which are usually found only in developed countries.[4] Sexual mores among the young are now much more permissive than those of their parents; they have set aside the myth of virginity. Dual morality is subject to permanent questioning. Such brusque changes inevitably give rise to tension.

The Federation of Cuban Women is promoting sex education through the press and television, the educational system, and in its own activity at the block level; the ideals are that both men and women consciously assume parenthood, to avoid hurried marriages, to correct the pejorative image of the unwed mother, and to create a situation whereby marriage does not interrupt education.

TRAINING OF WOMEN WORKERS

Whereas in the 1960s women joined the labor force with the knowledge and capabilities they had acquired spontaneously in their homes and in the existing educational system, in the 1970s the participation rate went up sharply and *at the same time* women began to be trained on a large scale for trades and professions in which up until then they had little or no presence.

The revolutionary process had begun with a strategy that stressed bringing women into tasks which tended to recover and develop traditional feminine culture, such as it was, in the craft work, organizing hygiene brigades, and the like. This line of work continues to predominate with housewives. While it still has a function for one sector of women and for the country as well, it began to take second place to bringing women into the forefront of the push for advanced technology.

Some of the transitional measures worked out in the 1960s, which channeled women into traditional "feminine" jobs, were abolished in 1973 after the thirteenth Congress of the CTC, since they were no longer congruent with the development women had attained by then.

The changes produced by the revolution in the social consciousness of the Cuban people made it possible by the 1970s for women to be incorporated directly into training programs in nontraditional areas on a large scale. The FMC, together with the State Committee for Labor and Social Security, began to plan the country's future labor-power needs, for new factories and other units. They set up on site training courses for skilled workers and middle-level technicians, so that local housewives could join the ranks of skilled labor without having to go through an intermediate stage of leaving the home and/or entering traditional "feminine" wage work.

In the polytechnical schools on the secondary level, quotas were established for women in the different areas of specialization, to make sure that women were not left behind in the expansion of skilled trades and technicians' jobs; the goal set in these quotas was 50 percent women in each branch, and this contributed to a rapid increase in women's matriculation in the 1975-80 period (Granma 1980); although the levels reached by the latter year were not yet considered sufficient, they make instructive contrast with the figures for other Latin American countries.

Women continue to study once they are working. It is significant that by 1980 31.5 percent of women workers were studying, while only 23.0 percent of the men were doing so. The breakdown of these figures by levels and types of education reveals that the tendency is quite uniform. In 1980 1.8 percent of all male workers were enrolled in secondary education, regular or polytechnical, while the figure for women was 4.0 percent. In higher education, 1.7 percent of the working men were enrolled compared with 2.9 percent of working women. And in schools for skilled workers, 4.2 percent of the men were enrolled and 6.3 percent of the women (Espin 1980).

These three different training efforts complement each other. The young women graduating from polytechnical schools, the housewives training on site in factories, and women workers who are studying together contribute to a marked shift in the occupational composition of women workers in favor of the skilled technicians and professional jobs. In 1975-79, the women entering technical and professional work were equivalent in number to 40 percent of the new female labor force in that period (Espin 1980). By 1979 women constituted 53.4 percent of all technicians and professionals (CEEDD 1981b:51). The change in the occupational composition of working women is reflected in Table 2.

This tendency continues into the 1980s. The proportion of women who are middle-level technicians and professionals employed in the civilian public sector, which was 24.5 percent in 1976 and 30.0 percent in 1980, has now reached one-third (Granma 1983). At the same time the total number of working women has increased steadily. According to figures released by the CTC (Central de Trabajadores de Cuba), there are 1,044,000 working women, which is about 38.9 percent of the employed population, as compared with 3.0 percent five years ago (Veiga 1984). Here again, the data probably refer to the civilian public sector (which in fact makes up the vast majority of the Cuban labor force), variations in which are monitored on a short-term basis. These figures make it possible to estimate the number of women working as technicians and professionals, as of early 1984, at approximately 10 percent of the entire Cuban female population over the age of fourteen.

It is important to note that this new participation has not been channeled into the service sector and that the increase in the number of women technicians was felt in productive sectors such as construction, the sugar industry, metallurgy and the mechanical industry, shipbuilding, textiles, and transportation, among other branches of industry.

The drift toward feminization in certain work areas, that is, the massive incorporation of women into a limited group of occupations that become feminine to the point where men cease to enter them, is a phenomenon that has been taking place all over the world, to one degree or another, wherever there has been more employment for women (Boserup 1970:217). Cuba shows a reversal of this tendency as women progressively invade all branches of work. Although in the first moment of expansion many women went into saleswork, public eating places, and services, this trend has been completely reversed among the newest cohorts of women workers. The tendency toward the dissolution of the sexual division of labor in employment shows up very clearly among the most qualified in each branch of work. And there is a growing concentration of women in intellectual work of all kinds.

Under prevailing world conditions, there often appears with the expansion of female employment what might be called a pyramid effect: women begin to enter a given sector at a greater rate than before and gradually take over the jobs requiring lesser qualifications and less responsibility. The key phase in the process comes when, and if, starting from what was perhaps only a difference in seniority, a new sexual division of labor crystallizes: whereas previously the whole sector was considered improper for them they become acceptable in the lower positions, but not in the higher ranking ones. The new structure may become permanent. Even with equal seniority and qualifications, the higher the rank within the given sector, the lower the number of women among the job holders. Another result would be lower wages for women, not only because their work is on the average less skilled, but because, as men back off progressively from a feminized occupation, it acquires the social image of a position requiring less skill and therefore less worthy of a raise. The Cuban practice of training women for widely diversified jobs needing high qualifications is thus particularly important in impeding the crystallization of such pyramids.

In order to test the trend toward the equalization of the sexes in the occupational structure, it is necessary to study the presence of women in the different occupational groups and, within each of them, at different levels of qualification. Under conditions of structural change, the decisive test is to make this analysis separately for the significant age cohorts so as to control the seniority variable and catch a glimpse of the new tendencies as they emerge.

Table 3 presents in consolidated form some new information relative to the presence of women among graduates in different areas of study recognized by the 1981 population census. It reflects the three fundamental levels of education that orient the students toward specific job areas: university, middle-level technician (12th grade education), and skilled worker (9th grade education). Table 3 does not include nonspecialized secondary education nor teacher-training programs, both of which are predominantly feminine. Figures are calculated from 1981 census data, using the specialization breakdown provided by that source. The table presents the percentage of women among diploma holders at each level, as registered in the census. The same percentage is also offered for two cohorts, the youngest graduated in recent years, and another older cohort, forty to forty-nine years of age at the time of census, who in the main can be assumed to have received most of their education in the prerevolutionary period. In analyzing Table 3, it is important to remember that it reflects one moment in, and one point of view on, the process of rapid expansion of education at these levels. Technical education was little developed before the revolution. This means that the increase in the number of women in the younger age groups, which the table reflects, is actually only one aspect of the growth in the number of skilled women in the younger cohorts; the other component, not reflected in Table 3, is the general rise in the number of graduates, women and men.

For degrees in higher education, the table compares the most recent cohort of graduates, who in 1981 were aged twenty to twenty-four, with the forty to forty-nine year-olds, who at the time of the revolution were aged approximately eighteen to twenty-seven; it may be supposed that most of them had begun their university studies or were recent graduates at that time. They represent the youngest cohort of graduates who in general had been through elementary and secondary education and had their orientation toward the university shaped in the prerevolutionary period.

At the level of technican and skilled worker, the most recent cohort is the group of graduates aged seventeen to nineteen at the time of the census.[5]

At all of these levels, there is notable rise in the percentage of women among the younger (and in general more recent) graduates. In higher education, the number of women among all graduates counted is 40.1 percent and 54.3 percent in the most recent cohort. Among the middle-level technicians, the overall percentage of women is 42.7, as compared with 52.2 in the youngest group; the figure for skilled workers is 30.8 percent with 35.8 percent among the youngest. Much more significant, however, is the distribution of these diplomas by field of study: Table 3 shows that the most rapid growth in the index can be found in the areas where before it was lowest (and this also happens with the absolute number of woman graduates). Tapering-off and stabilization can be observed only where women have already become the majority or are near that level.

When these data on graduates are examined in the context of the census information on occupations for 1953 and 1981, it can be seen that the growth in women's participation has been much faster in skilled work than in unskilled, in each occupational grouping. In the light of the data for the prerevolutionary situation (TSE 1955:204-05), as well as of the most prevalent tendencies in Latin America, it is no surprise to find that whereas in 1953 women were only 31 percent of all professional nurses, by 1981 they held 75 percent of the middle-level technician diplomas in public health and physical culture; but it is quite another matter to find that the percentage of women who are doctors, dentists, and the like has climbed from 10 percent to 40 percent of all university degrees in the field, soon to be a majority, and that even in surgery there are areas such as ophthalmology, where the women now outnumber the men.

Most notable perhaps is the expanision in the different branches of production and women's full participation in the development of the country's productive forces. In 1953 (TSE 1955:204-05), not one woman was counted as employed in the manual work of repairing and installing machinery (which at that time was all imported), and there were very few among the technicians and professionals in this field, about 4 percent of the total; but in 1981, although the presence of women is still scant in the physical labor of machine building, in the youngest cohorts they have accumulated 30 percent of the university degrees in the field, 40 percent of the middle-level technicians diplomas and 20 percent among the skilled workers graduated. The stituation is not dissimilar in some other branches of industry with more tradition in the country, such as construction and transportation. Even in long established production systems like the sugar industry and the food industry, women are a majority among the young graduates at all levels of qualification. In agricultural-livestock production, women have increased their presence in the same period from 1 percent to 11 percent in manual labor and from 5 percent to 28 percent among all university graduates; in the youngest cohorts, they hold 56 percent of the college degrees.

According to 1984 figures for the major occupational groups in the civilian sector (Granma 1984b), the area where Cuban women have most displaced men is clerical work, in which they hold 84.7 percent of the jobs. Manual service work is less heavily feminine, 62.6 percent. Women constitute 53.9 percent of the technicians and professionals, and 21.7 percent of the managers. The major occupational group where women have not yet taken a large share of the employment is manual labor in the production of material goods, where they have only reached 16.3 percent.

The weight of tradition and myth about the female can still be perceived in the area of hard physical work and the handling of heavy equipment, which is still considered masculine. Thus, there are few women operators on cranes and caterpillar tractors and cane harvesters, and few women automotive mechanics working as such. There is quite a struggle now to get over the prejudicial effects of tradition in this respect. At this point, the tendency is still to avoid having women doing what is considered the heaviest manual work.

The preference is to have them study first and then take on some lighter work, so that they reappear as technologists, quality control experts, inspectors or engineers, and though usually not classified as managers, they in fact go on to direct the male operators. In this way, the survival for a time of one particular limiting feature of the traditional image of women, the idea of their physical weakness and the need to protect them, has been part of the process of debilitation and elimination of other related traits, such as the notions of the generic inferiority of women, their incapacity for holding responsibile jobs not directly analogous to some domestic chore, their supposed lack of authority, leadership, command capability, and so on. Such notions, once firmly established in Cuban mentalities, have been sharply undercut in recent years.

Protectiveness toward women is strongest in the old shops that were set up before the revolution with an all-male workforce and in the midst of massive unemployment: the collective behavior patterns and values took shape on this basis, while at the same time all the seniority was accumulated by men.

The situation is different in the new factories, built after the revolution, which have contingents of higher-qualified, young workers, the most skilled among them graduated from the polytechnical schools, where women and men are trained together. There traditional restrictions about women doing work classified as hard or heavy have slackened off.

The potential influence of the rise in women's skill levels, as a factor of change is clearly reflected when young women are graduated as technologists and go on to direct the work of older workers with considerable experience at the point of production. One of the principles instilled in the young middle-level technicians is to respect and assimilate the workers' practical knowledge. The young people, sometimes very young, who are directing the work of groups of older men, enter into an interesting dialectic thanks to their training. The young technician transmits and implants the new, more scientific, techniques and at the same time learns from the practical wisdom of the older people. When such a relationship is set up, for example, in road building, between a twenty-year old woman and a gang of male workers aged over thirty, their perception of women, the old-established concepts, are transfigured, producing a profound change in the attitudes of the male working population, which impacts on the whole range of the personality of the adult male worker. We have had the opportunity to observe this in different contexts, among them shipyards, machine-building and repair shops, and some sugar mills, as well as in agricultural-livestock production.

Such changes are not easily measured and are often not transparently visible through the surface phenomena. Just as an iceberg hides the greater part of its bulk, much of the mutation going on today in the situation of women is located in mentalities, and only visible peaks of behavior make it possible to gauge the force of its advance. The effort, now beginning, to incorporate inactive young women into volunteer military service would be one of those points of reference. Another, to our way of thinking, would be the active campaign for sex education that is conceived of not only as mental and physical hygiene, but also as ideological education. At the present stage, there can be no doubt that one of the main contributions to the profound change in attitudes is the training of women at all levels for nontraditional areas of work.

The increase in women's labor-force participation and their demonstrated technical effectiveness is not mere happenstance, nor is it due to any intellectual superiority of women. It is the result of the implantation of *a democratic type of development*. In contrast to capitalist underdevelopment, this process is *not* based on exploitation and inequality betwen the sexes, between the different ethinic groups and the different parts of the country, between city and countryside. Quite the contrary. With respect to women in particular, in consonance with the basic orientation toward an equitable and rational development, what we have seen is a sensible policy that has developed through different stages without losing contact with the slow, fundamental evolution of the psychology of the broadest popular sectors. These results would have been impossible without the activitiy of the Federation of Cuban Women (which by now includes more than 80 percent of all women). A key element in this has been the FMC cadre, their training and their spirit of self-sacrifice; not until 1974 did full-time organization workers receive a wage.

In sum, there has been a gigantic change in the structure of the work activity of Cuban women, with the sharing of housework, the massive incorporation of women into the labor force and the rapid rate at which women are taking highly qualified jobs. Tentatively, this change can thus far be said to have occurred in two stages, the first to about 1970, in which the old social framework was broken and new channels of development were found, and the second in which family relations were reformed and the great advance in women's labor statistics has appeared.

THE PROMOTION OF WOMEN TO LEADERSHIP POSITIONS

The political participation of women was limited before the revolution, as occurs normally in a capitalist country. Promotion to positions of authority has made an important contribution to the contruction of a new feminine identity. Publicity has been given to women's presence in the armed forces and police, where some have attained high rank and held important posts.

The push toward the practical realization of equality, which gained strength in 1975, included a careful study of the problems of women's promotion to leadership positions (PCC 1975), an aspect which has since received much emphasis. The study pointed to material difficulties, which may be summed up under the heading of domestic labor, plus subjective ones such as traditional prejudice and women's lack of confidence in themselves. The eight years that have passed since then have witnessed the joint effort of the party, the government, and the Federation of Cuban Women to achieve the greatest possible upgrading of women in all fields and at all levels. Among the measures adopted was the creation by the National Assembly of People's Power of a permanent commission, Young People, Children and Women's Equality, which is one of the nineteen permanent commissions of the highest state body.

By 1980 encouraging results had been obtained, among them 22 percent women among the delegates elected to the National Assembly, and 50 percent women among the leadership of the committees for the defense of the revolution at the block level. As of early 1984, there are 45.8 percent women among the leadership of union locals (Granma 1984b); this figure is higher than their participation in the wage work force as a whole, as has been the case for some years now.

However, the elevation of women to elected posts of some authority must be described as slow, although there has been steady progress in recent years. Thus, the Central Committee elected by the First Party Congress in 1975 included 8.9 percent women, counting full members and substitutes (FMC 1980:25): the succeeding congress in 1980 elected 12.9 percent. The number of women elected to public office has been very low. When this trend appeared in the first People's Power elections, it gave rise to the party's investigation of the problems of women's equality (PCC 1975). The percentage of women among delegates to municipal assemblies was only 11.5 percent in 1984 (Granma 1984a), up from 7.2 percent in 1979 (ANPP 1979, FMC 1980). It is worth noting that, in the step-by-step electoral system which is characteristic of People's Power, where the lower bodies elect the higher ones, women have the largest representation at the top, in the National Assembly; this is of course the level that is most removed from spontaneous voting patterns, which are heavily influenced by tradition, and the level that best reflects the direction of revolutionary policy.

There have been changes in the composition of leadership and administration as the revolutionary process advances. This can be seen in the data from national statistical reports. The 1953 population census (TSE 1955:204) identified 94,000 managers, directors and non-agricultural administrators, of which only 5 percent were women. Participation has increased, although it is still low. Women make up 12.7 percent of the more than 200,000 people classified by the State Committee for Labor and Social Security as leadership personnel. (Granma 1984b). The 1981 population census used a more restricted concept of *dirigentes* of organizations, enterprises, and leading goverment agencies; they counted 20,000, less than 1 percent of all employees, which can therefore be taken as pointing at the mass of middle-level management. Women constituted 18.4 percent of these *dirigentes*. In the central state apparatus, the highest-ranking officials, from chief of agency to chief of section, women are 16.3 percent (FMC 1980:23). These figures tend to indicate relatively little decrease in the percentage of women from the lower levels of leadership up to the top of the state apparatus. However, the figure was lower at the head of big enterprises, where production is governed in a more direct way, and as yet exceptional among the administrators of large factories.

The frequency of women *dirigentes* is closely correlated with progressively rising educational levels and the succession of new population cohorts. The 1981 census reports occupations by age groups, and from this it can be seen that of the *dirigentes* under age twenty-five, 40.1 percent are women, as compared with 17.3 percent to those over that age. This tendency reflects both a concerted effort by the party and rising popular sentiment for the correction of the previously existing, traditional situation of discrimination (PCC 1981:493-99).

The younger generation is growing up much less encumbered with prejudice than its forbears. It is significant that while women have reached 19 percent among party members, in the Union of Communist Youth, the UJC, women are more than 42 percent of the membership, 45 percent of the mass of *dirigentes*, and 29 percent of the National Committee (although representation among professional cadres is still low) (UJC 1982; Granma 1982). In the Secondary School Students Federation, the majority of the leadership is female, as well as in the Pioneeer organization, which includes children through ninth grade (Castro 1980a).

The education program plays a key role in Cuban development strategy. This priority is especially favorable to women, since equality of opportunity increases along with educational accomplishment. Through education, many women have been promoted to highly qualified positions in government, in the economy and in scientific research as well as in teaching at all levels. Women *dirigentes* are more frequent as educational requirements increase.

Women's achievement can be most clearly seen in higher education. In addition to the tendencies already pointed out with respect to women graduates in different fields, the situation can be described synthetically by a statistical analysis of the distribution of the sixty-six different fields administered by the Ministry of Higher Education, which we have classified according to the percentage of women in the respective student bodies. Among students registered in the given field for the academic year 1981-82, the first quartile was at 33 percent women, the median at 47 percent, and the third quartile at 64 percent women. The degree areas governed by other ministries, not covered by these figures, are much fewer in number and would not in any case modify the general trend, in as much as they include medicine and the arts, where women are again in a when this chapter was written, ratify this advance in listing 32.8 percent of the women over 15 years of age as economically active. The most recent figures (Veigal 1984) indicate that women are now about 38.9 percent of all civilian employees.

[2] The theoretical development of the concepts of domestic labor and private reproduction of labor power (Larguia 1970, 1973) need not be reiterated here. Their presentation in English by the authors can be found in Larguia and Dumoulin (1972, 1975).

[3] Rural women often raised some chickens or a suckling pig on their own account, generally for sale; but they would not take part in the commercialization of these products. There was in the middle sectors, both rural and urban, some tradition of embroidery and making one's own clothes, but by the time of the revolution this was almost totally eliminated.

[4] Compare, for example, recent figures for the United States, which, although they represent no absolute ideal, may certainly be taken as a respectable yardstick for any backward country now trying to overcome underdevelopment. See U.S. Bureau of the Census (1978:59-78) and Comite Estatal de Estadisticas, Direccion de Demografia (1981a), as well as more recent sources. In the principal vital statistics, including fertility, early death rates, life expectancy at birth, and others, Cuba has reduced or even eliminated the substantial lag that once separated her from American levels in any given year.

[5] In using Table 3 to evaluate the progress women have made, several limitations should be taken into account. First, the youngest cohort, which is presented here as representative of the progressive elevation of women's participation, includes almost all the graduates of the regular daytime university programs, but not all the workers studying in night school, many of whom will graduate at over 25 years of age; men are heavily represented in night school because there are more men working, and this will contribute to some readjustment in the composition of the graduates in this cohort in a few years time. On the other hand, skilled workers, especially in the older cohorts, acquired their skills on the job rather than through a program of formal study; in trades where there were very few women, it was exceptional that they acquire skills on the job, and this could mean that the difference between cohorts is really larger than what is reflected in the table. Second, the figures for the older cohorts are not strictly representative of the professionals trained before the revolution because of the strong out-migration from the educated strata that occurred during the years of basic restructuring of Cuban society and the rise of the counterrevolution opposing it (about half of the doctors left in the early years); there has also been some

majority. There is, then, an extraordinarily strong tendency toward equality of the sexes in the different fields of Cuban higher education. And it should be remembered that this occurred along with a profound change in the class composition of the student body, which is now drawn mainly from families of humble extraction, which before the revolution were working class, from the countryside, and even illiterate.

To mention only a few areas that are very significant for the training of future leaders of a socialist society, women have reached 27 percent among all engineering students and 55 percent in economics. In philosophy women constitute 81 percent of the students. This is the most selective field--the one that requires the highest academic and political qualifications. Cuban women have a long-standing interest in this field, which no doubt contributes to their predominance in it now, but there has been a very important change in its social significance. Marxism-Leninism attributed to philosophy an important role in the construction of the future, as the highest form of synthesis in knowledge. Marx, in his *Thesis on Feuerbach*, wrote that "The philosophers have only interpreted the world in various ways; the point, however, is to change it" (Marx [1888] 1973:95). Does this mean that today's Cuba is handing over to women the task of projecting the future of society? It would perhaps be rash to say so categorically, but these figures tend to point in that direction.

Women do not yet play a role of full equality in the country's leadership, but the problem is recognized as such, there is a struggle to overcome it, and the logic of the development of Cuban society lends credence to Fidel Castro's words when he says: "The day must come when we will have a Party made up of men and women, and a leadership made up of men and women, and a State made up of men and women, and a Government made up of men and women. And I think all the *companeros* are conscious that that is a necessity of the revolution, of society and of history" (Castro n.d.).

NOTES

[1] According to decennial census figures, the participation of women in the American labor force rose progressively from 17.4 percent in 1890 to 30.9 percent in 1950. The corresponding data for Cuba indicate that the economic activity rate for women of 14 years and older went up from 17.8 percent in 1970 to 31.9 percent in 1979. The American rates are taken from U.S. Bureau of the Census (1975:128). Those for Cuba come from Comite Estatal de Estadisticas, Direccion de Demografia (1981b:13); they are based on the 1970 population census and the results of the 1979 National Demographic Study.

The results of the 1981 census, which had just been made public replacement within those same cohorts through adult education. As yet, there has been no detailed research on these processes that would give an idea of their influence on the present composition of these professional groups; it is possible that they may have raised the percentage of women to some degree in the older cohorts, especially in some fields at the secondary level. Third, Table 3 reflects the compositon of diploma holders, whether or not they are working. However, this should not significantly reduce the value of these figures under present circumstances.

REFERENCES

Agrupacion Catolica Universitaria. 1972. "Encuesta de trabajadores rurales, 1957-57." Economia y Desarrollo, July-August. (Originally published in Carteles, March 16, 1958.)

Asamblea Nacional, Poder Popular (ANPP). 1979. Informe sobre el resultado de las elecciones de delegados al Poder Popular. Havana.

Boserup, Ester. 1970. Women's role in economic development. London: Allen & Unwin.

Castro, Fidel. 1980a. "Discurso en la clausura del Tercer Congreso de la Federacion de Mujeres Cubanas." Granma, March 10.

_____. 1980b. "Informe Central al Segundo Congreso deel Partido Comunista de Cuba." Granma, December 19.

_____. n.d. "Discurso pronunciado en la clausura del Segundo Congreso de la Federacion de Mujeres Cubanas." Boletin FMC. n.p.

Comite Estatal de Estadisticas (CEE). 1982. Anuario Estadistico de Cuba, 1981. Havana.

Comite Estatal de Estadisticas, Direccion de Demografia (CEEDD). 1981a. Anuario Demografico de Cuba. 1979. Havana.

_____. 1981b. Principales caracteristicas laborales de la poblacion de Cuba, Encuesta Demografica Nacional de 1979. Havana.

Dumoulin, John. 1977. 20 anos de matrimonios en Cuba. Havana: Editorial de Ciencias Sociales.

Espin, Vilma. 1980. "Informe Central al Tercer Congreso de la

Federacion de Mujeres Cubanas." Granma, March 7.

Federacion de Mujes Cubanas (FMC). 1980. Tercer Congreso, Proyecto de tesis sobre la participacion de la mujer en la vida economica, politica, cultural y social de pais. Havana: Editora Politica.

Granma. 1980. Interview with Jose Ramon Fernandez, Minister of Education. August 14.

______. 1982. April 5.

______. 1983. "Laboran en todo el pais un millon 28 mil mujeres." July 30.

______. 1984a. "Elecciones de delegados a las Asambleas Municipales del Poder Popular, Resultados Finales (Primera y segunda vueltas)." April 24.

______. 1984b. "Intervencion de Vilma Espin." February 23.

Larguia, Isabel. 1970. "Contre le travail invisible." Partisans 54-55 (July-October): 206-20.

______. 1975. "The economic basis of women's status." In Ruby Rohrlich-Leavitt, ed. Women Cross-Culturally: Change and Challenge. The Hague: Mouton Publishers.

Larguia, Isabel and John Dumoulin. 1972. "Toward a science of women's liberation." NACLA Report 6, No. 10:3-20.

______. 1975. "Aspects of the condition of women's labor." NACLA Report 9, No. 6:4-13.

Marx, Karl. 1973. (orig. pub. 1888) "Theses on Feuerbach." In Karl Marx and Frederick Engels, Feuerbach: opposition of the materialist and idealist outlooks. London: Lawrence & Wishart.

Partido Comunista de Cuba (PCC). 1975. "Investigacion sobre la mujer y los poderes populares en Matanzas." Primer Congreso del Partido, Tesis No. 3, Sobre el pleno ejercicio de la igualdad de la mujer. Havana: Departamento de Orientacion Revolucionaria, Comite Central.

______. 1981. Segundo Congreso, Documentos y Discursos. Havana: Editora Politica.

Pino Santos, Oscar. 1961. El imperialismo norteamericano en la economia de Cuba. Havana: Imprenta Nacional de Cuba.

Tribunal Superior Electoral, (T.S.E.) Oficina Nacional de los Censos Demograficos y Electoral. 1955. Censos de Poblacion, Viviendas y Electoral, 1953, Informe General. Havana: P. Fernandez.

Union de Jovenes Comunistas (UJC). 1982. "IV Congreso, Sintesis del Informe Central." Juventud Rebelde, April 2.

U.S. Bureau of the Census (USBC). 1975. Historical Statistics of the United States, Colonial Times to 1970, Bicentennial Edition. Washington, D.C.: U.S. Government Printing Office.

_____. 1978. Statistical Abstract of the United States, 1978. Washington, D.C.: U.S. Government Printing Office.

Veiga, Robert. 1984. "Informe al XV Congreso de la Central de Trabajadores de Cuba." Granma, February 22.

TABLE 1

Female Economic Activity Rates, by Marital Status*
Cuba, 1970 and 1979

Marital Status	1970	1979	Percentage Increase
Total**	16.9	31.6	87.0
Single	21.8	25.0	14.3
Married	16.3	36.7	124.9
Common-law Union	9.2	24.8	169.0
Divorced	41.5	63.2	52.1
Separated	n.d.	45.3	n.d.
Widowed	7.7	9.1	18.2

* Women over fourteen years of age
** Excludes women of unknown marital status

Source: State committee of Statistics, Demography Section (CEEDD) (1981b:22).

TABLE 2

Occupational Distribution of Female Labor Force, 1976 and 1980*

Major Occupational Group	Percentage of Female Labor Force 1976	1980
Production workers	26.1	22.1
Services	28.0	24.4
Professionals and Middle-level Technicians	24.5	30.0
Clerical	15.1	16.6
Dirigentes (Government officials, managers)	5.3	4.7
Other	1.0	2.2
Total	100.0	100.0

* Data are for the civilian public sector, which includes 98.8% of the women listed as economically active by the State Committee for Statistics (CEEDD 1981b:32).

Source: State Committee for Labor and Social Security

TABLE 3

Percentage of Women Among Graduates of Three Levels of Education by Field of Study and Selected Age Groups

	Higher Education Ages			Middle-level Technician Ages			Skilled Worker Ages		
Field of Study	20-24	40-49	All Ages	17-19	40-49	All Ages	17-19	40-49	All Ages
Geology, mining, metallurgy	50.0	12.1	28.5	22.9	11.5	20.7	20.2	11.8	13.9
Energy	26.0	7.2	11.9	23.8	6.2	13.4	25.3	14.0	20.7
Machine building	30.0	6.9	11.2	40.1	11.2	21.5	19.7	12.0	14.0
Sugar, chemical, and food Industries	64.2	27.6	41.0	59.3	45.0	50.7	60.3	11.8	43.7
Electronics, automation, communications	25.0	9.6	18.0	33.4	19.8	22.1	37.8	27.5	28.3
Transportation	17.8	5.4	11.4	19.2	4.9	9.7	16.2	6.6	11.2
Construction	43.9	16.1	28.1	41.9	13.5	28.8	21.1	7.0	15.3
Agriculture, livestock	56.1	15.0	27.8	35.8	12.7	24.2	21.1	13.3	14.6
Economics	64.7	24.9	37.3	71.1	49.0	55.5	78.1	51.6	65.4
Public health, physical culture	51.3	31.3	40.3	74.2	64.3	75.0	76.4	70.3	74.6
The arts	47.2	40.8	41.7	80.5	62.6	67.4	--	--	--
Natural and exact sciences	57.9	53.3	52.8	--	--	--	--	--	--
Social science, humanities	56.7	32.8	41.1	--	--	--	--	--	--
Education	57.2	68.1	58.2	--	--	--	--	--	--
Other	52.5	37.2	46.0	45.2	33.4	37.7	61.3	62.9	59.1
All fields	54.3	33.1	40.1	52.2	39.0	42.7	35.8	29.1	30.8

Source: Compiled by the authors from the 1981 census of Cuba, population over eleven years of age holding diplomas and certificates, by sex, age and diplomas obtained.

Index

Related Books

Women's Work

Development & the Division of Labor by Gender
ELEANOR LEACOCK, HELEN I. SAFA, & CONTRIBUTORS

This vibrant survey of women's work analyzes reproduction and production in industrial capitalism, nonindustrial societies, the Third World, and Socialist societies.

304 Pages Illustrations

In Her Prime
A New View of Middle-Aged Women
JUDITH BROWN, VIRGINIA KERNS, & CONTRIBUTORS

"These ethnographies are fascinating, heartening, and provocative."
— WOMEN'S REVIEW OF BOOKS

240 Pages Illustrations

Nicaragua — *The People Speak*
ALVIN LEVIE
Introduction by Richard Streb

"Outstanding . . . For everyone questioning Nicaraguan self-determination."
— ED ASNER, ACTOR

224 Pages Illustrations

The Politics of Education
Culture, Power & Liberation
PAULO FREIRE

"Here speaks a teacher who lives life, a revolutionary with hope."
— CHANGE

240 Pages Illustrations

Applied Anthropology
An Introduction
JOHN VAN WILLIGEN
320 Pages Illustrations

Now in Paper!

Spiritualist Healers in Mexico
KAJA FINKLER
Foreword by Arthur Kleinman
272 Pages

Crisis in the Philippines
The Making of a Revolution
E. San Juan
Foreword by George Wald
288 Pages Illustrations

Recalling the Good Fight
An Autobiography of the Spanish Civil War
John Tisa
265 Pages Illustrations

Beyond Revolution
A New Theory of Social Movements
Ralph Larkin & Daniel Foss
Introduction by Stanley Aronowitz
256 Pages

The Struggle for Rural Mexico
Gustavo Esteva
320 Pages

Sex & Class in Latin America
June Nash, Helen Safa & Contributors
352 Pages Illustrations

Women and Colonization
Mona Etienne, Eleanor Leacock & Contributors
352 Pages Illustrations

Political Anthropology
An Introduction
Ted Lewellen
160 Pages Illustrations

The Nicaraguan Revolution in Health
From Somoza to the Sandinistas
John Donahue
188 Pages Illustrations

Women & Nutrition in Third World Countries
Sahni Hamilton & Contributors
160 Pages

Now in Paper!

Transnationals & the Third World
The Struggle for Culture
Armand Mattelart
192 Pages